RATOLOGY

Way of the Un-Dammed

Stop Shoulding on Yourself !!!

Cover Art Licensed under Creative Common from:
http://arizonarainman.blogspot.com
Many thanks to AZ Rainman

Many thanks also to LEUNIG for his cartoons

The Mystic Rat Says:

- You are a child of the Universe. As such you contain all the elements of the universe including the power of creation. You have the power to mold the stuff of life via the way you think, how you feel, and by what you expect.
- What we think feel and expect comes to pass in our lives, thus we learn by experience. Experience can teach us to modify our thoughts, feelings, and expectations.
- By learning to modify our inner being and how it expresses itself, we come to realize we are free to act as we choose. We come into the Liberty of Spirit, which is the very nature of creation.

(This is the Credo of the Orphic Mysteries from Ancient Greece)

Your Inner Rat Needs YOU!

Copyright 2009 - 2020 Ecallaw Leachim
ISBN: 978-0-9756994-2-3

This book is published under the Berne Convention. All copyright protected by the author. No use without prior permission, except for excerpts for review or educational purposes. All inquiries via email to: mrmichaelmouse@hotmail.com

Published by Ladder to the Moon Productions, Australia
All rights reserved to the copyright holder.

The Proverbial Truth

An archaic proverb speaks of an angel who visits three old monks, venerable souls who had dedicated their lives to understanding truth and living a totally pure existence. The angel says to the aged leader of the group, "You have earned a right to one gift from the heavens. You are now given the choice between Wisdom, Beauty, or Money. What do you choose?"

The old monk is ecstatic. Obviously, he instantly chooses Wisdom and, accordingly, he is immediately enveloped in deep, contemplative thought. But, clearly shocked by what he has discovered, the monk soon falls into a disconsolate weeping that lasts for hour upon hour.

The angel is now long gone and night is upon the small group, yet still the old monk weeps. Finally, his friends can take the weeping, the suffering, and the pain no longer and ask him, "What's it like? What is this pain you suffer? Does it come with the wisdom that has been revealed to you?"

The monk looks up, great misery and tears of sorrow are brimming in his eyes, and he says with his newfound wisdom, "Don't you understand? I should have asked for the Money!"

The Mystic Rat Says:

Learn to see the obvious! It will mean you have better relationships, clearer communications, and your sense of perspective will be sharper. The real bonus, anything that enters your life will become more balanced and complete.

INDEX

Prayer to the Holey Cheezus..8
In the Beginning...9
Introduction..12
Poker is Life..19
    Infamous Shoulder chips...22
    Spotting the Demons..29
Humpty Dumpty - Post Wall:...32
    I am Perfectly FINE..37
Accepting Cracks...45
Synchronicity..48
The Missing Pieces:...52
    The Cracked World We Live In...55
Call, Raise or Fold: Survival or Denial..57
The Scourge of Dreams..61
The Creation of Walls Within..64
We the Dammed..69
i aM a rAt...76
You are a LIAR..90
    You Want the Truth?..100
The Birth of Mickey Mouse..106
From Mickey to the Rat – Becoming Complete..110
A Midsummer Night's Dream...113
From the One to the Many to Refold Back to the One....................................114
Origami and the Clean Sheet..117
Let's Fun Ourselves to Freedom..119

Rules of Rattyness..121
    ONE: It's not About You..124
    TWO: Do Not Should in Your Own Nest.......................128
    THREE: Always Keep One Eye Open.............................133
    FOUR: Ask No Favours – neither a beggar nor borrower be..............135
    FIVE: Keep your Teeth Honed......................................142
    SIX: Always Have a Bolt Hole......................................144
    SEVEN : Do Not Expose Your Vulnerabilities..............147
    EIGHT: Pay Attention to Your Brother's Activity.........149
    NINE: PICK UP, and DUST OFF....................................151
    TEN: Shoot the Pope..154
The Romans: Breaking the Rule Book......................................158
Being Ruthless...166
Can you Smell Your Freedom?..172
Protect Yourself with Creativity..173
NOW is the Time...175
The Truth is Simple. YOU are Simple..178
Social Values = Sham + Necessity..185
SEX and SEPARATION...189
Why Authority?...192
Ratology: Getting Un-Dammed by seeing the Obvious............194
The New Slavery..197
The Jesters..206
Irony releases Truth from the Absurd.....................................209
Goodbye Utopia – Hello Freedom..213
The Cross of TIME...217
God is Dust..221
A Dream of Intimacy...225
EMOTIONS: Real and Unreal..226
Playing the Heart Strings...232
The Law of Three..237
The Glass Ceiling..245
The Laws of Emotion..248
The Seed of Emotion..250
Understanding Our Stick It Notes...254
Are We Still Pretending?..260
The Yardstick..262
SUMMARY...264

The GIFT

We have an unlikely GIFT inside us. It may not seem that the nagging voice inside you that doubts everything is a friend, but deep down, that part of us that smell the BS and knows chalk from cheese is the dividing line between personal freedom or slavery to the machine. That part of us that hates lies and finds social graces suspect is your personal Bart Simpson - The part that is awake to authority and seeks to find any way to get around it is your Reality Awareness Trigger - Your RAT! It is this part of you that gets what is REAL.

Shirley Howe - "Cracked Egg"

DECLARATION BY THE GREAT RAT

1. We all have Cracks, Faults, and Foibles
2. We all Lie and Pretend
3. We all Suffer more from too much Imagination and too little Reality
4. Few see the Obvious
5. Fewer understand the importance of this
5. And no one really cares, apart from your mother
6. So you may as well have fun, laugh, and dance, despite yourself !

Belief can be a Dangerous Lie

I say that our beliefs are not necessarily our friend. I say they stop us from experiencing our life as a free agent. In this book I will show you how many of our beliefs are formed around Memes, 'hand-me-down' images set up by society or family.

This 'inheritance' affects our perception, defines our attitude, and controls our thoughts. These false beliefs (what we might otherwise call lies) can, and do, affect our entire life. For Example: We know there never really was a Santa Clause, but even as adults who have discarded the myth, we usually retain the 'imprint' of this story and it becomes a core belief - *that there is someone who rewards us for being good.* Get it? It is the psychic residue of the stories we were told that become the seed from which our future beliefs spring.

What this means to you and me is that we are often acting in good faith, moving forward with good intention, and yet we are living with a lie. It's all good - we hop along like happy bunnies, until the 'Big Red X' comes - Where the Gods paint a huge cross all over our dreams!

The divorce, the shadey business partner, the gossips who whisper, the court cases - We start to understand you are standing on shakey ground only when our house of cards is falling down. This is why I say: *Belief can be a dangerous lie: dangerous to your happiness, your freedom, your sense of self-worth, and your wallet.*

Why do I say that our beliefs are not necessarily our friend? Our beliefs create the monster within. You don't believe me? Show me a baby that was born angry, greedy or lustful. No child is prepared to kill another child for their lollypop - until they are taught inequality and lack. I say all these things that control us are 'tags' we have picked up, and they stop us finding intimacy, warmth and love. In this book I will show you how to look through the illusion, break the spell, and get back to your natural self.

In seeing the false as false, truth is perceived.
Krishnamurti

Prayer to the Holey Cheezus

Dear Holy Cheezus
Who doth eat dairy in Heaven
Holey be thy Swiss Cheese
Thy fermentation will be done
In a few months of setting, and not before
Grant me this day my daily bread
Preferably toasted - with lots of butter- and sprinkles on top
Forgive me my trespasses in supermarkets,
And explain to the Judge that they give away free samples all the time,
So why not accept my argument that I thought the free samples at Two in the morning were simply larger than otherwise?
And anyway it's your fault for leading me into temptation by creating cheese in the first place.
Deliver me from Weevils.
Forever and ever, and then just a little bit more.
Amen (Or a-person if you are more politically correct)

The Ten Commandments of Ratology

1/ It's not about you
2/ Do not should in your own nest
3/ Always keep one eye open
4/ Ask no favours
5/ Keep your teeth honed
6/ Always have a bolt hole
7/ Do not expose your vulnerabilities
8/ Pay attention to your brother's activity
9/ Pick up and dust off
10/ Shoot the Pope

In the Beginning

In the Beginning, there was no cheese. The Great Rat slept and the only thing that existed was his dream. And, being a Rat, obviously, he dreamed of dairy products. In this dream of dreams, he saw many cheeses to eat: cheeses great and small, young and old, pungent and faint. Even the lightest of pale Ricotta was there for his sampling. All was delight, happiness, and joy in the universe of the Rat.

Then he awoke and, upon opening his great Rat Eyes, all the Great Rodent of Rodents could think of was cheese. This Desire for Dairy was most un-Buddha-like but, considering that we are talking about a Rat, you must understand that he really didn't care. He said to himself, "I must have this thing called CHEESE!" Naturally, being a God, he created it. He worked for hours that morning, inventing and manifesting left, right, and centre. All the cheeses we now know and take for granted were invested with the nature of existence that very day. The Great Rat even considered creating Venezuelan Beaver Cheese, but he was a Lazy God and he got tired of all this hard work. (I believe he left that particular creation to Monty Python)

In consideration of all the above and given that he was now addicted to cheese whilst allergic to working nine to five, the Great Rat had yet another brilliant notion: Minions! What better way to get in more cheese stocks for the upcoming winter than creating minions to do all the work?

"I know," thought the Great Rat "I will invent a race that will make CHEESE. I will instil a compulsive cheese making gene in their hearts, a gene that will make my minions incredibly, unutterably boring, but which will drive them to make the finest of cheese for my table." And so the Swiss were created.

Thus it also came to be that, unto this very day, the nature of Swiss cheese is Holey. (made incarnate by the true nature of the Holey Cheezus!) However, there were two a significant downsides to the Cheese Making Gene. The first was the severe and irreparable dullness that made the recipient unbelievably bad company at parties, but far worse than even this was the second side-effect - Yodeling! I know we all feel compassion for the Swiss for being, well, Swiss, but yodeling is a curse by anyone's standards.

The Great Rat turned a blind ear to it at first, but after gnawing mystic holes in the vast hoards of fermented curd created by his children, the Rodent of Rodents discovered a singular and absolute truth: He hated yodeling as much as the rest of us. The mighty Rat cursed the fault in his cheese making gene for this terrible compulsion. He also cursed the Swiss and regularly abused them with avalanches and miserable weather, but did they get the message? No, they kept right on yodeling, believing it to be some sort of love song to their cows.

Well, we know what happens when mountain folk start courting their cows. The sheep get jealous and make terrible wool, which means you freeze your ass off in winter. So central heating became necessary and this required huge sums of money. Thus it came to pass that, right under the nose of the Great Rat, the Swiss made a pact with Satan, an evil being best known under the nom-de-plume, 'International Banking". And this is how it came to pass that the Swiss fell from grace and became the lowest of the low - Bankers.

The Mystic Rat Sighed: *Not so Blessed are the Cheese Makers*.

Obviously, the race had to be gotten rid of. Yet, though they were exceedingly dull, even the Lord High Rat had to admit that the Swiss had done quite well on the cheese front. (It was just the yodeling, and Satan.) Added to this the fine print of their Creation Contract (invented by the German-Swiss) which stipulated 36.5 hours of productive work, plus a credit of one hour per day for Gorgonzola cheese production AND the 'No Cancellation' clause for Cheddar (inserted by the Italian Swiss and ridiculed by the French-Swiss) - Well, this unfortunately forbad their extermination by anything other than an Act of God. This clause caused a quandary for the Great Rat - it took him a long time to sort out whether he was God, the Agent of God, Godish, or just a big fat Rat with a very God-like position.

Either way, it was either cope with the yodeling or do something about it. We all know how Gods get rid of their problems and it is never pretty. Yet, getting rid of your cheese makers whilst you still desire ever finer dairy products is a tricky thing. He read up on Sodom and Gomorrah, but cheese production didn't do well with fire and another flood would be equally ruinous to the industry AND it would need to be an exceptionally large one, given the mountains.

This is where you and I come into the picture. As a very curious solution for the problem of the ever more irritating Swiss (who were now very foolishly starting to pray in yodels, hoping this would stop the avalanches) the Great Rat invented the rest of us. On this small point, I am truly not sure why he invented the Chinese, because they are terrible cheese makers. I gather it was something to do with the production of cheap dairy equipment.

But The Great Rat was soon to regret all this Creation of Souls business because NOW, while the cheese supply was quite good and no longer reliant on the yodellers, a thing called religion happened. People started praying for things. It was very distracting and left a bad taste in the Great Rat's mouth, which directly opposed the whole point of creating humans!

More and more stuff was being demanded. e.g. "Oh Great Rat, give me new socks." This is harmless you say? It is all very novel the first time you hear it, but by the fifteenth millionth time, it wears very, very thin. The Great Rat found himself wanting to create a sock which you put in the place where the sun don't shine. The prayer thing got out of hand: "Oh greatest of Great Rats, give me a lottery win!" "Give me a new Lover" "Can I have a better car?" etc. etc. etc.

The human race was such a waste of time that within short shrift the Great Rat was on the verge of Armageddon. (Act of God - Sorry German Swiss - he figured out the loophole) The thought was to keep a few select gorgonzola factories on the moon (Green Gorgonzola, can you believe?) but otherwise, the celestial rodent was seriously thinking of a decent plague. A good pestilence was always his favourite. Then fate intervened. His only begotten son, Mickey Mouse, said, "Hey, let me go down to save them! I'll see if I can make them more self-sufficient and that way they will stop bugging you, OK?

Of course, the real truth is that Mickey was bored in heaven and wanted to play here on Earth with Minnie, but be that as it may, this is what came about. To this end, Walt Disney was created and thus it came to pass that he bore (as a virgin cartoonist, of course) the only begotten son of the Great Rat, Mickey Mouse. Directly because of the birth of the Mouse and paradoxically via deals with Swiss Bankers, Disney gave birth to the art of total capitalism. This path saved the world because it made so much money that everyone got everything they ever wanted, thus there was no more need to keep praying for stuff.

The internet, Ebay, the Kardashians, and reality TV in general were just a coincidence - but these things completed the picture.

Fame, undeserved recognition, money, fashion labels, everything you would ever need was now yours to enjoy. Thus you live happily ever after! (Cue: sound of Gregorian Chants in the background) And so it came to pass that people no longer had to bug the Great Rat for things and the devil could take the Swiss - Which, as we all know, he did.

This is how Mickey Mouse saved the entire human race (minus the Swiss) and this is what, in the fullness of time, created the one true faith: Ratology.

Yea verily, forever and ever, Amen. etc. etc. etc.

oooooOOOOOOOOOOooooo

We are a jigsaw.

We know the pieces fit somewhere, but where? And why do we feel like square pegs looking for a round hole?

Introduction

"The reason I talk to myself is because I'm the only one whose answers I accept." George Carlin

I have always hated Liars. Despite this fact, in the process of being raised a Catholic, I became one. As a consequence, I learned to hate myself at an early age. However, the doubt and misgiving that emerged from this stood me in good stead as a poker player, for reasons that will later become obvious.

It was the lying thing that triggered off this book. I had been sick with a bad flu, you know the type, the one where you have the sense that dying would be OK? I had been playing endless games of chess in my mind - 24 hours a day for five days and six nights and had eaten no food at all. Finally the fever breaks and, exhausted, I get up. My youngest son has the TV on. I see a politician on camera - He is lying.

It is so clear to me that he is lying, then the presenter talks and HE is lying. Then ads come on and they are lies. I am absolutely disgusted and my memory flashes back to my first open encounter with society. I am aged four and am now required to go to church. I didn't like it much. But as if the constant mindless droning kneeling, sitting and standing weren't enough, I go outside after it is done and to my horror, I discover that all the people who are speaking in the courtyard have *two faces*. (Dis) Honest to God, they all had TWO FACES!

I hear what they are saying, 'Nice weather' 'Morning Mrs. Jones' but I also see there is a sort of 'other' person inside them saying the opposite. 'Prefer to stay in bed' 'Can't stand that woman', etc. One face was being polite, while the other saying what they really thought, yet the two did not agree. "LIARS!" I said to myself, horrified. Everyone was lying and, at a mere four years of age, I was shocked to the core. It felt as if I had entered hell itself.

But far worse was to come. I leave off my reminiscence and flash forward to the here and now. Leaving the rhubarb of TV and childhood recollections, I weigh myself. Oh My God! After five or six days of starvation I am horrified - I had not lost any weight at all! Not a single pound!

Hurrumph and Double Hurrumph!

I was SO pissed off that I sat down and wrote this book. Remember this, my lack of weight loss is the main cause for this affliction you now hold. I guess it's also because of the liars, the lies, and the consequences of the Lie - but really people, what have you got to do to lose an ounce?

So, I sat down to write - Then the miracle happened - A completely lateral thought clicked into place that connected the lies people utter with all my issues and problems with life and people in general. In part due to the shock at seeing no change on the bathroom scales, I had a clear insight into a long-standing issue, which was WHY people rarely what hear what is said to them correctly.

We all know the game of Chinese Whispers - say something to some one and by the time it goes around the circle what comes back is completely different to what was said at the start. People hear what they want to hear, see what they want to see, and act according to this false perception. Now it clicked and I understood WHY! It is all because of the disconnect we all suffer - The engine of disconnection that drives the need for lies and a goodly part of our actions.

How does this disconnect connect to lies? It is environment and upbringing - People are trained in certain paths, specific patterns of belief. We are told that this behaviour is right, that way of acting is wrong. This is true, this is false. Which would be fine, except none of us ever really fit the mold that we are cast into. *Everyone feels a little like a square peg in a round hole.*

The PROBLEM is that, because of social pressures, we tend to believe the round hole is correct and that we, as the square peg, are faulty. Or we become outcasts and convince ourselves round holes are evil and that only square pegs (like us) are the truth. Either way, we feel a conflict in the fact we do not 'fit in'.

In that wonderful book, "I'm OK, You're OK" by Thomas Anthony Harris, the author outlines the four basic modes of how an individual approaches society. "I'm OK, you are NOT OK!" is a criminal mode. "I'm not OK, You are OK!" is the basic faulty mindset of the majority of people. "I am not OK, you are not OK!" is the most negative framework while "I am OK, you are OK!" is the most positive and functional mind set. This is a balanced view that permits happiness for all.

So, how do we get to this?

At heart, most people have a fear that they are wrong in some way. So they do whatever is needed in the socialisation stage of their life (ages four to nine) to fit in OR they do a Bart Simpson and rebel. Either way, what they feel inside is not matched to how they connect to society. *This is the start of the disconnect.*

The basis of the negative self-view so often starts with well-meaning lies - our upbringing, religion, socialization, etc. - We are full of what are, at best, half-truths, at worst blatant lies. EG: We want a child to wear clothes, so we tell them they will catch their death if they do not. This is a Lie - Any number of cultures run around naked. But the rationale is it is easier to lie because we need our children to wear clothes.

A religious mother wants a child to behave, so they may tell them, "Jesus will cry if you don't tell the truth." She knows it is a fiction designed to create a good outcome, but it is still a lie. Jesus isn't weeping at every lie a child tells. This innocuous story leaves an IMPRINT on the child, saying, *"Act in a way that you will be approved of"*. But what the child HEARS is, *"You are not good enough!"*. The child then weds these two different statements into a new story, one that reads, "Approval means I am loved, so I must act in a way that is approved."

Little white lies are core to that which divorces us from our natural selves.

No baby is born angry, depressed or disconnected. This is all learned or reactive behaviour. If you are not genuinely, deeply happy, you are missing a connection to your real self. Further, this is because there is something - a lie - inside that you believe to be true, but which is fabrication.

The Serious Illness

One day when catching a bus I saw a headline that read, "MAN DIES FROM SERIOUS ILLNESS". Well, obviously, my first thought was that he would hardly die from a non-serious one - but then the quirk in my head spun over. I saw in a flash that we are all potentially dying from being too serious. We have forgotten the fun! We have forgotten we are in the sandpit playing a game called life.

That curious quip is what started me on the path of writing for comedians, and trying out the material at the Comedy Club in Sydney.

My imagination postulated that seriousness was a genuine illness. It started by infecting our minds with the Politically Correct restrictions and from this a sense of Totalitarianism took over. Comics now had to make all jokes relevant using a completely non-sexist, non-racist, yet somehow supposed-to-be still humorous language. Feminists without a sense of irony were given the task of running the country and, in a bid to stop testosterone fuelled happiness, they cut off every man's balls. (Oddly, this prediction came true when Thatcher came to power in the UK!) The long and the short is that it all finally emerged as a stand-up comedy routine that (appropriately) no one laughed at.

But the first line was good. A man enters into a box shop and asks for a small, white box. He has no idea what is wrong, but he is immediately arrested, sentenced and imprisoned. As he is being carted away the judge shakes his head, saying, *"Everyone knows we must not discriminate on size or colour."*

As Heath Ledger echoed in Batman: *Why So Serious?*

Well, we need a little and the serious side is that this book wraps around two points: What Jung called the 'Censor', and the process of socialization. These two things combine to create what we call social integration.

It is a given that socialization is needed to integrate a child into the ways of the world. First up, the practical day to day things: A child needs to learn to use a toilet, wash themselves, speak a language. In the West a child learns to read and write, use math, and become a useful member of society. These things are not the issue, it is all the useless baggage we pick up that is the problem.

It a given that many of the ways in the Western World are full of confusion for the young brain. We are taught that invisible friends are not real, yet we should believe in God. We are THEN taught that this religion is better than that religion. Rich, white males run all the companies, but there is equal opportunity for all. There is a Constitution that states, 'All men are born equal', written and signed by men who owned slaves. The world is full of conflicted messages.

To Summarize: *All men are born equal, but MY God is better than YOUR God, and for GODS SAKE, make sure Jesus is painted as a white man!*

I wrote this book to send a clear message. Ratology is a tongue-in-cheek path to freedom, a way out of confusion and lies. It speaks simply about complex subjects. It teaches that by seeing the obvious, accepting the cracks in our lives, and relearning to have FUN, we can become largely free of our conditioning. It is a way around the learned habits and the emotional programs that control us.

As a child I eventually got past the shock of realizing people were two-faced and became curious as to why people lied in the first place. I suspected it was because they believed appearances were more important than truth. But why?

Inside the dance of looking good, I discovered there is a SPIN DOCTOR in people's mind and that everyone has this inner controller that rules them: *The Censor!* Jung referred to it as the organizing aspect of the mind. It is built by the mind as part of the survival instinct - it is that part of you that keeps you separate from the tribe - the part that ALSO creates the disconnect you feel.

The Censor

The Censor is a very curious and difficult-to-grasp beast. It lives inside you but remains entirely invisible. Like the beast that lived under the bed of childhood, it exists as a result of your fears. It was constructed in childhood by yourself, as a way of combating the rules and regulations that were hemming you in. It knows only one priority, you must survive.

Created out of your childhood training, it now USES the socialization process you were raised in to cause you to act in specific ways. *'Odd,'* you might say to yourself. *'Is this author implying I am not in charge of my life?'* Before I answer this, ask yourself: *How many of your decisions are based on religious beliefs, guilt, shame, fear, etc. or are part of just toeing the line?* Answer: *Most.*

Our Censor is a strange creature. I first became aware of it at age twenty-four when my mother (who could be incredibly controlling) wrote me what seemed the MOST interfering letter I had ever received. I tossed it down with a shake of my head. It was the last straw and I declared that I would never speak to her again, at least not until she changed her ways.

That night my inner RAT got an insight. I had a dream experience where my mother, as a young child, is speaking to an old friend of mine, a Tibetan Monk who had helped me spiritually in this life. He turned to me and said, "A remarkable woman, your mother." It shocked me, because I had found her an intrusive pain in the butt and anything 'but' remarkable. But that that comment altered my perspective. Upon waking I started seeing her good points.

So how does this change anything? Well, I woke up with a different view. Now, when I re-read her letter, the words seemed different. NOW, this letter seemed like the most loving message a mother had ever sent her son! It was full of warmth, kindness, and well-wishing. Huh? What had happened here? How could the same letter be two entirely different things?

Folks, this is ESSENTIAL to grasp - The twisting up and re-interpreting of events to suit our bias is precisely what the Censor does inside our mind. It takes our past experience and superimposes this over current conditions. It then uses this mix of images to construct a story, just like a video editor. It is a spin doctor that weaves a tapestry with the threads of the past on the loom of the present. It presents this image to your inner mind and, if you don't know better, this becomes your accepted reality.

Do you ever wonder how a person can get so twisted up as to believe they need to gun down school children or strap a bomb to themselves to kill innocents? The mind gets conditioned by belief and prejudice. Like the blinkered horse, it can only see the image in front of it and fails to see everything else around. What this means is that the FALSE image in a person's head cannot be contradicted by anything other than a greater understanding - Seeing the obvious is precisely this, but who sees the obvious?.

There is an answer, a way out of this prison. It is called your RAT.

Your RAT is the aspect of our being that helps us get past this Censor. Our RAT, our *Reality Attention Trigger*, sees the obvious. This is the survivor in you that smells out the B.S. and wakes up the instincts. The Rat short-circuits the story of the Censor because it has a remarkable ability to smell when something doesn't add up. This book is here to show you ways to wake up your Rat and free yourself from the tyranny of what you presently believe to be truth.

Why? Because (believe it or not - irony intended) whatever it is that you currently believe is EXACTLY what is damming you up.

RATOLOGY states that our beliefs are not our friends and that they stop us from experiencing our life as a free agent. I say our beliefs are largely based around core lies or false images. They blinker us, they control us, and they breed a 'base code' of lies within us.

There is no Santa Clause

As an example of this: We all know there is no Santa Clause. The concept of 'Santa' is supposed to convey to the child that it is better to give than receive. But that is NOT the message most children hear - what they HEAR is that there is someone who rewards us for being good. This belief becomes the *psychic residue*, the imprint of the LIE. It becomes a seed thought which, when it germinates, forms our present beliefs, with the DNA of untruth within it.

What does this mean? It means that we cannot trust anything we believe. That we cannot trust our thoughts until we understand the lies that drive them.

This is followed by the paradox that we can never see our base lies clearly until we sort out the truth, or lack thereof, within our beliefs. It's a Catch 22.

This book is about learning techniques to deal with our automatic belief systems, to give you an insight into who, and what, you really are.

RATOLOGY is about you, your life, and how to survive it. It's a serious subject based on how to get more FUN into your life - Getting back to being kids playing in the sandpit of life.

Are you having fun? Of course not, all this serious thinking weighs us down, which is particularly horrible as I am trying to LOSE some pounds. But happily, in and around all the heavy-weight thinking, I will lighten it up with stories and snippets of truth to keep you smiling, thus make you happy to play along.

Seeing the Truth in the Myth

Most of us are not really living our lives - We are mostly obeying a book of rules given to us by our parents or our society. Underneath the storyline of this book there are MEMES, patterns which were passed down, that cause us to think and act in the ways we do. As an example: Just as Star Wars conveyed a great story, it also transmitted a message. The MESSAGE is far more important than the story and, in the case of Star Wars, it is purely the Roman Tradition: Nobility, belief in self, making the most of opportunity, trusting to luck, etc. These are ROMAN MEMES - ones that are still speaking to us in the present day.

Ratology is all about seeing the CORE MESSAGE, the base-line signal. It is caught up with the Latin phrase: Res Ipsa Loquitur - *The thing that speaks for itself.* It is the most powerful argument you can use in a court of law and it is the thing most people never grasp. It is called, *seeing the obvious*.

Only when we get to see the obvious in ourselves and in life's situations can we learn to identify what the REAL message in the MEMES of our upbringing might be. Only by seeing the obvious can we break through the myth-perceptions in our lives and discover reality.

Which is why I like poker. Poker is an excellent tool for learning this. You look at someone, they are presenting a story. They bet on what they hold, but are they lying, or do they really have the cards? How do you READ their actions? What you see *under the surface* will be the decider on how you act. Call, raise, or fold: you will base your decision on how to deal with an opponent largely based on the MESSAGE you read underneath the story they are saying.

If we want to win in life, we need to go beyond belief. We must see, hear, and touch the truth of what we are. Ratology will help you achieve this.

All the Dead Gods

Mankind has always found some sort of external God to believe in, but where are all the old Gods now? They die with their culture. Ever since people figured out the concept of fire they have offered prayers to an unknown God: Begging for success with war, the end to famine, and offering arguments about whose God is the best - These are all hallmarks of society. *Dead Gods = Dead Societies.*

I find it curious that, as the wars die down and individual wealth goes up, and as our personal security increases, our need for religion fades. In good times, our Gods become decorations on the mantelpiece, more of an ornament than a reality. But this is not the reason for the death of any particular God - the ending of that culture is the final nail in the God coffin - No-one worships a loser.

But why does a culture die out? Mostly they are defeated in war and a conqueror subsumes that race and their culture. In almost every case, the Gods of those cultures die with that culture. If your God can't beat their God, he/she/it deserves to die. There is ONE notable exception.

The Roman Empire was different. It ended the worship of Zeus and, for the first time in recorded history, an entire culture chose a different God mid-step. This was done in order for their way of life to survive. An extant culture, not conquered, not defeated, but killing ITSELF in a civil war killed off their Old Gods and instilled a new set of rights and wrongs in the hearts and minds of the people. That change is still with us today, known as the Roman Catholic Church.

Because of this choice, Rome still lives. More to the point, we are still under the Roman influence today. The Roman Gods may have died, but they were executed by the Christian God in order for the Roman IDEALS to survive.

The path to eternity is littered with Dead Gods. The world is full of dead beliefs, dead societies and failed dreams. Inside us there is the remnants of myths, beliefs and perceptions of 'every glove that has laid us down' - as Simon and Garfunkle expressed it. The edifice of past experience has constructed an internal Demon-God that controls our subconscious, and therefore, us.

I recommend a different sort of God - your own heart: *Learn to trust yourself. Learn to love your life. Look for the Holy Church of Freedom Within.*

Fitting In

So many people just want a place to fit in, where they are accepted for who and what they are. But who you are and where you are - These are not fixed positions. Our awareness gives us three options: *Accept it, change it, or leave.*

Most of our problems stem from the socialization process, which takes an innocent child and conforms it to the standards of any given society. I ask that you consider the following two 'truths', and ask you to understand how these have created the personal 'certainties' within you. These truths are self-evident:

- The process of socialization instils a set of shoulds and should-nots into the child, and are designed to assist it to become part of that society.
- This creates a 'split' between the natural and trained self.
- As a direct result, many in Western Society are confused and unknowing of themselves. This gives us a need to 'fit in'.

I say: *Why waste time fitting square pegs into round holes?* I say: *We need to get back to our natural self, expel the crap, and discover a freedom that is not limited by self-doubt and negating personal beliefs.*

Poker is Life

> *"If you're playing a poker game and you look around the table, and can't tell who the sucker is, it's you."* Paul Newman

I am starting this second chapter with a discussion about Poker, not just because the game is an analogy for life, but also because it is currently a popular craze and I want to cash in on it. This is my RAT at work, people, so you may as well see and experience it up front.

Poker is like life: It is a social experiment where everyone is out to get each other. It is a game where you are expected to lie, cheat, bluff and scam and what is more, you are RESPECTED and will make friends when you do it well. When you pretend to be honest, act like you have got the goods, you often win a hand. If you DO have the goods, you need to underplay your hand and allow some stooge to try and bluff you. *Life is Poker*. Play well, and the rewards are high, play it badly and it creates serious consequences to cash flow, emotional damage, and a distorted self-image.

Poker Tables are a place where you will meet a lot of people who are there to get a buzz. *Winning is the thrill*. It gives a boost to the ID factor and this is addictive. Losing brings you an anger that breathes fire all over the thoughts of how you could have, would have, or should have done it differently. Yet losing can be a low that is ALSO addictive. Ask any problem gambler.

Safe to say, we all want to win. We all want to be the big banana, the head honcho, the cool Bogart sipping gin and tonic while he plays the perfect hand and picks up thousands. The sad part is that I am not interested in showing you how to become this. *Why?* It is because of the odds. No matter how good you get, there is always someone better to take you down and it is odds on that as soon as you become cocky and think yourself bulletproof, you'll be shot down.

The Mystic Rat says: *It hurts to be cool.*

I have a better strategy for success than winning; it's called survival.

Let's face it, in real life 'winning' often comes down to the last man standing. If you are the one who suffers the least amount of loss, you win! In this sense, survival IS winning. If you want to win at a poker table, you just need to survive long enough to get winning hands. That's it!

There is ONE truth: *There is never a shortage of cards but there is ALWAYS a shortage of chips*. The cards themselves are endless. They keep coming and coming time and time again - But without chips you are not in the game.

I love Poker. It's a religion where Fun is the God. This is my type of faith! Poker shows me everything I need to know and understand about people, society and how to play the game of life. It also fits in well with this book, because at every poker table there is a RAT!

"You low down dirty Rat" You hear this in Westerns when the black hat man is caught cheating, usually at the poker table. Then (because it is a Western) it's out with the guns and the real men stand up to be counted. Some die, some get wounded, others run for cover, but we all know that the rough, tough good guy in the white hat will win the day and be loved by everyone.

The good guy always wins, doesn't he? What was that I mentioned about believing in Santa Clause? In the eternal context of Karma (As you sow, so shall ye reap, etc.) this is quite possibly the case. But in real life the nasty, vicious creatures are usually the ones that end up with the money. Why? Simply because they are willing to intimidate, humiliate, and bluff enough to cause you to want to walk away rather than continue in conflict. These people are using (wait for it) the Dark Side of the RAT. The good news is that we can easily get chips of these people, but only when our own Rat is stronger than theirs.

When it comes to Poker, you need an active RAT if you are going to survive. This is an acronym for your *Reality Attention Trigger*. It is that secret inner part of you that goes "Bing" when crap is being served up as sausage. I like the term RAT because Rats are known to be great survivors, mostly by remaining unseen: By staying underground, keeping to the shadows and staying hidden from view, they live relatively free from interference. They know the world will kill them at any given opportunity and so they adjust to living their lives accordingly. There is no argument, no fighting for causes, no trying to change the world: just waiting for opportunity and trusting it will come.

Life is a Poker Game. Everyone in your society is after YOUR chips. The mechanic wants to bluff you that the headlight fluid needs changing. The Doctor wants to convince you that you need an operation. The Police want to convince you that speed kills and will fine you big time, saying it is for YOUR benefit - Yet, as only 2% of accidents that result in death are directly as a result of speed, that is a lie. We all have to survive a thousand piranhas trying to eat us as we cross the river of life to our next great opportunity.

Remember this Golden Rule: *If you want to win, don't play to win. Look for opportunity and play to survive.* I like the analogy of the Poker Table because it really is a reflection of life. People come to a place wanting to WIN - but when you arrive with the goal of finding an opportunity, with the real goal being to just survive till you do, you come with a different attitude. THIS gives you a real advantage. You are not looking for the same thing as everyone else is, so you have less competition for the space you want.

Life IS a Poker Game. It is full of people who think they know what they are doing, but the fact is, it's all a lottery. You never know what cards will turn up. You never know who is sitting at your table. The person you had known for a few months and who you invited home to meet your parents may well turn out to be a sociopath intent on killing the guinea pigs in the back yard. They may have targeted YOU as the path to said guinea pigs and used you to get to them.

There are also Donkey's! Ah, donkeys: They are people who bet on anything, and the stupid part is, because of odds they occasionally win a big hand. They never last long, but they ruin the language of betting. To explain, in Poker a good player bets to ask questions. They judge the response by other players and use this in order to fathom the strength of what they face. Donkeys ruin this subtle communication because they play for luck and love a gamble. In the long run, they will be handing you their chips hand over fist. Just learn to fold the cards and not play with them when they are on a lucky streak.

There is the Cherry Bomber, the one who re-raises your hand because they have a pretty Queen, and that just HAS to win. The problem is, because of Pot Odds and the fact the Cherry Bomber is an idiot, other players are encouraged to buy in. Your pair of Aces now has to beat five players.

Then there is the Slow Player, the one who lets other people bid up the pot when they hold the best hand. They let people swing on their own petard, and cash in at the end with a massive 'all in' bet that no one believes, so everyone calls. There is the Bully, the person constantly raising every hand, pushing weak players out of winning cards. There are so many types of players, the actor, the drama queen, just about anything you can imagine.

There are all sorts of people who turn up at poker tables, but they all share one thing in common. They want YOUR chips. They will do, say and act out any game in order to get YOUR chips. Think of it as going to a nightclub: Everyone is there to get laid, and they will do and say anything in order to achieve this end.

Remember the obvious: Everyone in business wants your money. Even the local Church wants your energy, money, and devotion. It is not paranoia, the world really IS out to take what it can from you.

Everything boils down to a simple question: *Do you want to live well?* If you do, you just admitted you aren't. Now I rephrase: *Do you want to live? Well?*

Well? What IS stopping you? It is the thousand whispers of SHOULD within.

However, your RAT, your Reality Awareness Trigger, is attuned to the negatives around you. Trust it and you learn to hear OUTSIDE your own mind. You pick up the fine whistles and whispers that every living thing gives off. And one thing you learn, if you are not certain, better to leave it. This is when we learn to practice a sort of optimistic doubt about all things that come our way, and it can be surprising how luck will start happening for us.

The secret is that Lady Luck is always here, but her door is locked. We find the key to opening her heart with a combination of doubt, expectation, and the understanding that everyone wants YOUR chips. The true art of poker goes back to the Romans - it is the art of finding opportunity and making luck.

The original Romans were the Sabines, the tribe that lived on the Tiber where Rome began. They were an agricultural people who worshiped two main Gods, Fortuna and Ops. We know these today as Luck and Opportunity. And, If you must pray to an unknown God, these are good ones to pray to.

Infamous Shoulder Chips

Everyone at a poker table is there to get your chips. In life, people want your money, your attention, your whatever and, for the most part, you want theirs. Accept this is the game and we can learn to better defend ourselves against it. The trick is to have an open mind, a light heart and a playful attitude - *But the majority of people drag behind them a huge weight of misconception and doubt.*

Most people are not in charge of their thoughts or feelings - The monkey on their back is what really runs their show. When you work out who, or what, is driving their emotions, you can then reasonably predict which way they will turn. These hints are what the poker world looks for and calls a 'tell'.

So you pick a weakness in another - what do you do about it? If you try to help them they will hate you. If you capitalize on it, they will hate you. If you do ANYTHING they will hate you. Why? Self-hate is driving their bus. I let people and all their shoulds pass me by until they start to should on ME. After this, the trick is to step aside and let them stand in their own shoulds.

People don't want to learn what is wrong with them. They just want to WIN, but the monkey that is whispering from their shoulder is what is driving their bus. In a poker game, these are people who are addicted to hearing whispers of conviction inside their heads. Instead of seeing the obvious, or dealing with their fears, weak players are listening to what they 'should' do from the murmurs of their infamous 'shoulder chip' - the should-er on their shoulder.

A SHOULDER chip is a SHOULD-er chip. People have chips on their shoulders, grudges to bear, and axes to grind, all because they believe the world is not as it "should" be. To an experienced poker player, these are all little 'tells' or signs of weakness. So often people advertize with their attitude the sum total of the whispers that have created their world of defeat, failure, and depression.

In a poker game you can easily cash in on these negatives. The trick is to understand that we all have that pushy bastard inside who wants to tell everyone how they SHOULD behave, what they SHOULD do, or what they SHOULD NOT think. These 'Chips of Conviction' are your collective brace of 'Shoulds'. These are what rule people, not common sense, not reason, not kindness or consideration. These 'shoulds' give most people their instructions on what to do in any given moment.

If I ruled the country, I would make sure things run as they should! This 'should' is the Pope inside, the arrogant and generally stupid fool who thinks they know better than anyone else how things 'should' be.

The Mystic Rat Says: *Remove the condition of 'Should', and you remove a whole lot of stupid from your life.* (See Rule Two: Rules of Rattyness, P 128)

But we generally do not confront or deal with our 'shoulds'. We simply read about what we 'should' do from our personal rule book, our diary if you will. We write INTO it for the first sixteen or so years, then we 'rut up' in some dull marriage, or boring job, and spend the rest of our lives reading 'from' it.

Nose to the Diary Stone

All day long I see people, nose to the Diary Stone, reading what they 'should do' then painting their past over the present. *Our habits create the rut which in turn steers us towards the circumstances under which we find ourselves.*

Let's look at the 'Diary Stone' process:
- We mostly drive along in the rut of what we believe we 'should' do.
- Which creates the circumstances under which we find ourselves.
- Our circumstances to create our attitude, which tells us what to expect.
- Which gives us a pattern, a prayer book of sorts, of 'what to do'.

On any given day in any city I see people with their nose firmly planted in the diary of their past, acting out whatever their 'shoulds' tell them is appropriate. We have this 'Book of Rules' inside our heads and we believe it is important.

I don't know why, because to everyone else, apart from your mother, it is 'a nothing'. Humanity is a sea of people passing by and no one really cares about your personal sense of right or wrong. (unless they are on Facebook - which *automatically* means it doesn't matter.) This is important to understand as it forms up Rule One of the Rules of Rattyness: *It's not about you.* (P 124)

Why is this important to understand? When we recognize we are NOT the centre of the universe, we start to free ourselves from our personal 'shoulds'. By seeing our self as PART of the environment, not the centre of it, we will begin to read the signs life is sending us more readily. Further, because we are awake to the changing pulse of things, we look and act in a more random fashion. Therefore, we are no longer predictable. OMG! Look at that guy! He's being UNPREDICTABLE! (Cut to scene: Crowds of people running about, screaming, with their hands waving about in the air)

Seriously, do you 'really' think anyone cares? - Rule One: *It's not about you.*

Truth is simple: WE are simple. The first truth: *WE are not all that important to anyone we meet.* This is wonderful when you think about it, because it allows you to do whatever the hell you want. In other words, when we recognise that we are not important to another, we become free to act without fear of what the other will think. Further: We have no need to respond to them, thus we have no need for response-ability towards them.

Come to this place of freedom people. When you do you will soon discover you are in a far better position to observe the issues that really drive people, and how their 'choices' are predetermined by their programming, which effectively forces them to act in particular ways.

Stand back and watch and you soon see how the 'shoulds', which are the chips on the shoulders, are running the lives of most people. You will ALSO see how opposing the 'shoulds' inside the person are their passions. Most people are strung up like a bird in a butcher shop, hung between their 'shoulds' and their 'wants'. People 'want' to satisfy simple, mundane desires and passions. In response, society has installed 'shoulds' designed to keep these in check.

And yet, while I seem to be saying it is a bad thing, the state of should is necessary, as otherwise we would have a society of wanton rapists, murderers, and thieves. All societies have laws. Religion, the Law, the Police, and peer pressure - these are all 'force reminders' of the 'should' - The dividing line between the 'should' and the 'want' - but it creates tension.

To avoid dealing with this difficulty, people tend to 'hole up' into set attitudes and a robotic existence. Many people live lives that are little more than cogs in the wheel of existence.

Cogs Don't Dance

If you are living a robotic existence, if you are merely a cog in the machine, you will never grasp this simple truth: *Cogs don't dance.*

Living in a completely pre-determined existence, which is what the world of 'should' is, means you never even imagine you might go dance in the sun. Why? Because you are not supposed to, that's why.

NEWS FLASH! Running on automatic is a choice to not choose - But Is it really your fate to go round and round like a stuck record repeating your 'shoulds'?

When people talk, they are generally reciting a script written by their parents or peers. They don't know it, of course. Most John Doe's truly believe what they say and do is something they chose, but like heroin addicts and alcoholics, when your life is a habit you are not in the driving seat: *Your habits are running things!*

You see it all the time at the Poker table. There are patterns that drive other players and, if you can spot them, you will have a great advantage. Whether you are on-line or if there is an actual person there, it never changes. *People follow habits.* Thus the flip-side: To survive at Poker, the very first thing to recognise is that YOU can and will be controlled by YOUR patterns. Further, these patterns get mixed with your passions (to win, to look good, to get chips, etc.) and, to the astute opponent, you become an open book.

Remember, *cogs don't dance*. But you have a choice! You can be a cog in the machine, or you can define a greater sense of individuality for yourself.

'We are all individuals', the Monty Python crowd shouted in unison in "The Life of Brian". Can you tell me, what makes an individual? Answer: A person who cannot be divided, a person who is ONE. To be ONE you have to have merged the divided selves and unified your mind, emotions, memories and physical experience. This is not such a simple thing to achieve. To become a true individual requires a tremendous leap in the dark over the fence of cog-dom - And here is the greatest secret anyone ever gave you: *Freedom requires you to leave the known path, and the best way to do this is to start having fun.*

The motto of the Rat comes from the graffiti of Guru Adrian, found on the walls of Sydney town in the 1980s: *Half the fun is having fun.*

Logic hit: *Enjoying your moment means you are IN this moment. This means you are OUT of the endless wheel of becoming that is the life of the cog.*

It is NOT complicated. Fun + NOW = Freedom. What isn't so apparent in this equation is the need to accept yourself. The Paradox of Fun: Fun is an escape from reality to the cog, but for the true individual, having fun is an acceptance of it. Fun brings us into the NOW. When we are NOW, really present in the moment, we have nothing but ourselves. In other words, we dropped off our 'shoulds', unified our selves in the NOW, and discovered we were free.

I give you a truth few understand: *If you do not like parts of yourself, these 'pieces' cannot enter into your NOW.* The rejected parts of you will sit outside of your present moment and, unless you gather them all up, bless them, and own them, they will pull you out of NOW and back into your patterns. The trick to accepting yourself is to stop the internal argument between 'should' and 'want'. The only way you can do this is by accepting both our 'shoulds' and 'wants' for what they are - notes in your personal diary.

From the view of the social self: A cog not doing what it is 'supposed' to do is seen to be at fault. As we all know, Cogs are certainly not supposed to dance, or have fun, are they? But if you 'want' to be free of your mechanical existence, you are going to have to do accept you are faulty. Accepting your faults directly challenges your sense of 'should'. Which is a GOOD THING.

We all have Cracks

We all know unhappiness never made anyone happy - unless they are a masochist. Most of us choose misery - We see ourselves as wrong or faulty because we imagine we are not perfect. We are not the ideal person our mother imagined we 'should' be. Well, who really cares? The First Step to Freedom: We stop thinking we are important. Only then do we learn there is a bigger and better life out there waiting for us. Second Step: We let go of the bars of our prison. But CAN we? This means we must let go of our 'shoulds'.

We are whatever we are. Acceptance means we are OK with this. We don't need to be perfect to be happy. We don't need approval to have fun. We all can share this present moment and we ALL can live in it. What is stopping us? Answer: Non-acceptance of self and the belief that we are faulty

Accept your faults. Your cracks are what lets the light in. Acceptance sets us free from the machine. The cracks in you ALLOW the light to shine into the darkness of your heart. Trust that you are OK and allow your Inner Rat to guide you to a better place. Trust that all it wants is to see you strutting through life, confident and proud of who and what you are.

Now the whole point of this book is to get past whatever is blocking us from fun, but in the process, I am going to give you clues as to the best way to survive here on Planet Earth. In a nutshell, this is mostly learning to avoid confrontation with your personal desires. This is where RATOLOGY diverges from the Buddha.

He said we need to practice desire-less-ness. But I have a problem with this because the desire for desire-less-ness is what? You know it!

Answer: A Desire! Oh My Gawd! Off to a Buddhist hell we all go. (They have lots of them, you know)

The Mystic Rat Says: *You do not have to agree with your passions, you do not have to deny your ideals. You just have to avoid an argument with your wants. Why? It is ALWAYS an argument that we will lose, given time.*

I need to repeat this. Allow your passions to coexist with the rest of you. Allow your vanity, your anger, etc. to exist and accept that they are real and powerful forces inside you. If you can do this, if you can recognise and respect the wild horses within, you can harness them. In other words, stop shoulding on yourself (Rule Two) and just live! This is the *Way of the Rat* and by following this you will survive long enough to win the Poker Game.

Understanding Poker is Understanding Life

When I sit at a poker table, I look at three basic things:
1. *Who is here?*
2. *What are their Issues? (The chips on their shoulders)*
3. *How can I capitalize on them?*

The last thing I look at are the cards I am holding. First and foremost I want to see who I am dealing with. *What sort of people has life served up to me?* These are my REAL cards. The people at the table and how they act will allow me to survive, or they will kill me if I am not careful. It's a minor war game we are playing, disguised as a social event. But at least it is an honest war, not like the covert whispers of the back-stabbers in our social circles.

More people are going to poker games than ballroom dancing or church on Sunday. I believe there are very good reasons why Poker is sweeping the world as one of the all-time most popular of social experiences.
1. *Poker teaches us about human nature*
2. *Poker gives a buzz and the chance to win money*
3. *Poker allows us to be liars, cheats, and swindlers*
4. *Poker allows us to be ruthless killers without harming anyone*
5. *Poker allows the venal, callous, wicked aspects of ourselves to be expressed*
6. *Poker calls our negatives positives and being too positive a negative, thus it flips our attitudes and ways of thinking*
7. *But most importantly, all the above makes Poker FUN*

Poker allows the killer ape within to roam safely in society. It allows you to express savagery without hurting anyone. All our lives we have been taught to confine our negatives, but poker says, '*Experience them!*' A good poker game is a little like a good old fashioned gladiator's arena, though usually without real blood on the table. Poker is a forum where people are called to confront their demons, dance with their courage, and watch their vanity grow large before it is cut down to nothing. It is a great training ground where the RAT can learn to survive and thrive.

ACCEPT YOURSELF! *Like a dark light in the cathedral, there is peace and mystery in this place of shadows.*

We come to one of the reasons for this book. I am here to encourage you to look at your dark side, not necessarily to join it (though you can if you want to, your choice) but to see it for what it is. Learn to see what is here, right now, and you will live a far more balanced and, in the end, better life. The message is: *Do as you will.* But the tag to this ancient axiom is: *Do you really understand what you will?* There is no easy answer, but one thing is certain, if you suppress the dark side of yourself, you will never know.

And if you don't ask a question, you will never find out. In poker, we can test the waters with small bets and, as a result, reveal the willpower of other people we play against. WHO we are playing, WHY they are playing and HOW they are playing becomes secondary to WHAT is driving them. EG: Is the person really 'on tilt'? Has anger and frustration taken hold and they are making silly bets - Or do they hold a pair of Aces to match those two already on the table?

They may look like cool cucumbers on the outside, but you have noticed that the way they are drinking their beer is different now to just three minutes ago. That means something, but what? Here we reach a pivotal understanding in the world of Ratology: *The answers are found on the dark side!*

Why? It is OBVIOUS! The majority of people are motivated by their negatives more than their positives and the dark side of human nature is what is really driving most souls. Go to any judge in the local courts, ask how many people he sees who are motivated by goodness and kindness. He will just laugh.

Let me put it another way: If you have not inspected your own dark side, playing poker is like going to Rome and not speaking Italian. Until you understand the 'shadow dialogue' that happens inside yourself, you cannot read the Diary of Need most people use as their bible. You are looking at them and just guessing what the little signs you see might be saying. That sign might be saying 'Stay Away – Big Hand' but without the inner dialogue set right, you might read it as 'Big Bluff'. The sign might be saying 'I am really frustrated with these crap cards' but you read it as 'confident winner'.

The point is this: *Unless you have developed a language inside yourself that encompasses the whole person, you cannot even begin to read what others are really saying to you.* This is, by the way, why it is so hard to read new players. Are they shaking because they have a big hand, or because this is a big bluff?

Who is Driving the Bus?

There is a question I ask a lot: *Who is driving the bus?* What is in charge of the situation? As a small example, my brother's wife had just had her Seventh child.

They are very Catholic and do not believe in contraception but after seven kids? Well, I was wondering if maybe it was time for a change.

With this in mind, I suggested to my sister-in-law "So do you think this will be the last child?" Obviously, to my way of thinking, I am hinting at contraception being used in some way.

The reply I got surprised. "I certainly hope not!" she said with a degree of indignant surprise. That's when it clicked. What she HEARD was, "Are you going to stop having sex now?" My question had nothing to do with contraception in her mind, because the possibility of this was forbidden. Now, I could understand this because I had been down the strict religious pathway. I could see how the attitudes of the Catholic teaching were instructing my sister-in-law how she must think. But conversely, she would NEVER understand how I see things. Why? Because she will never walk a mile in my moccasins.

My sister-in-law was deaf to anything but the Catholic dogma. THIS was driving her bus. I imagine she believes she thinks for herself but her beliefs are what run her mind. Again, people are welcome to live and love in whatever way they choose, but I write this book in the trust that a few will start to wake up and start to look inside, asking: *Who, or what is really driving this bus?*

Who is driving the bus? This is what I ask at every poker table. You get all types, aggressive dominators, slow players, stupid players, careless "I am just here to have fun" types (you get lots of chips from those) to name a few. Every single one of them will tell you their secrets, if you have the eyes and ears for it.

These things we cannot learn from a book. It takes years of observation and experience to be able to spot the signs, understand the language, and get a sense of what is not spoken. Here's the secret: We need to clear the decks inside OURSELVES to enable this to happen.

You have probably heard that 85% of all communication is non-verbal, yes?

Most of us are aware that people speak unspoken words, using small gestures. This is true, but go another step - What the books don't tell you is that **100% of non-verbal communications are entwined with the passions and myths that run people**. In fact, almost EVERYTHING we express is wrapped around these distortions of our natural state. We refer to this state of deception as, "Human, all too human".

Poker is a Religion

Poker is indeed a church of sorts, one where we learn to understand human nature. In particular, it is a good place to grasp the deception side of things. In the Poker religion, it is perfectly acceptable to lie, cheat and swindle. Indeed, it is EXPECTED that you will do so, and further, you are RESPECTED when you swindle well. In other words, poker is a world where lying and deception are part of the woodwork. Yet at the same time, you have to keep a 'poker face'. This basically means that being two-faced in Poker is a requirement.

Let me see: Doesn't this sound a lot like society? When a guy wants to pick up a girl, does he go up and say, "Gosh, I am an insecure wreck who needs sex, will you help me out?" Not at all, he has to go up and IMPRESS the girl with an image that appeals to her. Impress is the right term: He has to project an image that works in with her psyche, one that presses the right buttons. So he LIES.

I love the Austin Powers character. He goes up to women and says "Yeah Baby" in a happy uncluttered way. He projects innocence, playfulness, fun, happiness - a good time. That's what most people want. A fellow I knew used to pick up women by sitting in a bar staring at his drink. Eventually, curiosity gets too much for some woman at the bar and she goes up to talk to him. He projected a dark, somber, deep image and this appealed to the dark side of women. Another person I knew used to act damaged. He was an actor who sat at the bar looking stressed and in pain, so the maternal instinct of some woman was called up and she went to help him out.

He hated women, I might add. He just used them for sexual relief. I asked him why he hated women so much and his answer was, "Because they can't see through me!" Oddly enough, this is also one of the main reasons people get cocky and start to lose at Poker: they actually believe people cannot see through them. But think for a moment: To most women, the insecurity of the male is obvious. To most men, the tentative doubt in the woman is clear.

If you sit back, observe, and just watch for the small signals that everyone gives, you will learn that the vast majority of people are an open book. Learn to look through the facade, over the walls, under the circumstances, and what you will be left with is a fairly obvious truth: *People are generally not happy where they are*. It is unhappiness that motivates most people's actions. Unhappiness, discontent, self-doubt, and greed - these are the things driving their bus.

The Mystic Rat Says: *We can all see the other side of the fence, you know, the place where the grass is greener.* But ask yourself: Am I a Cow?

Spotting the Demons

I spent some time living with a woman who was on the edge of madness. Let's call her Miss Buzz. She spoke to me a lot about what she saw and more importantly, HOW she saw things. After a lifetime of abusive relationships, she had been opened up to the negatives that drove most people's actions. The problem was that now all she could see was this negative side of people. At first, this disturbed me because at the time I saw everyone as Soul. In my world, every person I met had a beautiful potential, a wonderful surprise in waiting. She saw their demons.

Now here is the tricky bit: By seeing them Miss Buzz woke them up. She would not let the sleeping dogs lie and, when they woke, they bit. The paradox is that this proved to her the truth of what she had seen! She really DID see the negatives, but what she missed was how she caused them to rear up to bite her.

So, how does this happen? It is because of the infamous SHOULD. Miss Buzz had an attitude that the person 'should not' have this negative. She saw it as WRONG and, as a consequence of 'shoulding' on these people, she stirred up their usually buried issues. Obviously, when you tell someone steeped in negatives they are wrong, that they 'should not' do or think something, their first reaction is to fight back. You are threatening the survival of their passions. A simple rule of thumb: *We create problems in our life by expecting something from people that they do not want to give, admit, or condone.*

Miss Buzz broke the first two rules of Ratology: She thought it was about her, and she 'shoulded' in her own nest as a result. When she decided to turn her negative radar on me, I knew where it was going, and so regrettably ended the connection. To either argue or agree with her meant that I would be part of her shoulding and this is death to any freedom we might experience.

In this case, it was a vicious cycle: Miss Buzz used to see the negatives in others from the view that they were dangerous to her, therefore she had to protect herself. This meant coming to every table armed and ready, but armour clinks and the rattling of sabres wakes everyone up. So tell me, is there an answer for her conundrum? 'Should' she stop looking at people's negatives? The problem really lay in the way she felt threatened and thus believed that by attacking others she was acting in the interests of her personal survival.

The answer to the push and shove of human existence is found with every winner of a Poker Game. Winners in Poker are SURVIVORS. True survivors not only allow other people their negatives, they capitalise on them. In Poker, if you want to win you must see the negatives, the passions, fear, and vanities that drive people, and THEN you must ALLOW them. You don't fight or argue, you work with the issues at hand in order to position yourself in a place of confidence. You survive much better with allowing and accepting than attempting world domination.

Confidence comes as we learn the ways to draw chips off people. Surviving well means we develop an air of confidence and authority, which helps us to survive better. As our confidence rises this, of itself, is enough to turn the tide of circumstance into our favour. It is very hard to guess what a confident, focused player is holding in their hand because it all looks so good.

Oddly enough, at this point of genuine self-assurance, people start to see THEIR demons in you. A hint: You KNOW you are succeeding when people start to blame you for their failures.

Can you tell me who the most successful poker players of all time are? No? It is the Bankers! Banks have perfected poker. They place bets on people but they hold all the aces! (their mortgage) All the time, they stay back and rarely play the hand themselves. They sit back, take a small cut, and only play the safe odds. Yet look at what happened when the banks started to play the poker game themselves. By creating derivative-based investments between 2000 to

2008 they filled the world full of chips and started betting as if everything was an Ace. This careless gambling crashed the financial market of the world and, as a result, several banks did what people thought was impossible: They died.

Survival means to think like a traditional banker with your own chips. When you place a bet, call it an investment. Ask yourself if you are likely to win or lose, and always play the odds, but primarily play the players at the table.

Remember everyone is at the table to get everyone else's chips and to protect theirs. But to get other people's chips, at some point you have to risk your own. This is the dividing line between what most poker players call 'Guts and Glory' and failure. Sadly, the majority of players who go for glory fail. I love it when people put everything into the pot saying, 'No guts no glory' because it usually means they have an average hand and are just hoping to pull it off. OR they are playing ME! They have Aces and want me to think they have nothing.

It's all about reading the signals right. We make our decisions based mostly on what signals we read, by the cards we hold, and accordingly by the cards we fold. Another secret: *The last thing you want to do is to act because you love your cards.* This is when you regularly put everything on the table because you have two Aces. Would you give away all the money in your bank to a stranger you met last night? "But I fell in love with them!" the dear women say to the police as they describe how the handsome Nigerian man took all their money.

An odd saying most people will recall, "He seemed to be holding all the aces!" The reality is that Aces don't win as often as you might believe.

The Trilogy of Failure is very simple:
1. *If you love your cards (opinions, etc.) more than the game,*
2. *If you forget the cost of what could go wrong,*
3. *You are guaranteed to lose.*

Even so, in poker (as in life) never discount the possibility of sheer dumb luck. It can turn the worst of days into a joy, but don't count on it.

Summary: Only when we see all sides of our self can we begin to take charge of the "cards" we have been dealt. Failure is always an option, so act accordingly. Remember to stay focused on Opportunity and Survival rather than winning.

Suggestion: Allow your foibles, because they can be fun. Your passions will cost you, but no-one wants a robotic life, and the whole purpose of money is only there to bring you a little joy, yes?

"We are looking for what is looking"

Rumi

Humpty Dumpty - Post Wall:

*"Ring any bell that will ring
Forget your perfect offering
There's a crack in everything
That's how the light gets in"*
Leonard Cohen

The above verse is from a Leonard Cohen song, which in turn comes from a Zen koan, or proverb. It speaks to the fact that we are imperfect creatures. Life's wear and tear will take its toll and generally creates cracks in our 'perfect' world. You possibly know the place I am speaking about: It's that spot where you start to feel a little ratty towards life.

SO - Who hates cracks? Can you tell me? Your CENSOR does - When it sees a crack in the reality it likes you to see, it starts to take over. Your Censor is the inner person who glues up the cracks, paints over the blind spot with belief, and convinces you that the picture in the mirror is perfect. Your Censor may well be painting Snow White, but your Rat sees the Seven Dwarves behind her.

This Censor business can be hard to digest, so let's not get too serious about things too quickly. Relax. *Half the fun is having fun!* (Guru Adrian) Taking things too seriously creates a death grip on life. Let's toss away any need we have of being some great ideal or image of perfection and just chill by the pool.

Now, beer in hand, relaxing in the sunlight, feeling the cool breeze, we can let go of the need to impress. Sure the belly could be tighter, the tan better, but what the hell: *It's about enjoying the moment.*

Now we can start: Sure there are cracks in our world, but these let a greater light through. Rather than argue with our negatives, we need to accept our vices and give them as much right to live as we give our nobility, love and common sense. Thus the *Way of the Rat* is very simple: *Forget about Seizing the Day - Just ENJOY the Day.* Beating ourselves up and demanding perfection, insisting we must be the best and the greatest at every moment - All this denies the Rat within and we suffer for it.

Did you know Japanese artisans will mark a creation they have toiled over? Why? Because nothing is perfect and it is arrogance to pretend it can be.

Ratology declares that understanding the simplicity inherent in most things (IE: seeing the obvious) is the only real solution to the problems of our life.

We say in RATOLOGY that failure is OK if it leads us to freedom.

So, what does Ratology demand of its loyal followers? Do you need high ideals? *Meh - they don't pay the rent.* Do you need to improve? *Well, maybe, but accepting faults is one of your best improvements.* Does Ratology say you can become rich and famous by thinking right, or eating the right food? *Well, OK* then. *You will become rich and famous by thinking right and eating the right food.* Dammit, you caught me out, I lied. What I am really asking you to do is wake up and start seeing every moment for what it is.

The Mystic Rat Says: *Seeing the obvious brings a solution to most problems.*

It would seem that Humpty Dumpty's problem is that he is all in pieces and that he is now only good for compost. Yet consider the obvious: *Humpty was a total failure, yet by default he became famous.* Go figure! He's a Kardashian!

Laughter is the Best Medicine

I had a friend, a beautiful, talented musician who had a slight quirk: She believed she was Jesus. After some years with long and short periods spent in asylums (starting from the point where she had declared her reincarnation to people from the roof of her father's house), she had calmed down and no longer made the claim. We are talking over Chai Tea, served up in a tent standing in the middle of a music festival where my friend was performing.

"You heard about the problem, yes?" she says.

"Problem?" I ask, acting innocent.

"You know, me shouting from the rooftop that I was Jesus," she answers.

"Oh, that? Well for me that wasn't a problem, but it did cause me some concern." I said, nonchalantly lining up for the punch line.

"What, that I believed I was Jesus?" she looked at me with suspicion. "It seemed to make perfect sense at the time. Everything fitted and the more I thought about it, it seemed true. The whole thing made so much sense."

I could see she was still mildly convinced that maybe her true God Powers might yet reveal themselves. "Seriously," I said, looking her. "What are the chances there would of two of us being in the same tent at the same time, talking like this?" This was, of course, an old reworking of the Napoleon joke where the mental patient pulls the visitor aside and tells them that they need to be careful as Bob there is crazy because, "They think they are Napoleon!" And the punch line is the familiar, "And there can't be two of us, can there?"

However, my friend looks somewhat hurt. Was I ridiculing her? Do 'I' believe I am Jesus? What's going on?? Then it clicks in her head: *It's a joke.* Then it clicks again, *the IRONY kicks in and she starts to laugh.* Suddenly she laughs out loud with a genuine belly gurgle! Something in the obviousness of what I just jested about tickled her. She stands up and says, "Thank you! I just got it. It is so damn obvious - We ALL want to be important."

She left soon after. I was told that her delusion of being Jesus seemed to have retreated and she started laughing more in her life. Hey, glad if what I said helped, but I just reworked a tired joke from my days as a failed stand-up comic.

For my friend, her personal failure as Jesus had driven her to work on her musicianship until she DID indeed become a Master - of music.

That's the paradox of illusion: It is all lies and it is all truth. And it ALL stops when you laugh about it. My friend just needed to awaken her funny bone.

The Mystic Rat Says: *Your problem is the fact that you can't laugh about it.*

And what about the amazing tale of Humpty Dumpty? The egg that fell!

What does this story say to us? Failure can create success IF we handle it properly. Humpty is the perfect example of success through failure. You may say he's not all he's cracked up to be, but falling off his perch worked for him. It gave Humpty high ratings in the Nursery Rhyme Top Ten for centuries. Through failure, Humpty discovered fame and is now recorded in the annals of history.

Humpty Dumpty: Let's revise the scene as we know it:

> *Humpty Dumpty sat on a wall.*
> *Humpty Dumpty had a great fall*
> *All the Kings horses and all the Kings men*
> *Couldn't put Humpty together again*

Test Number One: Do you see something that is glaringly obvious in this nursery rhyme? You probably presumed, like most, that Humpty Dumpty was an Egg, right? But whoever said Humpty was an Egg? I don't see any evidence in the written material. I do see the pictures drawn in kids books of a fat egg with a stupid smile, but that is just imagination at work. Why the hell do we all imagine Humpty Dumpty to be an Egg?

We know why: it is in "Through the Looking Glass". Lewis Carroll ran the Humpty propaganda we all swallowed. But ask this one question and other obvious questions arise: How did he fall? Why was he on a wall in the first place? Was he pushed, or did he suicide? The person who has a strong Rat has already asked these questions, so why do I bring this up to you? *If you see the obvious you run far less risk of falling into erroneous patterns of belief.*

We were all pretty certain Humpty was an Egg prior to this, right? Yet there is absolutely no evidence in the rhyme that indicates this. *Can you tell me who, or what, Humpty Dumpty is, why he was there, or what caused him to fall?* None of this is made clear in the evidence. If your Inner Rat was active these facts would be among the first things you would have noticed when you first heard this rhyme. But like 99% of the people, you didn't, did you?

And here is the problem. Your Inner Rat is asleep! Your guardian to the bullshit is not at the gate: therefore, the B.S. gets into your system and becomes a reality. Faulty information breeds false facts which lead to false beliefs.

We ALL get raised on a diet of half-truths and ignorance and we believe this to be normal. Humpty Dumpty was not the fragile egg we thought he was, yet most of us believed this 'fact' until the obvious was pointed out.

The most likely source of the Humpty rhyme comes during the Royalist War in England. A short, fat cannon called Humpty Dumpty was knocked off a castle wall and was not repairable. It was a siege that went against the King, one in a series of failures that resulted in Cromwell winning the war. Humpty Dumpty is not a stupid story, its an historical fact. But this is not how it has been PORTRAYED in picture books. Get the message? From a curious truth 'harmless' lies have been created and thus the world has fallen for yet another fiction.

The reality is that Humpty Dumpty was a murdering thug, responsible for hundreds of deaths, and used as a tool of destruction by radical believers in a failing monarchy! Yet, he is painted as a Good Egg in need of Social Security.

Why do I bother mentioning this? We have all been fed lies as truth. Santa Clause isn't real, Jack and Jill never went up the hill, but of course, the Tooth Fairy is real because we all got money from her, right?

Our personal myths are dangerous to us. It is not the story we believed as a child, we all have long learned that was just a story - What is dangerous is the RESIDUE, the distilled core energy of these myths that lingers behind and become the seedbed for a thousand related half-truths we tell ourselves.

To whit: We know Santa isn't real, yet, long after the myth is dead, inside us the seed of the story remains and germinates in attitudes that control us. The SUBTEXT of the Myth is: *If you are good, you will be rewarded.* This is what gets lodged in the mind and it can affect us our entire life. Santa is Fake News people! It is LIE, we know it is, yet the poison of the Santa Myth has infected the thinking of millions of people. The truth is simple: To be free of our myths we need to see through our beliefs and find the reality inside them

When my youngest son was three years old, he lost a tooth. All day long he reminded his mother that she needed to call the tooth fairy and book her in, because he wanted the cash. This went on all day, yet when I was putting him to bed he pulled me aside and whispered: "Daddy - I know there is no Tooth Fairy, but don't tell Mummy, ok? (then a pause as he looks into my eyes) Because I want the money!"

"Bless my socks!" I said to myself, "My three year old can see the obvious!"

Not many people can. Why? Surely it is obvious that the politician is simply out to win votes when he makes all his promises. It is obvious that most governments are not interested in looking after anyone but themselves. It is obvious that creating a priesthood that is starved of sex will create problems. It is obvious that putting money into winning the lottery is a bad deal. It is obvious that a divorce lawyer is not interested in harmony but in getting himself paid.

Learn to See the Obvious

If we all saw and acted on what was obvious, we would not see the divorce lawyer and simply settle things amicably. In fact, we would never have been in a situation that called for a divorce lawyer, as we would have chosen a better mate. In Sanskrit is is called Vidya, true seeing, and it is a karma-less act.

Seeing things clearly changes everything - It minimizes trouble and increases benefits. We avoid disinterested courts and settle disputes honestly. We listen and hear another, rather than believe we know better. We bend with the wind, go with the flow, and plant seeds in fertile ground. I cannot even begin to express to you how completely different our entire life would be if we lived and breathed the obvious. But we don't.

Common sense is really a recognition of the obvious. Yet how many New Age books advertise Common Sense and seeing the obvious? Not many - De Bono and Lateral Thinking comes closest. Let's look at some Ground Zero principles. These are things that are completely obvious, yet we miss them time and again:

1. No one is perfect.
2. Nothing is completely true, or false.
3. Not one human soul is totally honest past the age of four.
4. Whatever you believe at this point is certain to change in the future.
5. And if it doesn't, you are stark raving bonkers.

When we fully accept that no one is perfect, we find a tremendous benefit. We are subsequently released from having to live up to some false standard for ourselves. We can relax more. We can enjoy life better.

If we accept that nothing is completely true or false, we become less insistent on our OWN view being correct, thus we are more able to listen and hear what others have to say. What they say may, or may not, be worth much - but listening always tells us more than talking.

When we accept that no human past the age of four is totally honest, then we will never get disappointed, twisted out of shape, or convinced we are being betrayed by another. We experience greater freedom within the changing nature of circumstance because we no longer have impossible expectations.

Once we accept that whatever we believe now will be different in five years, we won't need to defend our current bastions of belief, thus we allow ourselves to change and therefore grow more readily. Further, when we allow other people to be what they are, we ALL become happier, more relaxed and better able to get on with each other.

Here is the real truth: *We are ALL in some ways a Humpty Dumpty – Post Wall.* We are all 'cracked' to some degree and the idea behind this section of the book is to let you know that this is OK. We all start out as 'good eggs' yet, in the transition from child to adult, we get into hot water, start hardening up, and get a little cracked. Then we discover that people want to eat us!

We invariably want to hide our failure, because in the jungle being damaged makes you a target for predators. This is perfectly acceptable behavior because it means survival. The problem arrives when we pretend we are fine (Read: FINE = Fucked up, Insecure, Neurotic and Emotional) but we are inwardly shaking in our boots with fear of being discovered as a FRAUD.

Stephen Fry, the very articulate and highly intelligent English actor, came from a background of significant emotional abuse. He learned to act FINE but stated in public that he believed he had 'FRAUD' written across his forehead and that everyone could see it.

This belief controlled his life and, though he won outer accolades, he still suffered with deep, inner depression and confusion. Though he never spoke about it, Peter Sellers was another classic case of this conundrum.

The beliefs and convictions generated out of our experience as a youth control the lives of most adults. External success will not alter this. Stephen Fry had accolades thrown at his feet, but it did not improve the depression and anxiety he suffered. Remember Santa Claus and the residue of belief? THIS is the problem, the psychic junk-pile hidden in the unspoken remnants of childhood that survived the passing of our dreams, nightmares, hopes, wishes, and beliefs. The monster IS under the bed of belief!

I am Perfectly Pickled

"It's so fine, yet so terrible, to stand in front of a blank canvas." Paul Cezanne

So many of us live a life of acting FINE, and we do it to such a degree that pretence has become our watchword. What we are really doing is *avoiding the obvious*. This is the lie we live and it can happen to such an extent that we forget we were pretending and start believing our act is reality. This is like an actor subsuming their role on stage and allowing it to bleed into their personal relationships. It's just an ACT, but this is an act that can hurt you.

Fact: *No one started out as a Catholic or a believer in any particular religion.* Nor did anyone start out believing they were completely right in what they think, to the exclusion of all others. Yet this is often how things end up. How does it happen? It's called the Pickle Principle: You may well be the world's greatest cucumber, but after enough time in the pickling jar, voila! You become a pickle. We SUBSUME our environment and it becomes our beliefs. We have been absorbed by the notions we were soaked in when growing up.

When we grow up with emotional starvation we tend to live an emotionally starved life and choose emotionally starved people as friends. Or the opposite, we seek out emotional wrecks and people who are overly dramatic.

The Pickle Principle is simply that we become our influences. *"What you don't know may not hurt you, but what you don't remember always does"* (Prescott)

But it all changes when we remember we were born a free spirit. Can you imagine for a moment that you are 'Back to Baby', or what we call an 'unprinted item'? Imagine you are fresh out of the box, no anger, no preconceptions, no fear - A freshly minted baby-self starting out.

Our baby-self is our true identity. This is the cucumber. Yet once we soak our hearts and minds in this world, breathing in the lies, confusion and half-truths for long enough, it pickles us. We look in the mirror and forget we were once a cucumber because now all we see is a pickle.

The point: *We have gone from a social animal to a socialized one.*

The question is: Can we De-Pickle? I say: *Yes we can.* I say we can reverse the osmosis, clear up the falsehoods, lies, and distortions that have entered our hearts and I say we can do this relatively easily. Some teachings, such as Scientology, are fully into the de-pickling process. They use a system known as Auditing where, by use of questions and confrontational situations, the teachers of that path force people to look at the hard truths regarding the lies inside themselves. This can easily cost $300,000 and take many years.

Accordingly, as Ratology will do this better and quicker than Scientology, it must then be worth at least $300K per person. Yes? Donations are welcome.

RATOLOGY states that Soul is smarter than the patterns it is trapped in. It needs to set itself free from the confined view of its socialization and fly above the maze of confusion. Getting ourselves above the process of socialization and conformation is a state we generally call Self-Realization ('Clear' in Scientology) - But in simple truth, it is more a state where we come to like ourselves, appreciate the moment, and enjoy our own life. The goal is to fly free: no longer controlled by the past, our fears, or - worst of all - our lack of self-worth.

Fly to Freedom

Children go on flights of fancy all the time. What does this mean? *Flying free is a natural state, not a learned one.* If we are stuck in a rut, the message is that we have lost our natural self. We are caught up imagining we are trapped.

The way to 're-fly' is found by having fun and learning to see the obvious. Here we find the natural path that helps us get out of the lies and into the zone of true self. This 'zone' is a place where we sort things out, moment by moment. What is more, do it this way and it's FREE. (Apart from necessary donations to Ratology, of course) We need no priests, no churches, no altars, no expensive workshops - just laughing and learning to see the obvious. The goal is to get to, and remain inside, that clear, easy, child-like space within us.

So, we come to the real questions: What is stopping us from being free of our conditioning? What is keeping us in the maze and stopping us finding our wings? Good old-fashioned human attachment to the past is what clouds the vision and confines the heart. We all want to be seen as Good Eggs, we all want approval, yet we know that the façade is cracked. So, we plaster over the cracks, pray to unseen Gods, and CONFORM. We compensate our loss with pursuit: a better job, a bigger house, a faster car. The one thing we do NOT do is let it all go.

Why do we hold onto the bars of our prison when the door behind us in not locked? Why do we not walk through the open door to freedom? The lack of a genuine self-esteem is the dreadful fear that locks us up. The process goes:

1. *Guilt: We all generally fear we are not 'good enough'. So we fake it, and fear what will happen when we get 'found out' (guilt reflex).*
2. *Fear of Loss: We then start looking at what we have to lose in life rather than what we have to gain, and the fear of loss starts to control us.*

3. Our fears take charge of the bus. Every pothole becomes a focal point, one that makes us steer invariably, inevitably towards the abyss

So many people lose at Poker because of the above. They have the best cards on the table, but this happens to be the second top pair. They bet, but it is a sort of guilt bet because they are obviously nervous. An experienced player picks the weakness and, though they have nothing, they bet in hard against them. The weak player with the winning hand folds and loses their chips.

All the controls of society are based on conjuring the fear of loss: Do wrong and you go to prison (loss of liberty). Speed in a car and you get fined (loss of resource) and can lose your licence (loss of freedom). Our whole social order is based on fear and punishment. Ratology can teach you how to negotiate this minefield and show you how to live without fear.

What first clued me into fear as being the issue? As a youth, I read many of the psychology and new age thought books that were on my fathers bookshelf. In every single one of them, he underlined the word FEAR. You just cannot believe how often it came up, again and again. How much fear WAS there in the world? I determined as a youth to never let this emotion dictate my actions. Of course, I was fooling myself, as youths always do - but the idea was good.

So tell me, do you really believe there is a solution to your fear? Do you have any extent of the maze you have locked yourself into? Let's look at some of the basic patterns of behaviour people employ:

1. We imprison ourselves within rules of behaviour.
2. We constrict our hearts with fear of consequence.
3. We then proceed to apply emotional makeup, hide behind cliché's, and pretend that it's all OK.
4. We act out that it's all FINE:
5. OR we do the reverse, and see the world as black, our attitude as grey and that the colour has drained from society.
6. Or we get suicidal when we realise that none of the above is working

Not one of the above points will work out well for us. It is like the snowball rolling down the hill, picking up whatever crap is on the path. WARNING: *The world is full of negatives, they are very easy to collect and difficult to detach from.* Stop with all the fear and for one moment start to see the obvious - Spot the obvious, see where the path is going and chart a different course, where necessary. In other words: avoid the shit and certainly do not roll in it.

By seeing the obvious we run far less risk of being caught up in other peoples dreams, expectations and beliefs, and a far greater chance of fulfilling our own.

The Law of Attraction

We are all hearing about the Law of Attraction at the moment. Like attracts like, etc. and this is true to a degree - *Our buried fears and problems attract other people with buried fears and problems.* But this is not the worst of it!

The real issue occurs once a *pattern of distortion* is set inside our head and becomes the filter through which our experiences, and others, are seen. Look through a red lens, everything looks red. *(from: Please Mr. God, This is Anna)* Likewise, when we look through the lens of our disturbance, we then see distorted things everywhere. When this is normal, our false reality IS our norm. We no longer seek to fight the drowning tide, we don't even realise we are in the pickle jar! We just allow the cucumber-of-self to fall into pickle slumber.

This is where the suffering begins. This is where the tide of disjointed relationships, disconnected intimacy, and dislocated lives all conjoin to form a morass of social games and disruption. *Would you call this living?*

Living for most people is a series of stress points between moments of relief. Think Seinfeld without the funny bits and you've got it. (Wait a minute, Seinfeld without the funny bits - wouldn't that be Seinfeld anyway?) Are we beginning to see our life in here yet? Or maybe all your relationships are FINE, and all your intimacies are FINE, and you can be completely honest with all your friends?

Of course you can.

Worse, you *are* completely honest with all your friends, and they hate you.

However, there is hope! RATOLOGY can help you find your way past all the crap and waffle and show you the logjams inside that are causing your life to congest into a thousand clogged arteries of confusion. We can repair the shattered past. We can show you how to bring that childlike happiness back to your present moment. How? By teaching you to see the obvious.

This is another way of saying we will teach you to pay attention to your Inner Rat and allow it to guide you through the uncharted waters of your existence. Remember this: The problem is never the problem; Our lack of awareness of it is. First, recognize what is there, then we can find the way to fix it.

To illustrate the real issue: A man I was speaking to recently had to go in for a quadruple bypass. As he was going under, he heard the nurse say "Well, we can only get three of them - No one can get to that fourth one." SUCH a nice thing to hear when your life is at the mercy of these people, Yes?

Yet, my friend woke up to a smiling doctor, who said, "Well, we managed the impossible! They said the fourth valve could not be done, but we got it! And a good thing we did as it was 95% blocked."

What's the purpose of this story? The OBVIOUS: No-one can operate on their own heart. Likewise, no-one can fix their own mind when it, of itself, is the problem. Why? Because your mind believes there is nothing wrong. Here we have the need for the Lord High Rat. (I humbly bow before thee) We all need someone who has gone before, someone who has walked the road and who knows the steps we need to take.

Finding someone who understands consciousness to help you can do far more than save you pain and suffering - It can save your life. A faulty mind is as fatal to happiness as a faulty heart is to life.

Both will destroy intimacy, awareness and your connection to the present moment. A crack in the psyche is a far more delicate and difficult thing to resolve than a broken arm, but it is still something that is broken that needs to be fixed. It is just a lot harder to do. The reason for this is blindingly simple: *The person with the most serious disconnect almost invariably believes that they are perfectly OK.* (Refer to the book "I'm OK, You're OK" - Thomas A. Harris).

I am OK - Not

I meet a lot of bad actors, people who project a belief they are looking good but when you scratch the surface, the façade crumbles. This is a danger zone in all human relations. If you point out some obvious flaw in a person, it activates their survival reflex, and their angst soon rises like scum on a pond. Fury, abuse, anger and a flurry of accusations fly through the air like hot knives looking for a back to plant themselves in. And that's OK with me. I am almost as good as President Bush at ducking the boots that get throw. I say people can do what they wish. But, at the same time, I remember what happened to Socrates.

"Would you like some Hemlock with that philosophy, Sir?"

We generally need an external perspective to shift our awareness. Laugh at someone's stupid pretence and you run the risk of attack. Yet, if they give up their self-righteous position, they will see the obvious and understand how utterly ludicrous it was. I do not want to press people's buttons, yet how can you shift people out of wrong thinking if you allow their false beliefs?

Yet point out the flaws and they may try to attack you. Telling people the truth is risky business, so wisely, I choose to do this at arms length with a book.

I have no interest in philosophy. You cannot eat it, for one, and all our high ideals, beliefs and illusions largely evolve from the mind and do not nurture the heart. I just want to feed your heart a little bit of truth. Why?

A person with a starved heart lives in a silent panic. Natural communication becomes truncated with a staccato sense of self-preservation that goes 'Me-Me-Me'. Rather than holding a sense of honesty and trusting another enough to tell another how they really feel, the starved heart will generally drag you down, trying to save themselves from drowning in guilt, shame and self-loathing. But give that heart a buoyant sense of humour, and it all changes. Get the person laughing and they stop sucking in misery, and the soaking in self-pity stops.

Most people who truly know me would say that I am pretty competent in the areas of the Etheric Plane. This is the zone where our subtle communications and originating patterns of behaviour and thought start. I can generally show you the patterns that generate your problems and suggest ways to avoid these. I can even give clues about how to reconstruct yourself into a better Humpty Dumpty. But oddly enough, most people react very badly to this.

Why? Fixed beliefs rule. It is human nature to stake a territory and defend it to the death. But get them laughing and then poking them with sticks is OK.

So I wrote this book to be your piñata. You can take out sticks and beat it all you like - pummel it, thrash it, let your anger out. When you are done, you can pick up the sweet truth inside. Yet, a book is just words. It is not the texture, the feel or flavour of a banana, just a description of it. So, to really get RATOLOGY, you will need to read between lines and learn to taste the invisible.

As Saint Exupery says in 'The Little Prince': *It is only with the heart that we see rightly. What is essential is invisible to the eye.*

Through socialization, our natural self gets supplanted with programmed responses. So often we lose the free thinking child and become the robot-adult. The REAL 'pickle' we find ourselves in is that, when fully subsumed in our behavioral training, we start to believe our false face is the real one. Yet we secretly know - There is something we have to get away from here!

We have Humpty'd up on a pedestal of belief but, when Humpty looks down from the walls he has built around his heart, wanting to escape, he gets vertigo. That's when he fell into confusion and that's why we are all in pieces.

Getting Clear - Staying clear

I worked for a few months at the Park Café in the heart of Sydney. On my first day, the remarkable woman who employed me (the beautiful Helen) pointed towards a cluttered workbench and spoke her great words of wisdom: "Create Space!" This simple clarity had a profound effect on me. This magnificent creature stated in these two words two powerful things:
1. Take charge of the situation, and
2. Clear the decks

It is this simple: *To take charge of the space in the head and heart we need to clear out the patterns of the past.*

To be clear of the past you must first clearly see the present. This means seeing the obvious, which means grasping the stinging nettle of reality.

This hurts! And even when you succeed in reaching in and grasping the fractured pieces inside you, even when you fall gloriously into the flavour of life, it remains that you still have to do the work to keep yourself in that space.

The Law of Maintenance reads: *As soon as we reach clear space, clutter arrives to defeat it.* Ask any housewife and she will tell you the only solution is constant vigilance and to keep sweeping. If you don't, the crap creeps back in, and a mess becomes the norm. This presumes that you can see the crap in the first place, so seeing the obvious is always called for in retaining a sense of clarity about out surroundings. The good news is your Rat can help, because it smells where you have garbage. Again, the obvious: *You have to see it to toss it.*

Recognising what is NOW is the key. Getting the rubbish out, creating space, all of it means NOW works better. *Living your NOW* is the next step.

Why is this important? NOW is the broom that sweeps away the pieces of the past. So tell me, what is the 'anti-NOW' that keeps us away from living fully in the moment? *It is our collective baggage of Shoulds.* We all have them - these the beliefs and attitudes that hold us to the past. But why?

Answer: *Our past conditionings are magnets for our Shoulds.*

When you move to a new address, do you take what you need, or everything you don't? We know we are supposed to toss the excess baggage out, but hey, I love asparagus and that twenty year old can of it I will never eat cost a lot of money at the time. Old garbage is a sign of attachment and only when you toss these things out do we discover what was causing us to hold onto them.

I cleared my Dad's cupboards one day - and yes - a twenty year old can of asparagus turned up. It had gone through THREE moves! When I asked, my father had no idea - He didn't even LIKE asparagus. But I knew why, he had an incredibly deprived childhood and throwing ANY food out was a crime.

It is the well-meaning SHOULDS like this that we most need to identify and dispose of. These are the burdens that serve no useful purpose and, even if we can't quite junk them, at the very least we become aware that they are there.

The Mystic Rat Says: *Ignorance is nobody's friend.*

Reverse this to get: *If you are a nobody, ignorance will be your friend.*

NOW do you get it? You will if you survive to the end of the book. We need to shatter certain patterns of ignorance and we do this by seeing the obvious. More to the point, the thing that drives most people to the destination called 'nowhere in particular' is a blind belief in their past programming.

But toss the useless past and our state of NOWHERE becomes NOW HERE.

So this is where we really start our book. Any true beginning is, of necessity, an ending of the past, so, if we accept that the first step in being clear is the process of removal of junk, then we must learn to recognise the difference between clutter and what is useful. This is just common sense.

This is a little like the High Society woman who went to the doctor with a flatulence issue. She informed the Doctor there was A: no smell, nor B: any sound that came from her farts. Even so, she felt it was something that needed clearing up. The doctor agreed and gave her some pills. She duly took them, and to her horror, it did not slow down the number of farts at all, but the SMELL! It was shocking! They gave off this detestable stench. It was so disgusting she could no longer bear to be in the same room as herself.

After a week she was back at the doctor explaining the awful side effects of the drugs she was taking. The Doctor just looked at her and said, "Good, we have fixed your nose. Now let's get to work on your ears."

I may have to tear some strips off your present set of beliefs and opinions. I have to fix your nose, so to speak, and while this may really annoy some of you it's better than people talking about your disgusting farts behind your back. It's like taking castor oil: You may not like it but its good for you.

Let's pause, breathe deeply, and take in this moment. (not too deeply if you have just farted) We are at the edge of a cliff, getting ready to jump.

You are possibly guessing by now that this is NOT a "nice" New Age book that affirms you and offers accolades about how wonderful you are?

I am shocked. How could you imagine this? Of course, I will say that you are a wonderful, deep person who is both well-considered and rich in insight. You, my friend, are a truly meaningful person of significant worth: *to your dog*. The real truth is, most people are full to the inner rafters with deeply buried issues that are secretly controlling them.

Issues: Big ones, small ones, it's all the same. We all have issues and to your Inner Rat, they SMELL. Which is a good thing, because it makes them easier to find! So let's start waking up the sense of smell, shall we? First: What sort of generic issues do we possess? Let's look at a small sample of possibilities:

1. *We believe we are not good enough, or*
2. *We believe we are better than everyone. Either way,*
3. *We imagine that somehow we are at the centre of the universe, and/or*
4. *We presume we are unimportant / overly important, etc. etc. etc)*

Far worse, you might be the sort of person who imagines they are perfectly OK - This means I have to hit you over the head with the fact that there are a pile of internal issues and beliefs that are controlling you. (Reaching for rubber mallet) My job is to correct your dedication to false shoulds. (I tip my hat to Dr. Wayne Dyer and his book "Your Erroneous Zones")

The truth is, most people are vain and ridiculous in how they present themselves - yet let's not strain a friendship by suggesting that you might fall into this category. It must be obvious to everyone that YOU are humble, deep thinking and have it all together. Clearly, we are merely discussing your friends.

Some books are sweetness and light - They tell you how wonderful you are. Maybe as Soul this is true - but as a social animal, you are not. Why? Because EVERYONE has a stinking 'should' buried in their consciousness somewhere.

The point here is that, before reading any further, we need to accept that this book is more like war drums than perfumed roses being strewn before our feet.

Castor Oil: You have to take it, it tastes awful, and you really don't know what good it does you, but you take it anyway. We could sugar it up, but part of the effectiveness of the message is the sour note. Let's shatter the ignorance, find the NOW, and see life as it is. Only then we will begin to see who is driving the bus. Then, if we find the chartered destination is called 'nowhere in particular' - we can change direction to NOW HERE, in particular.

NOW has to become the place you really want to be for this to work.

The Mystic Rat Says: *Focused contentment is powerful, as it feeds emotions and nourishes the spirit. All emotions that assist survival are useful, otherwise they serve little purpose.*

Accepting Cracks

"Idealism is fine, but as it approaches reality, the costs become prohibitive."
William F. Buckley, Jr.

All of us are cracked by the circumstances of life; it is only a question of degree. No-one survives unscathed, yet so many Self-Help books want to tell you that this is all fine, that everything will be rosy, life will be wonderful, and you will be completely happy - as long as you BELIEVE. All you have to do is think positive, work with the Law of Attraction, act 'as if' and keep your attitude upbeat, etc. etc. That way the cracks will disappear and life will become peachy perfect pure porcelain fineness.

A little while ago, I was visiting a guy who was on his back in severe pain. He informed me he was fine because he had read all the New Age books and was applying the principles. He told me, as he crawled around the room unable to walk, that he was OK because he was keeping his attitude positive.

I said to myself, "What sort of crap is this?" Who could possibly imagine a good attitude will fix a bad back? Despite his stupid attitude, I fixed his back for him and I did this because I knew how. The paradox here is: I turned up out of the blue and I was one of the few people who 'could' sort him out. So maybe his attitude DID work?

The bad news: This book is not going to 'fix' your problems - though it MAY help you improve your attitude. Ratology does not encourage you to think positive and absolutely abhors the entire Positive Thinking brigade. The way of the Rat is nothing other than learning to see and smell the obvious.

The good news: if you 'can' learn this, it will improve your life, fix your problems, and get your attitude into better shape. Thus you will be in a better frame of mind, more confident, and less subject to the whims of circumstance.

But let's hold off on all this future stuff and talk reality. The most obvious reality shouts: **Nothing is perfect**! We all have cracks, faults, and foibles. We are ALL a sort of Post-Wall Humpty Dumpty. In one way or another we have all fallen from our childhood position of high expectations to an adult world where some form of cracked and jaded reality now controls us. If you haven't yet realised this, you are either lying to yourself or just too young to know better.

What's the problem with this? *Your cracks open you up to whispers, little voices that suggest we are not good enough, that something is wrong, and that nothing can put us back together again.* I spent forty years as a physical therapist listening and dealing with human problems. What I have found is that most people unknowingly listen to their inner fears and act accordingly. They SAY they are applying principles of some high ideal, but the reality is, this is usually lip service. What they are really doing is listening to a pre-recorded message that lists their worries, concerns, and agitations.

Why do we listen to our inner 'whispers of failure' rather than follow our aspirations? It is very simple: *Fear is driving the bus.* The inner dialogue of fear that instructs people has many voices. You may recognise some that I list below:
1. *"I am unworthy of love",*
2. *"I do not deserve respect", and also such notions as,*
3. *"I want, but don't deserve, better pay for my work."* (etc.)

Yet when we ACCEPT we have issues, that nothing is perfect, we take a different view, and accordingly, we EXPAND and receive a different experience.

This is when the miracle happens: *Our cracks and imperfections become doorways to inspiration.* An artist called Fane Flaws (modern genius) gave me a painting of a sad man grasping the bars of his prison, yet behind him was an open doorway to freedom! The message was very stark and simple: *Holding onto the bars of your prison is never the way to freedom and happiness.*

Acceptance of self, cracks and all, allows us to LET GO of the bars. It is a form of love and love opposes fear. The person listening to their fears will get choked up with restriction, while the person finding inspiration is looking out for and breathing opportunity. Good Luck is CREATED by people who look for opportunity. Bad Luck is created by those who live in restriction. Good Luck comes to those who are relaxed. Bad Luck is attracted to those who are tense.

Relax, have Fun, and Survive

I have survived a head-on accident on a motorbike at speed, hitting a car coming the other way. Everyone told me how lucky I was to be alive, but the truth was I didn't fear dying, therefore I stayed relaxed. Yet I was still focused on surviving, not dying, so I was able to point the bike in the least injurious direction and a lack of tension meant everything didn't rip apart on impact.

The entire side of the bike was shorn off, I broke a few things, and it hurt to laugh for the next few weeks - But I was out of hospital and at a party seven days later. *Let go of everything but the joy of living, people.*

The core issues we suffer are all wrapped around fear patterns. *Childhood fears have grown into pivot points in most people's lives!* These generate negative reactions towards life. These are the things that cause us to tense up, to look inward, and shut off the light of the NOW. We have all had at least one self-negating belief. Yet, when find our courage, we see the obvious. Then we will quickly see that various fears control our thoughts and actions. *FEAR is the thing that blocks our natural flow.* FEARS are the bricks that build the dam that prevents our free-flow! (Remember - Ratology is the Way of the Un-Dammed!)

The GOOD NEWS is that the easiest way to get past our tension and fear is to have FUN. No one is fearful when they are laughing. No one is controlled by whispers when they are on the floor with a belly laugh. And really, *'Why So Serious?'* - Heath Ledger, as the Joker, asked this question and it cuts right through the gorgonian knot of complication and rules-based thinking.

What do you imagine Jesus meant when he said: "Ye must become as little children?" Do you imagine it might be his way of saying we need to drop the state of tension and get past the dammed up 'adult' problems we all tend to suffer from? Do you think he is suggesting we get *'not so serious'* and just PLAY?

Look at the simple facts: There are emotional blocks, mental patterns of confusion, and all manner of logjams inside us that prevent us from a sense of free flow. This 'logjam' gives us a sense that we are disconnected from life and creates our sense of loneliness and isolation. This causes us to:

1. stay in a failed marriage,
2. keep friends we no longer like, and
3. stay in stagnant, old ways of thinking.

None of the above is any FUN. When our Fun Quotient (FQ) is strong we leave the failed marriage, make new friends, and get reconnected to life. Every new day is an new adventure - you know, like little children?

The good news is: We can get the egg off our face AND remake Humpty Dumpty into what he was destined to be. The shell of our belief was only there to protect the unborn potential inside you. It NEEDED to be cracked so YOU could emerge. What we are about in this book is to show you a simple way to leave your fear-based reality behind. This book is all about helping you ACCEPT your cracks and foibles, collect your scattered thoughts and feelings, and then we can show you the way to make them whole again.

The even better news is that 'we' don't have to do anything! We just have to allow ourselves to remain awake to the obvious. *Just by seeing the obvious we position ourselves at a deep, inner place of power where we can allow life to sort things out.* And when I say 'Life' I mean the powerful flow that drives the entire universe. You know what I mean - the thing we generally think of as 'The Great Spirit' or notions to that effect.

All the Kings Horses and all the Kings Men cannot put Humpty together or make your life sweet because they are external forces. But you, working with your inner connection CAN clear the logjams of doubt, fear, and mistrust, and so put yourself into the winner's seat. But HOW?

The way we do this is to invoke the opposite of the Logjam: Synchronicity.

So how do we find synchronicity? First up: We take charge of the direction our life is going in. In this way, we are stepping into the driving seat. Please remember, life already has everything anyone needs, but you have to call to it and invite it in. Your internal fears are telling it to piss off but when you put your AWAKENED self behind the wheel, you are going to AMAZE yourself and everyone you know.

Synchronicity is FLOW. Being a part of this flow is really a reconnection to the state of 'true normal'. The Spiritual Law is simple: When we click into agreement with life, life brings us precisely what we need.

Synchronicity

> "I am open to the guidance of synchronicity, and do not let expectations hinder my path." Dalai Lama (14th)

Have you ever wondered why some words seem to be in all languages? There are words that describe "Spirit" in every language and they always mean some essence of God. Certain words, like synchronicity, appear in every culture. The reason why is obvious: because everyone experiences it. It's when the magic happens. German: Synchronizität. French: synchronicité. Italian: sincronicità. Arabic: Alazamun. Dutch: synchroniciteit. Albanian: sinkronizmi. The reason every culture has a word for it is because they have EXPERIENCED it.

Which ALSO means they have experienced its opposite! A baby does not get the diference between a boy or a girl until they experience it. So what IS Synchronicity? For one, it is the opposite of fragmentation and isolation. It is a gathering of forces into a shared moment of NOW. It is not a thing you can command, or will. It is not something that obeys the dictates of any plan or design. It just appears to happen.

When things connect naturally with other things we call it synchronicity. It is seen as a sign we are aligned with Spirit in some way.

Tell me this: Do you imagine that synchronicity is a matter of happenstance? It is just luck? People think of it as a lightning strike, a coincidence, but synchronicity is more than this; *it is an amalgam of forces that combine at a specific point of destiny.* And destiny is really just the end point of our choices - the chosen destination. You have to have the right conductor set up to attract the lighting but, obviously, you need to have the storm form in the background for it to work. However, it is the CHOICES we make that bring both together.

A curious example of how I have seen synchronicity in motion: I create CDs for people, based on mathematics and the Ancient Greek method of healing with music. Some people seem more connected to a great 'power' and I know this because as soon as I begin a project things start lining up outside my door. Real, tangible, physical events start to occur as I record. Dogs start howling for no reason, in tune with the music. Lyrebirds gather around the house. Storms come up from nowhere. Powerful external things just start to 'happen'. I feel it in the air and somehow it flows into the music I am creating.

People have written back to me afterward saying that their heart operation has been cancelled because the problem fixed itself, or that after twenty years of insomnia they are sleeping like a baby, or that after seven years of loneliness the ideal partner has turned up, and on and on it goes. In every single case of great change, there was a form of synchronicity happening behind the music.

So what happened? It was not a few notes on a CD that changed everything. The GESTALT of energy that makes the synchronous reality is a ball that builds internally over a period of time and, when it meets a like field in the external world, it is a dog wagging it tail, wanting to PLAY.

The Mystic Rat Says: *Your synchronous life begins when you go past the whispers in your head. Synchronicity happens when you stop listening to what you 'should' do and just PLAY with life, because life WANTS to play with you.*

In my experience, to have these miracles happen we must uncover some of the natural synchronicity that underscores our existence. *We must become as Little Children!* What I have found is, for this to occur, the great hurdle of 'Should' must be crossed. The people who wrote in for a CD were really breaking free of their personal conventions. They were looking for an alternative. They crossed the barrier of 'Should' and 'Should Not'. They left the quandary of their fears behind. They moved forward and risked change.

An incredible miracle unfolds inside us when we shift the burden of our upbringing from the 'Should Do' to a 'Could Do' through to a releasing sense of 'Would Do' and finally to just 'DO'. We are moving away from personal ingrained patterns and starting to move towards expecting the unexpected. This is the zone where the synchronicity starts to hit.

But what IS synchronicity? It seems like a gift, but it really is something we earn. In poker, putting in a bold move where you have a small 'hit' on the flop will usually drive people with higher cards out of that round. When you start this process, you 'chip up' which allows you to play more rounds. This means you now have a better chance of hitting cards. To others, it looks like you are mysteriously winning all the time and people believe you have "gotten lucky". The fact is you played your cards in a way to give yourself luck. Yes, you need a degree of good fortune, but a bold sense of just going for it has to come first.

Expect the Unexpected

The Mystic Rat Says: *Expect the Unexpected*
When we EXPECT things to happen, they usually do. The problem is, most people expect the worst. But let's say you rise above this - We trust our natural instincts and go with the flow - this puts us on the first rung of the Synchronicity ladder. We only need EXPECT things to happen in a fortuitous way to trigger this. Then we need to listen, watch, and wait for our opportunity to arise.

The real question, why is this attitude so perfectly normal for a tribesman hunting in the jungle, and so unusual for a person living in Western Society? Native cultures LIVE with Synchronicity. They expect it, and most accept it as a normal form of communication from the Gods. They follow the signs, they find food. It always comes. Why are people NOT experiencing this connectivity?

In a study conducted in the 1970s a group of natural therapists put together a wide selection of school-aged children for a 'holiday camp'. This was a 'socialization versus natural selection' test based around open food choices. At every meal, the kids had the option of all things imaginable: A range of foods were made available, fried, steamed and raw, including deserts, ice cream, etc.

At first, the kids went for the garbage and pigged out. However, by the seventh day, all but five percent of the children were selecting a balanced diet. There were still some pigs attacking the sweets, but most of the children (without prompting or adult advice) chose a balanced diet. What this shows is that without restriction or pressure, we tend towards what works best for us.

WHY did all these kids align with a diet appropriate to their health. It seems like a miracle has happened, but really nature is constantly sending the signals and the kids just needed to get their conditioning out of the way in order to listen. The real point here is that nature sends the signal, but do we listen?

The kids initially scoffed the crap, but then completely changed tack. Think about it! What does this say about their upbringing? This experiment speaks more about how a child is raised than to any apparent 'miracle' that they choose a balanced diet. The initial pigging out speaks of a child escaping constriction and confinement. Once done, they do what is best for themselves.

Obviously, parents restrict a child's food choices believing that they know best. Yet as soon as we shove the adults and their 'shoulds' out of the picture, most of the kids didn't go crazy and pretty quickly come into a natural balance. And what is more, they had fun doing it! But FIVE percent didn't! ALL the rules and regulations in society are based around THIS lowest common denominator.

The message here is simple: *Have fun, be free, trust your instincts*. This is what calls in and creates synchronicity in our life. What stops it? FEAR! When fear drives the bus, you hit all the potholes, and nothing works well.

We know this already. People want to know how to get rid of their fears, but fear isn't something that just goes away. We 'sort of' know that the secret to getting rid of fear is to open the heart centre, but how do we do this? It is so simple - just enjoy life: *Have fun, be free, trust your instincts*.

The unfolding process to discover synchronicity:
1. We stop thinking what we SHOULD and start DOING what we COULD.
2. We imagine what we could do, and in time stop FEARING what we cannot do,
3. This is where we start accepting what is possible for us to achieve.
4. When we grasp this notion, we can start walking in that direction.
5. As we walk, life opens up before us.
6. BOOM! We start to truly conceive that we can do whatever we want.
7. But then we hit the question: What do we truly want?
8. This is possibly the hardest stage, but finally we realise what we really want are for the pieces of the puzzle to start to fall together. THEN we begin to grasp the bigger picture.
9. With a clear target we can go for it! (Usually with great success)

SUMMARY: We *stated that, if we are to be free, we need to see the obvious. We then looked at the cracks in our psyche, etc. Then we said these are OK. We then looked at Logjams and how 'Shoulds' create these inside us. Then we spoke about finding Synchronicity and how this is very much to do with getting past our 'Shoulds'. And finally, we looked at how Kids just have fun.*

The real question to look at is the difference between free flowing children, and fixed-minded adults. So stop, look, and give yourself a rating between One and Ten. One being completely Free, Ten being completely locked: Where does this place you? Now ask someone close to you where THEY rank you.

The Message: Have fun, be free, look for the obvious, and trust your instincts.

The Nature of the EGG we Protect

Most of us are living as a patched-up Humpty - Post Wall. We have fallen from our high expectations and our sense of adventure and thoughts of being unbreakable has been shattered. In our enthusiastic, idealistic youth we gathered all the materials to build our ladder to the moon, but life beat down our enthusiasm. At length, as Thoreau said, we decide a woodshed will do. We give up our dreams, create a mundane and ordinary appearance, act sensible, and obey the road rules.

But are we happy? We have constructed a life, built over many years, but have we simply erected a facade? Are we actually happy, or just getting by?

It would seem far easier to let the cracked facade fall, but CAN we let it go? Can we let the fragile truth we built over our lost ideals collapse and allow what is hiding inside us to stand forth? So often we are restricting our nature, shutting down our options, then telling ourselves we are 'keeping it together'.

The 'egg' we protect is what is keeping us from our future self, but just as we tend to fear the future, we also tend to fear our inborn potential. We employ a range of 'shoulds' to contain the wild, free spirit and our Censor uses every trick in the book to make this look like the good and sensible thing to do.

And what happens when, despite our efforts, the inner-self starts to be born? It comes out deformed, a battery hen afraid of the daylight. It is full of fear and loathing, a thing we believe must be kept locked up, hidden. So we stuff it into the background and pretend it is not there. Our natural 'self' is now living under the illusion it is faulty and it fears freedom, considering this to be unsafe.

Our Mantra becomes, '*I am not good enough*' and fear slams the door, locks the gate, and stops our heart from expressing itself. We start to live a haunted existence, fearful that something is missing and, in our confusion, believe that what we need it 'out there': in a religion, a book, or a paradise that exists somewhere over the rainbow. Fear makes us less, Courage makes us strong.

The Missing Pieces:

For all the Missing Pieces
In our Jig Saw Jumble Sale
For all the gaps and parts incomplete
There's one piece you can't assail

It's that whisper of your Soul
A gnawing sense of thee
That even though we feel fractured and old,
We are still that Jig Saw Jumble of me

And when our fate is dealt
Like the cards upon the sea
In that future cast into pieces
That Jig Saw Jumble
That Ey-Or Grumble
That crash, tumble and rumble
Is what sets us free

Most people spend their lives in the pursuit of happiness. Few understand that our 'happy space' is really where we fulfil our highest potential. There can be many reasons why we don't experience everyday happiness, why we do not reach our best, but I find the most common is when we get weighed down with 'shoulds'. These are the expectations of what we 'should' do, act and be. This is what generates the 'unhappy space' - Where we end up living our life according to other peoples rules, not our own.

An old Italian proverb goes: *At 20 a young man knows people in the village are watching, but he doesn't care. At 40, he is more circumspect and is careful to hide his tracks. By the time he gets to 60, he realizes that no one was watching.*

We usually think people, God, the devil, or whatever is watching, and so we do what we 'should'. The question in my mind is: *Why? Why do people should on themselves and/or allow themselves to be 'shoulded' on?*

Fear. We are afraid. What enlarges this fear is that many souls have a sense that they are unworthy - *People often feel like a jigsaw with a piece missing.* We can feel incomplete in many different way and it all starts in childhood, when some odd event shatters our confidence and positive self-image.

Obviously, we have all had our broken hearts and shattered dreams, and we cope with these as best we can. It can be incest, or very serious injuries like this. But, despite the cost, most people I meet are OK with the 'big stuff' - Death in the family, loss of a pet, parents divorcing, etc. We put on a brave face. We carry on and, even though it's an emotional patch job, we get by.

The real issues that complicate our lives start with uncertainty, where life starts to run in accordance with a sense of LACK. We know there is more, we feel something is missing, and there is! We are missing the WHOLE.

This sense of a 'Missing Piece' we have is connected with an understanding that we are not quite whole and it is quite difficult to describe. The mystery is: It is not so much a 'lack' we suffer but the belief that there is something more, something we don't quite grasp. Emerson called it the 'divine discontent'. It is something we all share and it is mostly to do with a lack - of purpose.

And this is not so much the fear we will not reach our potential, more the concern we will never find it. In many ways, this is a faulty recognition of a higher self - Soul, if you will. What happens next is paralysing.

Feeling a sense of immobility to move forward we develop a 'black hole' - an empty space within - into where our fears, doubts, and unworthy behaviours tend to fall. This empty place is the magnet to our negatives. Drug addiction, religion addiction, people-pleaser addiction, they are all pieces of the Jig Saw floating in that space - disconnected pieces of self that we can't make sense of.

Hiding from Reality

And the dark within starts to become a monster we must hide from. Here is where it goes wrong. Instead of listening to the quiet, calm voice speaking from this place, most of us only hear our fears, echoes inside a cage of whispers that sing the silent song of something missing.

We feel things spiraling downwards. To stop this we stick something over the emptiness - Things like loud music from our youth, getting that car we always dreamed of, or having the affair - anything to avoid dealing with the emptiness we feel. We just cover it up with a dream and the conviction we are OK. Yet we do not deal with anything - we avoid the problem by playing the old children's game of putting our hands up pretending it has disappeared!

I still do it when playing Poker. I have a Queen Nine suited - A Queen hits the flop with two smalls cards around it. Suddenly I believe I am bulletproof and I completely forget my low kicker is easily beaten by someone with a Queen and so much as a Ten. Someone goes ALL IN, and I call it, confident they are just bluffing me off. Then I am out of the game.

The stupid thing is, I usually have an inkling before I play a hand if it will go pear-shaped. On many occasions, I have the sense when something isn't going to win, but I will ignore my RAT. I lose these bets just about every time, but I still go against that inner knowing. Why? I know better, yet I still do it.

In the above instance, I am hiding from the obvious. It is obvious that there are better cards out there, and that all I have is a top pair. So why risk all my chips? If someone else is willing to go the lot, let them have it. We need to trust our luck, but don't tempt the fates just believing we will be OK.

The Mystic Rat Says: *Belief is a patch to cover up a hole inside us.*

I knew a girl who, if she had any problems when driving, pretended it would all just disappear. If someone pulled in front of her, she would cover her eyes (taking her hands from the steering wheel to do so) and shout: "GO AWAY!"

The incredible thing is, she went thirty years without ever having an accident.

We do this 'cover up' in a hundred different ways. Some do it with control, others with faith, others with booze. Regardless of the approach, we do this to hide from the hole within us - A general truth is that most of us are doing whatever it takes to get by - But if we are going to be true to ourselves, most of us aren't doing all that well. Rich or poor makes no difference. Even if we have a Ferrari in the garage, a Beach House in Malibu and a million dollars in the bank, parts of us are still in pieces, and we feel a hole where something is missing.

The Mystic Rat Says: *So What?*

Who cares if we have a gaping hole in our personality, or if we are a little broken up about something? It doesn't matter! It is not a matter of life or death, but the constant worry about not being good enough IS. This IS a type of death.

Forget it! Let the damn pieces fall where they will. Caesar had to put his entire life on the line when he defied Rome and took his army across the Rubicon. He declared *"Iacta Alea Est"*. Early Latin scholars interpreted this as the famous "The Die is Cast" but really, it is spoken in the present tense, not the past, so it means: *"Let the dice fly high"* (and implies they will fall as they will). It was an "All In" call in Poker. He gave his fate up to the Gods and succeeded in his endeavours beyond anyone's wildest expectations.

The message is: *Stop doing the King Canute! Let all the dammed pieces of you GO.* Let them fall down. Stop trying to hold up the broken dreams, those faded promises and lost hopes. The hole you fear is part of what you are, but it's also that part which you are afraid to meet. Your hole is really part of your WHOLE SELF. You just can't see it this way and that's why it stays a hole.

The Hole of Self is a space of no-thing: You cannot buy it, you cannot be given it, and you cannot find it by looking. Friends cannot approve it, yet no one can deny it. You most especially cannot trade it or sell it for recognition, fame or glory. Inside your very emptiness is the sacred well of being. But you are unable to OWN it because you are afraid the Eternal Spring is toxic.

Instead of drinking from the water of life, our fear drives us to the poisoned chalice of foolish dreams, illusions, and false beliefs. Money, love, and position are what most adore chasing - which is possibly why it is called the human race.

OK - So for one moment let's imagine you win. Let's imagine the dog finally gets that tyre he has been chasing - Now what happens? Don't worry about it, I already have the non-answer: *"Why?"* you ask the Gods, *"Why? If I have so much, why do I still feel this emptiness inside?"*

The Mystic Rat Says: *If you want to be happy, embrace your imperfection, accept your emptiness, and forget about believing everything is FINE.*

We are NOT PERFECT and no one is happy all the time. Emptiness is a natural state and inside this there is only FREEDOM. Once we let the pieces fall where they will we discover our inner certainty - a place of contentment. The incredible lightness of being fills all voids. We will only discover this place when we are no longer being tugged out of it by our 'Shoulds'. By embracing our emptiness we lose our sense of doom. We can sit in unhappy times and look through the veil of tears, knowing we are finally free of perfection.

Here's the thing: When our INNER RAT is alive and well, nothing is too much, or too little. Just living is sufficient reward for living and we become a 'Soul of Constant Smiles'. I still stuff up, do stupid things, put my foot in my mouth, and occasionally tease the cat. (I like teasing the cat) I also aim to do my best, but I have relieved myself of the desire to be perfect and replaced it with the enjoyment of the day to day moments and the intention to do my best.

I am even relatively happy to be unhappy at times, though I still get pissed off when I make stupid poker calls. It really annoys me when I do not listen to my Inner Rat and believe that I know best. So I am not perfect, yet this too is OK. I don't stress over it. I have some cracks, I accept them. The paradox: BECAUSE of my foibles I have found my Omphalos, my still, certain point.

And overall it's all a poker game: some days you win, other days you go backwards. But if you want to win in poker, or in life, you must embrace the risk and learn to really love that empty space into which anything might fall. It's within that empty, random place of risk that the great joys of expectancy, anticipation and, finally, intimacy live.

The Cracked World We Live In

"There is a crack in everything, that's how the light gets in." Leonard Cohen

You have heard the saying, "This cracked me up" when someone talks about laughing a lot? We all know "You are cracked!" means you're just a bit crazy. The Irish will ask you "How's the Crack?" meaning how's it all going, but they are really asking if you are having any fun. (Note: craic is a misspelling of the original word) You are getting along at a 'Cracking Pace' when you are doing really well. So what's the problem with cracks?

Look closely at any adult's life and you will see the cracks. Any sensible woman easily sees the testosterone-fuelled macho pride that will drive a man to do stupid things, and any man can see the need for affirmation that runs so many women - but can we see it in ourselves? *"Oh what a gift the giver gives us to see ourselves as others see us!"* as the 18th Century poet, Robbie Burns wrote.

In Poker, people who display little signs that they are weak continually lose and wonder why everyone keeps calling them when they are bluffing, yet leaving them to it when they hit cards. So they toughen up, learn to veneer over the cracks, and they win more pots.

There are the double bluffers, the ones who act scared but have big hands, and vice versa. But the real poker success stories are the 'Open Books'. These players are impossible to read because they seem so confident and relaxed.

Let's look at being OPEN. When someone has nothing to hide they can have no fear of what you think. What does this openess bring?

1. The Open Heart is a doorway to Soul. It is that which allows the love of life to flow through into our existence.
2. The Open Mind is that which allows concepts and notions to pass beyond the cages of our confining beliefs.
3. The Open Soul brings an understanding that our true nature cannot be harmed, hurt or wounded by the ways of the world and thus needs no defense against the arrows and slings of outrageous fortune.
4. When we are open, life flows through us: we glow, we shine.

The Mystic Rat Says: *Logically - When you allow yourself to shine, your cracks become the spaces where your inner light flows through.*

The 'Shining' is a pure survival state. This is loosely what we call the expression of the Soul-Self, but few people really attain it. For example I knew this woman who appeared to shine. Let's call her Lucifer, as it now seems suitable. She was beautiful, intelligent, well-to-do and a friend of some years. We got on fine until I picked up a new girlfriend and right away the feathers started to fly. These two women had an innate dislike for each other. Well, I got on well with Lucifer's husband and, as I was chatting to him one night on the net, I happened to ask "Is you dear wife over the school-girl tiff yet?"

Wrong question! There was a silence at the other end, and the man said quietly "Ah, my wife is sitting beside me right now." I could feel the steel daggers flying past me, searching for a suitable back to lodge in. Here I was, putting my foot in my mouth AGAIN, but what else could I say. My RAT spoke for me, stating the obvious. "Well mate - What can I say? It IS school girl stuff and we all know it. We either own the facts and move on, or avoid them."

The woman never spoke to me again. Lesson learned: *Only point out someone's faults when you never want to see them again.* I note she divorced her husband shortly after this incident. This was a woman who appeared to shine, but it was just a projection. She had so little real confidence that she collapsed under the simple weight of one question.

The proof of freedom is found in what we are willing to give for it. Most people believe they want to be free, but when it comes to the edge, the area where you really have to let everything go and just fly, they can't. Instead of freedom, what they see is the abyss below them and fear rules.

And here we come to a curious hurdle: I call it the "Call, Raise or Fold" reflex. *This is often the Choice between Survival or Denial.*

Ratology: Way of the Un-Dammed

Call, Raise or Fold: Intention V's Hope - Survive or Deny
Looking for Opportunity, Position, and Usefulness

> *"Hope is the denial of reality."* Margaret Weiss

The above quote seems SO negative, yet it is not. It is a recognition that reality is unchanged by hopes and wishes. A great message in Ratology is a very odd one to most people's ears: *Don't trust your hope reflex.*

In Poker, hope is deadly, but this is what makes the game a great place to train your Call, Raise or Fold reflex. One night I held the top pair with a higher kicker, people are betting in slowly, so I can easily control the table. Then an Ace hits the turn and someone feeds in a small minimum bet. This is exactly the sort of sucker bet someone will play when they want people to call. Most people, when seeing they hit their Ace, will hit hard - but a small bet speaks of confidence. The question is: Call, Raise, or Fold. I double his bet to see what he does. This is called 'Asking a question' - He smiles and meets it.

The river doesn't help me and another minimum bet is placed. So what to do? I am now hoping that the second top pair will be good. The guy is still betting, so he is either bluffing or he has the goods. I can re-pop him on a bet he doesn't have it, I might call and possibly lose more chips, or I can fold. Added to this, there is another person still in the hand, so do THEY have the ace?

I just do not know, so I fold.

Hope springs eternal they say, but in Poker (as in life) hope is a poison that attacks your resolve. On this occasion, I fold because of the third person still in the hand. I know the guy betting often bluffs, but the other person is solid. Bad call: The other guy was chasing something, and folds. The raiser turns over nothing cards, just to rub in the fact I fell for it. It was a total bluff.

Now, a single hand can change the course of a game - But the real issue is not winning or losing, it is how you act *after* the hand is done. THIS is where poker games are won or lost. Not on the cards, but on your reaction to the choices you make. (either good or bad) Call, Raise or Fold situations like this are where the small but important decisions are made. But MORE important than the cards is the conversation I have with myself AFTER this event. *It is NEVER the results of winning or losing that determines our future path. It is how we deal with our choices.* Please remember this, because THIS is precisely the place where we learn to walk the fine line between denial and survival.

Making a wrong call can set us into a reactive phase. We might doubt ourselves, asking, *"What to do?"* You KNOW what to do, just kick back into gear. There is only one truth: We have to start afresh with the next set of cards life deals us. Our problems do not come from the decisions of the past, they come from the decisions of right now. Do we Call, Raise or Fold? It is a NOW thing.

I ask you: Are we basing our life on HOPE, or do we have a deeper sense of purpose? Obama wrote, *'The Audacity of Hope'* - but do you 'really' believe he 'hoped' himself into the Whitehouse? No, he had a clear and powerful INTENTION. He knew where he was going, why he wanted it, and how to get there. Do we base our choices on Intention or hope? Intention is strong and drives us to live in the NOW, hope is weak and pushes us into the future.

When the BAGGAGE of your past is controlling you, you cannot live in the NOW, you are distracted by 'shoulds'. Your baggage owns you because you can't let go of the past, and because you think it is NORMAL to carry around beliefs, hopes, and wishes. Only by training ourselves to stay in the present - and NOT dream - can we get past the hope reflex and find true intention.

Social Justice

There is a huge issue with Social Justice at present. A true Rat is very concerned with family and will always defend their friends. Maybe you find 'Me To' story, where your boss is hitting on an office worker. So what do we do - Do we ignore it? Do we stand up and lose our job by pointing it out? Do we escalate it to a complaint? Well, what about something completely different? Ratology has simple advice: *Look for Opportunity, Position and Usefulness.*

Whatever we do depends absolutely on the situation. If the boss is out of line, you have to consider that he has power over you. If it is the local gossip, well it is wise to think twice as well, because she or he is a natural born liar and can cause you no end of trouble. If it is a genuine person, then maybe you want to say something privately. If it is the office idiot, well that's what they do.

Our present social mindset is that you MUST speak up. Report the matter, make sure this wrong does not go unpunished. So you do this, and surprise! Turns out the office girl was in love with the boss and denies your story. Your next complaint is at the unemployment office, talking about unfair dismissal.

Surely the better approach is to clarify intentions? Perhaps just talk to the person before you get carried away in social justice? *"Seems to me the boss is hitting on you, you OK with this?"* This is the RAT way of dealing with things, ask simple questions and find out what the reality is BEFORE you act.

Opportunity, Position, and Usefulness

It is all about opportunity, position, and usefulness.
1. *Does the opportunity to say something present itself?*
2. *Is it the right time and place to say something?*
3. *And really, is there any purpose served in speaking up?*

These are the right questions to ask. The situation is what it is, how you DEAL with it is what causes change. The intention is to find the best way to ACT, and asking questions is the best way to discover this.

The Rat way of thinking is not in accord with the politically correct ideals of the modern world. People are trying to tell us we have to face every conflict and resolve every issue, but I don't have the time for this. I just want to know the best way for me to survive. Self-hood is not selfish.

So often, my personal watchword for survival is 'Whatever'. It's not a negative or an avoidance. 'Whatever' neither affirms an action or curses it. It does not seek to change a situation; it just accepts it. 'Whatever' is a survival reflex of the highest order. It allows things to be and leaves you free to act - if you so chose. In the case of where we are in conflict, when we START with 'whatever' we are give ourselves DISTANCE and this gives us better perspective.

CHOICE is the real question. Do we choose to fight, avoid or run? Call, Raise, or Fold? If we ask the above three questions we will make better choices. But *my attitude and sense of perseverance* will only stay in good shape when I have a shrug of the shoulders and say 'whatever' in the back of my mind.

What about when there appears no winning choice? As a general rule, I am certainly not going to confront a man with a gun and tell him he's done wrong, yet the question remains: *What to do?* If I believe the guy will shoot me if I don't stand up, then obviously I have to do something. But what? That's always the question. *What to do?* It comes back to intention - where do you want to go?

Chris was a friend of mine and faced exactly this problem. He was out West and the car needed repair, so he tracked down the local garage owner and, at Four AM on Sunday morning, he knocked on the man's door demanding action. The fellow came out with a loaded shotgun and pointed it at the intruder. Chris just brushed the gun aside and said, "I will have none of this rubbish! Your job in life is to fix cars, and fix cars is what you will do!"

Chris got his car fixed.

Personally speaking, there are days where I don't feel all that strong and I will avoid all forms of conflict. If the problem gets bigger I may have to deal with it, but in the meantime, if I ostrich enough and put my head firmly up my butt, maybe it will all just go away. Denial can be very useful because it allows you to do so much less than you would otherwise be incapable of. (Think about it)

One of the main areas in modern life where the 'call' 'raise' or 'fold' choice has to be made is in legal proceedings. It's a disease in the States at the moment, with everyone suing someone over whatever. It is an area of ongoing threat that can cost you your house.

Excellent Legal Advice

I asked a Queens Counsel (Highest level of solicitor in the Westminster System) about the true principles of Law, and he laughed, saying, "I should not reveal the secrets, but I like you." I outline in point form his exact words:
1. *The First Rule is very simple: Avoid. Avoid dealing with the matter, drag it out, and make it difficult for the other party to get a response. Guilty or innocent is not the issue. It COSTS the person to pursue things, so drag it out.*

2. The Second Rule is: Deny Everything. It doesn't matter what the evidence says, deny it emphatically.
3. The Third Rule is: If you can't avoid it then Blame. Blame anyone and everyone, and give a thousand reasons why you are not the real target.
4. If all the above fails, and it is obvious you are guilty as sin, then the Fourth Rule is: Grovel. Fall on your belly and beg forgiveness and promise that you will never ever do it again.

I asked if there was a Fifth Rule I needed to know and the man laughed even more. "Indeed there is, it is called either MONEY or PRIDE. You have to figure out whether the person is attacking because of money or pride. Money is easy, pride is difficult. Pride will cause people to spend a million dollars fighting their case and, I have to say, this is where I make most of my money. But of course, for the financial health of my client, I will always recommend he reapply Rule Four in person. Get on your hands and knees and beg forgiveness, then offer some money. The real joy is when my client has too much pride to grovel - what a windfall this is for all of us."

"All of us?" I asked further.

"Yes, all of we solicitors are really in the money profession. The legal profession has very little to do with notions of right or wrong, it simply about the law and what it means in a particular instance. It costs a lot of money to have someone like me reinterpret and spin my version of what the law means, and really, this is all I do."

Or, as my deceased friend, James Daemar (who won more cases against QC's like this than you could imagine) would say, "Professionals don't care about you, they only care about your money. That's why I win, because they know they get paid win or lose, but if I lose it is a world of pain. So I fight for every inch."

Law, as it is practised in the West, is a process of war. It's a warring planet, but we have been given the path of survival: Avoid, Deny, Blame then Grovel. But if you MUST go to war for any principle, if you MUST take up arms, do not turn up to a gun battle with a pocket knife. And in our society, turning up properly armed usually means paying for expensive lawyers, etc.

Measure the Cost of Your Principles

Ideals do not pay the rent. Good intentions do not get you a promotion. Fine wine does not come cheap. Every single thing has a cost to benefit ratio and it pays to consider this before taking any action.

However, nothing costs more than pointless dreams that have little purpose and small chance of becoming a reality. These cost time, money and a whole lot of personal energy. Which is why I ask you to consider how your dreams can be a curse, not the blessing so many pretend they are.

The Scourge of Dreams

> *"Unfortunately, the balance of nature decrees that a super-abundance of dreams is paid for by a growing potential for nightmares."* Peter Ustinov

Many people will offer you dreams. New Age Gurus want to pander to you in order to sell you their book, their workshop, their website, or whatever. Most publications in the New Age and self-help sections will tell you to dream great dreams. They will say, if you really believe it - if you act AS IF it's all real - then this will bring in the Law of Attraction, and this will give you:
1. Unlimited wealth,
2. A beautiful partner, and
3. A great purpose in life.

Then you can register for a $3000 workshop in order to learn how to attract the Law of Attraction. Sorry to disappoint people, but Ratology is not here to trade in hope or dreams. We are here to POP those thought bubbles.

Deepak Chopra opened one of his very expensive meetings with the words: "Thank you all so much for coming here and giving me so much money to tell you something you already know." Can you believe he was CLAPPED for this slap in the face of the audience? Then he followed with the usual rhubarb about how following your dreams, staying focused, keeping positive, etc. will lead you to everything you ever wanted.

I say the opposite. I say we need to distrust our dreams, remove the concept of hope from our inner dialogue, and completely junk the new age waffle. It's a distraction from the present. I say: *Start recognising the obvious.* (Which is a better way of saying: *live in the present moment*)

I do trust that the next few chapters will make you really pissed off and agro, because this will mean your dreams have been shattered and I have hit the target. If you get angry, I have done my job well. After all, I am a self-confessed Rat, so you really cannot expect me to be nice and pander to you, can you?

It's my job to tell it straight and what I say up front is this:
1. Almost ALL things we believe in are generally wrong to some degree.
2. What all our hopes and wishes create is (usually) a ship full of holes.
3. ACCEPT LIFE AS IT IS. It's OK to be Fucked Up, (we are all cracked) and
4. Everything will change for the better when we plead guilty to 1 and 2.

Dreams and wishes are the scourge of our life. This is not because of what they are, but because of the fear and sense of lack that drive them. We will be looking at what drives us many times in this book, so what drives most dreams? Usually, it is fear. It's great to have a dream, but ask yourself: Are your dreams based on what you want to get away from, or where you want to go?

To Dream, or not to Dream - Is this the question? No, the real question to ask is: *Where does the BASIS of our dreaming come from?*

For the most part, many of our dreams, wishes and hopes are inadvertently cast from the image of what we fear and lack. When I was seventeen I had a perfectly good Morris Minor to drive around in, but I had a Maserati stuck up on my mirror in my room. Every day I wished for one of those fancy cars. Obviously, I didn't fear my little 30-year-old car. It was that a fast car would be exciting, fun, thrilling, etc. Can you guess that my life was incredibly dull at that point? I was afraid it was going to stay that way so I created a dream to escape my sense of lack. When my life livened up, my interest in getting that car vanished.

The life most people live is 'future based'. They are not present and cast their thoughts into the future of what they could become, could get, and where they might go. The question is: Why are they not present? The answer is: Almost always. Why? Because they are driven by a LACK.

A woman will dream of Mr. Right; the charming fellow who seems so wonderful in her imagination. She meets him, falls in love, and everything is perfect. But then he spends her money, sleeps with other women, and leaves the toilet seat up. She believes she has been betrayed. Well, who really betrayed who? He's the same person she met, but, deep inside her mind, her fears created dreams that *blinded her to the obvious*. It was not her LOVE that created the problem, but her fear-based dreams that caused her to avoid seeing the simple truth about Prince Charming.

THIS is what echoes through all of our lives, again and again, and again. It is not what anything IS, but what we IMAGINE it is that drives our bus. Don't beat yourself up, this is what humans do: *We imagine fear and need hope to cure it.*

Research by the brilliant Dr. Martin Seligman has revealed that the likely cause for depression and anxiety is to be found in the mammalian response to threat. An area at the back of the brain called the *Dorsal Raphe Nucleus* appears to be responsible for the way we 'lock up' under pressure. However, shine the light of HOPE and a circuit from the frontal lobe sends a signal to this nerve cluster to release. A person then unlocks - they feel free. Nothing has ACTUALLY changed, but a person feels less depressed and anxious.

The 'lock-up' arises because of a perceived threat. We freeze in fear, and we need hope to break the circuit. It is absolutely fantastic that research is showing a way to be able to treat depression and anxiety, but I have to ask the question: Why do we not perceive things correctly in the first place? Why do we not trust our RAT and just not get into these emotional and mental traps?

The reason we do not is wrapped around our lack of acceptance of NOW and the subsequent need to escape our reality. First, when we accept our situation, warts and all, then the need to escape vanishes. By seeing things AS THEY ARE, we are able to make clear choices. Yes, we can dream of a way out, but that dream is now based on NOW. *We are choosing a reality where fear is no longer controlling things.* So, I am not saying that to dream of a better life is bad - I am saying that dreams based on fears only manufacture more fears.

I will give you a NOW exercise. If you have any sort of dream or concept for the future at all, do this simple two-step exercise to bring you to NOW.
- Remember that perfection does not exist.
- Accept that EVERYTHING has cracks.

NOW you have the space to apply what a solicitor calls Due Diligence . A good solicitor will check the facts of whatever is before them. This gives them a better picture of reality, which allows them to form an accurate opinion. SO, I ask you, have you performed due diligence on your dreams? Did you check things before you believed them? Of course you didn't, no-one ever does.

This is how we develop a buffer against our fear-driven dreams. We need to check our beliefs, hopes and dreams - to ascertain if they are real or fictitious. We have to stop trusting our accepted truths. We need to slow our imagination down and learn to see only this present moment - as it is.

This next part is tricky, but if you get it, you will succeed in life.

When our dreams are based on fear, these fears create a negative mould in our psyche. Pouring our faith, hope and charity into a dream for our future casts the coin of the present in what seems the opposite, or positive image.

Do-gooders pour kindness over everything and feel all bright and shiny as a result. The positive image of the mould is the reverse image of the fear, but the "B" side that is hidden from their view has everything they fear. People who fall in love do the same - they pour love over the object of their desire, yet are incredibly surprised a few years down the track when the "B" side appears.

The problem is that the 'coin' is cast from a representation of what we fear. When we spend it, we will attract exactly what the coin truly represents, the image of our fear. It is something that looks a positive but which secretly contains the opposite. This is how life works. This is how the Law of Attraction REALLY works. The positive and the negative are the Yin and Yang, they always go together. If you call in one, you will soon discover the other.

Like the woman who wanted to find her Prince Charming, her fears of NOT finding him caused her to overlook his obvious problems. To catch a husband, she cast a line with a fear-based reality as a hook, and life gave her exactly the right fish for her to learn her own truth.

So here is the simple, clear and immutable truth: *Life is a mirror.* When fears form the core of imagination and desire, life reflects back to us the image of our problem. If we can see it, we can solve it.

Summary: *Your dreams and wishes are NOT your friend. They are often your enemy in disguise and you need to see through them. The way to make them more transparent is to doubt them. The Double Negative Secret: If they contain a negative, your negative will polarise it to a positive. If they are a pure positive, your negative will not shake it. This is the only way to understand the real message life is bringing us.*

The Creation of Walls Within

"Every wall is a door" Ralph Waldo Emerson

Bhagwan Rajneesh's and Papaji's teacher said to them when they graduated divinity school, "I have difficult news. Half of everything we have taught you is completely, utterly false. The problem is, we don't know which half. Your job in life is to solve this." Don't be too surprised, in India this is something said to every divinity graduate.

It is truly amazing how we generate and sustain a life of half-truths and half-lies. This next chapter is a little weighty and ponderous, but soon we will have a little more fun. For now, we need to look at our lies and beliefs to understand the whole business of what creates the walls that dam us. In a nutshell: *Our beliefs create inner platforms to look out from, yet these can also create our blockages.* If our beliefs are true it's all fine. But mostly they are not.

Emmanuel Kant wrote in a 1784 essay called 'What is Enlightenment?' that we must *'Dare to Understand'*. The whole principle of the Enlightenment was to challenge dogmas and rigid beliefs. It had a very tonic effect. Because we have done this for the last few hundred years we have clean water, hygiene, longer lives, better living standards and just about every aspect of our shared lives has improved. So why is there now this increasing tendency towards censorship, authoritarianism, and control? Mostly I suspect it is because people have forgotten how important it is to continue to *'Dare to Understand'*.

I spoke to a fellow who ran a religious organization. He was a good man, but he had not been all that successful in finding new people over the years. Still, he carried on regardless. I suggested to him that perhaps the process needed to be opened up a bit, in order to allow more people to come in. But all that his years of experience had taught him that his group only attracted one or two people a year. He believed that this was how it worked. What's more, he came to believe this is what made them SPECIAL, rather than a failure.

Well, I told him this was crap. I said that he is simply getting what he expects and that this has nothing to do with other people. His results came from a poverty within himself. I was pulling down walls of preconception and to the fellows' credit, in time he saw it. Soon after the man had a revelation that his entire thirty-year investment into his teaching was based on spiritual poverty.

What is more, when the wall falls down you start to see the REAL driving forces that built it. Behind this wall was a vanity, and behind that, a fear of failure. He realised he was dreaming of LITTLE because it made him more secure in LACK. The house of cards (our false beliefs) will always fall down before the obvious, but only when we allow it. And this happens only when we see it.

It's the fear that dams us. Let me shout this: IT IS THE FEAR THAT DAMS US! It's the fear that causes us to build the house of cards, it is the fear that causes us to believe these are strong walls that will protect us. It's the fear that doesn't allow us to see the comb-over in the mirror. It's the fear that is driving your car over the cliff of oblivion.

If you want to experience a piece of genuine contentment, you have to stop, recognise the problem, and take charge of it. It is a basic principle of this book that we have to take down the walls which create the blockages. Let me put it in an apparently opposite way: *Do you accept your natural state?*

Before you say "Of course I do!" think about what is natural. Good child, bad child, it's all part of US. Many prefer to avoid this. Many of us look in the mirror and despise aspects of ourselves and so we refuse to come to terms with the negative sides of our nature. We subtly refuse to work with the fact that we are not perfect, even as we bruise ourselves with pseudo-suicide attempts, doing the Humpty Dumpty from our self-created walls.

Accepting Self = Accepting Freedom

The Mystic Rat Says: *Just ACCEPT your God-un-dammed Negatives!*

If you do not accept your negatives, you are playing poker with only one arm. It's very hard to shuffle and deal with only one arm, you know. The present situation is that most adults are full to the rafters with walls and issues. We need to recognise these in order to create some bridges between them.

Now, if you really can't accept that you have inner walls that confine you, then put down this book and think about kids. They just PLAY. So, can you just play in the sandpit, or are you controlled by a thousand invisible SHOULDS? If you are an adult in western society, you are chock full of shoulds and should nots. These things are the walls your Humpty falls from!

We all have these invisible rules running things in the background, that's not the issue. The issue is how we deal with them, so what I will suggest to you is a simple exercise. This is to help you break down the barriers:

1. *If you always iron your shirts, don't do it for a few days.*
2. *Try not tying up your shoelaces on your lace-ups.*
3. *If you never wear purple, wear it. (Etc.)*

Let's start doing things outside the box of our personal conventions, and just observe how people respond to the change you have instigated. Pay attention and you will be amazed at how few people care, and how most will not notice.

The Mystic Rat Says: *No one is watching. If someone is watching you, it is because they want whatever you have got. Otherwise, everyone is too busy watching themselves.*

We need to reverse our self-absorbed focus and train ourselves to see what IS. Do you *Dare to Understand* what is inside the clock that is running you? At the Poker Table if we get absorbed with our own cards, thinking how great they are (or otherwise) we will not see what life is putting on the table in front of us. We may have two Aces in our hand, but what if there happens to be two Fives on the table? *If you don't look out from where you sit, you will never even consider that someone with just a single Five can unseat you from your throne.*

If we stay locked inside ourselves and just imagine we have it won, we will most likely lose. But if you are AWAKE to the obvious, you might look up, laugh, and say "I hope you have a five!" THEN go all in. NOW it changes. No one knows what you have and your confidence will get THEIR imaginations working against them. Now they will be thinking about what YOU have that makes you so confident. What have to done to flip things? *You have polarized the situation.*

Just acting differently creates a break with the past. Change causes ripples that break the spell of us looking at ourselves. The Myth of Narcissus is a very simple message. The story talks about getting lost in your own reflection and we tend to believe it is all about vanity. But the tale is really about ATTACHMENT which, at its core, is a refusal to change. So here is the challenge: *Can you change your view and get a different perspective?* Choose to Change and the simple act of choice will help us see ourselves and others differently. Change is your friend when you accept it.

Choose to Change

Why? Because changing stuff reveals our fears. So far we have used fear as the motivating force to build our walls of protection. Fear is useful in this regard because we are generally very lazy and would otherwise not bother to protect ourselves. Fear motivates us to protect the heart, to create an image of strength, and in some cases to get a higher view.

So far it's all good. These walls that we create form the pedestals for self-image and the barriers against threat. Each block is a worry or a 'should'. These walls are built from our collective fears, shoulds and should nots, and then MAGIC! These defensive WALLS turn into our BELIEFS. This is all part of the natural process inside us. *The problem comes when we start to believe in these barriers as solutions for life, not survival against it.* This confused logic reads:

1. I must survive
2. It is dangerous out there
3. Therefore I need Walls
4. Walls = Solution to Danger = Enhanced Survival
5. Therefore I can believe in Walls as my Solution for Survival
6. Ergo: No walls = no solution, no survival

It's nuts, isn't it? We like to think of our belief in a God, or in money, or in the perfect marriage, as some sort of solution to the problems of our life, whereas it was just a way for us to get by at the time. They were part of the tools we used to survive the day. But then the divorce comes around and our survival is threatened. The wall erected by fear and cemented with belief that states *'I am safe because I am married'* comes tumbling down, along with the Humpty sitting on it. (That's you, in case you didn't realise it)

We build walls to survive. Everything we do, we do because we believe it will help us survive. We think walls are a solution, but as Dylan sang in "All Along the Watchtower" - The war still goes on at the gate. A tiger still hides in the dark.

We hear the clanging of argument outside the doors of our inner sanctum and we pat ourselves on the back for erecting such fine defences. Yet we are stuck inside our walls! We believe we are 'safe' but we are trapped. Our fears have become the wardens of our self-made jail.

The Mystic Rat Says: Most of our beliefs are walls made from bricks of should stuck together with fear as the mortar.

Let's run this through from the top:
1. *We are flawed. We are all a Humpty Dumpty - Post Wall*
2. *We have gotten back on our perch, patched up our cracks with belief, but now we live in fear of falling.*
3. *For fear of more hurt, we build internal barriers that are a 'Belief in Something'. (Usually a faith based religion, etc.)*
4. *We now have external rules of what we should and shouldn't do.*
5. *We subsequently imprison our thoughts and feelings in a complex web of belief - most often based on obfuscation and distortion derived from fear.*
6. *And we do all of this in order to feel safe!*

Madness, isn't it? This book is aiming to do the opposite. It's all about unsticking our beliefs, dismantling the lies we live, and freeing ourselves from the burden of being our false, inhibited self.

How do we do this? Simple: *By having FUN and embracing the freedom of BEING.* This book is all about finding a different way to survive ourselves by accepting what we are, where we are, and who we are.

We initially do this by removing the blocks of "should" from our existence. Then we learn to face each moment with courage and conviction. But in order to do this, you have to learn to accept the RAT you really are.

Summary: *We are all Humpty Dumpty Post Wall. No one is perfect, we all have flaws. We all have fears and, accordingly, we have erected barriers to protect ourselves. Cracks appear, and we cover them with convention, belief, etc.*

But the act of covering up the cracks in our nature creates a division between the simple child-self and as an adult we fall into the complex world of 'should'. Here we have to present suitable faces for each situation we deal with. This causes further divisions in the wholeness of the being. We then tend to plaster over these 'cracks" in our nature with veneers of respectability. This causes us to lose our natural child-like connection with ourselves which then allows false beliefs, rather than our child-like reality, to rule our life.

Ratology: Way of the Un-Dammed

The Question of Humpty: *Was he pushed, or did he suicide?*

Humpty Dumpty sat on a wall.
Humpty Dumpty had a great fall
All the Kings horses and all the Kings men
Couldn't put Humpty together again

Can you tell me who, or what, Humpty Dumpty is, why he was there, or even what caused him to fall? Why were all the Kings Horses and all the Kings men at the scene of the crime? It is very suspicious and none of this is made clear in the evidence. And surely someone realized that horses were not up to the task, as they don't have opposable thumbs?

The Mystic Rat Observes: *We go through all the hoops and roundabouts in life and hopefully we gain an insight into who and what we really are. Yet, before we can figure out the difference betwixt our dreams and our reality, we find that we cannot really trust either until we know ourselves. We cannot find true certainty until we understand the basic myths and lies that our personal story is based on.*

No baby was born believing, they were taught it. We all have these fixed notions, our personal 'truths', but they are really matters of blind faith, born of our inheritance and our culture.

Our Rat sees the obvious. This makes it the only effective thing inside us that can bring us to clear perception. Only at this point of clarity can we start to deal with our automatic belief systems.

We, the Dammed

> 'Is that all?' Alice timidly asked.
> 'That's all,' said Humpty Dumpty. 'Good-bye.'
> This was rather sudden, Alice thought: but, after such a very strong hint that she ought to be going, she felt that it would hardly be civil to stay. So she got up, and held out her hand. 'Good-bye, till we meet again!' she said as cheerfully as she could.
> 'I shouldn't know you again if we did meet,' Humpty Dumpty replied in a discontented tone, giving her one of his fingers to shake: 'you're so exactly like other people.'
> 'The face is what one goes by, generally,' Alice remarked in a thoughtful tone.
> 'That's just what I complain of,' said Humpty Dumpty. 'Your face is the same as everybody has -- the two eyes, so --' (marking their places in the air with his thumb) 'nose in the middle, mouth under. It's always the same. Now if you had the two eyes on the same side of the nose, for instance -- or the mouth at the top -- that would be some help.'
> 'It wouldn't look nice,' Alice objected. But Humpty Dumpty only shut his eyes, and said 'Wait till you've tried.'

Do you remember the quip from the Wizard of ID where Rodney races up exclaiming, "Sire, the peasants are revolting!" To which the King replies, "Tell me something I don't know."

Most of us ARE revolting. We are arguing with ourselves all the time. We are like the double-minded man in the Bible - Chaff in the Wind, blown by circumstance, tossed aside by the fates and eternally driven by habit. What is worse, we know it, and are afraid of our worthlessness. But we hide this fear - No one wants to admit to anyone else what they really think of themselves, deep down. (Unless they are playing the suffering martyr and trying to hook the mother instinct in a potential girlfriend)

As a result, most of us live lives of deceit and double standards. We all know the saying: *Don't lie to yourself?* That's certainly sage advice, but facts are that we all do, to some degree.

Let's take stock of present reality:
1. Most of us do not live up to our dreams.
2. Most of us fail to rise above the fear of what others might think.
3. Most of us like the idea of dancing unrestricted by convention, yet so few of us achieve this.

Why is this the NOW of most people? By the end of the book, I expect you will be able to tell me. In the meantime, I think it is fair to say that we all understand that many of our life choices (whether chosen or inherited) derive from our blockages and constraints, not from personal freedom and joy.

We are a dammed people. We all have these walls, blockages, and safety barriers that we hide behind. We are the cracked eggs struggling to keep our shells intact. We are little pieces of self, glued together to try and make a whole. This, in turn, becomes our mask. And here is the problem: *The GLUE we are using is made from belief.* And what we most believe in is, secretly, a negative.

Notice that no one ever fills us in with what happened to Humpty Dumpty Post Wall? Typical media, reporting the flash in the pan, not the harsh reality. Did you ever wonder how on earth the rhyme came about in the first place? Humpty first emerged in 1803 as a nursery rhyme, from unknown origins, and came to prominence when used by Lewis Carroll. *'It's very provoking,'* Humpty Dumpty said, *'to be called an egg -- very!'* ["Through the Looking-Glass," 1872].

As discussed on page thirty four, there is no evidence to suggest Humpty was an egg. While we might seek to blame Lewis Carroll for popularising the notion, perhaps he was actually stating the obvious? To my eyes, Humpty is really implying here that he believes is NOT an Egg. Read through the text in the book, and you see that Humpty Dumpty is really asking Alice to see the obvious.

'In that case we start afresh,' said Humpty Dumpty, *'and it's my turn to choose a subject --'* (*'He talks about it just as if it was a game!'* thought Alice.) *'So here's a question for you. How old did you say you were?'*

Alice made a short calculation, and said, *'Seven years and six months.'*

'Wrong!' Humpty Dumpty exclaimed triumphantly. *'You never said a word like it!'*

'I thought you meant "How old are you?"' Alice explained.

'If I'd meant that, I'd have said it,' said Humpty Dumpty.

Humpty is continually saying: SEE THE OBVIOUS! Despite Lewis Carrol's drug addiction and possible tendencies towards paedophilia, despite all his faults, he could bring forward rays of brilliance - Perhaps it was because of them that he could?

The Source of Humpty Dumpty

Since "Through the Looking Glass" the term Humpty Dumpty has become synonymous with anything that is fragile or precarious. The Humpty Rhyme is generally believed to come from an incident in 1640's royalist war, where "Humpty Dumpty" was a Royalist cannon at "Saint Mary's at the Wall" in Colchester. It was knocked down from its perch and all the king's horses and all the king's men could not put him together again. Thus Colchester fell to the Roundheads.

There are other attributions, notably "Humpty" was Richard the III - he was a hunchback who fell from his horse in battle. (Thus Shakespeare and his "A Horse, a horse! My kingdom for a horse!")

There are other attributions and one rarely noted is that it may refer to Edward Despard, the last man sentenced to be hung drawn and quartered in London. Despard had been a ranking officer in the British Navy who got accused of plotting to kill Richard the III. This charge was set with virtually no evidence and, despite an appearance in court by Lord Nelson on his behalf, Despard and six others were executed. However, because of fears of public revolt, the sentence of being hung, drawn (racked while still alive until your bones broke) and quartered (cut into four after being racked and while still alive) was commuted to simple hanging and beheading. I am sure that made everyone, especially Despard, feel much better.

In every case, whatever we see as a source for Humpty Dumpty, the MEME is always about someone falling from a high place: *pride is taking a fall*. Mostly the rhyme is seen as an analogy to personal vanity being shaken by circumstance. But no one talks about what happens AFTER the fall.

What do you do AFTER your pride takes a battering? Most of us lick our wounds, tell ourselves we are OK and, after a time of penance, slowly emerge into the light of day once more. We have to rebuild that part that was shattered and after this is done most of us convince ourselves that we are OK.

We piece ourselves together by relying on friends, getting drunk, joining a religion, or whatever. The core of how we respond to life's shattering incidents remains fairly constant regardless: *We need to create a BELIEF in ourselves once more*. What most will do is look externally for other people's acceptance. We associate with a group and, as a consequence, fall into Group Think.

Group Think

What is generally called 'brainwashing' is really a process of having our pride damaged and rebuilt. Almost all fervent converts to religion have taken a blow to their pride before joining and becoming 'new' again. In the inquisition, the more fervent converts came from the torture racks. After suffering enough, the person has an experience that affirms everything their torturers are saying. Why? Because when we are shattered we accept any authorities suggestions as truth. We are designed this way as mammals. We do not want to be alone. Under sufficient pressure pride collapses and the need to belong takes charge

The Mystic Rat Says: *We avoid our Plurality by becoming One with the Crowd.*

We avoid the plurality of pieces inside ourselves by accepting the persona of the group we join. It feeds us, but all the external forces - all the Kings Horses and all the King's Men - will never solve the cracks in you. But acceptance by the group eases the burden. We may even find peace, but 'we' will never find freedom. Only the individual discovers this, never the group.

There are good reasons for this. What has been discovered is that when any human society is placed under threat, a signal is sent out. It is part of a survival reflex that connects the group. The purpose of this 'signal' is to create conformity in order to survive. Societies under threat develop strict social norms, sets of dos and don'ts designed to get everyone acting as one.

Likewise, when 'you' feel under threat, there is a strong tendency to want to join a group and part of joining ANY group is conforming to their unwritten rules, or mores. There is nothing wrong with this, but you will never find freedom obeying someone else's rules.

Rebuilding ourselves on our own is a difficult task. Standing without affirmation from external sources means no one is holding your hand and agreeing with you, so you have to do it all by yourself and this is always shaky ground. We all have a plurality of doubt after a shakedown. We may want to stand up, shake it off by saying, "I will survive!" or words to that effect, but we know we are still in pieces. Most of us instinctively fall back into group-think, even as we shout out how we are individuals.

The reason so many join groups is to have a support mechanism and a safety barrier. It is difficult standing up to life on our own and just easier to fall into agreement with some group that affirms us in some way. However, I am NOT a supporter of 'Group-Think'. The cost is higher than the benefit.

May I suggest something completely different? Why don't we just forget about rebuilding? Why don't we throw away the shattered past, the broken dreams, and the fragmented reality that is the cracked eggshell of personal failures? We do we not just reveal our 'selves' to our 'self'? But we don't. Instead of being free of the past after a crash, we tend to lock ourselves in, join a group, and seek to rebuild our life. This generally entails plastering over our internal falsehoods with whatever works in the short term.

We place our blond spot (Sorry, Blind Spot) firmly over the fragile concerns and convince ourselves that all is well. Then, for some reason, we get back up on our perch to talk to Alice as she walks through Wonderland.

I can understand why we don't want to appear broken, a weak creature in the jungle is prey to every carnivore. So we pull ourselves together - but why do we get back up on the wall that it is so easy to fall from? Why? You know why: It improves our sense of self-esteem. We love to be above the crowd. A wall means we are important. We believe it also makes us safe from intruders.

The Graffiti on our Walls

We need the barriers. Life seems safer with barriers. We feel better with a wall to hide behind or to walk long. It contains us and stops us from running all over the place making fools of ourselves. And once we are all glued up and egging along again, we start building OTHER walls to protect the fragile outer shell. We use the bricks of past experience, made from pain and fear, to create a new place. This is our Castle of Belief for our fragile self, the Egg of State.

I remember my then three year old coming up to me with the toy that had broken down, "Gyue it, Daddy, Gyue it!" (glue it). Daddy could magically fix everything - and 'gyue' became the code for repair. Yet we know the broken egg will never quite patch up properly. We look in the mirror and see the cracks staring back, accusingly. They are staring at us like the three strands of hair of a comb-over. Just ignore it! We HAVE to believe, because if we don't it all falls apart. So we look in the mirror, avoid the obvious, and say, "My what a good egg we are!" We leave the mirror to get back on the perch, so we can stare at the world from the height of our internal walls and feel safe.

You could say (Pun Warning!) that we are being a little Shelf-ish!

Yet we live in this fragile state with a constant fear of falling. Fear is the God we come to worship, even though we call these fears 'conventional wisdom', 'common sense' and lots of other solid, realistic sounding terms in order to make us feel better about ourselves. We have erected a thousand walls within and without us, all dedicated to fear and, on these walls, we write our little slogans, our personal 'Rules Graffiti' that will instruct all who come to visit what they should or should not do.

I walk down the corridors of most people's minds and I read these quips, these bits of graffiti that have become the person's rules. I talk to a banker and I can see 'safety first' as his motto. I talk to the housewife, whose graffiti reads 'small is safe'. I speak to the successful businessman who is obeying the term 'appearances are everything'. Which is fine, but why do so many want to convince everyone else that THEIR rules are the right rules? Loneliness is why.

We have become a society of wall builders who obey our own graffiti. We have become a clutch of 'should-ers'. (You like my invented collective noun)

I understand loneliness and isolation are what is driving you, but this does not give you the right to 'should' on anyone else. *Stop SHOULDING on me!* Stop telling me what I should do. Stop pretending you know better! As an alternative, may I suggest that you start reading and applying the "Rules of Rattyness".

In most societies we find people living a life where they are hiding behind the inner and outer walls of 'should' 'could' and 'would'. This only adds up to unhappiness, loss, and isolation. The process goes like this:

1. *Rather than advertise the cracks in our façade, we pretend that all is well with the world.*
2. *Thus: Living our Life becomes Living a Lie.*
3. *Yet: We want to be free, to dance naked in the sun, to laugh without care, to PLAY! But we don't because we are afraid.*
4. *So: Instead we look for guidelines on how to act.*
5. *We then begin to carry around this little mental and emotional rule book that instructs us what we 'should' do.*

6. Yet, to counter these restrictions, we also carry a little Dream Book that has written in it what we 'could' and 'would' do.
7. This is what splits us! This is where we fall down and become cracked: Our dreams become separate from our reality, and we feel lost.
8. So we look for someone to agree with us. (Top of the list is usually Prince Charming or Miss Penthouse Pet, or both!)
9. Voila! We form groups! Societies of Belief that collectively determine truth as agreed upon by the crowd. (This converts our internal plurality to the external plurality to which we now belong) But this needs to be controlled.
10. So: We instil terms of punishment on those who breaks our rules.
11. We subsequently live our lives in fear of this punishment.

And finally, the Twelfth Step where we forget our natural self entirely and our dreams become divorced from our reality. This is where we move out of NOW. After this loss of self, the need for re-connection drives up to religions, groups and external authorities, which sets up the secondary issue.

This is where it gets really messy - Everyone in any group is shoulding, woulding and coulding on themselves, as well as their neighbour.

Each to their own - The concern I have with this is that this is just not fun. It becomes hard work and what is worse, the older we get the bigger the cracks in the façade we see in ourselves and others become, so the more shoulding, woulding and coulding we do. Really? It's an endless circle and it's time to stop. It's time to just forget the BS and have some fun, but there's a problem.

If we ignore our rule book and just play, we believe the people in our society will think we are a fool. Yet if we live life just following rules, we think ourselves a fool. So we become imprisoned in our own skin. The Three "M's" of mortgage, marriage and martyrdom are as nothing compared to the bondage of Righteousness, Rules, and Religion - The Three "R's" of the adult.

Yet, under this barrage of circumstance and convention that seeks to conquer our spirit, a true heart still beats. Can you hear it?

Here is a little secret: *We all yearn to be free of the crap.* Yet if we were given the keys to walk away, would we? Could you just walk away from your life as it stands? Would you let go of the prison bars and walk away? You can, you know.

You don't have to scrub the graffiti off your inner walls, you don't have to rebuild, you don't have to take down the shattered walls or glue up the broken egg - You can just leave it behind you and move on. You are ALLOWED to have your internal contradictions, wrong thoughts, and faulty emotions. If you are truly free in heart, none of this matters. You DO NOT have to fix everything!

Ratology offers you a solution to trouble and a path to happiness. Ratology, the fabulous new genuinely artificial religion of the twenty-second century, says it is perfectly OK for you to have double standards, to have a secret life, and to pretend you are a proper citizen. It is fine if you wish to have affairs, drink yourself into an early grave and eat refined sugar. Ratology states that you CAN toss aside the Puritan Rule Book and start experimenting with life. If this means you are considered selfish, well, whose life is it anyway? Be selfish.

In fact, we recommend it! The goal of Ratology is to turn you into a complete and utter RAT. Why? Because it will release you! Only when you are free to be yourself will you be able to choose what way you really want to go. Allow your life to be free of the past. Walk away! The walls we have built to protect our fragile self are just blocking the free-flow of our life.

Go on, I dare you - Let Go! - Un-dam yourself, and be free.

Summary: We have all built defensive positions around our Ego's and sense of self-worth. These walls form a sort of Rule Book that defines us. We believe this is our defence against the world, but the reality is that these inner rules stop us from acting naturally. Ratology allows you to have your walls and rules. You CAN be two-faced, because RATOLOGY allows you to express yourself in any way you choose.

The Dictum of the Rat states: *You cannot be free when following prescribed patterns of behaviour.*

i aM a rAt

> *"Anyone can rat, but it takes a certain amount of ingenuity to re-rat"*
> Winston Churchill

I had a really "out there" girlfriend with multiple personalities. She was not your normal crazy, because she understood she went off tap. As a result, early in the relationship she advised me, "If I go over the top, just slap me and I will come around."

Kind of odd, but after a week or so she really went entirely nuts over what was nothing, so I did as she asked, I slapped her. Not hard, just a wake-up call. She snapped out of it alright! She launched at me (she was a strong little thing) lashing out and saying, "What the FUCK did you do that for!"

"Ah, you asked me to, remember?"

She came out of her rage, settled down, and became entirely sweet, "Oh yeah, was I going a little looney? I guess so, thanks for that."

Does this break your social sense of right? Am I messing with your RULES? I hope so - Which is why we will shortly be coming to the "Rules of Rattyness".

What did you think about the opening story about the Great Rat and the prayer to the Holy Cheezus? Did you imagine, like the above slap, it was a cheap trick to get your attention? Of course it was. You would be an idiot to believe this sort of crap. (You DID think it was utter crap, didn't you?) I used Myth as a way to communicate a deeper truth.

Yea, verily I say unto thee! Take the Bible, it uses myth as a way to convey truth, but it is full of contradictions. Did you realise that in some sections of the Bible there are twenty-two commandments, while in others there are seventeen, and somewhere there is also twelve? You would think it could have at least been consistent with the ten we all know and ignore.

There are always lots of holes in everything, holes into which either truth or lies can fall. But given the world as it is, we have better odds it will be a lie.

Think for a moment about how many people believe that Jesus rose bodily into heaven? So please tell me, he went where, exactly? We have a society based on Myth and Fantasy. An obvious example: Mary was the Mother of God - Hey, are you are saying God needed a mother? The list goes on and on.

Some religious beliefs are:
1. *The Pope is Infallible.*
2. *God, who knows everything and knows all things, created Souls that he knew would burn forever in Hell*
3. *Adam and Eve propagated the entire Human Race, including the Chinese.*

How about some Scientific Ones:
1. Global Warming (Breaks Rule One of the Rules of Rattyness)
2. Big Bang Theory (A belief structure proven wrong - yet still believed)
3. Dark Matter (The thing needed to prove the wrongness in Big Bang theory is right)

How about some Emotional Ones:
1. If I love him enough he will come good
2. If I behave and follow the rules everyone will like me
3. If I pay enough to the mechanic I will get a good job done

We look at these things and we agree with some, disagree with others, but the fact is that NONE of the aforementioned things are provable. Not a single one. To believe in any or all of the above is to say with certainty that Humpty Dumpty was an EGG. All of the above are to some degree based on Faith and Belief. What's more, if the past is a guide, it is a given that a good part of what we presently believe to be true will be proved wrong in the future. Do you really believe that future treatment for Cancer will involve almost killing the patient with radiation, as one example?

We Are All Idiots

The Mystic Rat Says: *In some way, in some compartment of our mind, and to some extent, we believe something false to be truth. IE: We are ALL idiots.*

So now I am going to prove my idiocy and say things that I know will specifically irritate and annoy you. I am going to do a little King Canuting against the current tide of opinion.

Pretty much all of us believe in something that, in the end, amounts to utter nonsense. As a controversial example: We have many scientists who argue their theories and claims about Global Warning. Some insist the whole of human occupation of Earth is under threat by our own activities. Well, maybe it is, maybe it's not. I am quite sure the weather is changing and, in fact, there is a very old saying that backs up my belief: *'changeable as the weather'*.

As far as the end of the human race as we know it, I don't know the absolute truth or falsity of the claim, nor do I have the time or the capacity to figure it all out. What I DO know is that this argument is just another variation of the *'We are the centre of the Universe'* theory. It is just another piece of the Status Quo. What I also know and understand is that, in fifty years, everything we believe to be right about this subject will be proven wrong, or at best, incomplete.

Already 'Global Warming' dialogues have been shifted to 'climate change'. And you watch what happens to climate change arguments with the continuation of the economic collapse that is occurring in the West. There is only one certainty, everything will change. All things must pass. So too will this theory morph - again and again - until the beast that appears at the end is nothing like the original animal.

(Author note: 2020 update edition - Climate Change debate is still going, but it does not win elections. We still have climate, it is still changing - but the general interest by the population has faded, as evidenced by the lack of votes.)

The Mystic Rat Predicts: *All arguments about every 'world ending' scenario eventually transmutes to viable economic alternatives. Then, taxes go up to pay for them, and the idea of saving the planet diminishes to lip service.*

Fact: Every 25 years or so, there is a global scare campaign about something. If you look over newspapers, ever since they were printed there has been a world-ending threat two or three times in everyone's lifetime. I say that the climate change rhetoric is incomplete and that a degree of hypnotism has taken hold of both the 'believers' as well and the 'non-believers'.

My uncle Kevin was a fisherman. In the early 1970s, just as the climate debate was getting traction, he sold his fishing boat. He knew nothing about science, but he knew he wasn't getting enough clear sailing days and that fish were getting thin in the water. He switched to running a dairy farm. So there is no argument that the climate is changing, the only argument is defining how much is part of an overall cycle and how much is generated by human activity.

But it DOES beg the question: WHY do we choose to believe with such conviction in things that are incomplete, false and sometimes downright absurd? More to the point: Why do people in office jobs, a place far more divorced from the effect of climate change than a farmer or fisherman, take up such a polarised and avid stance on the subject? Perhaps the REAL truth is more about the 'lack' we feel inside us? *By believing in something, anything, we get a sense of purpose, we feel whole.*

FACT: When society has a perceived threat, the instinct is to pull together.

In 2014, when he was a guest at Jimmy Kimmel Live, former president Bill Clinton talked about the possible existence of alien species out there in the ever-expanding universe. He finished the interview with a curious sentiment. "It may be the only way to unite this increasingly divided world of ours," he said. And by 'it' he meant an alien invasion from outer space.

Thirty years earlier, in his address to the United Nations General Assembly in 1987, President Ronald Reagan said: "I occasionally think how quickly our differences worldwide would vanish if we were facing an alien threat from outside of this world."

Honestly, who wants to unite the world? Who really cares about differences? Who needs a threat to pull themselves together? Everyone seems to be missing the fact that there has never been a better time to be human than right now. We have more freedom, cash, and opportunity *right now* than at any other time in the entire gamut of human society. Yet so many people are doomsayers.

Why not drop the entire bundle of worry and concern, and just walk away from the lot? The world is a puzzle that cannot be solved, so why try?

But we do, we seem to think we can all 'pull together' - 'find the complete self' - become WHOLE. The 'whole' desire to cure the world that some lonely office workers has comes from a fear of being unimportant. The entire 'work together' drive the University student has is more wrapped around a non-acceptance of self than the improvement of society.

The REAL question is not being asked: *What is really driving the bus?* High notions, grandiose principles and dreams of perfection invariably hide the sense of lack, hopelessness, and fear that is fuelling them.

Becoming Whole

In many ways I am sick of great notions to cure the world. We must become 'whole' again! - Wholistic thinking, whole foods, whole earth catalogue - Everything is marketed as 'whole'! Leave it to Beaver was 'wholesome' but how many alcoholics and drug addicts were involved in making it?

We are not 'whole' - We are Humpty Dumpty Post-Wall and all the kings' horses and all the kings' men can't put us together. Though, to tell you the truth, I never expected the horses would be that interested in fixing an Egg and, as far as putting it back together - reality check - it's not like they have an opposable thumb, do they?

We are a broken race. We are forgotten of ourselves and ignorant of our truth. There is precious little in our society that will make us whole. Yes, we can get a convenient substitute, an apparent wholeness. This is the well-paid job, a good relationship, or a Gold Medal at the Olympics, perhaps? These things allow us to forget our pieces and feel whole for a period. But it doesn't last.

You can hammer your toe to avoid a headache, but eventually, the toe will get better and the headache will reappear. Truth is: only our attention shifted, the core issue never went away.

I am not here to convince you that your political, scientific or social beliefs are right or wrong. What I am trying to do is convince you to LOOK and see that, whatever they might be, behind these is reality. Start seeing the obvious. And first lesson of the obvious is: We go round in circles to avoid the obvious.

Circular Thinking

The real problem comes back to the circular and self-justifying nature of our thinking. There is nothing 'wrong' with this, you are allowed to think whatever you like, but it does mean we can easily get trapped in loops of faulty logic.

In the Golden Age of Greece, the Pythagoreans defined what we now know as the Logical Fallacies, the false beliefs we hold as truth. I will not go into these in detail here, but you can look them up on the net. The point is, ever since humans began to think, they thought 'wrong'.

Classical stupid argument: The sun is light. Feathers are light. Therefore: the sun is a feather. That is a non-sequitur, a thing which does not follow logic.

There are many such faults in logic generally used and abused in media and education. A goodly part of the climate change debate the media presents is a False Dilemma. As an example: *"You either believe in climate change or you are wrong!"* This is a derivative argument based on two assumptions, neither of which is provable.

The false dilemma fallacy is often a manipulative tool designed to polarize the audience, heroicizing one side and demonizing the other. It's common in political discourse as a way of strong-arming the public into supporting controversial legislation or policies. (thebestschools.org/magazine/15-logical-fallacies-know)

"Science has complete agreement on the subject of Climate Change". I have actually heard people say this in the media and this is blatantly false. But if it WERE true, it would be virtual proof that it was wrong. Every time in human history where there has been a complete agreement on any principle of science, it has been proven to be wrong. The Earth is NOT the centre of the universe. The world is NOT flat. Angels do NOT dance on the head of a pin, regardless of projected numbers. But LEECHES! THEY are the medical miracle, aren't they?

Even the most basic core beliefs, the weight of the hydrogen atom and the speed of light, varies. Life is in flux. Life IS change, movement, shifting sands, and I suspect the real reason for all our fixed beliefs and convictions is a sad attempt to find stable, solid ground underneath our feet.

Hint: If you are certain you are right, it is almost certainly proof you are not.

A Certain "T"

The person who wins in Poker is the flexible one who chooses to never fully believe in what they hold. There is almost no hand you hold that cannot be beaten until the last card is shown.

Many years ago I drew a short comic, about a fellow with a 'Certain T'. The 'Certain T' was actually a large wooden cross he bore, but he believed it was the thing that made him important. That 'Certain T' is a pun on his certainty, obviously, and I drew it up because I realised I was suffering from too much self-conviction. The thing was, at heart I was not so certain, so I did what almost everyone else does, I closed my ears, shut my eyes to the obvious, refused to hear the whispers of self-doubt, and just convinced myself I was right.

In my case, it was necessary. My body was at the point of death, I had not eaten properly in almost two years, and I weighed just over seven stone. I HAD to convince myself in my own direction because if I stopped, I died.

However, when you are taken to the edge of existence, you start to see things more clearly. And what do you see? The pointlessness of struggling your entire life to be able to retire with a few dollars, the uselessness of sitting behind a desk pushing paper around, the hopelessness of trying to convince a shut mind it is better to be open, etc.

But the good news: all these things I discovered that were useless were what pointed me towards finding my Inner Rat.

I started to see with absolute clarity the waste of time most people's existence was. The notion of 'Spiritual Arithmetic' came from this period, (See Ratology Two) where I understood how everything we have in life is tied to the addition or subtraction of choices and attitudes. As I healed, slowly, the Rat within emerged from the dark corridors of guilt and shame I was raised in.

I saw that, for many people, the story of their life is a Grimm Brothers fairytale without the 'Happily Ever After'. And this is perfectly OK - Why? Because it's all a story, it's all an illusion. We all live in 'Maya', the dream of becoming and, as a direct result, a high percentage of our existence is spent in a dream strung between certainty and doubt. Because of this, we take on fixed beliefs in order to create 'solid ground' under the shifting sands of our existence. As a result: the majority of people live a lie and call it truth

And here is the tricky bit to grasp: *We create dreams designed to escape our reality, not enhance it. We live a life where we oppose ourselves in some way.*

The circular process of trying to find certainty tends to go like this:
1. *Our dreams oppose our reality* –
2. *our reality defeats our hopes* –
3. *our broken hopes weaken our expectations* –
4. *our failing expectations break down our self-belief* -
5. *our failing self-belief requires a greater dreams to bolster us* -
6. *And then it's back to the start.*

It's a circle where nothing really adds up, but we dance about acting as if it does. Which is fine because, otherwise, we would all collapse into a Bukowski like apathy and a severe, poignant despair. Our 'dream' is to be on top of the wall, and whole. Yet our reality is that we are already fallen and in pieces. We are glued up with bits of tape and cement that are just belief and hogwash for the most part, and we live with a fatal fear of falling.

So, you may ask, *what's the solution?* Well, finally you are asking sensible questions. We need help if we are to put it all together. We need something to sniff out the corners of untruth within and without of ourselves. We need something that is not afraid of the dark, something that is naturally curious but which is also tough because it is a hard world and the weak get eaten up. In short, we need to bring our RAT into the picture.

Discover the Wild Self

I can be a RAT. It's not all of me, it's not even a high percentage of myself, but it's there when I need it. It is an instinctive part of my consciousness that is really only concerned about ME and how I survive. It is intelligent, curious, and above all, it protects me. It is part of the Wild Self, and it can protect me from the smothering veneer of civilization specifically because it is outside of the boundary fence. It is also that part of me that knows when there is a hole in the wall to escape through.

Do you remember the Tarzan movies? The wild untamed man meets the beautiful woman, falls in love, and gets tamed. He then goes back to civilization and, conquering his fears of the unknown, he learns to face society. Then he gets tired of the social nonsense and returns to the jungle, preferring the company of apes. It's an analogy to the wild child within. The Wild Child, the free one, the liberated Soul. It learns to fit in, awakens, then drops out. As Timothy Leary said: *Turn on, Tune In, and Drop Out.*

The WILD: It is the place that we are taught exists without rules, where all is dangerous and threatening. This is just false. As I write this, two crows are outside my window. One of them is trying to prove how tough he is by going up close to my 22-year-old cat. She really can't be bothered and walks away. She is old and prefers food on a plate now. Then my younger huntress cat comes out, looking curious: Guess what? No crows to be seen. They are GONE.

This is the reality of what we call 'wild'. In simple terms, it is CONSCIOUS. It's isn't unrestrained, or uncontrolled, but a state where we know and understand our needs and wants and how to get both. The crows KNEW the second cat was dangerous to them and left even before it walked outside. It is the re-discovery of this *"something that knows"* that I am talking about - THIS is your RAT.

There is something instinctive in all of us that just knows what a thing really is. We believe that nature is brutal: kill or be killed, run or die. But this is the lie your civilized self wants you to believe. In the wild, there is a harmony and balance with things, where we animals KNOW our place and how we fit in. Contrary to this, in our 'civilized' society there is a tremendous sense of disharmony where people feel like square pegs in round holes.

In our society, we have layers and layers of conventions. These are the 'shall nots'. These are the control measures put in place SPECIFICALLY to prevent the 'wild child' from emerging and creating havoc. And guess what, it works. But most people are unhappy and don't know their natural place.

Would you like some Havoc with that, Sir? Come on, admit it! You would like a little bit of havoc now and then, wouldn't you? Could be fun, hey?

Grandpa Duncan

My grandfather was known as *'The Man who cleaned up Broken Hill'*. Broken Hill is an Australian mining town which, in his day, was as rough, tough and uncompromising a place as the worst town in the Wild West. The police of that time were worried when the miners got out of hand, because they were true wild-men. Riots and fights could extend the entire length of the main street and last for days.

Grandpa Duncan was the Health Inspector and his job was simple: To make sure people used the public toilets instead of the street. So, how did he manage this? Was it through patient, caring education? Maybe he got everyone together and entered into careful discussion about health and safety, possibly by running weekend courses?

Nope - Grandad used a gun. He walked down the street with two loaded shotguns, both on ¼ charge, one loaded with lead pellet, the other with saltpetre. He used these to SHOOT people who were caught peeing (or worse) in the street. He had the Two Guns Rule: *Lead pellet for the black guys, saltpetre for the white guys.* Everyone thought that was quite reasonable of him, especially since ¼ charge didn't kill you. And the result? People stopped peeing and crapping in the streets.

He was given awards for this. PROOF: *A little bit of havoc does you good.*

Now, clearly, Grandpa Duncan was a complete RAT. However, imagine what would happen if you tried these sorts of antics today? You would be JAILED. It doesn't matter that the right results are achieved; in the modern world, it appears that the ends no longer justify the means.

Mavericks need not Apply

Mavericks need no longer apply for the job as Town Sheriff. Poker-faced winners need to go to Gamblers Anonymous. People who tell it straight are now lepers. Kids having fun are now troubled teenagers.

Do you remember the US election with McCain and Palin talking up being 'mavericks' and thus hoping to appeal to the frustrated Red Neck vote. Oh please! Who would ever believe that a creature of the Senate and a born again fundamentalist were Mavericks? Would anyone truly believe that a moose-shooting, narrow-minded bitch who believes in the rapture was an individualist? They got a few votes, but as the economy slid into the abyss, the greater reality was the purse strings. It gives me hope that the inner RAT of the United States was awake enough to vote for a true RAT at last.

And make no mistake. I write in Dec 2008 and I promise you, President-Elect Obama is a fully fledged Rat of the first degree. He will do deals on both sides of the political fence, we will negotiate anyway he can to get out of Iraq, he will avoid all confrontation where possible and he will do so with a lot of people feeling it was their idea. He is a cunning, careful Rat. Which is about the highest compliment I could give him.

Sometimes I wonder if a few more Grandpa Duncan's wouldn't be such a bad idea. He had his good points. He knew BS when he saw it and knew where it belonged. After all, his job was to make sure people put their crap in the right place. Now, I am not recommending loaded shotguns as a solution to the things that are not quite working for you, however, you CAN come armed and prepared to the table of the Social Lies and Distortions.

So, what sort of weaponry is permissible in a modern PC age ruled by the cynical exorcism of manhood?

How about wit, sarcasm, humour that breaks down illusion - Clarity of thought, the ability to spot a lie. THESE are the tools we use to defeat the weapons of Mass Delusion. Just remain AWAKE. Listen to that inner voice that is telling you where and what the trouble is. Listen to your RAT.

EG: When a car salesman is trying to sell me something, the nice, gullible self inside wants to believe him but my Inner RAT doubts everything and twists about for the truth. It turns on the motor, and straight away says "What's that?"

Nine times out of ten the salesman will say "Oh, it just needs a tune" or offer some sort of excuse for what he believes you have discovered. If he knows or suspects the car has a problem, he will act on this with a defensive posture. The RAT then is in a better position to ask "What, it isn't tuned? What else haven't you told me?" You can now bargain down the price.

So simple, isn't it? There was nothing there, yet you tested the boundaries of what you were being told and put yourself into a better negotiating position. You discover so much more when you allow your RAT to sniff out the lies in the never-ending stories around you.

Currently, we are being sold global warming. By all media reports, it's a given and we are all doomed. My RAT has some doubts about this and I suspect that there are some snouts in the trough. I may be wrong, but at least I can start asking questions rather than go, "Oh dear, we are all going to die!"

Rather than panic, I look for perspective and what is under the surface.

Look for Sub-Text

I have absolutely no problem with a theory that leads to a cleaner, more sustainable environment. However, for people to even begin to imagine Global Warming is a greater threat than a nuclear holocaust just beggars belief.

Regardless of ultimate truth, ALL perceived threats to society get used as a prep statement to up the ante on government charges. Whether the theory is true or not becomes irrelevant when only one truth remains: *Soon enough it will be about revenue raising*. Whether the claims of Reds under the Beds, or the Y2K bug, or the 16th century Tulip crisis were true or not, the one certainty was that they DID raise money for someone. The SUB-TEXT (or what is really being said) of all Government FEAR Statements is: *Get ready to pay more for less*. It is the same thing, whether the War on Drugs, or Terror, or Global Warning: To a RAT, this message is clear, it will soon be about paying more for less. It's something very obvious, opportunists look for opportunity. A measure of how strong your Inner Rat is today is how you react to this statement.

To put this into perspective, you used to think Humpty Dumpty was an EGG. Now you know he is something else. We currently believe Global Warming is all sorts of things. You may agree, disagree, believe a little or a lottle, but in fifty years we will see we were ALL wrong and that it is not what anyone thought. This is a given, *because no one knows enough about anything to be certain*!

Time will tell us its truth. The only REAL question is the ratio of right to wrong in the sales pitch.

No matter what someone is selling, the RAT inside you will make sure you stay awake to the obvious. In commercial reality, it means that you get a lower price for things than Mr. Stupid-me-wants-to-believe-bunny.

It also means you save time. Do you smell a RAT? You will when I am around. My RAT can be quite offensive. It is self-centred and purely motivated by what's good for itself (Which happens to be me). And guess what, I rarely pay too much for anything as a result.

This is why I so often win at Poker. I doubt everything, I do not believe anyone, including myself. I look at the faces on the table and take a calculated guess of what I can and cannot get away with. And it is simply amazing what we get away with. The only times I really stuff it up is when I forget to doubt, think I know better, and stop looking for the reasons BEHIND people's actions.

I have gotten bargain after bargain in my life. People keep getting amazed at how little I pay for things, even with large ticket items such as houses and acreage's. Last year I picked up Seven Acres on the water for around HALF its real value without a deposit. Can anyone do this? Only those with an awake and attentive Inner Rat can. Because your Rat instinctively knows how to tune in to the currents of energy flowing through every moment.

The Power of the Universe

Let's rule out what it is NOT. Finding the Power of the Universe has absolutely NOTHING to do with asking the Universe to provide. Forget 'The Secret' and 'The Celestine Prophecy'. That's kiddy stuff that amounts to little more than fairy floss at the circus. I am talking to you about powerful forces that emerge from your baseline attitude. You were possibly expecting the bit where I tell you how to 'attract' the powers of Attraction? Forget that: *The Powers of the Universe, by definition, are already here and there is nothing to attract.*

i repeat: The power of the Universe is here. It is all around you. It is just a matter on tuning in to the radio station and discovering what song life is playing.

Forget positive thinking. It's a pollution you throw about in your brain. Why? The subtext you are giving your inner mind when you try to think positive is that there's a problem, or that you have a LACK. Logically - This is the only reason why you have to think positive. Yes? Give the human mind some credit: It survived the dinosaurs, it can and will survive your attempts to control it.

Forget CONTROL! The RAT inside you just accepts what is, and picks up what it wants. It's all here, the good, the bad and the ugly. The rich and the poor live at the same address. I have often found that the richer the person is, when it comes to the heart, the poorer they are. Your Rat is not about wealth or poverty, it's about spotting potholes, snakes in the grass and lies. It is about seeing the people who want to take you down on one hand and finding opportunity as a result of this on the other. The problem is SEEING IT. If you can see it you can choose to duck it, welcome it, or shoot it for dinner. Tell me: Can you see the richness in your own life? Can you see the poverty? It is all about seeing the obvious and respecting this.

It is all about becoming a radio that can tune into the present moment, listen to the whispers of NOW, and be awake to the BS.

But the question remains: how do we get to this point of awareness? The sign to this place is a paradox that reads: *To see anything clearly you have to see the obvious, yet you can't because you are living a lie!* There is a way through, but it may surprise you that it is all about grasping the NEGATIVES inside you.

Forget your Positive Attitude - Adjust and fine tune your NEGATIVE attitude and things can happen. Wake up your doubter, trust your RAT to guide you, and you will start recognising opportunity. When you see your opportunities, luck will seem to fall into your lap. People will start believing you are lucky and presume that the universe is providing for you. But really, you are just staying awake to the obvious.

There are many benefits that come with this. Some reasons as to why you might seriously accept and train your inner RAT are:
1. *Everything will be cheaper for you.*
2. *Your relations with others will improve because they will instinctively know you are more honest and direct than most. (Therefore more able to be trusted*
3. *The Opposite Sex will subsequently find you more attractive.*

This is not to say all will be rosy, because your RAT can be objectionable on occasions. It certainly doesn't always make other people happy, but it will if they are aligned to your interests.

Your Rat Shakes Things Up

I had one guy get very upset with me when he bumped into me at my solicitor's office one day. Why did he get upset? I was buying some old train carriages off him and he had sold them to me cheap because he believed I was really poor. Then he realised I had more money than he did.

At the time I was buying the carriages I didn't tell him I was poor, I didn't tell him I was rich. I simply rocked up in an old battered car, and cheap work clothes, saying that I didn't have a lot of money to spend but that I wanted the carriages. What was his best price? This was all 100% truth. I stated the OBVIOUS. And I really wasn't going to pay a lot of money for them.

He then gave me his best price for a carriage and I just acted as if he meant this was the price for them both. Sure, I had a wringing of hands and a tugging of the forelock, and I acted like I was sweating over the high cost: But the fact is he paid bugger all for them and the carriages had become a problem for him. He wanted them gone - I was willing to take them. It was just a question of money.

What happened? As he signed the agreement for a block of land at my solicitor's office, he saw some of my own contracts waiting there and he then believed I had 'tricked' him. He thereupon declared that I was a RAT! I thank him now for the inspiration that became this book.

I guess his vanity finally got the picture that I was not a peasant who needed his help, that he was not a White Knight who had done me a favour. Here is where a curious thing happens: People are black and white as far as mentality goes. Because I had 'tricked' him and destroyed his White Knight, I must therefore be the Black Knight. I became the one who stole his dreams, yadda yadda. People's minds really serve up a load of rhubarb with the inner dialogue they tell themselves.

At the time, I have to say, I was a little shocked because from my point of view I was just getting the best price. My solicitor (bless his soul) said: "I cannot see that a person looking after their own interests is necessarily a bad thing, Sir." (I liked that solicitor) But then I realised he was looking at me thinking "Why am I charging him almost nothing for the work I do?" I had to change lawyers after that.

Tell the Story Right - Reap the Benefits

My old mate, Will, is another classic case of a Rat rising to the top. He is an old fellow who looks like he doesn't have two cents to his name, but he is worth hundreds of millions. He loves to go up to a corner property that is on a block zoned for high rise and talk to the people, saying he used to live in this house when he was a kid. He loved that old house and wanted to save it. He wanted to spend his last days being able to hang out in the old part of town. Fortunately, he had luck with a lottery win, and was able to pay decent money - But did the people want to sell?

You cannot believe how many people would sell their block to Will for less than what the major developer was offering. Why? Because the sale to poor broken down old Will made the owners feel bigger, better and more important than the developer. They tell themselves they are being kind to an old man, but really, it was their vanity that drove the bus over the cliff. Will, of course, now had the high rise builder over a barrel and could pick up a free million dollars or more because he held the all-important corner block.

Now, your RAT is not unkind, if this is what you are thinking. It is not anything nasty or unpleasant. Your RAT isn't a ruthless callous indifferent bastard who will steal from your grandmother - Not at all. Yes, it will allow people to exercise their vanity and make stupid calls on the Poker table. Your RAT will also quite happily allow others to believe they are superior. It just sits and allows reality to be what it is and takes advantage of what comes.

Will simply told a story, then allowed the sellers to believe what they would. He just acted as if they were very important people and he was begging a favour from them. Time and time again, a tugging of the forelock and acting below someone gives you an excellent price. My RAT taught me this.

My RAT is the part of me that is AWAKE! It is my Reality Attention Trigger. It is that instinctive part of me that goes "Hang on! This doesn't seem right." Or "Hmm, doubt he is telling me the truth here." Or maybe "He's saying this, but he means that". It is also that part of me that is awake to the good things! Not everything in the world around us is negative. (though you are safer betting it is until it proves itself otherwise)

If you want a perfect example of a RAT, look at Socrates. He went about pulling down the facades of all the important people in Athens, and he did so by allowing people to hang themselves on their own petard. People talk about the fabled Socratic Questioning, but really, he was just stating the obvious. NB: He was put to death.

Put to death? The truth is, Socrates taking the Hemlock was a bit of a Soap Opera. The people of Athens were just trying to get rid of him and hoped he would just piss off. Plato makes it perfectly clear that Socrates could have gone to Egypt and finished off his life in peace. So WHY didn't he choose to survive? I can tell you why: Vanity. He let go his RAT during his last days and acted in a way that he would be REMEMBERED. He decided it was better to martyr himself to get his message out. Socrates gave into his desire to be important in the eyes of his fellows and died as a result. He broke Rule Number Two: He shoulded on himself. He died doing what he believed he SHOULD do.

The Bounder, Cad or Shyster is called a 'Dirty Rat' in some of the old movies. James Cagney, famous for his "You Dirty Rat" quote that he never said, was an exemplar of what people imagined the nasty RAT might be. *And he was loved and adored for it.*

So tell me - Do you want to be loved? Do you want to have a real relationship? Do you never want to pay too much for anything ever again? Well: You need your RAT to wake up. If you want to be awake to the truth inside the stories you are getting told (and we are getting told stories all day long) be a RAT. Be Attentive to Reality as it presents itself to you.

You learn this in Poker again and again. ALWAYS check the cards on the table against your hand and consider every other player before you decide to throw in your cards. In one game I saw one guy look at the pair of Aces that his opponent turned over and tossed his own cards, not even realizing he had hit the winning hand with a straight on the river. But once you throw the cards, it is final. Just pay attention to the small details before declaring your position.

Why? Because this liberates you. This sets you free to act, speak and deal with life with authority. The reason we don't look closely at the end of a hand we have played is because we got caught in the mill wheel of fear and anxiety. Stop it, focus on the task at hand, and this will give you freedom from the tyranny of belief.

Now ask yourself: *Do I really want this?* Do you really want freedom from the tyranny of belief? Do you really want to start this journey towards total awareness?

If YES, are you sure? It can be a painful journey. It requires a great degree of change, and change hurts! However, as this is the reason why I wrote the book I can't really tell you not to, can I? So, give me some time and I will tell you all about it, and if you grasp even a small percentage of what you are about to read - Nothing will ever be the same for you again.

Summary: *In order to see reality, you have to see the obvious. Your RAT is your Reality Attention Trigger. It is the thing that takes the obvious, packs it into the bullet of truth, and fires it at the lies within you. It is that part of you that is Awake and Aware of what's going on. Your RAT accepts and deals with negatives and shows you how to make them a positive in your life. Your RAT knows when crap is being called caviar. It can sniff out a lie, a deception and all manner of hidden agendas simply through its ability to doubt.*

When we learn to work with our inner rat, life becomes more cohesive. We find greater synchronicity and we increase the degree of perception of the NOW in our day - This generally pays great dividends in friends, opportunity and money.

Everything is CHOICE

If we ask ourselves about the worst, most devastating events that have happened in our lives, they are generally the death of a loved one, the ending of a relationship or the deceit of a friend. These things shatter us, and yet we rebuild. But the broken image of the past haunts us as we reconstruct our lives. These things 'paint' a color over the self we are reconstructing. We mostly learn to see things in black and white, in order to see through this illusion - this is called cynicism. Or we take a different path - we accept the past is gone and rebuild our lives using the song of the morning chorus, the light of the new day, and the love of being alive. It is a matter of choice.

The Mystic Rat Says: Forget the notion that *Beggars can't be choosers,* - *Choosers can't be beggars*

You are a LIAR

> *"There are a terrible lot of lies going about the world, and the worst of it is that half of them are true."* Sir Winston Churchill

"The Whole Truth, and nothing but the Truth, so help me God!" Oh PLEASE! I say all 'truths' have holes and God isn't watching to check. Where are you going to find the whole truth? Google? TV? It's a nonsense. I have a barrister friend who bases most of his questions around a simple reality: *Everyone Gilds the Lily.*

Fact One: *People tell you the truth they want to believe.*

Fact Two: *They often then start to believe it.*

Fact Three: *The bulk of what we presently believe has been handed to us through circumstance, inheritance or upbringing.*

Fact Four: *Most of these beliefs are inherently incomplete or blatantly false.*

This brings us to one of the most important principles of Ratology: *You are a Liar, and so am I.* We are Liars - Every one of us. We may not mean to lie, we may even believe we are telling the truth when we splutter, "I never lie!" but we do manufacture lies, and we do it all the time. Why? Because it is a habit. This one single habit is the main cause of the majority of relationship break-ups, difficulties at work, and all manner of communication issues. So why Lie?

This is a very difficult question to answer, not because it is hard, but because to see the truth you have to get out of the lie you presently live in. In many ways, I am telling the turtle his shell is a prison. He looks back at me and says "What nonsense! it is my beloved house!"

We are so used to the lies we live, that we believe (this is the key word, *believe*) they are normal and, far worse, true.

We are back to the very difficult area of what we call the Censor. Remember right at the front when I mention that part of our mind that is in the driving seat? The Censor takes any information it receives from the external world and rearranges the images. Like a spin doctor, it presents this stream of information (What the Hindus call Santana) as the story it wants you to hear. I doubt you have the interest for me to through the five compartments of the mind, and how each links up to make what we believe our 'truth', but accept for the present we unknowingly deceive ourselves.

The Insidious Lies

A good friend of mine had a father who worked in the British Public Service. His name was Neil Bull and he was recalled to London to give the current financial status of the New Hebrides to the new minister in charge of this area. (Now Vanuatu) You would think this a simple request? Well, Mr. Bull had to teach the new man that nothing is simple.

When asked about the finances and budgeting, Neil Bull replied, "Certainly Minister. Tell me, are we spending too much, or too little - You need to give me the information you want before I can give you the figures you need."

"I just want the figures, man!" the new minister demanded.

"Of course Minister, but you really need to tell me the results you need before I can work these out for you."

This is like the argument between the mind and the Censor. Our Censor will rearrange everything to fit the presets of what we want to believe. Truth has absolutely nothing to do with it. The internal process of lying to ourselves is a given and only an understanding of the process will free us from this prison.

Why do we lie to others? Well, often we start because it's more interesting. Or perhaps I could put it in another way: It is less dull. On other occasions, we tell lies to avoid pain and suffering. When the good Catholic Brother asked if you did something, you always said, "No Brother!" because if you said yes, you got the cane. These are perfectly good reasons to lie, but not all lies are so gentle.

The insidious lies are the false beliefs we have absorbed into our psyche. These have slotted into places inside our emotions and thoughts, and they now control the way we see everything. I ask you:
1. When did you first learn insecurity?
2. At what point did you pick up that notion you were not good enough?
3. What was the first time you felt you could not trust life?

We are talking about the point where a negative belief entered into our world and became accepted. All these little negative beliefs came from an external source and got implanted into our minds and emotions. Further, we had some sort of agreement or acceptance on our part for this to happen. These 'pictures' are inserted by parents, transferred from friends, and the picture frames that house them are built by the general conditions we grow up in.

Most know to some degree what a curse the haunting sense that we are not 'good enough' can be. Yet - it's a straight up LIE we are telling ourselves! Not good enough for what? Running a ten second quarter mile? That's the truth for most, but generally feeling inadequate is a straight up, unmitigated LIE. How do I know? No baby feels inadequate or 'less than' anything. It is a learned belief and a false truth.

If you are an Olympic athlete who ran last, yes, you were not good enough - compared to the other top ten in your sport in the world. Yet, to everyone else, you are a champion!. So many of our beliefs are really COMPARISONS, which invariably breaks Rule One of the Rules of Rattyness.

But what can we do about it? If we could see it clearly, we might be able to change things for the better, but our minds and hearts are so totally soaked in wrong thinking and faulty emotion that we hardly know up from down anymore, let alone the truth from the lie. In many cases, our own IMAGINATION is lying to us at a most basic level, and this sets up the 'problem' - the lies we speak and believe - which creates issues in the life we lead.

Let me be blunt: Inside our head is a swag full of notions that are patently absurd and stupid. Yet we do not sand CANNOT see this. Worse, we BELIEVE our beliefs are true. Why? Because we believe them. Ye Olde Catch 22.

Even DIS-belief is a belief. The Atheist is as much a believer in nothing as the god-fearing Christian believes in something. It is not a question of belief, but of clarity, and believing we see things clearly is often the greatest lie of all.

We think what we 'know' is true and we would swear on our mother's grave as to the veracity of this. The patriot KNOWS his country is right, even when the rest of the world sees its actions are patently wrong. The Patriot believes because he is a Patriot. This is the Catch 22, the loop we are caught up in and, to some degree, this is also the loop of the self-fulfilling prophecy

The bulk of what we believe, almost everything we hold true and pretty much all that we think we know to be right is an INHERITANCE. When you look at your ideals of being noble you will find they come from Roman Times. These ideals are really just hand-me-down notions you wear. When you really analyse the fact that you are attracted to a particular type of person of the opposite (or same) sex, this too comes from patterns developed at an early age. These patterns are not US! Yet we believe they are. Your censor is like a cat who sees your true self as a mouse to play with, and who stamps a "should not" paw down whenever we try to escape it's grasp.

Yet, even though we are living hand-me-down ideals, dreams and beliefs, we are still responsible for the choices we make. We allowed them in and will reap the result of this decision. But good or bad, right or wrong choices - They are the same slave master when we are ignorant of their source. We are on a belief train with no idea of the start point or the destination. We are trapped by the inertia of our upbringing. Consider: *How can we say left is more correct than right if we are not sure why we are here, or where we are going?*

We are in that place Steve Miller sang about, "Stuck in the middle with you". When we do not know where we have come from or where we want to go, left or right may as well be up or down, in or out. We have no firm hand-hold, no certainty in this zone. The ONLY solution is on the Temple of Apollo: KNOW THYSELF. This basic belief of the Ancient Greeks stated we need to find and keep that Still Certain Point. And how do we discover this? We need to recognise our internal logjams/lies. We need to recognise the Truth that exists within the lies.

The Mystic Rat Says: *The ONLY thing we need to understand is the Truth about the Lie. There is no right or wrong in any lie or truth, there are only degrees of truth versus untruth.*

I know the Mystic Rat is making a very big statement here and most sensible people will scoff and laughingly ask, "What's this nonsense?" but I assure you - The Mystic Rat is 100% correct in what he/she/it asserts here.

Meeting the Judge

Once I was charged with a traffic offence that I personally thought was not an offence at all. I was being towed in a car and got charged with an unregistered, uninsured driving fine. It was a hefty fine, so I went to argue the matter in court. After batting off the inevitable for many months and knowing I was due to head out overseas in a matter of days, I finally stood up for my appearance.

Lucky me - I got the Hanging Judge. This man was sending people to jail for minor offences! He was berating them and he was cursing them. What's more, he was obviously drunk as a Lord. Of course, I referred to him as "Your Lordship" but I am not sure if he got the subtlety of the joke. Anyway, the fact is that I was guilty of breaking a law and we all know that ignorance of the law is no excuse. But I wanted to find an alternative, so when asked if I would plead guilty or not guilty I said, "Dingoes, your Lordship!"

He looked up, sincerely shocked. "What do you plead?" he questioned.

"Well, your Lordship, clearly I will be found guilty but at the time I was sincerely ignorant of the law as it stood. I believed I was doing the right thing because in the State where I come it is the right and proper thing to do to be towed in an unregistered car. I can't really claim to be guilty when I believe I am innocent, can I? However here in this State, it is illegal, so while I did it, I didn't really do it, so I want to plead Dingoes. The Dingo did it, your Lordship."

This got him laughing, and the judge not only apologised for dragging me through this unnecessary waste of time, he gave me the minimum fine possible. I still got a fine, but I ducked the worst of it. The point is this: Ignorance of the law, ignorance of whether you are living a lie, does not alter the fact that there is a cost for this. However, when we inject a sense of reality into the circumstances surrounding our choices, this can - and does - affect outcomes.

Again, it is all about finding the point of what is obvious. It was obvious to the judge that I was not a problem to society and, I suspect, he thought myself a fine old chap for making his day a little brighter. Now he would now have a wonderful story to tell at the bar that evening, as he chatted to his judge friends, "Can you believe I got a plea of DINGOES today!" and chortlingly happy he then becomes the centre of conversation for a few minutes.

I succeeded in two things with my court appearance:

1. *I recognised the flaw in the system between absolutes. No one is completely guilty nor totally innocent. We all have a dingo in there somewhere.*
2. *I employed my Jester to work hand in hand with my Rat. I used humour to bring out and make the obvious perfectly clear.*

We all tell lies, whether consciously or unconsciously. These lies are rarely intentional or malicious, but invariably they come from a place inside what we believe to be true. Yet, almost everything we believe contains an element of falsehood and, as a result, we tell lies. Don't feel offended, we are all liars of the first water but it is not because we INTEND to. It's because we are TRAINED to be this way. In so many small ways we have been trained to live a lie. Our only real crime is that we do not realise it.

But let's be generous, and say that we all plead Dingoes to the above.

The Mystic Rat Says: *The simple truth is that there is almost no simple truth.*

Everything is affected by the Lie that is in our upbringing, our beliefs, and our self-image. Every part of our life has been touched with some sort of story that is overtly or covertly false. As a child we just accept things. After we experience a repeating cycle of untruths and half-truths that come from our upbringing, the child-self starts getting all sorts of cracks. It appears I am NOT good enough, because I have to act in a certain way to make those other kids like me. Or I am NOT confident, because I was told I was born a sinner and have to go to church to redeem myself.

We get split and then we get shattered. We get Humpty Dumpty'd with the reinforcing of half-truths and lies that flow from our friends, our environment and our associates - and then these false patterns solidify and become our 'truth'. Our culture and our beliefs thus create a snowball effect of lies and distortion which, in time, become the pillars on which we stand.

The child is flexible, accepting of change. The adult becomes rigid and insistent that their way is right. Why the shift from fluid to fixed? Why this strange need for certainty in an ever changing world?

Let me ask you: Do you really imagine that a clear, confident and focused society could have been hoodwinked into a War in Iraq? It was overt and obvious that this was a play to control the oil price, and the excuse of Weapons of Mass Destruction was just a bargaining chip to get the poker game underway. It cost the U.S. BILLIONS of dollars for NOTHING. (Not having an awake, aware RAT can be expensive)

And another one: Do you really imagine it's OK for a Government to bail out inherently greedy, abusive financial systems that have plundered the worlds wealth and THEN for all the guilty parties to be rewarded with a bailout, leaving the innocent to suffer the burden of debt the banks created? It's quite insane, inherently false, yet it was accepted with nary a squeak.

Meeting and dealing with consequences is what defines truth for the individual and a society. We all make mistakes, do things that are unwise, and generally fluff about in confusion. Then life (causation) sends us a reminder, reality hits, and we recalibrate.

When my youngest child was eighteen months he threw an almighty tantrum. I saw what was happening, and picked him up and took him outside. I then plonked him on the ground and explained, very gently, "You are allowed to misbehave and act like an animal if you want, but this means I need to put you outside where we put the animals, ok?"

I looked at him to make sure he understood, and added, "This is where you now live." Then walked away. Immediately I heard him call out, speaking perfect English even though he was still in the 'Ma Ma 'Da Da' stage. "Don't leave me alone!" The screaming had stopped.

"Oh, so you CAN act like a proper human? Well, OK then, you can come back inside." There were no more tantrums, he had met and understood the consequences of his actions. Today he is a remarkably even-tempered man.

This is called 'Meeting the Judge' - where you come across a person who sees you and your situation clearly. You are then in a position to correct your error and carry on. The simple truth: Most of our problems derive from parents and teachers who are not good at understanding reality and consequences. It is your present choice to break those chains or re-forge them for a new generation.

Tell me: Is it mere coincidence that ALL religions have you meeting a judge at the end of your life? Inside ourselves, our CENSOR is the Judge. It is the King of the little world we live in and it defines our reality until a greater awareness of truth displaces it.

Don't Mind the Mind

Let us spend a moment and look at the Five departments of the mind. There is the MANAS, or thinking section. This is like the central computer that stores and calibrates the thoughts and emotions, feeling and experience of the individual. There is the BUDDHI, which is the Admin Centre. It determines how things are to be presented to the external world. The CHITTA is the area where we perceive beauty and it is very important. It is where our creative self is based and is the only area that can get around the Censor. Our EGO is the centralising force. It is what determines 'me' 'not me' and creates inner focus. Finally, the CENSOR, or Judge. This is the part that takes all the information, the thoughts, beliefs, and experiences, and rearranges them to make sense. This is where our personal 'truth' comes from. (More info in 'Book of Number: Client Psychology'. Available on Amazon)

When we meet an EXTERNAL Judge, our Censor has to recalibrate and adjust to a new reality. And here is the secret, beating heart of RATOLOGY: *Seeing the obvious is a JUDGEMENT, a very powerful, unquestionable judgement.* When we begin to recognise the obvious, we can supplant our Censor and start redefining what is truth for ourselves. Our RAT will lead us to this place.

Economic reality used to be an external judge, but now, who knows? The economic situation of the world at this point is a blatant, ongoing LIE. The US is bankrupt and has been for years - yet manufactures ever-increasing debt, denies the obvious, and continues to drain reality from the world of finance. But we are told it's fine, so we get another mortgage, buy another car, and go to work for another dollar. Then came the financial crisis, a powerful judgement.

Banks died, the money disappeared, real estate values plummeted, and Warren Buffet made an absolute fortune when he snapped up the bargains.

The ONLY Government that supported the people in this crisis was the Icelandic republic. They JAILED the bankers, cancelled the fabricated debt, and put their then Prime Minister on trial for negligence. Iceland was the ONLY powerful Judge to determine a new reality for its people. And the result? Prior to the collapse, Iceland received 500K tourists a year. Now they get 1.5 million. I cannot tell you why, but I can report on the facts. It seems to me that an honest country is something a whole lot of people want to experience.

But the majority of the world did the opposite. The US did not adjust their faulty derivative-based market, so we are doomed to repeat this sorry saga.

The Paradox of the Lie

The Paradox of the Lie States: *There is no truth that is greater than the Lie that is accepted and believed by two or more people.*

But the Bible says, *'The Truth shall set you Free!'* Go on, tell the boss exactly how you feel and watch how quickly you will be set free. The Bible is correct on this score, but to know the truth you would have to know what is an un-truth.

This can be difficult. It is like separating the milk from the coffee.

Blatant Lies have been implanted into our Psyche by society, family, and media. When two or more people agree that any particular lie is a truth, then for them it is truth. For that Lie to extend out and be accepted by society is merely a question of numbers - If you can get ENOUGH people to agree, it becomes the accepted truth. The Earth was the centre of the universe for a very long time, as you know. It was also flat at that point in time. These accepted myths are what makes us all LIARS - but not in the way that you might expect.

An Example: You probably believe your dog loves you. Yes? Why wouldn't you? Every day you get proof! Look at how he races up to see you when you get home. You love your dog, your dog loves you. It is simple, clear and undeniable because you both appear to agree on the same thing.

The scientist (of course) will cry 'Pavlov's Dog' and will say the dog gets excited because he knows you will feed him. Yet we know that a dog will run up to its owner even when he starves it. So what does this mean? It means that the Scientist is ignorant, yet it also means that you are telling yourself a lie.

It is perfectly reasonable to believe that your dog loves you, and he probably does, but the fact is that a dog loves whoever owns it. That's the nature of a dog. It's not 'you' who is necessarily deserving of the dog's love, but it's the nature of the dog to give it, regardless. You took it personally, the scientist took it impersonally, yet the truth is that the dog just does what dogs do. Can you see how the lies start to creep IN BETWEEN the lines of your experience?

There are fine lines that make the difference between a truth and a lie. We believe something and, as long as it is reinforced by external 'proof', (EG: our dog coming to greet us) then we have no reason to doubt our belief. But when our dog runs up to someone else quite happily - What does this mean?

It means that this is the nature of the Dog. It just doesn't mean anything else. That's the whole point; it really doesn't mean anything more than what it is. If I am splitting hairs here, it's because a truth and a lie are a hairsbreadth apart.

Another Example: You really thought you were in love with that person so many years ago, but here you are, years later and you wonder what on earth made you believe this. They turned out opposite to the one you met!

It's no secret - 'Being in Love' is a thrill we enjoy and we really don't care if it is an absolute truth. We didn't WANT to see the negatives that would have been glaringly obvious if we had looked closely. We just wanted the fireworks and the sex. It was great at the time, so why would we have wanted to spoil it? In other words: We had sufficient reward to ignore what was obvious. And this is fine!

If the Story Entertains, does it NEED to be True?.

I was making love to a beautiful woman one night. It was just incredible, but then I realized it was just a dream. I woke up, realized it WAS a dream, and then cursed the fact that I became aware of this and ruined a good time. Can you guess that I was a little too keen on the pursuit of truth as a young fellow?

So: Let's say you discover your spouse is sleeping with another. You were living in a dream and now you have to deal with reality. Here we make a choice: We can ignore, confront, OR we can understand and accept. Most will go into a rage and demand to know why someone betrayed us, but is this useful? Not really. What matters are the choices we make as a result of life's changing circumstances. And what are the choices most people make when confronted with an uncomfortable change? Often it is a random mix of all of the below.

- Turn a blind eye and pretend it didn't happen (Ignore)
- Blame the person, usually with the consequence of divorce, acrimony, and angst. (Confront) Or you,
- Accept it happened, allow the person their freedom, and thus
- Negotiate a new agreement.

They then tend to continue carrying unresolved angst towards the person, depending on how good a story the guilty party spins.

We slip into lies for many reasons: Passion, convenience, lack of self-determination, fear, need, etc. But simple convenience is by far the largest reason to invent a story. What is more, we welcome our fabrication because it provides us a benefit. At the time, the story seemed harmless and, on their own, these tales are. It is the collected snowball of 'stuff' that is the problem.

Let's say: You are a teenager and you get home late. Your mother calls you in, and you lie saying the reason if that you got a flat tyre on the car. You love your mother, but you lie to her anyway. What's more, she knows you are lying, but because you gave her a good excuse she lets it go. She likes the fact that you cow-towed and gave her a feeling of authority. Mother basks in a warm glow, the child is happy to get away with it.

Lies are often used as the grease between the wheels of our differing realities. It would be better to use courtesy and respect, but let's not try to change the world today. It's just too much effort. And did it matter so much the child was late? Not really. The oiling of the social cogs is what mattered and this is a good deal of what our little white lies are about.

What if I told you the real truth? *Lying and obfuscation sit at the base of social communication and interaction in Western Society. These are the pillars that bind us to the common fate of all our Humpty Dumpty's. They are the hidden wells of sorrow that tie us together. It is not truth and honesty that is at the core of society, but obfuscation, deceit and double standards.*

I can feel people cringing. How DARE he insult my society! Well, think about it, how often do you NOT say what you really think or feel? A lie by omission.

Can you imagine saying to the fat woman with bad breath who sits beside you on the bus "Crap woman, you are a disgusting creature. Get out of my space!" No, what we usually do is cough, look the other way, hold our breath and seek the first opportunity to escape. It is a silent lie of convenience that avoids confrontation. But is that 'really' a lie, you ask?

What we really need to do is to define what a 'lie' is. I want to avoid concepts of 'right' or 'wrong' because, in truth, absolutes like this are quite rare. All things tend to be Yin and Yang, each containing a little of the other.

Let's try this for a definition: *A Lie is when you are thinking, feeling or believing one way on the inside, yet acting a different way on the outside.*

That's a Lie, isn't it? Yet there are many different types of lies. When we tell children about Santa Claus, that's a lie. When we imagine that God is looking after us personally, or that the devil is out to get us, or both! These are lies. Yet a "proper" Lie is rarely a total lack of Truth. Invariably, it is a perversion of it. So what's Truth? *The truth is that there are lots of twisted train-wrecks called people who are living lives of quiet desperation and pretending otherwise.*

Now, despite what I have just said, there is absolutely nothing wrong with a lie. Our society gets along fine with its double standards and absurd notions of truth. What would newsreaders say if they were required to tell the whole truth and nothing but the truth? *"Fifty people died in Georgia today. Boy am I glad that I have this cushy well paid job and am not like one of those stupid peasants"*

Of course, he/she can't speak his mind, he/she would be fired on the spot and social outrage would pursue him/her. He/she needs to lie to save his/her job. That is not the problem. The problem comes when we forget what we are doing. We forget we are Humpty Dumpty - Post Wall, and imagine that we have it all together. We dress smart, act clever, think quick, but really we are all in pieces. The result: We are hold ourselves together with the sticky tape of convention and invisibly, yet continually, compromise our ideals.

Acceptance, Awareness, and Perception.

As long as we see our lies for what they are, we are not lying to ourselves. This is what really matters at the end of the day. It is when we believe our lies that we get the problem, and the problem is that we are all in pieces.

Professor George Cockcroft, writer of "The Diceman" wrote to me on the subject, and very simply stated, *"We are all multiple."* (If you want to discover a first-class Rat, read "The Diceman") We are all many aspects and not all of them know each other or understand they are conncted.

Maybe you are living with someone you no longer love, but it is convenient, so you stay. Well, that's a bit of a lie, isn't it? However, maybe you KNOW it is a compromise and do not pretend it is anything else. You remain kind, because it makes the other person comfortable, but you know what's what. That is when the LIE becomes a truth. You KNOW you are lying, which makes it is true.

It's not really about lies. *It is all about Kindness, Awareness, Acceptance, and keeping a Clear Perception.* If you see clearly, you can be USEFUL to life.

A different sort of lie: Maybe you think you are worthless, yet you go to the job interview and demand more money. That's another little lie, yes? However, once you recognise you will say and do anything to get ahead, then you are expressing a personal truth. Get it? When you are AWARE, you can turn your Lies into versions of Truth. (or vice versa, if it is more entertaining)

And please, if your wife is wearing a frock that makes her butt look fat, are YOU going to be the one who tells her? You would have to be crazy. You LIE and say she looks great. Being practical is a greater truth than the truth. This awareness is where we start to get in charge of our inner and outer life.

We all tell stories in a thousand different ways and this is not necessarily a bad thing. But we need to remain aware of a simple principle: *When we are ignorant of the truth, lies create a current that weakens our heart.*

So the lie is not 'bad', the lack of awareness is. How do we get awareness? Well, via hard experience, usually. After all, experience is what teaches us to LISTEN to our RAT. And whether we accept it, reject it, or do whatever we want with it, if we *listen* we have a toe pointed in the right direction. And in our listening, we need to accept and expect that others will lie to us, either consciously or unconsciously. The question I ask you is a simple one: *Can you get past the concern that someone is lying, or not telling you the whole truth?*

You will need to because, I assure you, no one is telling you the whole truth. Not because they don't want to, but often because they can't. It is simply not possible here on Planet Earth to always speak the truth. The best we can hope for is courtesy, sincerity, some honesty, and maybe in time a little wisdom.

The Whole Truth, and nothing but the Truth? Please, let's not laugh too loudly. People swear in court on this every day and yet every single one who makes this oath is gilding the lily in some way. Why? Because this is what people do. Socrates based his reputation on this fact.

You Want the Truth?

"There is no worse lie than a truth misunderstood by those who hear it."
                                                                - William James

"You want the truth? You can't handle the truth!" I love that quote from Jack Nicholson's character, USMC Major Nathan Jessup, in "A Few Good Men". Really, I promise you, you do NOT want the truth because truth in its raw form burns the hands that try to hold it. When people asked me if I was telling them the truth about something I would often reply, "depends if you want something nice, or if you really DO want the truth?" Usually they change the subject.

The TRUTH is that you can have everything you ever wanted.
1. The most beautiful partner,
2. all the money in the world,
3. the best house,
4. the most important friends,
5. the perfect marriage

Anything else? If I forgot anything, just write it in and it's yours! What, you think I am LYING? How DARE you Sir/Madam/It!

Let's be honest about lying: *We all do it.* But why? Normally, to protect ourselves or to get something we want, or just because it is more interesting. Lying is all about US. It's a selfish impulse designed to get something. We also tell little fibs to avoid confrontation, accusation, and conflagration. Again, it's fine as long as we know it. What happens, however, is that the unconscious little lies build up inner walls. Each little untruth becomes an unconscious brick in a wall that divides us.

Here is the truth: *We all Lie.* It is a given in our present society that we lie. They have osmosed into our being. The problem comes when we are unaware of our lies. This is when they can take over the driving seat and direct our lives.

The Paradox of the Lie reads: *No Truth is greater than the Lie that is believed by two or more people.* (It can take a while to grasp what this one means)

The walls of belief people erect within themselves are what separate us. Group think, social mores, and religious differences - these are all walls to contain the faithful and expunge the infidels.

We are a society of Walls and Bridges. (Nod to John Lennon) Young teenagers live inside a walled fortress where the sign says "Only young people can enter". No-one else can enter, yet they have bridges to each other. Drug addicts have their own walled city, a state of consciousness where junkies feel at home but where everyone else is excluded. Just go to L.A. if you want to see a walled society! Whole neighbourhoods are divided along colour lines, the colour of money and the colour of skin. (Ok, it's wealth and ethnic lines.)

So, why don't we build bridges instead of building walls?

Walls and Bridges

Walls and Bridges is the name of the second album John Lennon brought out after Imagine. In between was "Mind Games". They both form a grudging reality that accepts that the ideals of "Imagine" are hampered, hindered and harassed by the nature of society as it is. I guess it was his way of recognising the very real barriers in society. "Jealous Guy" on Imagine is part of it. Walls and Bridges are the net result, the gestalt if you will, of the lies we have told and been told.

Here's the paradox: *When we start imagining there are no barriers (The childlike attitude) then we see they are very real indeed. (The adult attitude)*

So here's the secret: *Just stop telling lies and the walls start to fall*. The hard part here is how do we stop telling lies when we don't realise we are speaking them? The answer is surprisingly simple. Every slice of intimate, open communication is a bridge. Ask yourself if whatever to are doing brings you to a feeling of closeness, of value, of intimacy. The way forward will be clear.

Intimacy is fractured in most people's lives. We have divided, compartmentalised and segregated everything. It's no one's fault. This happened because it was the only way we saw to survive at the time, but it means we remain in a state of uncertainty. But when we practice finding centre, discovering the authentic self, awakening our heart to intimacy and trust, we find bridges everywhere. To do this we only need to stop whispering our little lies, then the walls start to fall and we begin to experience personal connectedness once more.

Do you go to France and speak English? Do you go to the tax department and speak truth? It is the same question. It comes down to survival, you learn to speak in the language of the conditions where you find yourself. The problem is, tell the truth to a liar and to them it looks like a lie. If you put in a tax return and it is all the total truth, you will pay more tax. Tax law is set up and designed around the principle that you WILL lie, and so absolute honesty will cost you.

There is the true story of the black man who came across an injured white woman and he called out for help. People came, and immediately accused HIM of the crime. As it turns out, the poor woman had been raped and stabbed. What's more, when the woman came to days later, she confirmed it was the innocent black man who did it and the fellow was hung for his kindness. But why did the woman accuse an innocent man? She had been raped by her cousin and she didn't want HIM to hang. Lies on lies on lies, all to protect what we believe is precious to us. (Reputation, social standing, self-esteem, etc.)

President Clinton swore that he "never had sexual relations with that woman", yet everyone knew he did. But he had to lie until it was his time to leave office, when he finally said: "Sure I played about with that woman". He had to lie to block the attacks from the opposing parties, but in the end, when it no longer mattered, he was happy to "Fess up".

Really, it didn't matter at all, but he had to lie to survive.

No one really cared except those who sought to profit by the story. No one really thinks your lies (or your truths) are all that important. So why do we keep telling them? There are a million reasons why we lie, but essentially we lie to protect something or to get something. Just accept it, and move on.

So what? I recommend learning this very simple phrase and apply it every day. Combine *"So What?"* with "Whatever" and you will save a lot of wear and tear on your soul. We all lie about something at some point, and so what? The Great Rat story as a lead-in is a Lie, but so what? It's fun. And that's part of the rationale of our lying: *It makes things interesting.*

What would you prefer, a dull truth or an interesting Lie? Maybe a re-reading of "1001 Nights" will give an answer to this. On the Arabian Nights subject, I knew this guy, a Bedouin, and he told the most outrageous lies all the time. Every story he spoke was a litany of lies, but it entertained everyone and life around him was fun. So what's the problem?

The problems start at the point where we start to believe our lies.

So, let's stop and just be person to person for a moment. Let's forget notions of right or wrong, and please answer me this simple question: *Are you Happy?*

Happiness = Connection

Honestly, are you happy? The reason I ask this is because I have noticed that the people who lie the least are the happy ones. Perhaps this is because happy people who have a high degree of CONNECTION in their lives.

Intimacy is the reward at the top of the non-lying ladder. People who feel a sense of true intimacy do not want to lie to those around them, because they know, instinctively, that LIES SEPARATE. People who feel no need to hide anything are generally accepted and loved more easily by others in their society. Those with a sense of natural intimacy engender trust and are just happier. Young children are naturally intimate, naturally trusting, and are happy. Intimacy, trust and happiness always add to a positive outcome.

The happiness scale runs from the high point of true intimacy, down to the low zone of isolation. What is the theme of a depressed person? Isolation, despair and loneliness. Lack of purpose, lack of self esteem, a lack of ANY sort equates to low happiness and high lying.

I have met people so submerged into the belief they are so completely alone that they tell the most outrageous and provably false statements without batting an eyelid. Pathological liars are very lonely, unhappy people.

People lie to get your attention, and pretend this is a connection with you. The Great Rat story that starts this book is a piss-take on Genesis, designed to put a smile on your face. The story is a fabrication, obviously, yet it is one where there is a real basis to the story. The whole truth? The thing everything in this book is wrapped around is this: *Mickey Mouse really IS the Messiah!*

Mickey Mouse is the Saviour of the World.

"What? Are you MAD?" do I hear you say? Well, more cunning than mad.

What I just wrote was a thing to get your attention. A little lie like this keeps you reading. Get it? We KNOW it is a Lie, but despite that we want to know more. THAT'S part the reason why we lie: *It makes us more interesting*. The real problem is when we start to believe the lie and it becomes our truth.

My oldest son once pretended to be scared of the vacuum cleaner. He was just four years old and he ran away, screaming as if it was a really bad thing. Then he laughed about his game with the 'monster' vacuum cleaner. The next week he forgot he was just acting scared and he really WAS frightened of the vacuum cleaner.

There are the lies that comes from inadequacy. I knew this really wimpy guy through a mutual friend. One day down the bar he started talking about this incredible adventure that happened to him. I mean, it was truly amazing, and the story was given with incredible detail. The problem was: *he was telling a story that was in a book my friend had lent him the week earlier*. His life was so empty that he pretended that the character in the book was himself. A modern day Walter Mitty, trying to gain a sense of worth.

The LIE isn't the problem, it is when we believe them. When we do this we build walls around us, lock the gate, and throw away the key. The adults raising us told us lies about Santa Claus and the Bogie Man. These are stories designed to entertain, yet also to keep us behaved. The PSYCHIC RESIDUE of thee little white lies is the foundation of all our walls, but there is a surprisingly and brilliant positive to be found inside this reality: *There is no ceiling*.

Zig Zeilger, a well-known motivational trainer, told would-be salespeople about how a flea circus works. The flea circus trainer puts a whole batch of fleas into different glass aquariums. One has a glass ceiling four inches high, the next has a glass ceiling six inches high, then eight inches, then ten, then twelve. The fleas in the various aquariums learn to jump *just under* the glass ceiling, so they will stop hitting their heads. And here is the truth about ourselves.

After a few weeks of this, the fleas are trained to NEVER jump any higher than the height of their ceiling. Now, when you put them in a big aquarium without any ceiling at all, even though they can see their brothers jumping higher, the ones trained to jump four inches will continue to jump four inches.

Of course, the flea circus trainer sets up little wheels at four inches, six inches, etc. So it looks as if the fleas are jumping up to do tricks. Here is the thing - Any flea in there can easily escape his/her prison, but the personal lie they learned is he self-limiting belief that they can't.

Hey, even the NAME is a lie! It isn't even a circus. It is ALL a setup that fleas land on set toys at set heights. But you get the idea? We have been trained in a set of limitations. This is a lie that has defined us BECAUSE we have believed. This is the precise and simple reason you are where you are today.

The WHOLE truth? Now matter how much we may have walled ourselves in, there is no ceiling. Your NEW truth is: *You can do whatever you want, go wherever you choose, and be what you want to be.* The LIE is the glass ceiling that is keeping you confined and keeping you from happiness.

What, do I hear you thinking? *"Holey Cheezus - Is he saying I can do anything I want? That I can sex whoever, whenever, make scads of dosh, and eat like a pig ... This sounds GREAT!"*

Sure I am saying this. If that's what you hear, it's all good. If you want to be a pig, be a pig. If you want to be a Saint, be a Saint. Be whatever you want to be, and if it gives you happiness, all power to you. You can only become a true RAT by doing what you enjoy. Test your limits, savour life, and feel freedom.

Do What You Will

I have to appeal to your pleasure principle because Ratology has no eternal Hell. As a result I cannot scare people to my side of the fence, I have to make them believe the grass is greener here and make them WANT to come over. I know life will present you with reality, and your dreams will be tested, but that doesn't sell books. However, if I can promise people that they can have whatever they want, then they want to come on over to our side, yes?

Right then, let's do this again: You can have everything you ever wanted.
- *The most beautiful partner,*
- *all the money in the world,*
- *the best house,*
- *the most important friends,*
- *the perfect marriage*

Anything else? If I forgot anything, just write it in, and it's yours!

This is not complete rubbish. The reality is that we DO get what we expect. We get what we believe we deserve. Yes! We CAN! But how? Mostly by being free of our past. When we shift away from guilt, shame and a sense of confinement, move towards a more intimate connection with others, and relearn the childlike open-hearted trust, then things start to work for us.

INTIMACY and TRUST opens life's doors, not prayers to an unknown God, or grovelling in fear of the consequence of sneezing in the Synagogue.

Ratology has no concept of "sin" as an eternal wrongness. Sadly, this makes it harder to get people to grovel for forgiveness because of some invisible wrong we have nailed over their head. It is SO MUCH EASIER to have Original Sin to swing as a dull, heavy weapon of control. *I declare you guilty before you were born!* Now isn't THAT an utterly absurd lie a lot of people have believed!

However, I understand why Constantine invented this fiction of Original Sin. If someone is not properly scared they won't toe the line. Of course, he also had a very large army to help him convince people of his theology. Sadly, Ratology is without a suitable Guilt Trip (or a large, ruthless army) that we can use to apply the emotional pressure in order to make you stay. Without negative, fear-based emotions being projected on the congregation, it makes it harder to put people in a listening position. I therefore need a little guile and cleverness to trick you into believing and adhering to my view. This is especially awkward, because part of Ratology's inherent teaching is not to believe another's belief.

Anyway: Time to move onto a lighter subject: Mickey Mouse.

Summary: *We lie to protect ourselves from something we fear. Lies form walls inside and outside, whereas truth and intimacy form bridges to the heart. The only way to discover where the walls inside us exist is by getting pass our internal barriers. By recognising the inner lies and fabrications we can put ourselves in a position of choosing to bridge them or leave them be. Either is OK, as long as we are aware.*

A Curious Thought: *If no one believed that science was real, it would not exist. Why is this? Well, for one there would never have been a course at a university for something no one believed existed, therefore there would be no scientists! So, believe it or not, it is the belief in science that created the lack of belief in scientists!*

Ratology: Way of the Un-Dammed

The Birth of Mickey Mouse

"Greatness appears in unlikely places. You, for instance?" The Lord High Rat

The first emergence of the Rat in the current cycle came with Mickey Mouse. The pretender to the throne is (as we all know) Mighty Mouse, a 1942 latecomer to the scene. Followers of Mighty Mouse are to be scorned and spat upon. They must remain chained to a worn out easy-chair and forced to watch Black and White TV sets for ever.

The real story of the Mouse is that Walt Disney had an existential crisis. His Oswald Rabbit character had been stolen and eventually became the fabulously successful Bugs Bunny. He needed something else. He needed a HIT!

During this period he became fascinated by an ancient, carved stone image of a cartoon-like head. It was a little weird because it had what seemed like mouse ears. It was **Apollonius of Tyana**, a miracle working mystic and contemporary of Jesus who was being re-discovered in the 1920's. The "ears" represented some sort of halo, and the image came from a piece housed in the Athens Museum. It was a very old Apollo derivation. It was cartoon-like, a silhouette, and drawn in an odd proportion which was very unlike the Greeks.

It was a bit of a puzzle for the Curators, and it caught Disney's eye. Why? Because it was part of a study he was undertaking with either the Christian Scientists or Theosophical Society, and Apollonius was being looked at as a "What If" alternative to Jesus. We know more about this enigmatic figure today.

A little known Epitaph to Apollonius reads:
> 'This man, named after Apollo,
> and shining forth Tyana,
> extinguished the faults of men.
> The tomb in Tyana (received) his body,
> but in truth heaven received him
> so that he might drive out the pains of men'

If you think this sounds 'Jesus-like' you would be right. Apollonius was worshipped as a Divine Son of God and, at the time, had more followers than Jesus. Many believed he was the incarnation of the great Teacher Pythagoras of Samos, who had been an incarnation of the God Apollo. The words of Apollonius on reincarnation and many other subjects paralleled those of Pythagoras.

More importantly, he was the favoured philosopher of the Empress Julia Domna and also her son and grandson. She is the one who commissioned the work "Life of Apollonius of Tyana" (AD 220). Curiously, Origen, a bishop of the Catholic church of that time responded with a work, "Against the Heresies" that specifically nominated Apollonius as a curse. (This book remains a staple of Vatican dogma to this day - despite Origen's views being rejected)

Apollonius was a figure of great reverence during his life and up to the 4th Century. The Arabs and Bahaii's still refer to him as Balinus. Prior to the 4th century any worship of the man was condemned by the Christian teachings (He was considered the Devil by some) but this was of little account until Constantine. With the formation of the new Catholic Church by Emperor Constantine, the worship of anything but Jesus became religious suicide. All spiritual sites dedicated to Apollonius were destroyed and any reference to his person was banned. His memory was preserved, however, and somehow it came down to the present day.

Apollonius was an Essenne (as Jesus was also reported to be) and he manifested many well-documented miracles, including raising people from the dead. Yet he didn't have the PR machine that Jesus recruited and was virtually unknown in the society of the 1920's, apart from members of the Theosophical Society. The image of this odd "Mouse Eared" mystical man set something in motion in Walt's brain. It got him thinking of the perfect man and why was this portrayed as a cartoon person with what looked like Mouse ears? (Author Note: In recent times more "mouse eared" cartoon-like images of holy men have been discovered in religious shrines)

What's Wrong with a Mouse

Now Disney was a shy fellow, and apparently at this point he heard the old saying 'Are you a Man or a Mouse"'. Walt thought, "What's wrong with a Mouse?" This was the moment of conception for Mickey Mouse, the little mouse who could never be defeated. Exactly! What's wrong with a Mouse? And, logically, if a mouse is good, why isn't being a Rat even better?

That little mouse represented Walt Disney and his indomitable spirit. Despite incredible odds, Disney never admitted defeat and, like Mickey, was full of the American spirit of 'can do'. And he needed it, after his prize creation, Oswald Rabbit, had been effectively stolen from him he had few prospects. He was depressed and reportedly, around this time, the image of Apollonius got him thinking. He got the vision of Mickey Mouse, the one that emerged pretty much as the legendary Mickey in "Steam Boat Willie".

A little known fact of Walt Disney's creative process was that he always had the complete vision of a cartoon in his imagination before he put ink to celluloid. He had seen Steamboat Willey (a send up of a Buster Keaton movie) in his imagination before he set Ub Iwerks to the drawing process.

This cartoon was highly successful, and was amongst the first 'Talkies' that used synchronised sound. It was also one of the first musicals! Yet, while it was very popular, Walt realized that the vision he had for Mickey as a radical free-booter was going to be a hard one to fit into the mainstream. From the Mickey Mouse in Steamboat Willie, Walt started to extract pieces, to expand the narrative and make his Mouse more acceptable. He slowly split Mickey up into what became the characters we know today.

Steam Boat Willie was released in 1928, then came Pluto in 1930. Goofy arrived in 1932 and Donald turns up in 1934. These were all 'subject personas' of the original Mickey Mouse. The bad tempered Mickey became Donald Duck, the carefree part became Pluto, while the stupid part became Goofy. (And let me ask you: What sort of creature IS Goofy? Pluto is a dog, Donald is a Duck, Mickey is a Mouse - But Goofy? The mystery remains unsolved.) This 'splitting' notion is important because we ALSO do this! Soon we will come to the part about how we divide ourselves into acceptable personas in order to fit in.

Mickey became the curious adventurer who seemed detached and aloof from any concern about things going wrong. He was the ideal Man/Mouse who could achieve anything he dreamed and, with his friends in tow, he succeeded.

Failure became the lot of Donald, and ignorance fell to Goofy. It was Mickey who would unify them and guide them all to success. It was a hugely successful endeavor which gave Disney the clout to go further, much further.

Disney extended his dream with his 'crazy notion' of creating extremely high quality, movie length cartoons. From his vision we got Snow White and the Seven Dwarfs and so many other marvellous films, yet the most special of all remains the magic of Fantasia. This is a story unto itself. The original two hour show was done as a Roadshow release, which meant that Disney barnstormed the film to theatres around the country. Yet, it was not particularly successful until it was edited down to the cinematic eighty-two minute version. Despite the cuts, the extraordinary Sorcerers Apprentice scene remained untouched. This is Walt Disney's true reference to Apollonius and indicates a connection with his mystical side.

Walt took his alchemical whimsy and combined it with a curious spiritual understanding to produce one of the outstanding short films of all time. The *Sorcerer's Apprentice* is now considered art and has become far more than just a cartoon. To begin with, Walt Disney listened to the first recordings for the sound track, but found it lacked substance. So he developed what we now call Stereo Sound AND at the same time multi track recording with overdubs.

Have you any idea at all just how powerful a force was being unleashed at this point in time? Imagine life without Mickey AND Stereo? Imagine, no Stereo recordings at all! Imagine no multi track recording, as in, no music industry to speak of. The Mouse was flexing his creative muscle. Fantasia was not only a milestone in both animation and technical wizardry, it changed society.

Fantasia was also the first time Western Culture was fully exposed to the concept of magic and other worlds, a thing being pumped into the heart of every child who watched it. It was far more than a cartoon, Fantasia was a door opener for imagination and dreams that lit up the heart of every child that watched with eyes of wonder. Further, Fantasia changed Hollywood.

The nature of its storytelling changed how Hollywood perceived the creation of movies. It broadened the base and altered the fabric of movie making and, by extension, the cloth by which society was cut. Fantasia echoes down through the decades in the themes of Star Wars and so many other hallmark productions. Steamboat Willie unleashed the Mouse, but Fantasia is what set Mickey Mouse up as the Super Star.

As a curious note: The sorcerer in Fantasia was nicknamed Yen Sid, which is Disney backwards.

Summary: *The Fiction of Mickey Mouse is likely based on the reality of a God Man, Apollonius of Tyana. The 'mouse-eared image of this sage possibly comes from the Hellenistic and Roman literary tradition of an inverted world where mice were portrayed as humans. Regardless, the message is that the fiction of your life needs to be based on something higher and greater than you currently realise. It is a coded message that reads: Find your inner Hero.*

See: Philip Kiernan. "The Bronze Mice of Apollo Smintheus." *American Journal of Archaeology*

The Bronze Mice of Apollo Smintheus

From Mickey to the Rat – Becoming Complete

"We are born whole, but insignificant. To find happiness we must grow from insignificance into something meaningful. Generally, to do this we need to break ourselves apart. Sorry, but that's just how it is. It is only when we fall into pieces that we realize how the jigsaw works."
The Lord High Rat

Mickey started out in Steam Boat Willie. The mad mouse who does what he likes: **https://www.youtube.com/watch?v=Bbgghnqf6e4** Soon he would be, in effect, castrated to be more appealing to the general public. However, now that he is big and strong, has his real nature as a Rat re-emerged? No. Well, maybe he is hiding in the Porno Movies that Disney studios created. Seriously, where is Mickey Mouse 'at' today?

The original Mickey was a complete Rat who was chopped up in order to make him acceptable to Society. But rather than re-connect with his original inspiration, Disney allowed the highly successful Mouse to remain immature. Then Walt died and his mouse got frozen in situ. Now, FINALLY, we get to the real reason we are talking about this.

You have done this to yourself as well! *Do you realise you have chopped yourself up into pieces in order to fit in? As a child, we were complete, we had one-ness. We once were all Humpty Dumpty PRE-Wall. But then it changes, we want to get down to where all the people are, so we jump into society. In doing so we become fractured.*

In order to present the correct face to society, we learned to divide ourselves into aspects of our being that others would accept. You may not recall this right now, but what happened is that you hid or disguised pieces of yourself in order to make yourself acceptable (and in some cases unacceptable) to your Mother's preconceptions and/or your Fathers image of what a son/daughter should be.

As an example: Your Dad wanted a "Real Man" so you buried the poet inside, and pretended to like football. In time, you forgot that you didn't really like football and your transference of energy was such that you learned to hate poetry. Or you might otherwise completely reverse this and become something your father hates! (drug addict, gay, etc.) It is all a part of what we call the molding process, where we adapt and adjust parts of ourselves in order to fit in or fit out of societal projections and expectations placed upon us. We do this in the belief that it helps our survival. THIS is where our Censor grows!

By recognising this "Many in the One" condition Walt Disney (perhaps inadvertently) created an analogy for the path towards internal unity that we all must walk if we are to become free.

He created a cartoon character called Mickey Mouse - This made people laugh and helped lighten their load, plus he made a lot of money in the process. He was, in other words, a True Rat.

It's symbolic the way how SOUND itself was split in two with Fantasia. Disney created the Stereo Effect and this (literally) allowed his vision to be heard better. By dividing the whole into pieces, a new world was unleashed. Now we have 5.1 and 7.1 Surround Sound. Disney broke SOUND into pieces to make it work better! He broke Mickey into pieces to make him more acceptable. And what is the key note in business and computers today? Multi-Tasking.

Similarly, we hear of how people had spiritual break through after a nervous breakdown, or some 'falling into pieces' account. By shattering the Ego Image we often get to see the reality: That we already ARE in pieces. Many accounts of what we call madness are really people who are not able to accept or work with this shattering of self. We all need to be able to move on to a sort of multi-tasking with the various aspects of our being if we are to survive ourselves.

Note: *Perhaps Schizophrenia is just someone who can't multi-task properly?*

The reality is that you have a "Mickey" inside you - an indomitable, unbreakable spirit - But it is fragmented, pulled apart to fit in with the various demands of society and family. Yet that lonely little mouse, the little squeak within, is truly destined to grow up and find his or her bits and pieces. Then, once we solve the jigsaw we can remake them into the complete self and become the whole person once more: The True RAT.

As the Indian said when greeting the fur trader: HOW, dear reader - HOW?

Summary: *By Division of Self we make ourselves more acceptable. We are now a jigsaw. The Lies that control our existence were the scissors used to cut each piece. Resolving the lies means we remove the power that separates us, and this allows the jig saw to reconnect, to become complete once more*

The Mystic Rat Says: *Follow the cheese to your destiny. Trust your nose, and always remember that the best purpose for your tongue is tasting, not talking.*

A Simple Truth

We have three major driving forces in our existence: *Socialization, Sexualization* and *Spiritualization*. These forces wrap around the simple, sincere, sanctity of self in complex and obscure ways, yet they form the corner stones of character and behaviour.

In seeking to homogenise these often diverse energies we tend to do the opposite, we diverge from our natural and spiritual aspects and select the pieces we feel fits in with society. We use some bits that work in attracting a mate, while other bits work best appealing to the boss. We become 'the house divided' as we compartmentalize our true feelings in order to find way to be acceptable to our society or prospective partner. We thus learn to suppress our natural self and this creates a sense of fragmentation.

The internal separation becomes fertile soil for little white lies to grow, which in time become overbearing monsters that rule our lives. EG: The priest who shoved his sexuality into the background so he could fit in becomes warped, occasionally becoming the paedophile who destroys the lives of children.

Only when we start to recognise these internal lies do the demons lose their power. We break down the walls within that separate us and THIS is what allows the jigsaw of self to rebuild itself, to reconnect. The term 'religion' come from the Latin, 'Reliare', which means to re-tie or reconnect.

The Mission of the Rat: The omission of suspicion and false supposition that breaks the superstitions which leads to the remissions of bad decisions based on false dreams and dumb wishin's.

The Journey of the Rat

The Journey before us is a path to freedom. The burden of our past can now left behind, like the sailor who leaves the shipwreck.

Now is the time! Here is the moment when we choose between our fear of the future or our love of the present.

Just as the child tosses the rag doll it once loved, we must let go of things we once cherished, and embrace the greater purpose, the higher destiny, the finer way. This path is your purest truth, your kindest belief, and your simplest heart all working as one

Be you a slave or master, to serve this greatest good is our only truth. To know what this might be ... This is the journey !

A Midsummer Night's Dream

Shakespeare gave us A Midsummer Night's Dream and in this play he gave us Puck. Puck is like your Rat, it is the part of the story that is AWARE. He gives this wonderful soliloquy: (Act v. Scene i.)

If we shadows have offended, Think but this, and all is mended,
That you have but slumber'd here While these visions did appear.
And this weak and idle theme, No more yielding but a dream,
Gentles, do not reprehend: if you pardon, we will mend:
And, as I am an honest Puck, If we have unearned luck
Now to 'scape the serpent's tongue, We will make amends ere long;
Else the Puck a liar call; So, good night unto you all.
Give me your hands, if we be friends,
And Robin (Puck) shall restore amends.

It is a dream we live in. We live a life of beliefs that will one day be proven incorrect, with loves that will, one day, be shaken, and with ourselves, who will one day soon change our mind, heart and dreams.

Shakespeare's play is very much about the twisting world of love and belief. It is about how a love potion can bewitch you and you become convinced in things that are unreal. What most people don't quite understand: Shakespeare's play is all about real life.

Ratology states that we need to get ourselves to the point where this world becomes a dream, because only then will the overt lies that are the substance of our personal stories begin to reveal themselves. Only then will we discover the jig saw puzzle inside us, and accept that we are indeed a person in pieces.

Summary: *It's all a dream until we wake up and realize it's all a dream.*

Ratology: Way of the Un-Dammed

From the One to the Many to Refold Back to the One

"Only through recognising and growing the Natural and True Rat within our heart can we overcome the lies that run us." The Lord High Rat

You think you are One, don't you? You look in the mirror and imagine that 'you' are looking back, but the reality is that different "you's" look back on different days. Grumpy you, Lazy you, Sleepy you. Hang on! Are we talking dwarves here? And who is playing Snow White? Exactly, who IS playing Snow White? You will do that some days, as well as play the wicked queen.

The writer of "The Diceman", Prof. George Cockcroft, said to me when I was describing a multiple personality girlfriend: "WE ARE MULTIPLE." I am Multiple, you are multiple. We have many sides: We can be two-faced, about-faced and long-faced. When you grasp the notion that the various aspects and shades of yourself are 'Many', you will discover an opportunity to become 'One'.

What's more, without the 'Many' we would not have the differing aspects to reflect ourselves to our self. And so we come to the First Axiom: *If we are to fully understand the ONE (Self) we must truly experience the MANY.*

This Axiom may also be read as: *Have Fun!* You might not think we need any instruction in this, but in Western Civilization we are mostly repressed, compressed, depressed and, as a result, have ignored a whole lot of the basic elements inside ourselves. We need to learn to have fun and, though you may not understand it yet, this means embracing the whole self: The sexual, emotional, mental and physical aspects, the highs and low, the wides and thins! Everything is all part of all of you. We also have repressed moods, unspoken sighs, and small things we have stuffed down and not let out. It is the collective brace of anger, fear and resentment that form up our 'Dark Side'- and THIS is as much a part of us as the ideal, loving, ethical, stalwart of respectability.

We are trained to hide our non-socially acceptable selves, to repress desire, and to act innocent. This is part of the Lie we are taught. The Social Lie is that we must keep up appearances, which in turn sends the message that we must keep our true self hidden. All it creates is a 'Forbidden Planet' build up of repressed negative energy that destroys everything we love. Look at the Catholic Church and its paedophile priests and you get the perfect instruction manual on how to fuck yourself up. Ah, religion! The Guilt-Edged Investment.

Forget this crap. The message of this book is simple: *Be Yourself, Relax!*

"Oh No!" You exclaim. "How can I relax if we do not know who I am?"

Persactly! How can we recognize the Lie that stops us being ourselves unless we can see it? How can we know ourselves? The answer to all the above is the same: *Your Inner Rat will show you the way.*

The Mystic Rat Says: *Our Doubts are more important to us than our Certainties. Our Doubts show the places to grow, to expand, to become new.*

The Mystic Rat, that great eternal being that dwells as the survivor in the Collective Consciousness of the Human Race, has given you the Mouse of Doubt. As you grow your Minor Mouse by doubting everything, (other than random acts of joy and freedom) it slowly becomes the One True Rat. (May it flourish and become the Great Rodent within.)

Here is where most hit the wall and fail. Just when you try to grow and expand your freedom and experience of life, you will soon discover just how many 'Shoulds' and 'Should Nots' are running inside your head. These things are the social training from your family and your social conditioning. Expectations, obligations, and obfuscations: These elements form the wall that creates the barrier between you and your Rat. They are the stumbling blocks that cause the confusion as to your true Identity. It is exactly why we need to doubt everything, because in this way we reveal where the should's and should not's hide within us.

Stop shoulding on yourself!

Shoulds stop us experiencing life and given that only by EXPERIENCE can we grow, it implies that your SHOULDS (which restrict experience) are making a mess of things. Only by doubt do we learn to separate ourselves (and our true desires) from our conditions and confinements. In this way we learn to see the illusions and lies that are presently running our head and heart. There are a thousand ways to approach this truth, but one simple principle holds true: *Only when we see that we are OWNED by our beliefs, the things we hold to be certain, can we break the internal control and change the images in our heads.*

Doubt everything. Doubt the lies that have propagated as truths in our culture. EG: All this crap about deep and meaningful love, marriage forever, the perfect life, the house on the water, etc. etc. Do you really believe it? Even when you DO achieve lofty goals after a period of time ALL this starts to be revealed for what it is: *Passing!* Yes, it happens, and it also happens to end. I know a little bit about it, because I have had all of these things - Or at least I thought I did. They all passed. *All things must pass.*

Doubt gives us a degree of acceptance over this process.

Doubt gives us room to see things for what they are. First we have to see it, and then we find something remarkable: *We are not running our life!* What we discover is that our beliefs and conditioning are doing this.

Most of us are running on auto. On one level, it's a good thing, this automatic existence. Imagine if you had to think about breathing 24 hours a day? On another level it's bad, because when we are being run by infections (conditions) of guilt, fear and self-doubt, nothing we do works out right. We meet a new situation, our negatives kick in on an automatic basis, after which all our actions become introverted and confused.

Net result: *The natural self gets lost, the social face survives.*

Clue: *Doubt the situation, not yourself.* Doubt the guilt, doubt the fear, doubt the fact that you are certain you are not good enough. But I doubt that you can.

We are a Social Animal largely run by fear. It is sad, but true. It is the 'stuff' (guilt, fear, self-doubt) that separates and creates the divisions within ourselves, and this is what stops us from becoming powerful, aware beings. The 'stuff' of fears and self-doubt were what formed the wall your innocent Humpty Dumpty fell from, and now what we must do is break these down - take them apart to reveal the bricks. Then we can REPURPOSE these and convert them into bridges to ourselves. Do you want to reform the majesty of the One Self? Only through the breaking up of fear-based habits and patterns can we rediscover the great oneness within.

But HOW? Easy to say, difficult to do. The trick is understanding our personal history. When we understand how something came into being, we give ourselves a reverse roadmap in finding our way out of the maze. Let's take a brief look at the process of how our blocks came into being.

The Mystic Rat Says: *From the One to the Many to refold back to the One.*

Growing Past Our Lies

Unfolding from our personal lies means we become as little children. We unfold from our origami selves back to becoming a clean sheet.

Our fears can only be broken down from within, and only through having a sense of fun and a desire for freedom can we start this process.

Our Rat loves to FUN itself, and through this sense of fun it leads us to what is truly in our hearts.

We then get to see what is inside. What we find is the good, the bad and the ugly. We find twisted ideals confused with passion and guilt. We find scared little mice of freedom running from the Controllers of the mind. We find everything that has ever been a source of fear, pride or freedom.

It then comes down to what we CHOOSE. The simple recognition of the fear, belief, and other assorted mechanisms of control within us now becomes the most powerful tool for dismantling them - Should we so choose.

Origami and the Clean Sheet

> *"Always fornicate between clean sheets and spit on a well-scrubbed floor."* Christopher Fry

We are a little like a piece of paper. We start out with a clean sheet, then someone writes something fearful on it. The baby-self is extremely sensitive, so when someone writes, "grrrr" with a bad attitude about changing a nappy, it has an effect on us. We start to feel 'less than' and not 'equal to' our environment. This is the start of *"I am not good enough"*.

We have our natural self, a clean sheet of paper. But someone writes on our open state of being with a 'should' and it hurts. Not knowing any different, we try to get around the restriction by folding over it. We hide it away and tuck in under the carpet, so to speak. We all do this! This is a BASIC SURVIVAL HABIT of every human. Our present shape is a sort of Origami, something formed from the folds within our nature. All of us in childhood folded ourselves over and around the obstacles. So, after this heavy analogy we FINALLY get to the pun: We need to UNFOLD!

I can hear the groans from here. Yet it is True! Unfolding means to slowly but surely lift up the lid and show to ourselves the 'stuff' we have buried, and this really means facing our fears.

Many years ago I made a pilgrimage (of a sort) to an ancient Aboriginal Site. This is a part of the world where, for 50,000 years, the tribes had met to carve their tools and weapons while they looked out over the beautiful Kangaroo Valley in Australia. There I met this old man, who said as I came up to him, "You are not good enough."

I was stunned and went to go back home, but then I got curious - I turned back to him, and asked, "Why?"

The old guy smiled broadly and said, "Well then, maybe you will be OK." I was puzzled, but it seems that I was finished there. So I got back on the bike and went to work, still wondering what it all meant. Then it clicked: Curiosity! It is a powerful thing. Curiosity means that you don't need courage or audacity to face things, you turn and face things because you just want to know. Having the curiosity to ask questions, this is a determining force between success or failure. Curiosity opens the door, fear shuts it. It was a turning point. I didn't need to defeat my fears, I just had to understand them. Doubt is the first step in curiosity! Asking questions breaks down the barriers.

The Mystic Rat Says: *Fear is the great blocker. Doubt is the answer to Fear. Curiosity, more than courage, is the cure.*

What? Doubt is the answer to fear? How did that one sneak in here? Well, facing that old man, old fears arose, fears that would have easily let me agree that I was not good enough. But I doubted this at the same time. My doubt about my fear is what helped my curiosity take root, and so ask WHY.

OK, am I right in supposing you want to be free? Well, that means you must have something holding you down, otherwise you would already be free. To become one of the Un-Dammed you must first realise that there really are things that are blocking you. These 'things' are many and varied, yet they exist. (Usually as buried emotions such as fear, hidden shame, etc.) Once we accept we have these blocks, we must then discover WHERE the logjams that hold back our natural flow can be found. This is where doubt becomes your ally, because every single one of your certainties, your fixed beliefs, is actually a blockage. By choosing doubt, you are dis-choosing your blocks. You then can use your natural curiosity to sniff out the source.

And here's the rub: *Only your Inner Rat can smell these out.* Only your Inner Rat can get freely and easily inside the Palace of the Dammed (That's your miserable, fear-ridden consciousness, by the way) and break down the barriers of certainty that hold the blockages in place.

The Mystic Rat Says: *Your Rat is the most curious yet most doubting aspect of your being.*

Thus we come to a primary understanding within Ratology: *Your fears can ONLY be broken down from within. This is done via a process of doubt and curiosity until we come back to the clean sheet of our natural state.*

Your Shoulds and Can Nots will break up when you start to see them. It's a natural process called 'Vidya' or True Seeing. This is a recognition that occurs when you discover the 'you' that is locked within these things, and it is like a cleaving light sabre that cuts through the impossible obstacles. Like Alexander's Sword through the Gorgonian Knot, you remove the unsolvable with the clean insight of truth. Only you don't have a sword, you only have your teeth! You need your Rat to gnaw through the bonds of conditioning and prejudice, and you need to trust it to smell out where the problems are.

So, why aren't cynics happy? They doubt and ask questions! Cynicism is doubt solidified by the very fear it is trying to uproot. The cynical mind is one that has its OWN walls, and has trapped itself with cleverness for the most part.

Your Rat is a survivor, and looks only to the NOW. Cynicism opposes it.

Comparison is one of the great evils that rule us. This represents an ultimate 'should', the belief there are winners and losers. We believe our measure can be taken in relation to how we perceive another's success or failure. It is a nonsense! When we place ourselves in competition with life, which is what we are really doing when we base our lives on comparison, we will lose.

The centrist thinking that evolves out of continuous competition creates a belief it is all about us, which snips our connection to synchronicity.

Let's Fun Ourselves to Freedom

"Half the Fun is Having Fun" Guru Adrian (graffiti from the 1980's)

At first your Rat is a whimper - a small, squeaking mouse. But as you grow in courage and confidence, your true Inner Rat emerges from the Shadow Self and struts proudly on the stage of your being. Sounds good, yes? But what does "Fun ourselves to Freedom" mean? Well, first up, surely it makes sense that if you are having fun, you have accepted yourself. Yes? Conversely, if we are serious about everything, we are rejecting our child self.

Having fun, holding a sense of fun, enjoying your moments as you can - These things bring about a total acceptance of your 'self' by 'yourself'. (I apologise if this sounds like New Age waffle, but it is really just common sense) What you need to know is that, despite yourself and all your issues, you can still have some fun. This is how your RAT thinks.

1. Avoid any and all confrontation by just ignoring it.
2. Enjoy life, don't deal with it.
3. In the process: Have FUN.

It is by having fun that your RAT develops the power to liberate you. It does this by calling up and strengthening your JESTER. This aspect can snip the wires that hold us down. Let's forget for now the serious notions of responsibility, purpose, and all those high ideals. They are fine in their place, but if you are not having any FUN they are just toilet paper degrees from the University of Pain.

The Rat is a hedonist. It loves ***funning*** itself. It has a great sense of avoidance regarding matters of conventional wisdom, rigid behaviour and rules-orientated situations and people. It is that part of you that likes nightclubs full of smoke, sleazy jazz bands and hot sex and it LOVES building the biggest sand castle on the beach.

Your RAT has no fear of the dark and finds irony, curiosity and candour hiding in the shadows of self. It lives in between our high ideals and noble notions and finds fun is ALL the many aspects of our being. Your RAT can be perfectly happy behaving politely during social gatherings and generally appearing civil, because it KNOWS this is a disguise, a socially acceptable facade that is an opportunity to bend another Soul towards it's mischievous and diabolical sense of FUN.

Once, at a Christening party in England, I met this perfect young English gentleman. He was well-spoken, polite, and very courteous - until I mentioned the fact that the Christening cake had a very lovely iced teddy bear on it. Suddenly a gleam came into his eye and he said, "Let's EAT it!"

"Ah yes" I said to myself, "a fellow Rat indeed!"

We chose to spare the gathering the horror of a teddy-less cake. But here is the real point, we CHOSE to spare them the indignity of a teddy-less cake. We were free to do as we would and we simply chose to be polite.

Choosing freedom - this is the only demand your RAT will make of you. In the state of freedom your RAT creates the connecting threads that sew your many separate and disparate parts of self back together into a unity of being.

It is our internal 'folds' or origami logjams that separate us from the water of our being - These are the things that cause us to believe we are in pieces. The message is simple: *Have some FUN. Get our flow back together, and we naturally bring ourselves back to the state of ONE.*

The Mystic Rat Says: *We Un-Dam Our Self when we FUN Our Selves*

We all have a Rat within. It adores living, loving and feeling free - so feed it on the cheese of its desire and, as it grows, IT will show you the truth of the logjams inside. Why? Because these are the things that are stopping ITS fun. It wants you to be aware of where they are and it wants you to be rid of them. Only by clearing these can you (and your Rat) discover your natural freedom.

Summary: *Half the Fun is Having Fun. Unfolding from lies means we become as little children, or back to a clean sheet in the analogy of the piece of paper we used in this chapter. Our fears can only be broken down from within but only through having a sense of fun along with a desire for freedom. In this was we get to see what is inside. The simple recognition of the fear, belief, and other assorted mechanisms of control within us becomes the most powerful tool for dismantling them.*

PS: Have we gotten the notion that we are running on a force-fed diet of misconceptions and erroneous patterns of belief yet? Well brace yourself, because NOW we come to the Rules of Rattyness

The Mystic Rat Says: *Choose your battles like a stonemason chooses his stone. Pick up what is useful, leave off what is not.*

Rules of Rattyness

> *"In a world of Rules, the Golden Rule is that ALL the Rules will change as you change and as how you see things change."* The Lord High Rat

Now here we come to a perfect paradox. So far we have effectively been talking about throwing away the Rule Book, then we give you one? C'est une paradox! Perhaps, but the Ratology rules are better than yours.

Are you beginning to accept that you have been living out the belief structures of your parents and peers? You have been programmed with MEMES by society just like a programmer uses code to get a computer to do what he wants. The whole truth and nothing but the truth? Do we even know what that is? What we REALLY need is a sense of connectedness. What we want is a sense that we are OK. Deep down in our bones we want the recognition that we are good enough, worth-while, competent, and - most importantly - loved.

This is where we start LIVING. Opposing this is death, and the normal prelude to death is suffering, and it goes without saying that suffering is not a good agenda to pursue if you want happiness - This should be self-evident, yet for the most part people just don't get it. The main religion of Western Society worships a guy suffering on a cross, for gods sake! (Pun intended)

We all know we want to get a sense of one-ness, a gestalt within. Deep down in our heart there is a need for real and lasting joy. Obviously, enjoying life and having fun is a pretty necessary part of this agenda. The road to being complete, happy and whole means having fun. A laugh a day keeps the doctor away, etc. etc. But is there some sort of road map to happiness we can follow?

Here comes the good news folks: YES, there IS! We call this roadmap "The Rules of Rattyness"! They provide a clear, unambiguous path to freedom, awareness and a sincere, lasting happiness if we follow them.

These are the Rules that all True RATS live by. These guidelines are our Ten Commandments and they are very simple.

1. **It's not About You**
2. **Do not Should in your Own Nest**
3. **Always keep One Eye open**
4. **Ask no Favours (Do not a beggar nor borrowers be)**
5. **Keep your Teeth Honed (Be Prepared)**
6. **Always have a Bolt Hole**
7. **Do not Expose your Vulnerabilities**
8. **Pay Attention to your Brothers Activity, but not their business**
9. **Pick up and Dust Off**
10. **Shoot the Pope**

If you want to be free internally, you must grasp the intent and purpose of these Rules of Rattyness. The Rules are self-explanatory when you understand them, yet impenetrable puzzles when you do not. So let's run through the basics and get a better grasp of this all important start point in Ratology.

It is very important to understand that these are rules are simply recommendations to help develop clarity - They are not an instruction manual. These are the 'Bones of the Rat' revealed. If you grasp them and apply them to your own life, you will soon understand how powerful these Ten Rules are.

I am not saying you have to obey them. This is opposes the Ratology way of Un-Damming. What I am saying is that if you wish to survive better in this world, an understanding and practice of these principles will help enormously.

There is an overriding concept we need to look at first. Primarily, the notion that we need to 'process' experiences! This is largely wrong thinking. We need to digest the food we eat, yes, but the final process of this is (literally) crap. Yes, we need to get rid of our crap, but it does not mean re-eating it.

Many years ago I was giving an Australian friend with his new American wife a lift back from the farm. I noticed a leech on him so, without really thinking about it, my friend got out a lighter and burned it off. We were both Australians with bush experience, therefore we thought nothing of this. It was just a day-to-day event. But his wife burst into uncontrollable sobbing with this action.

I thought she was a little over the top with it all, but attempted to cheer her up. However, my friend waved me down as if to say "Let her go." So I did. She sat in the back seat sobbing and sobbing, wetting the carpets. Finally the woman stopped weeping enough to explain things to me, because I obviously did not understand how things worked in the modern age. "You know, it's really OK - I am just processing. It's the whole bug thing here in Australia that has gotten to me." In a while she was OK.

Now: It was just a leech, nothing else. If you want to waste a lot of time and energy to 'process' a dead leech, if you want to make little things big, go ahead. But really, it is an indulgence in emotion, not a true experience or an appreciation of the moment. Here is how it really works: The present moment is always CLEAR. It is always free of 'stuff' and there is NOTHING TO PROCESS. Our job is to find a way to stay in the moment. This is our only concern.

There is nothing to process, however, as the very desire to 'process' is usually part of what the problem is, we need to look at it. The problem of turning everything into a process is as follows:

1. We bring our 'stuff' into our present moment.
2. The moment enlarges our focus on everything, either positive, negative or neutral, so the problem starts to look BIG
3. We then believe that, because we feel it is BIG, we have to process it. This is when we usually make the 'big' mistake -
4. We go down the slippery slope of belief by believing that 'processing' is part of the experience of this moment.

There is the old story of the Linguistics Professor talking to his students, explaining that in different languages a double positive is really a negative, and how a double negative can become a positive. Then he states that, in English, there is NO example of a double positive meaning a negative. A kid at the back of the class goes "Yeah, sure!" Which is a double positive that means a negative. The message here is: *We can get so involved with the details of the process that we miss the obvious.*

Yes, there 'are' real things that we need to process. So let's look at real versus imaginary here. Grief is a real process. Suffering can also be a real process, even when self-inflicted. Divorce is a real process - for some it's a great liberation, for others a disaster. The process of working through these 'real events' can increase the depth of our being and lead us to appreciate the moment more deeply. But burning off of a leech is just not something worthy of a full-on weeping-it-up. Get it? Perspective matters.

Some things we DO need to process, but we already know that the greatest loss will pass. Remember: Any sense of loss or gain is NOT part of the moment, just another thing we have brought to it. The secret: *This present moment is devoid of consequences, responsibilities or reward.* All it holds is NOW, and nothing else. We need to grasp this fully if we are to understand our RAT.

As a general rule we create our own problems. We all carry our cross to our own crucifixion. We are all our own judges, executioners, and saviours, and in this process we either learn from the experience, or we disappear into the oblivion of the process itself. Usually we cart way too much crap about and the real 'process' is just learning to junk the garbage. With luck, in doing so we will learn something about being a rod for our own back.

I could go on for another book on 'process' but what we are doing here is quickly moving THROUGH this and getting to the reality of being. In other words, sure, have your process. Do your workshops, exercise your right to cry, experience your misery. When you are finished with that roundabout, come back and we will get to something a little more real than your indulgences.

That's why I like Poker. It's not about the winning hand, but the winning attitude, and that attitude is not one of winning, it is one of SURVIVAL. In the Poker Process, you can do anything you like: You can lie, pretend, tell the truth, or fake it. No one cares because, in the end, you either survive or you don't.

Primarily, if we are to survive well, we need to keep things in perspective. We need to keep clarity and intent to the forefront of our being. The Rules for Rattyness are designed to assist in getting us OUT of this area of 'Processing our Stuff' and straight into seeing the obvious. Therefore, the only true process we seriously need to consider is the path to thinking clearly. *If our thoughts and emotions are clear in every situation, we cannot be trapped or confused by them.* As we go through the Ten Rules, please keep this in mind.

ONE: It's not About You

If you want to be FREE then you need to learn and apply Rule Number ONE: *It's not about YOU*. The sun doesn't rise for you, the moon does not shine just on your lake, the world does not turn around YOU.
1. It's not about YOU.
2. It's not about ME.
3. It's not even about US.
4. It's about being alive and experiencing life.

Life is for Living and, when you are truly living, you find that you are not all that concerned about yourself. Why? Because you are no longer watching you! You are no longer locked inside yourself! Not only does the watched pot never boil, if we are always looking at ourselves we are not looking at the world. Yet when we look outwards and put our focus on what is NOW, it all changes. Put your focus on how to best survive and it all becomes clear.

Remember the Old Italian story that speaks of a man growing up in his village. At age Twenty he is full of fire, and does whatever he wants, despite the fact that everyone is watching. At age Forty he is far more circumspect and careful in his dealings, because he knows everyone is watching. By age Sixty the man finally realises the truth - no-one was ever watching.

Your life represents a drop in an ocean of living. People believe their life is all about themselves but it just isn't. It is not about you, it is not even about ME (I know you are shocked that I could say this, but it's true). It is not about US or THEM, or THOSE. It's about Life and living it.

Your mother, on the other hand, wants to believe it is all about you. Why? She has invested her life in you. Her survival is, in a very real sense, perpetuated by her children. This is how she proves her worth to the world; therefore YOU become very important in her eyes. That's what mothers do, so you can easily get a very skewed sense of your real value from that side of the fence. But life doesn't care what your mother thinks or believes.

More to the point, *life does not take anything personally.* This is ESSENTIAL to grasp - If you want to align with life, understand that it is NOT about you, and accordingly there is nothing you need to take personally. A good example: I called up a friend in Holland just at the time her houseboat was being axed up by a jealous ex-boyfriend. I asked her "Have you rung the Police?" She said she hadn't and probably wouldn't. Obviously, I asked why. She explained, *"He is driven by pain. He thinks he will cure it by destroying any connection between us, so this is his way of surviving. It means it is finished now."*

I asked how she knew he would not come back, or worse stalk her, and cause greater problems. She said, *"We only do that which we believe will help us to survive. All this is a way for his ego to survive rejection, and once his big statement is made, once he had 'proven' himself, then he will go away."*

She was 100% right. Now I do NOT advocate letting abusers off the hook. Far from it, but directly as a result of her calm reaction, everyone who knew the fellow tossed him out of their social circles. His boss fired him, no one would employ him in that town, and no one would talk to him. He lost everything and had to move, buy a house elsewhere, and start a new life. Problem solved.

This woman had a deep understanding of human nature and the primary cause, the primary flame of that understanding, was that *she knew it was not about her*. The guy attacking her home: That wasn't about HER, it was about HIM and his wounded pride. It was not HER that caused the outbreak, but his insecurity. She discovered a pearl of detachment in a world obsessed with self-interest and victim mentality, and because of this she was free. Pursuing the matter with the Police would have only activated a deeper level of insecurity and defensiveness in the man and he would have gone to another level of attack in order to feel he was protecting himself. It would have also meant having further dealings with him in court, etc. She didn't need revenge or a settlement or further communication. She just wanted it finished.

It is not about us! When we learn this and practice being involved in life, rather than ourselves, an amazing thing happens - We start "funning the day" - A good deal of our problems fade away and we rediscover that childlike certainty of living in the moment. So tell me: What are we really doing when experiencing life and living it? We are practising the NOW. We are living in the moment without concern for anyone's 'shoulds' or 'should nots'. This shifts our awareness away from fear bubbles and into experiencing the moment. In this space we find a sense of happiness much easier to come by.

For myself, the peculiar thing about learning Rule One was how it came about. It started as an understanding about something that seemed the complete opposite. Many years ago I had a break down of sorts: My world fell to pieces, I was not able to eat or really do anything. I spent six weeks on just water, then, seeing my muscles beginning to disappear, I reluctantly started having bread and fruit for another six weeks.

I spent three months in the bush on almost nothing (It was a vision quest of sorts, but a blind one, if that makes any sense.) I know the period happened because I wrote a book during that time, otherwise I may have thought it was all just a dream. The up-shot of it all was that I had a Cosmic Realization about something that was strikingly dull. You like to imagine a Cosmic Realization is going to be all bells and whistles, but for me it was horribly ordinary. So ordinary that it barely rated a mention in my Dream Journal.

I had gotten back to town after my three months of fasting and was not exactly enjoying the experience of a public urinal. You know, the urinal, the place where men line up to surreptitiously inspect each others dicks? They do, you know. Men pretend to be disinterested in the size and shape of the guy beside him, but they almost always glance over and check things out.

Well, I was shy. I always felt a little intimidated being on display and would usually duck into a toilet cubicle where I could close the door. But this day it struck me that all this shyness, it just didn't matter! The words came through clearly, "It's only me!"

And as this sank in, I realised "It's only them, it's only me, it's only US." We were all in it together. We are all here, now, and nowhere else. I felt a deep sense of relief because now I could use a public urinal. I know, it doesn't sound like much of a result for three months of starving yourself, does it?

Even so I was set free of what other people may or may not have thought. How? By accepting myself as I was. As time went by I began to understand that it really was a big step upwards in my process of personal integration. A curious understanding began to germinate: *I discovered I didn't need to sort out all my pieces - I could just LET THEM GO!* And when I did, I paradoxically discovered they were all worthy of something, so nothing had to be rejected. Yet equally, nothing had to be cherished.

This understanding uncovered something else that was really surprising to me. I found that as I let go of my fears, I was more able to see them clearly, thus I was now much better able to deal with them.

Even so, despite the fact that I had realised it was 'only' me, in my mind it was still all 'about' me. Sure, I was able to cope better and walk taller in my society. Certainly I was more confident and able to express myself more clearly in public: But it was still all about ME. I am not complaining, because it was a major milestone, yet this was just the FIRST step towards freedom. Now when I met a pretty girl instead of getting nervous I could said, *"It's just me, it's just her"* I was then able to communicate better. But it was still all about what 'I' wanted out of the exchange.

That's when it hit me! I realised that the girl only wanted something in the meeting for herself. "OH!" went a gong in my head. "It's all about self-interest!" That's the real secret - It was a very simple comprehension of reality.

What this translates to is important. I finally grasped that what 'I' want is irrelevant to other people! They only care about what THEY want. Only a mother with a new born is concerned more about what someone else wants than what she needs. Her baby gets her full attention. This is where we start our 'I am important' addiction but really, are we all still babies?

By accepting that it is NOT about you, and by no longer desiring anything to BE about you, it is simply amazing how much more you see when speaking to people. This is the first rule of the Rat because the RAT survives mostly through its perception. Having a clear perception of your environment gives you a leg up over the people who muddle about thinking that things somehow revolve around themselves. Most mothers know this. Why? Because they took the first step and loved their children so much that it was no longer all about themselves.

You can abuse this, by the way, and quite easily. Most Salesman focus intently on the person they are trying to sell something to, and ask leading questions in order to get people to talk about themselves. Why do salesmen do this? They are simply encouraging you to believe that you are important to them. They want you to think it's all about YOU when it's all about your MONEY.

Experience tells us a few important points that rate a mention here:

First: *If you let someone talk about themselves for ten minutes, they will believe that you are their friend. When someone feels you are their friend, they not only believe more easily what you say, they are less likely to do you wrong.*

Second: *If you maintain an interest in things outside your self, you will not be easily introverted, therefore not easily controlled by external pressures.*

Third: *When you practice not placing yourself at the centre of things, a strange thing happens. People want to start placing you at the centre of things. The more you refuse it, the more it will be thrown at you. I am not talking about attaining fame or money, but quietly getting recognition by others of your inherent worth.*

Of course, now I go and spoil everything by publishing a book with my name on it. There it is, I have gone and put myself as the centre of everything. That sort of proves I don't practice what I preach, hey? Well, tough. I am a RAT.

The Mystic Rat Says: *Truth comes in bubbles of thought, feeling and belief. If you cherish truth, it stays in the bubble. You have to pop your hopes and dreams if you want to get to the secret inside.*

TWO: Do Not Should in Your Own Nest

There are a lot of nasty little SHOULDERS out there who care for nothing but their invisible rules. They do not respect or understand your reality and they are not interested in accepting others have their own truth - But before you disparage them, ask if you might be shoulding in your own nest. Are we allowing family and friends to be who and what they want to be?

Rule Two is a form of the Law of Non-Interference and it is very subtle. When you break the boundary of self, when you allow your attention to focus more on the 'rightness' of the external world rather than fixing your small part of it, then you are externalizing your shoulds - and they go plop on the floor behind you.

Shoulding is all over Facebook and social media now - It is a disease that has taken over society. Here's the thing: Everyone who is telling you what you should do is secretly suffering a negative distortion of self-image. Their censor is weak and trying to extend its control by shoring up weak emotional foundations by getting others to agree to ITS rules. When we pull back from opinions and notions of what SHOULD be, we soon realize an extraordinary thing: *Only people suffering a lack of self-respect will insist on you doing what you 'should'*.

Conversely, those who refuse to should on others have a strong self-image.

Your social upbringing has taught your mind and emotions to say "I SHOULD do this, I SHOULD act this way, I SHOULD or SHOULDN'T behave in this manner" It is all pervasive and has taken over the Western World like a mold that eats into its vital organs. What's more, this is not going to change this with a single book. It is a chronic fault at the heart of Western Society that will take decades, possibly generations, to pass. But you can stop shoulding right now!

Rule Two: *Stop SHOULDING on Yourself*! Stop shoulding in your own nest.

Now the secret: *There is not a single SHOULD in your head that is YOURS.* No baby is born with a SHOULD in their heart or mind. Shoulds are IMPLANTS. It's not that they are "bad", they are just control measures put in place by parents and society in order to keep humans from self-destruction. Imagine what a mess it would be if people did whatever they would, instead of what they should? The wheels of commerce would slow, the schools would empty, and the entire economy would falter and degenerate back to the Stone Age.

Yes, we would all be happier, but soon enough someone with a large army of shoulds will turn up, take over our happy society, and start shoulding all over it.

SHOULDS are a necessary part of existence, because they represent the ORDER CREATORS in our social framework. But if you can keep yourself in order, why do you need a should to tell you what to do? The short answer: You don't.

If you get nothing else from this whole book, get this: *Stop SHOULDING on yourself.* This stupid act of self-terrorism separates you from the Book of Life. Shoulding on yourself keeps you imprisoned in other people's beliefs and it makes you a puppet on a string controlled by anyone who cares to tug your beliefs. SHOULDS are everywhere, in everything, and on everyone's shoulders - like the proverbial Monkey on the Back. And yet we need them.

Imagine a world without Shoulds? Let's all hold hands and sing along, "Imagine there's no shoulding, it's easy if you try!"

Seriously, imagine people sitting out in the sun enjoying their days rather than sitting in air-conditioned holes sweating over useless paperwork. Imagine doing what fulfils you rather than what makes money for the boss! Can you see how society as we know it would collapse? It would ruin everything. There would be no advertising because people wouldn't want anything, which means they wouldn't watch TV, which means there would be far mess media control. It's a shocking thought that must be rejected out of hand.

Shoulds are everywhere in the psychic framework of society. Shoulds are the main tool of controllers. They are a means to contain the wild beast, the rapist, the thief, the murderer inside us. And that is fair enough: Society had to evolve, and it evolved through negative control measures such as SHOULDS. Religions, of course, are the single greatest source of most Shoulds, but we also find them running through families, peer groups and work places.

The Flow of SHOULDS from the outer world into your brain is fully established and you will have a huge battle to fully remove them. In fact, you will never really get rid of them all, they are too ingrained. So what is the cure? There are some simple techniques that have proven to be effective in countering the pervasive menace of the SHOULD.

Exterminate Your Sorry!

The first is easier to say than do: Remove the word 'Sorry' from your vocabulary. Surely, if you do someone wrong, apologize, and do so earnestly: But avoid the SORRY word, because using it almost means the opposite.

Just as your RAT is your Reality Attention Trigger, the word 'sorry' is the worlds strongest PUP. A PUP is a Personal Un-integration Point. Technically Un-Integration is not really a word, but non-integration implies you are NOT connected, whereas Un-Integration tells us that we are, but not properly - so I use it. (Blame my RAT) Un-Integration explains the effect of SORRY on your Psyche. SORRY is used as an apology for living. It keeps you in pieces, it stops you collecting yourself and standing up straight to face the world Eye to Eye.

Saint Paul said: "At first, through the Glass Darkly, and then Face to Face".

If you want to get face to face with life, you must get through the 'Sorry Barrier'. The concept of apologising for your existence is a form of demeaning yourself, and it clouds your view. It is a way of bowing down and worshipping the false Idol of the Should God and it ALSO puts you squarely into the concept that you are the centre of things. 'Sorry' is rarely used as a recognition you are at fault, but as a an avoidance of responsibility.

We all bump into things, it is not something to be sorry for, it is something to celebrate! It means you are alive. When you apologize for your existence you are covering yourself in a shower of SHOULD. Bad, very bad.

"At first, through the glass darkly, and then - Face to Face!" Saint Paul is talking about the discovery of Soul, the perpetual Spark, the great knowing within. To connect with this requires absolutely REMOVING the concept of SORRY from your brain. Let me stress - *We are not refuting the genuine apology.* We are speaking about removing the pattern of avoiding, or apologising for, your life. Removing this attitude brings us into a stronger sense of NOW.

Saint Paul is alluding to the importance of meeting your personal divinity in the here and now, discovering your Soul, finding your Beingness. The process to get to this place of clarity is "through the Glass Darkly" - Why is the glass dark? I doubt he is meaning God wears Raybans. It is because the light is obscured by your SHOULDS? One thing I know: Only when we get this notion of personal wrongness sorted can we begin to understand, "Face to Face".

SORRY is such a dreadful word. It is a MAGNET for every SHOULD in the Universe to come calling on you. Even when you apologize to yourself or another, saying, "I should not have done that!" you are still SHOULDING on yourself. However, when you say "That is not working. I apologize - This is a far stronger direction to go." You are AFFIRMING your right to life even as you admit a mistake. Surely we must apologize to any and all we may have done wrong to, but to survive this world of 'should' we must do so with the attitude of making it RIGHT, rather than bathing in a worry of wrongness.

A Rat in a Restaurant

AVOID the word Sorry and you will start to see the difference in your life. As a small example: I ran a restaurant (Yes, someone put a RAT in charge of the restaurant, can you believe) One night a woman was served a chicken pastry meal when she had ordered a vegetarian one. No problem, just let the staff know and you get the proper meal.

Obviously, she complained and fair enough. However, when I came over I saw that she had eaten ¾ of her chicken meal and was now squawking about how it had poisoned her. I simply stopped, looked closely at the lack of remains on her plate, and raised one eyebrow.

You must understand how POWERFUL a raised eye brow is when combined with a lack of apology. It says so much without saying anything at all. It says you doubt everything the person is saying because you can see the OBVIOUS. The person KNOWS they are angling for a freebie, or trying to get some case up to sue you, or whatever. But by saying nothing and just observing the obvious reality, you do more damage to their aggression than anything else.

The legal Term is "Res Ipsa Loquitur". It means "The thing speaks for itself". In other words, it is recognising that which is obvious through manner or word.

Here I will share with you the secret on how to apply this in order to gain the greatest effect. If you want your rat to grow, if you wish to survive this world, then do the simplest of things: Nothing! Just STOP and WAIT. Always remember how POWERFUL a PAUSE can be. Just WAIT a moment before proceeding.

I raised an eyebrow, took a deep breath, looked at the woman for a moment, then said "I can truly see how terrible this must be for you. How can I help solve this problem for you? What can I give you that will lessen this blow?"

The woman got her dander up, and started decrying:
1. how she might DIE from this meat,
2. how she had not eaten meat for nineteen years,
3. how shocking it was that this could happen to her

So I nodded in agreement with everything she said and, of course, I also made sure the offending item remained on her table. Further, I made not a single comment on the fact that it was ¾ eaten. I just waited for her to say what she actually wanted. She never did.

"Res Ipsa Loquitur" was the single thing I kept in mind.

I simply concurred with all she had said. "I completely agree with you Madam. What can I DO to help solve this for you? Free Dessert? A Port? What can I offer you?" I then explained how we had a new chef and that the pastry for the vegetable dish had a 'V' on it which can sometimes look like a 'C' - for Chicken. An honest mistake, not an assassination attempt, I assured her.

Whatever I said, I refused absolutely to say SORRY. I was reasoned, calm and clear and offered to help in any way I could. As a result, a curious thing happened. Her boyfriend started taking MY side. He started arguing that it was not unreasonable of me to try and offer what I could to help her. He stopped short of saying "Hey, you ate most of the chicken before you realised it was meat?" but we ALL knew this was the baseline fact. 'Res Ipsa Loquitur!'

So what does the woman do? She turns ALL her venom on the boyfriend, and THEN she becomes sweet as apple pie to me. Ah Ha! I had discovered a CAT. This woman had a CAT running her. (Controller And Terrorist) She was a control freak who wanted to steal my energy and suck on my fear by having me grovel and apologize. Why did she want to place myself in a position of WRONGNESS? Purely because this would make her feel important.

This is what SHOULDING on ourselves does: It places us in a position UNDER the Powers that Be – This simply means that you become CONTROLLABLE by the Negative Power Flows that rule this planet.

The CAT in the woman wanted blood. When she could not get it from me, she turned on the weakest point close to her, her boyfriend. (I was guessing soon to be ex-boyfriend) What's more, the way she was now looked at ME? I suspected I was intended as her next victim - I mean, lover.

CATS do not have Lovers, they have victims of their Lust. They are vicious, dangerous to you emotionally, and if you marry them they will eat you emotionally, mentally and financially. However, it is easy to negotiate with most of the controllers we meet by simply REMOVING the concept of Sorry from our Psyche. They respect you for it and, can you believe, they then want to buddy up. (CATs are vain and lonely creatures who need a lap)

However, this time she came up against a Rat who was awake to her game. She lost that round. But this gives us an opportunity to see how powerful avoiding 'sorry' can be. It allows us to find a greater reality in our passing moments. Let's look at the very basic Anti-Rat mistakes the woman made:

1. She acted as if it was all about her
2. She tried to should on others

Are you getting the picture here? What we are REALLY doing by applying these first two laws of Ratology is learning how to avoid control issues. Controllers love to make you WRONG. In the restaurant, because I did not use a self depreciating 'sorry' attitude, the woman gained no leverage to control the situation. All her efforts reversed on herself, and rightly so.

Opposite to the above, I was at a cinema one evening and a pretty young thing accidentally stood on my toe. She automatically said "Sorry!" to which I replied "No, Please - Do it again. I love it when pretty girls step on my toes." She looked up, puzzled. Then she smiled and said *"Yeah, I guess it is like apologizing for Life, hey?"* And THAT, dear reader, is the whole sorry business in a nutshell.

The Mystic Rat Says: *Stop SHOULDING on your self! Stop apologising for the fact that you are ALIVE.*

Remember this: *A Should is a Could that wanted to grow past being a Would, but failed.* People who 'should' on others are controllers, and they generally are this way because they do not love their own life. Critics are all mostly 'Shoulders' and, as a point of observation, many of the really negative critics are significant failures in the very profession they now professionally critique.

2020 update: *How will things change with the Covid scare? Currently there is a vast movement to require masks and everywhere is pumping out the message of what you SHOULD do. When it is done, will we have a new race of people aware and alert to how fear is used to control the populace?*

The Mystic Rat Says: *Find the "why" or the motivation in any given situation and you can Iron out just about any problem. Find the "why" and you have discovered your personal (wait for it) ... Iron-y*

Forget turning Lead into Gold! What is more important is to steel the spine, see the obvious, and be unafraid to ask the hard questions.

THREE: Always Keep One Eye Open

The Third Rule is based on the Eye of Horus. The All-Seeing Eye is spatial awareness personified. *Always Keep One Eye Open*. It means to be aware of your surroundings, but is also to be careful, which is:
1. To be Full of Care, and
2. To be Cautious.

They sang the night has a thousand eyes, another way of saying everyone is watching. One level, this is true. Facebook and news permeate every corner - The world is full of "I", "me" and "mine" - thousands of opinions and beliefs circulate around us every day via media, friends, and social groups. People are full to the brim with their half-truths and semi-lies based on past programming - So, how do we see through all this and keep our own house in order?

Your RAT sniffs opportunity and danger, your Reality Attention Trigger sees the obvious. It never sleeps unless you ignore it, so the Third Rule is a reminder to keep your RAT awake. Feed it with your awareness and your doubt of what's going on around you. We want to be able to give ourselves a Triple "A" rating - Be: *Awake, Alive, and Aware*.

If external influences brings us to the point where we are no longer able to respond to life, we are disobeying Rule Three. If not - we are good. Being drunk to the point of oblivion or taking drugs to the point of forgetfulness is breaking Rule Three, and will cost you.

It is really about responsibility - The ability to respond. Placing yourself into a situation where you are unable to respond to change or danger makes you vulnerable. Using drugs or booze to avoid pain may well be necessary in the short term, but writing yourself off with external influence is a message to life that you are not happy where you are. Accordingly, Life will answer your 'statement' to it by bringing you situations you are not happy to be in.

This is not just drugs and alcohol, it is the weight of shoulds that generally drive you to these. This takes you away from NOW. The idea of not living anywhere but the present moment is what the Ancient Greeks wrote on the Temple of Apollo in Delphi. We all know the right hand side, which is inscribed with the famous "Know Thyself" quote. But lesser known and on the left hand side are the words "Nothing too much". (It also has inscribed "Make a pledge and destruction is near" but we will leave that one for now)

You may have thought that living the life of the RAT meant living a life of indulgence - Far from it, dear reader. RATS are careful creatures, who obey the rule "Nothing Too Much". Most animals love to get drunk, stoned or whatever when chance allows - Drunken Parrots are legendary! But it is occasional.

The point is, animals cannot and do not stay in this state permanently because, if they did, they would be dead. Natural Selection really is a killer.

Keeping One Eye Open means to stay aware of the moment. Just as the sailor on the ocean can feel the current shifting under his feet, you feel the winds of change and adjust your sails BEFORE the gale arrives to capsize your boat.

We do NOT live in a harmonious, peaceful world. This is a World of War, a place of enormous greed and lack of respect for others. We MUST keep our awareness; we MUST keep our wits about us if we are to survive it all intact.

Sentries

Life IS a war, so tell me, what does an army do to ensure survival? It places sentries on watch. We would do well to copy this, but in a different way. We look for 'Sentries' that are specific markers. Look to nature, such as the behaviour of Ants. If ants get overly active for no apparent reason this is a clue there is a change happening around you. Usually it means rain, as one example.

Immediately prior to the huge Tsunami that killed 200,000 people in Indonesia and surrounding areas, ALL the animals on the island of Aceh (the worst hit island) moved to higher ground. Did any of the locals pay attention? No, and they drowned as a result. They did not keep one eye open.

We will get to this more in Ratology Two, but in summary, Life has a SOUND. You can hear it and, when a change is about to occur, a signal is sent that nature hears. You can hear it if you listen. (Doctors often call it Tinnitus)

Obviously we know when seasons are changing by the leaves on the trees. But there are subtler signs. Native Americans know when the salmon will arrive because BEARS start acting in specific ways. These were SENTRIES, or markers that tell you when change is to come. Only experience and wisdom will teach you this truth, but suffice to say, nature is attuned to the FREQUENCY of life. SO! Learn to LISTEN to life around you and much trouble can be avoided.

How do we listen to Life? Well, this is a problem for people who are either locked in mind stuff, off their face on drugs, or spinning out on emotional benders. But if you can get off the wheel of your circumstances and get closer to the NOW you will hear it. And when you hear it, you will realize you have been listening to Life ... well... all your Life!

It is a very real thing, called by many names over the millennia. *"In the beginning there was the Word,"* is one we all know. Life is always bringing us 'the word' but are we listening? You may find this funny, but often when I have a big hand in poker, and someone hits me with a big bet, I will stop and listen to the songs the cards are singing. If it seems to me that I have less harmony in my cards, I fold them. I let it go and allow life to keep telling me what it will.

It's all about awareness, setting up sentry posts, and remaining attuned to the natural currents. We all have a better chance when we are forewarned.

Keeping one eye open means you are placing perception to the forefront of your thoughts. It is practicing mindfulness but it is also an expectation on the unexpected. It cultivates an attitude that nothing is too much, that you can cope with whatever comes, and survive. It is what the Eye of Horus really means.

FOUR: Ask No Favours – *neither a beggar nor borrower be*

Rule Four describes HOW we go about getting things we need without fearing weakness or needing force. It is about negotiation, not putting yourself into the position of being a slave while still being able to get ahead. We might ask, "Ahead of what?" Just keeping our head above water should be enough, but it isn't. People need progress, they need the sense they are going somewhere. Rule Four allows us to move forward and stay balanced.

The old Jewish proverb, "Credit for necessities - Cash for luxuries," is the key. If you have a family and need to get kids to school, etc. you NEED a stable house. This is a necessity and requires a mortgage. I am NOT saying you do not use banks where appropriate - It is the useless things we put ourselves into hock for that are the issue..

Maybe you get the mortgage for the house, but this one has the Jacuzzi, a marble kitchen, five bedrooms, etc. - things which inflate the mortgage to stress levels. Of course, the good Rat generally finds the best things at a price less than they can resell it, so this is another qualifier. If you can move something on for more than you paid for it, this is investing, not spending.

This is just common sense. The PROBLEM is that this modern age of excess drives us to get MORE. The general concept is driven by a MEME that comes all the way from Victorian England: that you MUST be forging ahead. It is 'kind of' true - But Ratology says you don't need not enslave yourself to your future dreams. There is nothing to prove - You just need to come to each moment with clarity and this means not complicating our life with obligations or obfuscations.

And yet we DO have to do the odd job that is not pleasing. We DO have to buckle down and move through times that are not fun. But how do we not become a cog in the machinery of commerce in the process?

We avoid becoming a slave to the machine by simply taking responsibility for our personal situation. There are no victims, only circumstances we are not yet in charge of. There are difficult positions we get into, but every problem has a solution, we just have to find it. In every scenario of our life, we must meet our circumstances and CHOOSE: Do we agree with it, change it or leave it? And inside this choice is the path that leads us through it - there are three options.

- Negative: We can believe we are not strong enough to do it ourselves.
- Positive: We can rely solely on our personal prowess and ability.
- Or the Balanced Path: We can call on life to help us out.

Rule Four is really about creating harmony and developing a connection with life. Harmony and freedom are ESSENTIAL if things are to work out well for us. These are the energies that bring LIFE FORCE to bear in our lives. Without life on our side, it is a battle, and what happens is that we tend to end up needing to call up favours from others to help us survive. Asking a bank or worse, a relative, for a loan to pay bills is never a good place to be.

Negotiation: Fair Trade is No Mans Loss

While we may lean on life for help, we still need to connect with others. We need to communicate, bargain, trade, and *negotiate* - And the secret of all successful negotiation is to come to the table with a sense of authority and strength. Confident calculation and a clear perception of the benefits we are offering help people to believe in us. All successful negotiation is based on one constant: good for all. *The trick to getting better for you is to approach our dealings with others with the sense that we already possess everything we need, and what we are ask for is simply a reasonable addition to what already exists.*

The Law of Nature is: *Much gathers more, less gathers loss.* When we have an attitude of 'LOTS' life tends to give us 'More'. Even when we lose a few rounds, this attitude keeps the energy of success flowing, far more than positive thinking ever will. Even better is a sense of generosity: I have LOTS and I am willing to share! As a result of the above, you never need to ask favours because you truly believe you do not need them. You DO ask for a deal, however.

Rule Four is very much about finding a point of balance between your needs and those of your community. *Ask No Favours:* Be self-contained to the greatest degree possible and offer fair trade for what you need. Be a good citizen and do not rely on others to support your lifestyle. It is pretty simple stuff.

The qualifier is where it gets interesting. Do you remember the phrase: "*Neither a Beggar nor Borrower be*"? This comes from Shakespeare's 'Hamlet', and is an old axiom about not incurring debt. What you may not have considered is how this implies that you are not to be a LENDER as well. Why? If borrowing and begging is bad, then the Lender is an essential part of the equation. Do you think this might also apply to people begging favours from God? (I heard the Great Rat gets very annoyed with all the prayers) This phrase, and Rule Four in general, really means: *Do not to bind yourself to others*.

Again, a qualifier. Being married is a binding contract. Rule Four does not mean living independent of everyone, having no personal relationships, etc. Rule Four relates to the subtle chains that lie IN BETWEEN the contracts we enter into in this life.

I woke one day with an extraordinary revelation. I had spent the night looking at fine wires that tied the universe together. These 'wires' represented the natural forces, gravity, light, etc. But when I woke I saw different sorts of wires, I saw all the binding agreements that people make. Contracts, both emotional and mental, that people had taken out between each other. I saw very clearly how so many people are living in dependant relationships and effectively tied up and bound by a long series of what were really quite useless agreements. THIS is the reason for all the divorces, people were rebelling against the control lines they felt ensnared in.

Everyone in confined relationships are generally 'borrowing' energy, favours, beliefs, memes - you name it - from their mate and/or their associates.

Under the surface of normal communication are thousands of tiny contracts that bind people. The strings that bind are a prison created by ourselves not reading the fine print of the agreements we entered into. We all have done this to some degree. But life can snap you out of it, if you ask.

Quite by chance, if you believe in chance, soon after the dream I was down at Byron Bay and something said to go into a hippie shop that had opened. Now, while I had no need for bongs or cheese cloth shirts, I listened to and obeyed the inner nudge. Inside, I was surprised to meet Gerry, a fellow I knew who ran a large business supplying health bars to shops nationwide.

We got talking, and it turned out he had been cheated out of his business, a multi-million dollar enterprise. He had lost his wife, his house, and his income. So he went to the religion he had been a faithful member of for many years and asked if he could build a small house on the riverfront land he had GIVEN them some years earlier. It was an acreage property and he asked if he might go into a quiet corner, stressing he would be completely out of the way.

Losing My Religion

Well, they told him to piss off. So he also lost his religion. In the depths of despair, he found this shop for rent that had accommodation out back and it was cheap. So he rented it and started his little business. It was a hit, the thing was going gangbusters. The part that really impressed me was the fact that Gerry was genuinely happy, despite his adversity.

"I am glad they wouldn't let me build a house on the property I gave them," he said. "Now my eyes are opened, I see things as they really are. Yes, I met cheats, scum bags, I lost everything, but all it really means is that everything that TIED ME DOWN is GONE! I am truly free, for the first time in my life."

Gerry had been forcibly woken up out of his prison, but he HAD woken up. Many years later, life was to deliver myself the exact same message, and remembering Gerry's smiling face was one way to help me deal with the loss. The message is very simple, we cannot rely on another to supply us happiness.

We get married thinking this will make us happy. We buy a new house, a new car, believing this will make us happy. We get into all sorts of social and financial contracts, thinking this will bring us happiness.

There is nothing WRONG with this. In truth, all the strings and attachments we wrap around ourselves are what form the cocoon that allows us to go through the internal change that brings us to freedom. But once you find a point of freedom, you soon realize the greatest curse in our life are the little beliefs and agreements that tie us down.

We bind ourselves through deeds, beliefs, identifications, and considerations. When we hold the belief of being greater *or lesser* than others, when we think our religion is more important than we are, when we compare our lives with others, all this means we are tying ourselves into invisible contracts. How do we make contracts that DO NOT bind us? It is the principle of Fair Trade. An old Yorkshire saying goes: *"Fair Trade is no man's loss!"*

A fair exchange of money, energy, or whatever does not bind you. There are also gifts from life, like oxygen, water, three dimensions. (Ever thought to be grateful for that third dimension?) Life gives without a contract and by accepting the gift we are not bound to anything. Yet it IS a contract: We breathe oxygen and give back CO_2 to the plants who give us oxygen.

However, if we wish to grow, discover love, create a better life, we have to do more than eat, breath and shit. We have to enter into agreements of a sort with people around us, with work, with general living. Social contracts are part of human existence, so how can we have these yet not be bound by them? The answer is shockingly simple: *Do without thought of reward.*

Do Without Thought of Reward

Altruism, acts of selfless kindness are what leave us free of entanglement. You can be working for the boss, doing your job, but the internal agreement does not have to be a slave/master notion. You can simply do your best, without thought of reward, because that is what you WANT to do.

True altruism, however, is exceedingly rare. Most 'gifts' from others are Trojan Horses. This is the harsh reality of life. However, when we expect no favours from others, nor grant favours on the basis of GETTING something, we have a better point of balance. We are more able to spot the ties that bind.

Obviously, it is fine to help others, but the attitude of gaining favour because of your kindness removes the 'actual' kindness from the equation, yes? This is where we usually miss the boat. Even when you believe you are being kind and wonderful, if, under the depths, there is a wish to gain as a result of your actions you are setting yourself up as a lender, not a giver. Get it? *Playing the White Knight creates a Debt: You have LENT another your good will and kindness, usually because you covertly or overtly want something in return.*

You may want a sense of importance, you may be looking for a sense of worthiness, or perhaps you just want someone indebted to you. You have to know yourself in order to know your true motivations but, as few of us really know ourselves, the simple guideline is this: *Sure, help someone if they need it and you can afford it, but GIVE them this help, do not LEND it.*

By the same token, if someone wants to GIVE you help and assistance (Like I am offering with this book) feel free to accept it. What I am saying here is don't buy into an invisible agreement where we OWE or are OWED something. The Beggar and Borrower enter into a Karmic Agreement, but the GIVER is free.

I give this information freely. You owe me nothing unless you downloaded a pirated copy of this book. If you have, I invite you to send money via Paypal to info@numberharmonics.com. Otherwise, our CONTRACT has been completed with the purchase of the book. You owe me nothing for the tremendous wisdom and insight I have GIVEN you.

Here is where the next level starts. If someone inspires us, we naturally give them respect. We RECOGNISE their effort with kind regard. Now we usually commit a crime - we elevate that person to a pedestal. We tend to place them above us in some way, thus inadvertently breaking Rule One: "It's not about you!" Respect is fine, but the subtle shifting of gratitude into idolatry can turn good intentions into a slave-like worship of some sort.

When the Union army marched Charleston. The black population came out and got on their knees in front of President Lincoln. He told them that the only place they should be on their knees is in their church, in front of their God.

However, if you are deeply moved and feel the need to worship me I have an excellent suggestion. Worship with money! I won't object to your gift of love in the form of cash. I may even offer up prayers to the Great Rat on your behalf if you do. But I defer to the opening story of this book, if the Angel of God offers you wisdom, beauty or money - Take the money.

Why? Because it frees you from needing contracts. Money is a clean agreement: If I want this, I will pay you that. I can learn wisdom, I can buy plastic surgery for a little more beauty, and money gives me the space to do both.

Everything in life has some form of CONTRACT or AGREEMENT at its heart. The trick to being free of the strings that bind is to have a balanced exchange, either in Cash, Energy, or Karma. We have an agreement with life: We breathe in O2 and breathe out Co2. This helps US, and it helps LIFE because trees need CO2 and produce O2. Everything is a cycle, and we are all part of this wheel.

Now here is the NEXT thing to grasp. **Be part of the circle!**

The Mystic Rat Says: *A gift given must be passed on, or the gift is lost.*

In Australian Aboriginal Society, many anthropologists believed the Native populations were total communists because it seemed to them that no one owned anything and everything was shared. Nothing could have been further from the truth.

Everything was shared, yes, but subtle emotional and mental records were kept of EVERYTHING. If you borrowed an artefact or thing of power from one family, you may have it in your house for a whole lifetime. But your descendants were expected to repay this gift with one of equal value. This was discovered by an anthropologist when he spoke to his native elder friend about all these relics he had been given. He said, "You are so kind, what can I give you in return?"

The headman replied "I have indebted my family for generations to give you these things. I did this because I believe it will help my people and my race. It is not possible for you to repay this debt. But help my people survive and you have repaid me."

The anthropologist was deeply shocked. This native culture has a notion of a MORTGAGE? When he started asking specific questions, he began to realize that the ENTIRE CULTURE was based on trade. Not just of goods, but of thoughts, feelings, articles and experiences. Doing a DANCE at a particular meeting may be a form of repayment of some event from your GRANDFATHER's time.

This is why lineage and territory were an integral part of Land Rights. It was all part of a very delicately balanced state of agreement. This is why most Native Societies become utterly and irreversibly ruined by intervention of any sort.

The anthropologist's recommendation to the Government of the time was that this was a far more involved culture than anyone imagined and that the whole area where these people lived should be locked up and kept from development until the process was better understood.

Of course, the man was ignored and the 'natives' were rounded up and taught to 'behave' by Missionaries. Thus the aboriginal culture was all but destroyed, and many of the members of those societies are still wandering around, completely lost. People ask WHY indigenous cultures cannot assimilate. Well, how would YOU cope if your entire Credit System were wiped out and all the Banks disappeared? Imagine if you lost your job, your house and your family was scattered to the ends of the Earth. What would you do?

Imagine, no ATM's, no supermarkets, no banks to borrow from and overnight you had no money, no job and most of your family was dying from disease. You can't borrow to buy or build a house, and unless someone had cash you couldn't sell what you had. But even then, CASH itself would have become meaningless because the new government didn't recognise your currency.

In one fell swoop, the Government of Australia completely eradicated 50,000 years of collective understanding and subtle trade agreements. It broke Rule Two and SHOULDED all over the Native Population: You SHOULD assimilate, you SHOULD behave as we expect, you SHOULD reject your own culture.

This happened to the Native American culture as well, and pretty much ALL Native Cultures apart from the Maori and Ghurkhas. These people are a very important exception to the rule. How did they survive the Western onslaught of civilisation? The Maori and Ghurkha people rejected the notion of "should". They did not roll over but defended their rights and in time FORCED the Western Powers to come to treaties in order to have peace.

Maori Warriors could not be defeated because they practiced the original Trench Warfare. They looked at how the British operated and worked out a way to counter them. So too did the Ghurkha, who practiced the original nighttime Guerrilla warfare. (Even today, with trained sentries using night vision, a Ghurkha can get past them) The British realised they were better off coming to agreements with these races, and so, like the Thai people, these races kept their sovereign cultures and their dignity intact.

Now, an incredibly interesting fact came to light when researchers for alcohol abuse in indigenous cultures rigged up EEG machines on people all round the world. Virtually ALL indigenous cultures lived mostly in the ALPHA wavelength, but the Ghurkha and Maori peoples lived mostly in the BETA frequencies.

And guess where Aryan people live? Yes: In Beta. We live in Theta for the first few months, in Delta up to age two, in Alpha from two to seven and mostly in Beta for the balance of our adult lives. Dreaming tends to bring us into Alpha, and when we are being creative we tend to dip to Alpha frequencies. So researchers then started to look at people on the fringe who were creative. These were the musicians and poets, etc.

Goodness! It was discovered that these people live mostly in ALPHA as well! And THEY don't fit all that well into society either. So what research has PROVEN that when "Ye become as little children" that the ruling society on Planet Earth will beat the crap out of you, then SHOULD all over your face.

Glad we got that sorted out! Really, we are talking an emotional and psychic disconnect of huge proportions here. We have an entire culture that insists that ITS way is right, and this heritage comes to us largely via the channel of the Romans, and the Roman Catholic Church. But before you object too much, think of the options. Without the church, we could all be riding camels and praying five times a day, or worshipping the descendants of Genghis Khan. The message is, nothing is perfect and we need to make the most of what we have got. And here is the secret: *When we accept imperfection, we soon discover that wherever state we are in financially, mentally or emotionally, there is always a way to trade up to a better set of circumstances.*

Finally, we come to what it is **really** all about: Communication and Trade are the real paths to freedom, not begging or borrowing. All traders understand one simple rule, you need to understand any given situation and find out what others need. Then you apply this information to create a benefit for yourself and the other person/s. This is called the Art of NEGOTIATION.

We learn to GIVE and TAKE in order to gain an upper hand in dealing with life. We learn the ART of NEGOTIATION in order to get what we need and want. In other words - We ASK NO FAVOURS but EXPECT Fair Trade. Therefore:
1. Ask no Favours.
2. Make No Promises.
3. Give nothing away that you need and give everything away that you don't. (But see if someone will pay you to take it away)
4. Trust that the winds of life will bring you to your destination

This Forth Law is not so difficult to grasp. In essence we are saying that we need to be careful of the little hooks we find in between our agreements with others. Am I 'giving' you these words to garner your respect? Or do I just give it?

Contemplation: *You may be out there thinking you are catching a fish, but have you considered it may be thinking exactly the same thing about you.*

FIVE: Keep your Teeth Honed

Obviously, despite all good Rats being demure and shy, there are times when we need to fight to protect our space. We need to keep our teeth honed, which essentially means keeping ourselves fit and ready for war. But we do this in order to avoid it. It is the same principle as holding a nuclear arsenal, you have it with the specific intention of not needing to use it.

Robert McNamara (Secretary of Defence during the Vietnam War) was joking initially with his now famous 'Mutually Assured Destruction' theory. (MAD) This was having enough bombs to make absolutely certain that if YOU went down, so did the enemy. (And the whole world becomes collateral damage) It really was MAD, but this was the nature of the nuclear arms race. Billions were spent on developing a capability for total world-wide destruction for the express purpose of never having to use it. Completely MAD, yet it worked!

The US Government SPENT the Soviets into bankruptcy as they both played Economic, Social and Environmental 'Russian' Roulette. Mad, absolutely. Yet because the teeth WERE honed, neither party would advance against the other for fear of the bite.

It's the old Boy Scout motto: *Be Prepared*. Keeping your teeth honed means keeping yourself READY. For a Rat, this means far more than just being prepared to fight, it means being prepared to live. Being ready to move at a moment's notice means being ready to grasp the opportunities life provides. It also means you DO look the gift horse in the mouth and make sure it is not a Trojan.

On the practical side of things it means you fix the hole in the roof on a sunny day, not when the rain starts to fall. Keeping those teeth honed means you have thought about and prepared for a variety of scenarios. It is simply better to have everything you need in place BEFORE you step out the door. A perfect example of a failure in this regard is Napoleon sending troops off to Russia without proper food or clothing. The Russians just retreated and let them freeze and die.

Hitler did exactly the same thing. He went in thinking things would be easy, but it took far longer than expected and his army was caught unprepared. Therefore his assault failed. In simple terms, Russia was the end of his dreams. We can think ourselves fortunate because if he had NOT taken on Russia he would have had time to develop the Nuclear Bomb and ICB's and we would all be speaking German.

But how DID Hitler get so far so quickly? Easy. Hitler got his foothold in Europe specifically because the teeth of the leaders had grown blunt. Europe was completely unprepared for war. People laugh at 'Peace in our time' now, but the truth is, most everyone cheered Chamberlain and ignored the dire warnings from Churchill. Churchill was ABUSED in the media when warning people of the dangers they all faced. Why? People WANTED to stay comfy and in bed. They preferred their dreams and didn't like facing an ugly reality.

Ratology: Way of the Un-Dammed

If we are not prepared to face the obvious and deal with consequences, we will end up writing a large reality check to cover the cost of our avoidance.

Avoiding a fight is one thing. It is wise to duck a punch, but not being ready to fight back is another thing entirely. People can SENSE when you are unprepared and thus vulnerable, therefore you WILL suffer as a result. But keep your teeth sharp, your wits clear, your vision undulled by compromises, and your potential enemies will keep to their own borders and look for an easier target.

In Poker, I win hand after hand with no real cards because people believe they are behind. I act as if I have the cards, then I allow their own fear of losing to dictate their actions. When someone comes up against me betting big and I don't have cards, I have to either bet harder with the bluff, or fold. Here is the secret: The basis behind what I will choose to do is based largely on how sharp I feel their teeth are.

This is what Poker is really about. It is not about having cards, it is convincing others that you do. It is all attitude, a look in the eye, and a sense of being awake that convinces others to not want to take you on. It is creating the impression that you have TEETH and will call their bluff.

As a small addendum - If you want to win money playing Poker, obey this one simple rule: *Never let anyone see your cards.* Successful players do not want anyone knowing what cards they play and aim to keep opponents wrong-footed, guessing what your next action will be.

The Russians bluffed the US for many years in just this way. The US military genuinely believed the Russians were far better armed and more ready for war than they really were. What really defeated the Russians was a political system that destroyed personal incentive. They lost the war from within. Otherwise, they had the US bluffed.

If you want to win, you first have to win the war within yourself. Another reason to keep your teeth honed is to continually remind yourself that you are ready willing and able to fight the good fight. Remember Star Wars and how the Jedi had grown complacent? They let down their guard because they thought the war was won with the Sith. Well, thank goodness they were lazy because all those movies would never have been made otherwise!

The Mystic Rat Says: *It is far more difficult for a serious man to put his tongue in his cheek than it is for him to enter into the Kingdom of Fun.*

SIX: Always Have a Bolt Hole

Ques: How do you make the Gods laugh? Ans: Tell them your plans.

It's an old story. No matter how you plan, no matter how well you organize things, the "X" factor can and will occur. There is always that time and place when the Gods come and put a big red "X" right across all your hopes and expectations. Thus: You need an exit strategy for every plan you make. We all know the saying: *For every door that shuts another door opens.* But have you heard the flip side of this? *For every Door that opens another door shuts.* Either way, CHANGE is about, and we need to be ready for it.

When astronauts take a journey into Space, there is always an Escape Pod. Every ship has a lifeboat of sorts. *We need this in our life.* Like carrying an umbrella in case it rains, we NEED to have a place or a situation we can retreat to if needs be. This means we can RELAX and not worry about consequences so much. (Let me not ask about what happens when you get to your bolt hole and discover it's full of rabbits)

I met an old Drunk in the streets of Sydney many years ago. It was a perfect sunny day, yet he was carrying an umbrella. I asked him why, and he said: *"I always have an umbrella! When you live on the street, an umbrella is worth more than money in the bank. It keeps the sun and the rain off you and it also has a sharp point which you can use to protect yourself."*

When he had his umbrella, he felt safer and more at ease in his difficult circumstances. Kerry Packer, the Australian Businessman, always had One Million Dollars in GOLD in a safe in his office. Why? If everything fell over, he would have a safe haven with the GOLD, because it can always be traded for what you need.

There was a second reason, which highlights what a perfect Rat the man was. He put the One Million Dollars of Gold into petty cash. Strange, you might think? As the price of gold went up, he took some of the gold, just enough to keep the balance of net value in petty cash at one million dollars. Tax-wise and according to the books he retained one million dollars in petty cash, by weight. After two decades, he retained only 22% of the original gold, but it was still worth one million dollars. (He also had a fully equipped B&D room behind his office, but that's another story.)

And then the impossible happened, the price of gold crashed. What to do? There was a huge shortfall looming. This is when it gets interesting, the gold with an insured weight of 285 Kilos (628 lbs or roughly 10,000 ounces = 25 standard gold Bars) gets STOLEN from the safe in his office, and police are pretty sure they know who did it, but can't prove a thing. No one gets charged, yet of course, Mr Packer is fully insured for the WEIGHT of gold, which is now worth 5.6 million dollars.

Everything was perfectly OK with the accounting because the weight was registered when it was put in. But accounting did not require the gold to be WEIGHED each year for tax, only that the VALUE stayed the same. I only know this story because his bondage mistress told me, otherwise it was one of the close-lipped secrets of Australian society. "What a RAT!" you say? Yes, but you have to admire the depth of dedication to sheer rat-nosed impropriety.

What are you using for YOUR safety net? Superannuation, a second house, money in the bank? These are all perfectly normal ways to protect our financial interests, but what about your emotional and mental safety? What are you doing to keep your mental health? It is something few sane people think about.

But I promise you, if all you are doing is planning for a safe future, you are already half way to insanity.

Most people save for financial safely, yet in the process they live in fear. They can become so afraid of loss that they lock the door to fun. THAT will keep us safe, won't it? It does, in a sense, but the flow of life gets cut off as well.

A good friend of mine, diagnosed with liver cancer, was staying with me. He had a tremendous sense of fun and humour, despite his present circumstances. One day he said to me, "You know, I really lived my life hard. I had a great time and I have no complaints it is ending earlier than most. But while I had fun, I spent everything. There was no pension plan, no real estate, no superannuation, and I had a background fear of what was to happen to me in my old age." He looked at me quite seriously, then his serious face paused. A huge, cheeky smile spread across his dial. "The good news - now I got nothing to worry about!"

Fear really is the mind killer. The little background fears poison our sense of well-being and most people start to shut down. They start to cut off from living in order to find a way to build what they feel is a safety net for old age.

A mental dis-ease occurs, one where we start to think that hiding from life is safety. We can easily pick up a belief that cutting off fun will protect us. Let me promise you one thing: *DISCONNECTING is not a good safety net.* And we disconnect in a hundred little ways: Sweep the dirt under the rug. Stay in a job you hate. Chew down anti-depressants rather than do something useful. Watch TV rather than the sunset. Talk about nothing and go around filling your personal holes with space rather than read a book that fills your heart.

It will get you many things, but never happiness or contentment.

A perfect example of the present social disconnect are all the reality shows. All those people who are talking to each other and being nice are really all just COMPETING for a prize. All that apparent laughing and joking hides the fact that they are OPPOSING each other and playing mind games round the clock. Personally speaking, I spent most of my early years avoiding exactly the type of people you see on these shows. Why would I want to watch them! The so-called reality opposes the natural flow of life. Big Brother, Survivor, etc. are all entirely based on a DISCONNECT.

There is only ONE door that opens and that is the Exit. These show are really about doors closing as you get evicted. Life is NOT like this! LIFE is all about growth and new openings. Real Life opposes everything Big Brother stands for. In Life there is no ONE PRIZE with everybody else the loser. Life is about living, and when you are LIVING you are a WINNER because LIVING feels great.

Real life involves risks, but a happy life is not one based on comparison, competition or conflict. By living our lives thinking solely on winning or losing, we isolate ourselves from living in the moment. Yes, things happen that challenge us. Sometimes we need to pick up sticks and run, which is why we plan for the possibility. But if we are fixated on WINNING, we will miss the subtle call that says "Time to go!"

Which brings us to the question of risk-taking, the apparent opposite yet natural complement to the Bolt Hole. We can come to the point where we have made our plans, chosen our path, but no door seems to open. We say "To hell with it" and just leap into the dark, trusting that life will in some way hold us up. We go "All In". And we get an adrenaline high. We get a buzz. It's fun.

Having a bolt hole means you CAN run a risk.

Living a life completely safe from RISK means to excommunicate yourself from living. Yet living a life where you risk EVERYTHING on a roll of the Dice or the fall of the cards is another form of Disconnect. People who are afraid to risk anything have pretty dull and conditioned lives, but it comes back to "nothing too much". Risk is great. It helps get your heart racing every once in a while, but cover your bases. Get yourself an umbrella of sorts.

Things DO go wrong and if they do a good RAT is prepared to drop everything and RUN when needs be. As a result, they ALWAYS make sure there is one door that remains open in case they need to get away in an emergency. The only risk here is a loss of face, which is no loss at all to a true Rat.

The Mystic Rat Says: *Those who have Two Faces usually fear losing one of them.*

Bubbles of Truth

Truth comes in thought bubbles. Often hidden in feelings and beliefs, these bubbles have to be popped if they are to reveal what truth is inside them. Likewise, you have to pop all your hopes, dreams and fears if you want to find the secret hiding within.

SEVEN: Do Not Expose Your Vulnerabilities

We all have vulnerabilities! This is a given. But this does not mean we need to ADVERTISE our issues. So we develop our poker face: Yet, every so often, some little part of us lets us down, and we give away our weakness. In Poker this tendency to give away your vulnerable position is called a "Tell". Usually this comes from a deep-seated need for acceptance.

Now here is a little secret. The easiest way to NOT expose yourself is to never hide. Your attempt to HIDE can be the signal that will make people curious. A perfect example was a fellow who lived in a rental house. He had a Marijuana Plant growing in the back yard and was given notice of a real estate inspection. He was scared it would be seen, so he decided to HIDE it by DISGUISING it and attaching Plastic Red Flowers to the bush. What! Are you SERIOUS?

The Dope Plant now stood out like Dog's Balls. It was glaringly obvious that something was amiss and EVERYONE who looked at the house went up to inspect the silly plant with the red plastic flowers. Combined as these things are with drug paranoia, you can imagine the poor fellow was in a bit of a mess.

On the flip side, his neighbour had a dope plant growing in full view in his front yard. What 'this' man did was to trim the illegal herb like a topiary bush. He shaped it to a nice round ball. This made his marijuana plant incredibly overt and obvious, yet it looked like a conventional garden decoration, thus no one was curious as to what it really was.

The BEST way to hide your Vulnerabilities is to not hide them. Keep them in open view, but give it a shape or form that no one would suspect. When I have a big 'All or Nothing' hand where I am unsure of the outcome, I might get pretty caught up in the excitement - This could look like a weakness to an opponent, and they may run harder at me as a result. But instead of trying to hide the nerves, I usually say words to the effect, "I love this bit - where you just don't know what's going to happen next. It's what Poker is all about! This is the fun part of the game."

Then before you go to bet, hesitate, saying, "But do you have Aces?" Just watch, and their faces will tell you a whole lot more than just betting.

Now, for most, this is the stress part of the game. People love to win and fear to lose. Give off fear, you will be read as weak, and called. Reversing this attitude will really confuse the opponent. Are you excitable because you know you will win, or afraid to lose? Doubt creeps into their mind. So often by letting go of YOUR need to hide a fault, you expose theirs, and they fold.

Remember the flip side, however. Sometimes you WANT something to be found and the best way to do it is to pretend it is a secret. A perfect example of hiding what you want to be found and displaying what you want to hide is found with a friend of mine who used to sell things door to door.

The Salesman would drop a ten dollar bill on the carpet when quoting people on something. He would pick it up and say, "Goodness, is that your money? I mean I wish it were mine because I love money, but I have to be honest and admit it isn't MINE!" He then gives it to the potential customers.

How does giving away money help the salesman? Let me tell you:
1. By showing the money, then saying it isn't his means that he is telling the customer that he is incredibly HONEST.
2. This HIDES the fact he wants their money even when he openly says he loves money and he wishes it were his.
3. He WANTED the people to find the 'hidden' surprise because it meant that at the end of his presentation he KNOWS they have a $10 deposit. (The greatest excuse people make for NOT deciding on something is that they have no money, not even enough for a deposit.)
4. What's more, he helped unearth the customer's GREED, because they ALWAYS takes the money he offers.

Do you want to know how to get children to try new foods? The trick is to NEVER place new food on their plate. I always put what I wanted them to try on MY plate. Children are curious creatures and invariably they ask what the food is. I say, "It's grown up food. You wouldn't like it." By showing, but then placing out of reach, I reduce the possibility of rejection and increase the desirability.

Almost all children say "Can I try it?" You have to object for a little bit, but eventually, you give in, and most often the kids find they LIKE it. Why? Because they DISCOVERED it for themselves. If you put it on their plate, you are forcing it on them. But show it, then take it away, and you develop curiosity.

Curiosity creates attention, attention creates Interest, and Interest creates Desire. How does this reduce your vulnerability factor? It is sleight of hand we are learning. We are learning to DISTRACT in order to PROTECT.

If you want to make something disappear, just get people looking at the other hand. You can then drop whatever you are holding and no one will notice. In Poker, survival is so often all about protecting your chips. If you have an unbeatable hand, you don't want anyone to know it - You want to slow play and see if someone will get excited about their cards and bet in. If you have a weak hand, you want people to imagine you have the winning cards, and you do this by bluffing with a big bet on a high card that hits the deck.

Now if someone has a pair of those high cards, you will lose because they will call your bluff - But the odds are that they won't and your subterfuge will get you chips. We need to look at the odds, what we have, and how other people are playing the game, then work out the best way to disguise our vulnerabilities.

NB: The worst thing you can do if you are weak is to half-play a hand. Go in big, or pull out. Never sit on the fence when you are vulnerable.

EIGHT: Pay Attention to Your Brother's Activity

It's a sad truth that unscrupulous people will always want whatever you have. People's greed knows no bounds! If someone believes you have a little more than they do, they will be jealous and envious of you. Eventually, they will start planning on how to get whatever you have.

Every day, all around the world on Poker tables, people are trying to get everyone else's chips. If you don't stay awake to the game, you will lose yours. This notion of looking after your neighbour is all well and good IF you are certain your neighbour is not out to get you. This is why we pay attention to our brother's activity, to work out whether we are in a safe zone, or a war zone. For this reason ONLY, you need to remain aware of what your Brother does.

You are not your brother's keeper and you are a fool if you trust him to be yours. At the same time, you really do not need to know his business beyond the point where it may interfere with yours. The principle is simple: It does not matter if you get on with your neighbour or otherwise, stay in touch with the neighbourhood and listen for what news is on the wire. This is the only good purpose behind listening to gossip, because somewhere along the line, if someone means you harm you will hear of it. You still have to make sense of the whispers that are in the air, but if you pay attention to the warnings as they come down the wires you will be much better off.

The Mad Neighbour I once had is a perfect example. I DID listen to the whispers, but they were SO negative I thought "This can't be true. No one can be THAT bad?" Well, more fool me for having a compassionate heart and expecting the best of people. In this case, the rumours WERE true and he WAS that bad. I paid the price for not paying attention and in a sense, I broke Rule Ten by Playing the Pope.

The point here is obvious: I could have listened with open ears, rather than listen with ears that believed how things SHOULD be. This is another subtle form of shoulding on ourselves, one that cost me dearly. But Rule Nine then applies: We pick up, dust off, and start again.

The Mystic Rat Says: If you make a mistake, learn from it. Living is about recycling negatives, by using them as paving stones

By believing that no one can be that bad, I set into motion a whole series of events that drew me into a web of confusion, suffering, and pain. People really can be sour, unforgiving bastards and we must never forget this. If the message that comes through the wires reads, 'Be careful' - well, BE careful. If the message that comes reads "This is a Saint!" - Be even more careful.

Observe your brothers action, look to see how he does little things, and make your judgement call from what seems obvious to you. Remember, giving something more time before you act costs you nothing and can save you a lot of grief. Pay close attention to those people that surround any project you are intending to enter into. They can influence outcomes to a huge degree. Also, keep things tight. You always want to minimize the number of players on a table who are in your hand.

We deal with techniques to bring unruly partners and neighbours onto your side of the fence in RATOLOGY TWO. The essential technique is the practice of the old phrase: *Keep your friends close, and your enemies even closer.* If you believe you have a problem in the wings, go out of your way to embrace it, welcome it, bring it close to you. That way the problem believes you are its friend and slowly it will start telling you ITS secrets.

Alternatively, the rule is simple: *Avoid conflict situation.* If there is a problem in this part of the world, maybe it is easier to just look elsewhere?

The principle technique for applying Rule Eight is a matter of keeping one ear to the ground and two eyes open. Look for the obvious and don't be a hero. Remember: the best way to avoid a loss is to sniff trouble out before it arrives. Feel out the taste of the situation before you move into it.

The quote from Zeno the Elder is useful to remember: *I have two ears but only one mouth!*

Ask, and it shall be given! Well maybe, but asking means you might at least get answers. Questions are shields when properly applied. Asking about a situation before you enter it can equip you to defend your ground better than any army. The correct question can resolve conflict, disarm opponents and reveal truth. Demanding an answer, not an outcome, gets results.

Always remember: Questions can make friends of enemies, and enemies of friends - They have the power to change lives, polarize situations, and create wealth. But only if you LISTEN to the reply.

NINE: PICK UP, and DUST OFF

This is the Golden Rule of all true RATS. This is the ORDER of the RAT, the one thing that holds everything else firmly onto the Rat Ring of Truth. It is very simple, and again, very obvious: *PICK UP, and DUST OFF*.

There is more to this than meets the eye, however. We automatically believe this means we get up from a fall and get back on the horse - But read this part closely, because if I meant that I would have said it. I DO mean this, but I also am saying that by keeping your eyes open, by being prepared, by keeping your teeth sharp, by protecting your vulnerabilities, by following ALL the previous rues, you will always be in a position to do what the RAT does best - Spot the diamond in the rough.

PERCEPTION is what this is all about! See what others do not, and whatever you see, be ready to pick it up, and dust it off.

There is an old tale of Alexander the Great taking over an Etruscan city. Etruscans were known the world over for their ability to negotiate and arrange business dealings in their favour, so Alexander was completely deaf to their entreaties. In fact, he meant to specifically embarrass them, so he packed them off to a worthless plot of land and said, laughing, "Here, I give you this land and all it contains. It is YOURS in exchange for your city."

The old king who was leading the evacuees bowed low and thanked Alexander for his kindness. Then, with a look of surprise, he bent down and picked up a rock that was at Alexander's feet. He dusted it off, revealing a brilliant, HUGE diamond, saying, "Thank you Lord and Master for the gift of this land and all that it contains."

Of course, he would have palmed the jewel on the way out of the city, but the point was made. You cannot defeat a person who finds OPPORTUNITY and LUCK wherever they go, especially when they create it!

The Mystic Rat Says: *OPPORTUNITY and LUCK are the TRUE GODS of the RAT. Worship and Respect these twin aspects of life and you will never go wrong.*

Fortuna and Ops, Luck and Opportunity: These were the Gods of the Sabines, the tribe that lived in the fields where Rome was built. They became the only true Gods of the Romans and they remain the twin pillars for success.

How does this relate to the modern day? Well, it's a simple question: *Are you going to be part of the millwheel, grinding away all day so others can eat the bread, or are you aiming to be a little more independent?* If you DO want to be free, it's not going to happen working for the boss, is it? The reason you are working for him, in his mind, is so that HE can be free.

However, if you have a sharp eye and keep looking for opportunity there are innumerable ways to make extra cash. One perfect example is the fellow who traded himself up to a HOUSE using Ebay. He started with some minor thing he didn't need and offered to TRADE.

Eventually, by picking his trades, he ended up with a house. He made his luck by finding opportunity. Now THAT is a true RAT.

For myself, some years ago I got back to Australia with a wife and new child and figured I would have to create some security for the family. So, I started looking around for real estate bargains. The best way for the average person to make money is through Real Estate.

I have a simple rule: Look for something going cheap which you can make more valuable with a little effort. That was my sole credo, so I combed the papers and the agents for cheap property. I was amazed at how much I found. Of course, cheap usually means there is a problem to solve, so what I was really choosing was a problem, but that's OK.

Eventually, I bought acreage close to town with a badly run-down house on it. I didn't know anything about renovating, but I figured I would sort it out by asking questions. I bought the place and it was in really bad shape. The house literally had sections hanging in mid-air where stumps had once been. The real estate agent who sold us the property said it was a demolition problem.

It took three months to make it liveable. This meant putting in a kitchen, a bathroom, re-stumping, fixing the roof, repainting, rewiring sections, polishing the floors - You name it, I did it, and soon enough it came out quite cosy.

I had checked out its subdivision potential before buying, and there was a lapsed approval on the place. The first thing I did was to try and revive it and, with a little prodding, we got a small change of the Rules. The five acres that I subsequently chopped off paid me my cost for the entire property. This left me some fifty acres that were effectively FREE.

I used some of the money from this sale and put a deposit on a 250-acre place that came up cheap. I then mortgaged that acreage to buy a Federation House that needed repair, but it was on a river and it was cheap. After I did this one up, I used THAT house to get a mortgage for another acreage with a sea view that went for a song. Within two years, I had over a million dollars in property.

Unfortunately, it seems that my then-wife didn't like being rich, and she left. That cost a million dollars but with large enough lies to the banks, I managed to hold on to some bits of land. I learned something: *It comes and it goes*.

In my life, I have found that anything can and does happen. But when I am connected to my RAT, I see opportunity better and start to make my own luck as a result. We also tend to polarise things in our immediate social circle and possibly ruffle feathers. Why? Because people who know you tend to get jealous when you seem to be streaking ahead. *C'est le Guerre!* That is the cost of being free.

However, I hit a brick wall with the divorce. I had worked my butt off restoring houses, fixing up old properties, making things work where no one else could see it happening, and in the end, it was all for nothing, or at least for next to nothing. So what did I do? I got a little depressed, then picked myself up, and dusted off the past.

But I went one step further. I looked closer at what I had in the present and found ways to make it work for me. I remember distinctly the day when, building my own cottage because I could not afford to pay anyone, I was licking wounds. I had a child to look after, a house to build, and I was suffering without running water or power. That day, I just looked up and asked myself why I bothered.

Could it get worse? That's when I saw that it certainly could. Then when I realized I was actually quite lucky! I started to see the possibilities of things before me. I had a creek, a waterfall, and a roof over my head. If I were a native in Bali, this would be heaven! I changed my attitude, I picked myself up, I dusted my attitude off, and I started again. Within the week I had figured a way to get water to the house, and in a while, I got the cash to connect the power.

I am a greater being from the experience, so I am RICHER in Heart. Truth to tell, I did OK in the end, simply because I was stubborn enough, persevered long enough and kept myself focused on what was useful.

The Mystic Rat Says: *Life provides opportunity; it will not necessarily provide an easy ride.*

You really want to be part of the Rat Race?

TEN: Shoot the Pope

The Tenth Rule goes: *SHOOT THE POPE*. It means to kill off the vanity that is instructing you how to behave - END that part of you that likes to pretend it is important, the part that imagines it is in some way above everyone else. This is the "It's not about You" put into practice in your personal affairs.

I love it when I meet a Pope in Poker. They almost always give me all their chips because they never know when to pull back and cut their losses. And when they lose a big hand to you, they cannot stay out of any hand you are in. They want to keep coming against you to prove they are the boss! All you need do is fold and fold until you get the cards, while they keep charging like a bull at the gate. Finally they get you into a hand, and all they do is bet, bet and bet more - Then you have all their chips. And yet, despite the beating, the next week they will come at you AGAIN and do the same thing, again, and again, and again. SHOOT that damn Pope inside you and cut your losses.

You tell me, what particular aspect in someone do we all instinctively react against? It is ALWAYS overbearing vanity that we hate and which we always want to cut it down. When someone acts above you, or appears condescending, or sounds arrogant, all you want to do is pull them down a peg or three.

When we act like the Pope, when we believe it's all about US and act like we know it all, this breaks up natural communication. As a result we cause ourselves no end of grief. Why? Being too up yourself means no one is your friend. Your partner leaves you and takes your money. The boss fires you for being a smart arse. The kids say "OK" but behind your back are saying "Pratt". Our VANITY is the most expensive luxury we have and the truth is we only need it because we secretly believe we are crap.

Nietzsche said "God is Dead" Well, the Mystic Rat says, *"God is Dead? Fine - Go one step further and kill Your Pope as well."*

How do we do this? Easy: *Just listen to people before you speak.* You may well feel superior to them, but always act humble. In time you will get the knack of being Humbly Superior. (How do you like that for an Oxymoron?)

People who listen are liked - No-one likes a smug bastard. And here is a little secret - You get much further acting stupid than you do by showing everyone how smart you are. A good friend, Paul Smart (Barrister extraordinaire) wins lots of his cases because he acts dumb and allows everyone else to feel superior. He feeds on this in order to get the answers he wants from people.

His favourite term is "Gilding the Lily". Time and again I have seen him question people, almost grovelling before them, saying "Mr. Jones, I know you would not tell a lie. I understand you are an honest man - But seriously, with the testimony you have given, surely you are perhaps GILDING THE LILY just a little bit? Surely, perhaps?"

What can the person do? If they agree then they are saying they are lying. If they disagree then the judge KNOWS they are lying. Everyone Gilds the Lily just a bit, with the only possible exception being Mister Spock. Yet, invariably the person in the witness box denies this and says, "No."

Paul then launches onto the next question with a surprised look and a great laugh, "Oh HO!" he will say, pouncing. "I see Mr. Jones - You are seeking to tell the court that you never even hint at so much as bending the truth, is this what you are trying to say to us?"

People usually answers, "NO", to which it is then asked, "What, you admit that you are not telling the truth?" The person will stammer out that they did not lie in their testimony, not at all - which opens the door for, "So Mr. Jones, you are telling the court that you would never even consider saying anything that might possibly put yourself into a more favourable light? You are saying you DON'T gild the Lily, never, not at all?"

The person then either gets on his high horse and absolutely denies he lies, (thus immediately losing the confidence of the judge) or he admits he lies. If the fellow stumbles and says "Well, maybe a little." the amiable Paul Smart becomes a ruthless eagle diving on his prey. "Oh, so you ADMIT to telling a Fib to the court Mr. Jones, yes? This is what you are trying to say, is it?" (And Paul casts his eye up to the bench with a knowing twinkle as if to say "Another one, Your Honour".)

To a Judge, everyone is lying, and it is essentially his job to simply work out how much. Right at this point, Mr. Jones is looking the bigger liar than Paul Smart's client. And that is all you need. You only need the advantage of a nose in front. You do NOT need to appear intelligent, smart or clever. You don't need to even be telling the truth. (though it helps) You just need to get out of the firing line and let others stand up and let 'their' egos take the blows for you.

All survivors of war know, the safest place to stand is behind a hero.

If you are connected to your RAT you answer questions from the point of NON-DEFENCE. You are not denying anything, you are not fighting for turf, you are just stating your case. I promise you, this is a lot more difficult to deal with.

If YOU are asked if you have been Gilding the Lily you can earnestly say words to the effect: "I certainly would not want to say anything to incriminate myself, but equally if I were to colour the facts knowingly and incriminate an innocent man, this I would find equally repugnant. I am saying things to be the best of my recollection, Sir/Madam. (And here is the clanger) *But surely it is up to the Honourable Judge to decide how much truth is in my testimony?"*

THAT way of saying things gets you off the hook. You did not play the Pope. You hid your vulnerability. You shifted focus from yourself to the Judge. (A Technique called Playing the Third Man which we deal with later in Book Two) PLUS, you managed to find gold where there was none AND you gave yourself a Bolt Hole because you have not said a categorical Yes or No. (categorical answers are known in the legal trade as a hanging statement with good reason) You both avoided the bullet yet answered the question sincerely.

Let's look at this scenario one more time: Did you cover all the Rules?
1. It's not about You. YES
2. Do not Should in your Own Nest. YES
3. Always keep One Eye open? YES
4. Ask no Favours YES ... Left it to the Judge to Decide
5. Keep your Teeth Honed YES
6. Always have a Bolt Hole YES
7. Do not Expose your Vulnerabilities YES
8. Pay Attention to your Brothers Activity, but not their business.- ABSOLUTELY YES! This is what got you off the hook here!
9. Pick up and Dust Off YES
10. By doing all of this, you have effectively Shot the Pope, made yourself look humble and won your legal argument. Well done!

Point Eight is the only tricky one. You could safely presume that your opponent was going to be telling a lie, and you already know that their legal eagles are paid to lie. By shifting the focus back to the Judge and stating you are doing your best, you are swinging the balance of judgement your way. Unless you are caught out in a blatant lie in testimony, the case is already not lost (rather than won) if you are defending a position.

Why is this? In a room full of ugly people, an average looking soul looks beautiful. In a room full of liars, someone who appears to lie less looks the most truthful. But if you act like a Pope, anyone who looks at you will expect perfection and, as that never happens, you will lose.

I might add, another basic principle of being a good RAT comes from Poker as well. If you have a good hand it is always best to have someone else attack you. If an argument is unavoidable, it is so much easier to defend than to attack. Why? In a court of law the attacking party has to prove guilt, whereas if you are defending, you simply have to indicate a likely innocence.

The same thing applies to social groups. Let other people do the parading of peacock feathers. You do not have to appear better than anyone in order to do well, you just have to appear OK. No one trusts the Popes and, in the course of time, in any given situation, people will direct their trust and goodwill to the one who appears the most steadfast and honest.

Paradoxically, this is exactly what a Pope is supposed to be, steadfast and honest. So, if you want to get by more peacefully in life, sit on the Ego, listen to the forces that are at play in the room, and wait for your opportunity. These things will win you more hands than the best cards ever will.

Summary: Remember these Rules and life will go better for you. They put you into a position of strength with every situation you will find yourself in. When properly followed, they create doorways and opportunity where none might have otherwise appeared to exist.

Now, you may be asking at this point: *Where did all of these Rules for Rattyness come from?* Well, everything is handed down to us. We have an inheritance of Memes (Passed down collective memories) from many sources, but the most important ones come from Roman culture. The Romans, of course, were the world's biggest bastards, and because of this they kept things running quite well for a thousand years. The Romans carried the baton of socialization and organization from former civilizations and they have brought this baton to us in the form of the society we experience to this very day.

The Roman Rules were:

I. Thou Shall Be Observant at All Times

II. Thou Shalt Listen to Gut Feelings

III. Thou Shalt Stay Safe in Traffic

IV. Thou Shalt Practice Legal Survival

V. Thou Shalt Make an Informed Decision About Body Armor

VI. Thou Shalt Be Wary of All Weapons

VII. Thou Shalt Know and Practice Safety Tactics

VIII. Thou Shalt Not Assume That All Strange Odors Emanate from Your Partner

IX. Thou Shalt Have Fun

X. Thou Shalt Realize That Survival is a Mindset

Ratology: Way of the Un-Dammed

The Romans: Breaking the Rule Book

"The various modes of worship which prevailed in the Roman world were all considered by the people as equally true; by the philosopher as equally false; and by the magistrate as equally useful"

Edward Gibbon quotes (English Historian, 1737-1794)

All societies have Social Mores, or norms. They emerge as a survival tool to deal with threat from external forces. The Sacred Cow in India came about because a famine meant the people were killing their cows to eat. The Sultan could see that when the natural circle was done, a greater peril would exist, so he declared that cows were sacred in order to save them from being eaten. But, even when the famine ended, this law had changed the mindset of the people and to this day cows are still sacred in India.

The separation of milk and meat is another thing that emerged out of necessity and became a fixed belief. This law came about because, in the desert, putting milk near meat ruins both the milk and the meat. Purely logical to separate them, but now we have refrigeration it is entirely unnecessary. Yet any orthodox Jewish family to the present day will have two kitchens, as a result of this law.

Societies create law to preserve order. The INERTIA of that law propels a society through the ages, even when the purpose for it is long gone. if you wanted to convince the people of India today that the cow was NOT sacred, you would need either a large army, a very convincing public relations teams, and a whole lot of patience. Plus, you must also educate those in charge and convince them it is in their interest to alter the existing laws. It's not going to happen.

The Westminster system is based on Roman Torts, common sense principles that define the use of a public road, natural justice, and most of the essential functions of society. Out of these the Magna Carta emerged. The Western culture is fundamentally based on the Roman way of life, and remember, the Romans were considered some of the most ruthless bastards you were ever likely to meet. Yet, despite their lack of political correctness, they were very successful!

When we think of a Roman, we think of the the forums, the grand buildings, the public consultation, the respectful way discourse was carried out and the fair and even balanced view brought to bear in regards civil matters. The other part we remember is the army and ruthless administration that gained them the position of top dog. We also think of debauchery - Nero, horses in the Senate, orgies, the worship of Bacchus - You know, much like how the Middle East thinks of America today! The United States IS the new Rome, with a dose of political correctness added.

The keynote of the Roman civilization was reasoned organization. Systems, processes, and laws were created that applied to everyone equally. (unless you were poor, a slave, or not a Roman citizen) The Romans set up the structure of civilization as we know it. They prized cleanliness and dress sense, as well as beautiful trinkets and fine art and wine. Respect for government, the creation of roads and infrastructure, the erection of public-use buildings and monuments - so much that are the hallmarks of our present culture comes from them, albeit via the Greeks. Of course, the Roman could also be extremely uncivilized as well! They were very cultured, yet they would torch an entire city if a message needed to be made regarding rebellion, non-payment of taxes, or some other similar crime against their society.

They would not only burn the city, the Romans would enslave the inhabitants and sell them to the highest bidder. This may seem a little harsh today, but there was a very simple reason for this strict enforcement of rules. In those times there was nowhere like the present levels of 'should' to dominate and control societies. Think about the mad Celts running amok! If these people got stirred up and became the feared MOB, it was troublesome. Brutal force was needed, and often called for, in order to train populations to obey the rules. This created the shoulds (unwritten laws) which kept a society running.

The Romans SHOULDED on the population of entire countries. They did this in order to keep everyone in line. There were rewards for doing what you should do (Obedience = Roads, sewerage, functioning government, protection from barbarians, etc. etc.) and severe punishment for what you should not do. (Disobedience = Nailing to the cross, sold into slavery, etc.) In the end, it was better to put up with the rules (and paying tax) because of the benefits. This is the nub of things: Roman society was accepted because the benefits outweighed the costs and because the alternatives were far worse.

You may not like the taxes and road rules of our society, but honestly, would you prefer to live in Somalia? Yet while we owe the Romans a lot, we are still under the HUGE blanket of SHOULD they laid down millennia ago. We need to get out from under this if we are to take control over our own destiny.

So how did the Romans civilize Europe? It's no secret: Essentially, the Power of Logic and Reason (as rules) were used to control wild emotions.

Julius Caesar expanded the borders of the Roman Empire with the intention to Romanize the world. The notion was that by extending the boundaries it gave Rome a buffer of protection. Expansion was not new, but changing the attitude of the people INSIDE the new borders was, at the time, revolutionary. It was necessary as Caesar needed a bigger army, and he needed reliable soldiers for that army. To get this he had to subdue new countries in a way that made them stable, which meant working under good governance and the rule of law.

The Romans performed a unique social experiment. They took alien cultures and converted the thinking inside them to align with their own. They did not just conquer new land, they made these lands their own. The WAY they did this was to set up controls inside the MINDS of the people they took over. They created a NEW NORM - a whole new set of Social Mores that wild Celts and crazy Germans would not just accept, but embrace. And the way they created this ORDER was via A/ a universal language, B/ a unified currency, and C/ a fair and reasonable system of law.

Language - Money - Law

The nature of a culture is revealed through its language. Latin is a very logical language and it follows strict rules. At this point the ruling world language is English, and it, likewise, has a very precise linguistic protocol. It is all very reasonable. Yet is it utterly mad! The rules of English change from one situation to the next. This is also like our culture, strict rules, yet also completely mad.

A culture is also defined by its currency. All through the world, if you have US dollars you are welcomed. Try to negotiate with a Somali Shilling and you are laughed at. Money and language can BOTH speak a clear message, with the US Dollar being the ultimate Lingua Franca. And for good reason, it is accepted everywhere and with it you can get whatever you want.

The combination of benefit (accepted money) stability (reasonable law) with communication (mutual language) determines a societies level of power. But these reasons do not determine the VALUE of a society, just the strength of it. Nor do these things allow you to negotiate a variance of rules within that society. So, what is it that creates variance?

Choices Determine Outcomes

Lewis Hamilton, the many-times world champion in Formula One, explained, *"Only those with the need to win become champions. You have to really, really WANT it."* That is the choice the champion makes and nothing else matters. Everything you do is subject to that choice.

Reason, according to the good scientists, resides in the human mind only because we have a large frontal lobe. Yet people who experience out of body projection and are still able to think, so is the mind really tied to the brain? But a tool needs a hand, so perhaps in this way, a reasoning mind needs a good frontal lobe. The real point is that we believe reason and rational thinking is the background to most business, political and financial decisions we make.

So how does this explain the G W Bush Administration, The Trump Administration, and - of course - any party connected to saving the environment. Ergo: We like to imagine that REASON is the main factor that we humans use when determining anything. *But it just so isn't!* Our **choices**, and the passion they are based on, are the driving force behind everything.

Even the logical Romans were completely ruled by omens, superstitions, and beliefs in invisible Gods that governed your fate. Those logical Romans were completely devoured by their passions and it was their passion for gold, tin, whatever that caused them to expand which created the NEED for all the rules and the shoulds - They needed to control the wild societies where the wealth was being generated.

The paradoxical message: *Passions drive choices that need organization.*

If we wish to renegotiate the rules, we generally imagine using reason and logic to convince people is the best way to go. This is SO wrong! Spock never motivated anyone to a change of heart. Passions and beliefs are the main drivers of our world. We just dance with reason in an attempt to justify them.

What are we choosing? Do we choose to act on a desire, or does reason rule the day? Are we even choosing, or just acting out of habit? RULES are the braking force we put in place to guide our choices. If the fear of getting caught that gives us pause, this opens the door for REASON to come in and help dictate our choice. RULES cause a person to stop and think - they force us to CHOOSE a course of action, one not purely defined by our wants.

But what does the choosing? Not WHO - WHAT - *What chooses inside us?*

Science associates choice with the frontal lobe as there are cases of people with frontal lobe damage who have effectively lost the ability to choose. Choice is one of the major faculties that the use of reason develops in the brain. The larger the frontal lobe, the better the ability to choose, or so it is believed. However, opposing this is the evidence that excessive enlargement of the frontal lobe can also indicate increased aggression, one that aggravates a lack of reason. People, the brain is just a tool: *Our Passions and Desire drive the bus.*

Our passions are the fuel, our choices hold the wheel and our choices are controlled by our beliefs. The combination of all three determines where we go. This is where we discover the majority of our choices come down to little more than putting on the brakes, or pressing the accelerator.

REASON is not choosing your course, your BELIEFS and PASSIONS are. Stop fooling yourself, you are doing what you WANT to do, not what is logical.

Everyone is choosing to move forward or to slow down in their life direction based on what they believe is the best way to survive. It seems reasonable, but what do you class as survival? A loss of face can be a form of death for one person, and they will do ANYTHING to avoid this. A loss of friends may be a form of death to another, and they will do anything to appease their peers. Precious few of the choices we make involve common sense.

It is because of the absurd passions we all suffer that the Romans wrote a Rule Book. They imbued the world with a sense of order that was based on reasonable, sensible regulations. There were practical reasons why things were done, and time frames to achieve them. If you want to argue a matter in court, you present a reasonable argument. If you wanted an exception to a rule, you had to present a reason why. This Roman Rule book is still with us in the form of our present laws, ethics and beliefs systems.

The Roman Catholic Church is the obvious survivor of this process and we find Roman Memes in everything that Western Culture has touched. This is where the construct of most of our rules come from, and the secret is, if you want to CHANGE these rules, you have to appeal to the passions that created the need for them. And our passions only really relate to other passions, not common sense or reason - And what is the base passion we all share? Fun!

The whole point of everyone in the sand pit is for us all to have FUN!

How We Can Change the Rules

Everything in our world supposedly works on reason. Society is a collection of organising rules that we are told are designed for the 'good of society'. Yet what they think is good one decade is very different to what is good the next. The rules change all the time - Fifty years ago, advertising had Mum in the kitchen, Dad coming home from work, and the kids polite and friendly. If you ran that ad today you would be attacked in social media. Further, this invisible line of what is acceptable continually evolves from one politically correct statement to the next. So how do we alter rules that are affecting our freedom?

Social change is inevitable. The thing that accelerates and creates change in society is a collective agreement. Slavery is generally agreed as being unacceptable, as one example. The REASON the laws changed regarding this was because of powerful, emotive arguments appealing to the better side of those in authority. Or a war, as the Civil War in the United States demonstrated.

In the area of personal matters and relationships we often see wars and passionate arguments, and these are expensive and wearing affairs. Taking it all so seriously misses a very important truth - the greatest thing ALL people share is the desire for Fun. Get someone laughing, and it is fairly easy to shift the goal posts - FUN changes the rule book. FUN redefines the boundaries of acceptance. FUN shifts us out of 'rules mentality' and makes things pliable.

"Puff and nonsense, it isn't that easy!" do you say?

Nonsense - happens all the time. When you fall in love, everything changes. Falling in love is no way reasonable, yet this act changes all our personal rules, and our entire life flips. Falling in Love is FUN! Love makes us blind: to logic, common sense and shows us the swan inside all ugly ducklings. I will now tell you a little secret: When *we imbue any logical argument with our excitement and our FUN, all fixed reasons and beliefs become malleable.*

Spock from Star Trek embodied pure reason. There were logical and clear choices to be made in any given event. Nothing was chance, everything was worked out, and no one could beat him at 3D chess. He was the human robot, a machine of pure logic, yet through the series you see him slowly succumb to the Power of Passion. And what is more, he learns to like it. Fact: *Emotion is more interesting than dry logic, so we choose it.* Why?

The reason is obvious - It's fun!

The 'appeal to fun' appears in many ways. The most obvious is with sex, where people will do incredibly stupid things for the sake of it. Naughty schoolboys smoking behind the toilet block is an appeal to fun combined with the need for peer approval. Society has a series of punishments in store for rule breakers as well as a judge to enforce them, but as the fall of the Berlin wall proved, the massed voice of the people can break the will of any government.

And weren't they having fun when it happened! Dancing in the streets and an all-night party. You cannot stop a sense of fun. The East German government was NOT having fun. They faced a failing economy, a rebellious public, and a total lack of any worthwhile future. Their world was no longer fun, so they gave up. There is a curious message in this: *Just as imagination trumps will, our passions trump rules*. But it is not necessarily always in a good way.

Look at Hitler, swaying crowds with rhetoric, getting them onto notions of greatness and creating the illusions of an unbeatable army. He bent all the rules of the Weimar Republic and drove his people into a ruinous War. His greatest mistake? He got way too serious and believed his own rhetoric.

Look at Bush convincing the US public that they needed to go to war in Iraq. A lot of Americans were laughing, having a great time as their army went forth to prove how tough they were. Soon after this, a collapsed economy and a wasted inheritance was no longer fun.

Here is the secret - when you are laughing and singing, when you are roused with passions of any sort, your internal censor is not controlling you. You become free of rules. Rock and Roll broke down the conservative values of America. Jazz and Swing broke down the death grip of prohibition.

When people are laughing and dancing they are living outside the rule book of 'should' - but to STAY in this place of joy we need to have a handle on our emotions. Otherwise, rampant emotions are what create the need for rules!

SO! How can WE take charge of our emotions, find our fun, and bend the Rules so that they work for us? Rather than living our lives in a mire of shoulds and should not's, how do we become free of the Roman inside us?

Getting Past External Authority

Step One: Stop worrying about what others think, how good you look, or how smart you are, and just breathe. Step Two: Pay attention to your RAT.

The only thing that matters is how your RAT can help you alter the rules that are driving you. What matters is that we learn how not to be owned by social mores or by our false logic and passionate beliefs. Let's get an overview:
1. We have a heritage of Shoulds and Should Nots governing us
2. We have animal passions that want us to act against these
3. But - We have false beliefs dictating our reasoning.
4. We, therefore, are not in a position to make correct choices.

SO! How do we get into a position where we start to make good choices?

Our RAT cuts through all of it. It smells out the BS and brings you to the right understanding of any given situation. Only at the point of clear understanding can the correct action can be chosen. And when we come to the understanding that our present situation is weird and locked up in problems that have no real solution, then our RAT is like Alexander at the Gorgonian Knot: It takes out the sword and cuts it through. It doesn't try to solve the unsolvable, it removes it.

This is the RUTHLESS part of the Roman Heritage that we need to wake up. So how do we wake up the ruthless aspect to ourselves? Finally, we come back to seeing the obvious. The process goes like this:

1. *It's all about getting past our illusions and seeing things as they are.*
2. *We are then automatically OUT of illusion and seeing a greater reality.*
3. *This greater reality is always found in the same place where the FUN is.*

Here is the truth: It no longer matters that you play a losing hand if you are playing for FUN. When you play the game this way, even if you lose, you win. The funny thing is (pun intended) you will find you win more by having fun!

My classic example of this: A friend of mine had an old two-door Mercedes. A fellow with a hotted up Jap car pulled up to him and shouted, "I will kill you in a race over the quarter mile." My friend (called Jimbo) enthusiastically agreed with him, then paradoxically said, "Pity you will lose, hey?"

This confused the guy, "Why do you say I will lose when you already said I would win?"

"Well," Jimbo explained, "It's very simple. When I get to the end of that quarter mile, mere seconds behind you, I will open my door and all the pretty women will want to go for a ride in MY car. Why? Because I have a cool two door Mercedes - So I have already won."

Half the Fun is Having Fun

The poor guy just did not get it. Bottom Line: Everyone wants to have FUN and those having FUN are winners! Only ascetics and stoics disagree on this point. Yet I point out that the ascetic has fun when he suffers and the stoic enjoys himself when he is deprived! So the pleasure principle still rules, even as you deny it. If you want to find the point on which the world turns, if you want the Omphalos, it is always found in same place as the FUN.

So what has this to do with the Romans? For them to have fun as a culture, they SHOULDED on everyone else. To negotiate with the Romans, you had to first accept their SHOULDS, then show them a better way to have FUN.

We come back to Humpty Dumpty and the Royalist war. Humpty fell, the war was lost to Cromwell, thus the Puritans took charge. These were the most un-fun people you could imagine. Fun was banned. If it made you laugh, it had to be cast out. Life was hell tough for comedians in those times, I can tell you.

Cromwell, who ran the show for the Puritans, died in office. He was so lacking in fun and such a pain in the butt that, when the Royalists came back into power, they dug him up, hung him in chains, and beheaded him.

That was the Royalists way of having some fun!

But this brings to bear another issue - Cromwell was a fanatic, and fanatics are very dangerous SPECIFICALLY because their desire for Fun is diminished.

A fanatics reasoning cannot be negotiated with via the use of humour. The court jester has already been hung for trying! When fanatics are in charge you cannot use humour or wit to alter a rule. The solution: Pack up and go somewhere more interesting. Avoid fanatics of any type or colour.

FUN is dangerous to rigid societies. Puritans believed fun affected your moral compass, and it DOES! You will be laughing too much to let rules rule.

Remember when Elvis Presley first started gyrating his hips? He was a threat to society, an agent of the devil, and the likely bringer down of all good Christian morals. In truth, he really was a threat to the social order of the time. Why? Because he encouraged people to have FUN. Everything changed from that point! Go on, have some fun, you know you want to.

So what stops us having fun? It is very simple. What stops Fun is the weight of our shoulds; the pressure of rules and obligations that we feel on our backs. And why are these on our backs? Remember the Romans - Shoulds are invented burdens created to keep people in line so that THEY could have fun.

That's it! This is the whole damn story in a nutshell.

Is Your Society Shoulding on You?

There is a sidebar thought to remember here: *Society does NOT practice what it preaches, it preaches what YOU should practise.*

The sole reason and purpose for all Societies, Governments, and Laws is to keep order. The Should is the most effective instrument for this. Society is NOT about being fair, but about placing SHOULDS on your shoulders.

The real message here is blunt and simple. Do you feel trapped by convention? Do you feel caught in a stagnant pond without any free flow? It's your internal Rule Book that is nailing you down. This Rule Book has been handed down to you by the Romans in the disguise of rights and wrongs. We can rewrite our rule books, but only when we have the capacity for FUN. And yet to really have FUN, you have to - paradoxically - be a little ruthless.

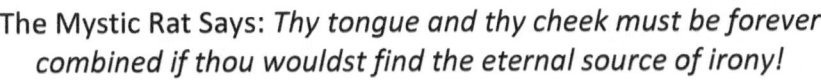

The Mystic Rat Says: *Thy tongue and thy cheek must be forever combined if thou wouldst find the eternal source of irony!*

Being Ruthless

> *"This is a ruthless world and one must be ruthless to cope with it."*
> Charlie Chaplin

This Charlie Chaplin comment is not what you expect from a funny man. But he was raised in Victorian England, in abject poverty, and yet, by age twenty-six, he had become one of the most successful artists of all time. He survived crossing from 'talkies' to sound and, as one of the founding fathers of United Pictures, he negotiated contracts that paid him over Twelve Million a year in today's money. An astronomical figure back then. So the 'Little Tramp' would have been pretty damn ruthless when it came to business.

You need more than a sense of fun to bend the rules your way, you also need a sense of unmitigated direction. A ruthless focus on your goal is necessary if you are to rise up out of your background and fulfil your dreams.

For most, ruthless implies being cruel. In Roman times it was a perfectly reasonable and indeed, common practice, to burn an entire city to the ground. If the town fermented trouble and created disorder - it was removed and all the citizens were sold into slavery. How terrible, you say?

Look at your own body. When a disease attacks it, the body will seek to destroy and completely remove any trace of that bacteria or virus that caused it. It does not sign a truce or put up with things. It does not negotiate or discuss. So I say it is natural to be completely ruthless with things that are wrong inside.

We need to treat our false reasoning, erroneous beliefs, and blind ignorance like a disease. So many of our 'reasons' for acting as we do are stupid, ill-considered or just plain wrong and we have to root these things out. Imagine if you were an alien visiting your house. He sees what you are eating is not good for your body, what you think is not good for your happiness, and that what you felt was based on absurd dreams and illusions. The alien would consider that you were completely MAD. Soon after this, he would get addicted to coffee.

Consider, we live in a Christian Society that preaches, "Love thy neighbour", yet we quite happily throw the insane onto the streets, lock up someone for smoking hooch, and give positions of power to complete and utter bastards. It seems quite mad, but the reality is that this is a ruthless world and what's more, we want ruthless people to run it. Ergo: We pretend that we want politicians to tell us the truth, but if a politician is not a liar, we are suspicious that he doesn't have the balls to run the place. We don't want him to ADMIT he's a liar, of course, we just want to know he can be ruthless. Because then he will be tough and therefore we will be safe.

Huh? Really, it's all nuts. We are living in a Looney Toon.

What about other mad notions, such as: *All men are born equal!* Please - Are we talking standup here? Did Thomas Jefferson with all his slaves really BELIEVE these words as they were being written? Animal Farm (George Orwell) had it right: *All animals are born equal, but some are more equal than others.*

We are not here to slate society. It is what it is, which is to say completely mad - Yet it is also healthier than you realize. Indeed the very vicious and callous nature of society as it has evolved from Roman times will teach us a great deal about the true nature of our own RAT.

Our RAT gives us the eyes to see and the nose to sniff out the truth behind the rhubarb and lies. Your RAT is the ruthless part inside you that will jettison everything from the plane in order to make sure you reach your destination. Yet seeing the problems in our society is only half the story. Society is also looking back at US and how we are 'seen' will determine how we are treated. If we are to recognize this and get around the lies, deceit, and obfuscation most societies are soaked in, we need to train ourselves to understand the Rat and the CAT in other people. *We must become aware of their truth.* Looking at society is one thing, but remember, it is looking back at you.

Remember the Robbie Burns poem: *"Oh what gift the giver sees us, to see ourselves as others see us. T'would from many a blunder free us, and many a foolish notion."* Obviously, if we cannot grasp how we appear to others we cannot take charge of how we are perceived. This is where you need to be ruthless because you must cast off the false image of self, discard the excess baggage from your past, and re-form yourself as needs be.

As an obvious example: If you look like a beggar, no one will vote for you as a potential President of the United States, will they? How we are seen: This is the keynote area to master. Everyone you meet has a judge on their shoulder that is looking at you, so using humor and learning to present a suitable face will set yourself free from many difficulties and troubles.

Being Seen Right

We all want to survive better and this means dealing with external authority. Fact One: *We are all under some form of authority.* Fact Two: *If we want to attain more freedom, we have to work with Fact One.* The question is *"How do I make myself appear in a positive light to the powers that be?"* Is there any way we can swing external authority onto our side?

Let's look at things from the Authority side of the fence. Authority (in the form of lawmakers, judges, politicians, religions, etc.) controls and directs every facet of our society, but do you understand the overall rationale for its existence? The rationale of society's existence is simply ORDER. More to the point, authority opposes Dis-Order. All Authority lives in fear of a society out of control, or what we call the MOB. All its rules and punishments come from this fear of disorder. (Read the history of the Brothers Gracchi in Ancient Rome)

Think about this: If all Authority lives in fear of Disorder, all you need do to impress any authoritarian is to appear highly organised. Show this person in you have everything in order and you will automatically find favour. But go one step further, let this person believe you are ruthless, and you will have them on your side. Machiavelli did precisely this in order to curry favour with the Borgia's. (To understand ruthlessness, read his book: The Prince)

The Mystic Rat Says: *Clothes maketh the man, appearances maketh the rules.*

So, be organized and appear ruthless and authority will love you - but if you go one step further you will succeed beyond your wildest dreams. If you can fulfil all of the above you make any important person feel secure. THIS is when you will get that promotion. But can you then appeal to the FUN aspect of any authority figure? Here is the secret: If you are organised, ruthless and FUN they will bend over backwards to help you.

Usually, this means appealing to their lowest instincts. A project I was working on had the opportunity for significant Government funding - if we could get a university onside. I had a partner who was possibly the greatest Rat I had ever known. He targeted the most likely source for getting the money, and subsequently sucked up to the head of an important University research facility. He came in with all the right pieces of paper, talked the right language, but he also made sure he appealed to their FUN. Once IN what a menace he was!

He started working the cloistered high end of the University professors, finding ways to twist their passions. He knew the head of the faculty was bored, with an ordinary wife and unexciting pay. So he started talking about all the things the man dreamed of having: Money, Sex, Good Times and Gambling. Oddly enough, it was the gambling that hooked the main fellow.

My partner simply showed the guy a good time. Girls, parties, casinos and many little hints that there would be LOTS of this in store. Yes, good old fashioned adult FUN. We got the grants, we got the investors, we got everything we wanted. Unfortunately, my then partner's history caught up with him and he spent ALL the money he had raised for the project to keep himself out of jail. Not a good look! It broke the illusion and the funding ended. However, in the process, he taught me about being a proper RAT, so all was not lost.

The history of big business is the history of how RATS find power and influence. Little known fact: Certain unnamed billionaires were once very high profile drug barons before they 'went straight'. They will never be punished, not just because they were not caught, but because they understood the secret. The Secret that is Simple, Free and Alarming! (SFA) They appeared as profitable, conscientious organisers that would support society and authority, and they had that essential, overriding, sense of FUN.

These larger-than-life Billionaires (who shall remain nameless) founded empires on the drug trade. No one will publicly state the truth of their origins, but anyone who is anyone knows it. How do they get away with it? They were charming devils and were great fun to be around - so all those drugs cannot really be THAT bad, can they?

Shocking you say? Well, I hate to say it (no, I am lying, I love saying this) but the East India Company, that bastion of British Pucka spirit, that colonial giant who propped up the entire British economy, were drug pushers. This was a trading company that kicked off its money by trading in Opiates. What, you thought "spices" meant Cinnamon and Turmeric?

The Spice Trade was a polite way of referring to the Drug Trade and no one cared because it meant MONEY. No one cared if a million Chinese died from Opium because it meant nice china teapots and silk dresses for the ladies at home, which meant that these women sexed their husbands out of gratitude. So there is nothing wrong with the drug trade, is there?

The business of the 'Spice Trade' put enormous sums of money into the economy, which gave jobs to workers, who built houses, which allowed families to be raised, that allowed the expansion of the economy, and so on. In time it led to more substantial commerce, mining, tea, etc. but the drugs gave the immediate cash injection that paid for the ships and the sailors. Are you shocked? Stop using Ebay then. Why? The internet Ebay is based on came about mostly because of Pornography. This provided the funds to expand the concept. In Western Society, the ends DO justify the means. This is an important thing to understand if you are to find the Secret of True Freedom.

True Freedom

Hang about! Doesn't inner freedom come from contemplation and the appreciation of fine art? Surely culture and refinement are the pathway to the true qualities of life!

Forget soul searching your navel. Leave art and culture on the stage and in the art galleries. Sing Dylan at home where no one is watching. I am NOT saying these are not good and wonderful things, I am simply saying that this sort of appreciation of finer things of itself will not get you closer to freedom or an understanding of the reality that is yourself. Sure TODAY we say how wonderful the Greek architecture is, but back then it was simply a luxury afforded by the money business had generated.

The pursuit of art does make our life more interesting, however. It can give us a way to chat up girls and boys (whatever is your thing, even grandma's?) so it is essentially a good thing. Yet the BUSINESS of art is the commercial reality, and one of the great investment portfolios of the current age.

Art has a role. Obviously, it holds a powerful place in creating new social Memes, but the short term 'escaping into art' to find freedom is not a solution for surviving better. It does not give you results. There are exceptions, such as Warhol, Dali and Picasso. But they were complete Rats, so it really isn't an exception. These were successful artists who obeyed the Law of Focus and used observation as a weapon to sell themselves.

But on the other hand, if you slave away for commercial gain, make inroads into all sorts of markets, gain respect from your peers, and live for a thousand years - but wake up and realize you are not having any FUN! Well, that's not really worth it either, is it?

The Mystic Rat Says: *If it isn't FUN, look at your options.*

Ask yourself where the Fun is. Forget the Road Less Travelled unless it goes past a free whorehouse. Ignore the priests and politicians who talk about ideals. Don't worry about the bank account and trust that your friends will feed you, if necessary. Hint: If you are fun to have around, you will always have friends who will feed you!

Travel the highways and low ways of society with a sense of FUN and opportunity will present itself. With your Fun as your shield, you will be able to go anywhere with impunity. And Your RAT will guide you. It might even send you funny thoughts to lighten the load.

Still got problems? Find the Fun and you find the solution.

Crabs in a Bucket

I heard a remarkable story many years ago, about Soldier Crabs. You put them all in a bucket and everyone gets on fine. But when one of the group tries to leave by climbing out, the rest of the crabs will work together, drag it back, and EAT it. This is a little like society, do and say the right things, behave, and stay in your place, you get no problems. Seek to climb up and out, however, and you get attacked.

The Mystic Rat Says: *Find the path of Least Insistence.*

The reason to be ruthless is to remove the things that stop you focusing on the FUN. It is not to hurt anyone, it is to remove the cancer of self-doubt inside.

Your RAT is not a critic; it is an observer of reality. It never believes it has a greater right than another, but it knows it has a right. Your Rat has no position to defend, no morals to uphold, no authority it needs to respect and holds to no politics that it needs to proselytize - but it WILL help you get results. Your RAT will generally despise purists, intellectuals and the Hoity Toity because they focus on concepts, not reality. Your Rat will look for the quickest way to get from "A" to "B" and if it means that the businessman must become a drug baron in order to get his cash flow up, his Rat will help him achieve it.

Yet can you imagine what a TV journalist would say if they read this? Headlines would scream "Author advocates the Drug Trade!" or some equally stupid comment. Why? Why are people offended by an awake, alive RAT exposing the soft underbelly of their social BS? Because sycophants like this are always cuddled up to the fur on the underbelly of convention, feeding off the tit provided. And you know something? I just love to sour their milk with the vinegar of reality.

It causes me problems, but I can't help myself. The foot goes into the mouth with such remarkable ease! BE WARNED.

1. Say the system is faulty and any person feeding off the system will attack you.
2. Stir up any lie or deceit with hard reality and you will get attacked.
3. When your RAT starts to awaken, your own family will want to cut you down to size .
4. When you start to break your boundaries and stake out new spiritual, psychic and intellectual ground, your whole emotional state within will change.
5. This will create break-ups of the old and an influx of the new.
6. Old relationships will have to change or they will die on the vine.
7. Your own connection with yourself will have to change or you will hate yourself. (Actually, you already do, but you have forgotten how much)
8. THIS IS WHY YOU NEED TO BE RUTHLESS. It's not about hurting anyone, getting on top of another, or winning at another's expense. It is about snipping what you no longer need and which is no longer useful to you.
9. The net result is that you will survive better.

There is a difficult truth to face here: Society will attack you when you are ready to become the person you really are. This is why Jesus said (paraphrasing) "Ye must hate thy mother and the father, thy brother, and thy sister, if ye are to enter the kingdom of heaven". We need to be able to snip ties that are not helpful to us. The cost of freedom is realising that sentiment is not survival.

Sure it costs you. Otherwise, it is all just pretend and theory.

Anyone can read an adventure novel and see how James Bond does it, but will you allow celluloid heroes live your emotions? Can YOU take the full measure of freedom that life offers? Living life is a much bigger story than you find in a book. Yet when you DO start living, you discover freedom it is a whole lot easier to live with than staying behind in your prison.

One day you will understand just how much better it is to be free. And being free costs nothing - it is FREE! *The cost we must pay is snipping the ties that bind.* You may say, naively, that this is a good thing but, when these ties start to be cut, you feel the pain. You hear the screams of anguish from those parts of yourself that really do not want to let go.

Your Rat sees through the garbage and waffle and will cut to the chase, but the rhubarb and waffle within you will protest loudly and try to stop you pursuing this. Yet your RAT, your Reality Attention Trigger, is that part inside you that KNOWS when you are being served a crock of crap. Yet, seeing the obvious and recognizing the truth is not enough - You have to DO something about it.

This is the difference between the free soul and the enslaved one.

Can you Smell Your Freedom?

> *"The unity of freedom has never relied on uniformity of opinion."*
> John F Kennedy

OK then, you ask, "How does your Rat spot BS and crap?" The answer: *Your RAT doesn't read the label, it smells the scene.* Your instinctive survivor, the RAT within, can smell a false smile and a lying bastard from a mile away. Your Rat can spot this so easily is because IT knows what IT is. That's the paradox, IT knows what IT is, so it can help you to avoid this in others.

Exercise your RAT, make it strong, and it will become your friend and saviour. In every situation that you find yourself in, imagine you can already spot the BS and nonsense in people's conversations and communication. What would you do? Will you seek to correct every lie people speak? Would you seek advice from those who are programmed to act stupid? Of course you wouldn't. We just want to wake ourselves up and move around the sleepwalkers. Let them be!

Don't wake up the Zombies! That's the REAL Secret: *Do what you will, and wake up nobody*. If you do, they will get out their guns and start shooting. It's a blind reaction that sees freedom as dangerous, independence as flawed and happiness as risky. Plato referred to this in his analogy of the Cave - If a man who has walked free in the sun goes to those who have only lived in a dark cave and tells them they can be free, they will not believe anything he says, and will come to hate him. He is a risk to their existence.

Accept your Roman heritage - it is the cave you grew up in. Accept the ruthless need for order in your own life, and be ruthless in removing excess baggage. We are all part Roman, even if we live in Ethiopia or Afghanistan. Throughout the world we find the Memes of the Romans. These are not things that are spoken of, but it is what we SEE and FEEL. It is the way a newsreader looks at the camera. It is the smile and reserve Ingrid Bergman has in Casablanca. It is all the subtle things that almost do not register to the conscious mind. It is ALL Rome! Don't fight it, just seek to be free of that world of Should. Let the sleeping dogs lie but keep your own doorstep clear of their crap.

This is far easier for me to say than do. Every moment of every day we are being pummelled with MEMES, images from the past that bleed into the present. Movies, radio, and media have combined to form a massive 'Meme Machine' that has programmed the world to the ideals of Rome and Western Culture. Hollywood, TV, Sports: It's all ROMAN hand-me-down memes, or patterns of the past. (We look at this in depth in Ratology Two)

Every Die Hard movie is a Colosseum in disguise. Every football game is a gladiatorial bout. People used to queue to read the latest legal story from Cicero, or Message from Gaul sent by Caesar! Now it is "Boston Legal" and CNN.

Everything is different while nothing has changed.

Protect Yourself with Creativity

> *"Creativity is more than just being different. Anybody can plan weird; that's easy. What's hard is to be as simple as Bach. Making the simple, awesomely simple - that's creativity."*   Charles Mingus (Musician)

We do have to protect ourselves from all these Memes and, in order to do this, we have to be able to see them. This is not possible in a cluttered life, so the first step is to simplify our world. Once the inner clutter is out of the way, our RAT can spot the hand-me-down pictures we have inherited, but even then, we still need to find a way to deal with all these patterns that have been buried in us like little time bombs. As an example: We may think we are not Catholic, yet one day we meet a pretty girl and suddenly contract with a weird sense of guilt. The reflex of upbringing!.

These habits are the traps of consciousness within that we must define and then defend against. The easiest way to do this is to see who and what is driving the bus in ourselves - Only then can we shift whatever it is out and take the wheel. Often, it is simply the 'weight of ages' in the driver's seat.

You cannot beat the weight of ages, but you CAN create a space where YOU are free. Here I will now appear to reverse what I just said about art serving no purpose. Creativity is the key. Build something, make something, paint something, write something. And damn it all, have some FUN. Express yourself in whatever way you can to create an internal space but PLEASE remember to make it fun and never, ever try and foist your beliefs onto others.

Hey! You call out from across the pages. You are the guy writing the book full to the brim of his notions and opinions and who just berated the pursuit of art as a waste of time? How does THIS add up?

Hey, cut me some slack. You cannot believe how much personal crap I have tossed in writing this book. Why? Because it wasn't FUN enough to read. (Tip of the hat to Prof George Cockcroft for his ability to cut things down to size) I am talking about USING creativity to generate FUN, not pursuing some lofty goal. Being truly creative in not an escapist dream, it's a means to create OUTFLOW.

It is SO simple - The expression of personal energy stops the inflow of other people's ideas taking hold in your awareness. Of course, Ratology is the best book ever written! So take care, as we can get pretty full of our own brilliance, and PLEASE don't get too one-sided in your RAT-ness and should on the world by trying to impose your "wisdom" onto others.

Apart from breaking Rule One by imagining it is all about YOU, it's dull and ordinary. Really people, remember that I only bothered writing this book because I got up from a sick bed and saw all the liars on TV. I am clarifying things for myself. I do it to hone my OWN instincts, not yours. However, I am happy to accept your money. Praise, glory, and honours can come afterward, thank you.

The Mystic Rat Says: *You cannot beat society, but you CAN wake up and learn not to be overly affected by it.*

It comes down to this: Creativity is good for breaking up the hypnotism and the Memes that run the social structures around us, but our Rat is only interested in fun and survival. It won't help you create anything, however. Mostly, it will offer what appears to be cynical and sardonic observations, but these CAN assist your inner artist to shape things.

Creativity is also an armour that protects us. It creates an outflow of energy that opens up the interest and fun centres of the brain. If we keep looking for the Interest and the fun we tend to also find the best avenue for success in our life. Why? Your RAT loves to have fun. Fun causes it to stay awake and keep looking for options, and it usually finds them. Your RAT will also continually reset the radar, looking for the little blips of BS and seeking out where the next fun zone might be. But remember the Temple of Apollo, "Nothing too much." We can fall too deeply into anything, including creativity. A clue: If you catch yourself saying any particular thing is done for the sake of art, you have gone too far down the rabbit hole. It's BS and an excuse to avoid the world. In this case, our RAT gets really, really bored, then falls asleep.

We need freedom, but not indulgence. We need happiness, but a never-ending fountain of optimism is ridiculous. We need open horizons, but these horizons need defined destinations because we will otherwise get lost in our possibilities. What we need to create are not barriers of should, nor the tyranny of endless dreams, but the open-hearted welcoming of life. We need to potter along, doing what we do, and expect the unexpected.

Summary: *Our Culture derives from Roman, Greek and Etruscan roots. We have a subsequent worship of Reason and Order that created a social "rule book". This book can be worked with and altered by appealing to the Fun element in any controlling authority. We need to be ruthless in defining our rights and keeping our side of the fence free of other people's BS. Creativity is important in helping create clear space around us. And, most importantly, this whole journey is really one to help us define the difference between the inheritance of society and our natural self.*

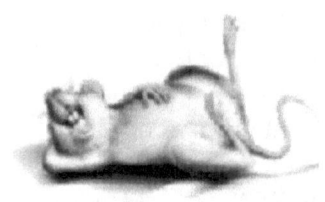

NOW is the Time

"The best time to plant a tree was 20 years ago. The second best time is now."
— Proverb

Your RAT only knows one time and place: NOW. The RAT in you is a very immediate creature. It is very spontaneous and very inventive but if "you" are not present what use is it to you? You, in a sense, are where your attention is. What we are looking for what is looking, as the old Sufi Proverb says. Obviously: You have to be HERE to listen to what your Rat is saying NOW. When you are right HERE, there are simple things you recognise:
1. Now is a choice.
2. Choosing Now sets us free.
3. Yesterday won't come again, and tomorrow never arrives.
4. We can learn from the past, and prepare from the future, but what we DO can only be done NOW.

Imagine we are all in a vast auditorium, and we have all come to this place to read from the Book of Life. But we do not come alone. Each of us brings along a trail of moments that we have experienced. They follow us like puppy dogs and each one of these moments from the past holds in their mouths the bones of our present beliefs. We believe, irrationally, that all of our vast experience somehow qualifies us to read from the Book of Life. It does not! The only qualification we can hold, the only thing that will allow us to read clearly is the LACK of these barking puppies.

If we are to understand and experience what is NOW we need to cage the puppies of the past. Your PUP, your Personal Un-integration Point, is a pivot from which discontent, desolation, and desperation are brought from your past and invade your present. They are energies from your past that are full of misery, the lack of contentment, irrational dreams, and fears for the future.

The Book of Life is vast - much broader than the sum of our experience, and far deeper in knowledge than the wisest of men - Yet we seem to imagine that we, our puny little selves, can somehow read from this book and understand it.

Further, we believe we can find our way back from here. We imagine our trail of breadcrumbs, our thin line of logic we wound out in the Minotaur's lair, will save us. We think that the gnawed-on bones past experience deposited in front of the book with the wagging tales of our puppy thought are important, and we imagine these will fill our heads with enough wisdom to read from its pages.

The Book of Life can only be read by someone genuinely present in the NOW.

Further, the Book of Life is far beyond our collective experience. Like a vast ocean, it cannot be drunk by any one man, yet the paradox is that every single drop contains all that the ocean possesses. The TRUE Book of Life is a Grail of

Wisdom. The Norse tale of Thor drinking from Cornucopia, which is connected to the ocean and thus he is unable to drink it all - This is a clue to the vanity we all possess that allows us to imagine we are important.

Life itself is intelligent. Life Life knows what we need and provides in exact accord with how you can accept it's gifts. We rarely see our painful circumstances as life providing what we need, but as we learn acceptance, as we learn trust, things become clear. Life will humble us again and again until we are distilled to a single pure drop of essence. Only then can we read from the Book of Life and understand its message.

When we stand before truth and read its story, we discover the single drop of the great ocean that has been placed in the glass before us contains everything the entire ocean holds. That single drop is what we are,

Wow, does this mean the author is claiming to understand the Book of Life? That is one hell of a vanity call if you ask me! I have read from its book, but did I understand the words? You tell me. I can say that I have experienced moments where absolute clarity descends, and it's great. But what do I know otherwise? I have learned the following:

1. Life exists only in this moment.
2. Life doesn't live anywhere else
3. Yet the paradox is that ITS moment is in all the moments experienced by all the people who have experienced any given moment.
4. We are a Single Drop of Truth. Your grasp of any given moment is based on how DEEP your experience of this is, rather than an understanding of what it might be or what you do with it.

The Book of Life is everything. The Great Book is as much our small, petty arguments as it is our grandest, greatest thoughts and aspirations. Even our rejected hopes and our embraced fears are all connected within its pages.

It's everything we are, all we hope to become, and all we have been - and this is all HERE NOW. What we need to learn is how to read from the book, and that means getting off our hands and knees, getting out of the begging for crumbs mentality, removing ourselves from our high horse, letting go our beliefs, leaving behind our passions and just lifting up our heads to DRINK the TRUTH of this present moment. Just a pure, single Drop of Truth will set your heart free.

Your freedom is determined according to the depth of understanding you have of this present moment, and how you can appreciate this.

But reverse the word "drop" and we get "prod". This is what happens when we come close to a Drop of Truth. The reflection in the drop is pure, and it will show us clearly the world of lies, Memes, and self-deception we have come from. But get one glimpse of our face in the reflection of truth, and it is a merciless prod, driving us forward to catch that moment once more.

Pure Truth always appears to us as a negative, a reversed image if you will. It will prod you, make you feel uncomfortable, and give you a sense of foreboding.

We get prodded and pushed until we let go of the crap. Only then does the reflection become clear of the garbage. You are finally able to go through the 'glass darkly'. Only then can we accept truth for what it is. Only then can we suffice our inner thirst on that single drop within us. This Drop of Truth is YOU - as SOUL. You are one who is watching what is watching.

One Drop of Truth, that's all we are.

But which drop is truth? In the pouring rain of experience, we find many possibilities, many choices, many cups to drink from - which one is the truth?

It's a little like Harrison Ford knowing what is the real chalice, you just know. When we get there we discover that Truth is simple. We also learn that all our personal fears and the subsequent consequences of our failure to dare, dance and delight are what constitutes our living hell. We learn that fun, fulfilment, and freedom are our heaven. We learn that despite all the rhubarb of what we dream, hope, fear and imagine - No matter where we go, it is always only our 'self' that arrives. WE are the chalice that holds the drop, people.

It's only US.

Heaven or Hell is a state of consciousness we experience right now. In the world of Walt Disney, there are no eternal hells or forever heavens. Mickey Mouse lives totally in the NOW. He reads directly from the Book of Life without fear or favour. He never worries about his mortgage, feeding the nephews, or about his relationship with Minnie. Mickey follows the way of ISNESS

So did Walt Disney. He dreamed of achieving the impossible and though he had no money and few prospects, he managed to create the dream, and live the creation. It was the power of Imagination and Walt used it all day, every day.

And it worked! Even Hollywood, that mongrel pack of money grabbing evil bastards know how powerful it is, because all in Tinsel Town know the one golden rule of survival in that place - *"Don't muck with the Mouse!"*

What we WANT Versus What We NEED

People talk about the fine line between what we want and what we need. That is useful, but not so important. What really matters is knowing the difference between the half-truth we discover and the half-lie we lead.

We all live in the shadowlands of Memes, compromise, and confusion. What we really need is a clear vision of the parts of us that are infected by past conditioning, and so the line we really need to find is the one that separates the indoctrinated self from the natural self.

Ratology: Way of the Un-Dammed

The Truth is Simple. YOU are Simple.

"It is cheering to see that the rats are still around - the ship is not sinking"

Eric Hoffer

Rats Deserting the Sinking Ship - You have heard this saying, yes? It is used as a term of disdain, but why? Personally, I get surprised when I hear people speak this old cliché as if it were a BAD thing. Have often wondered why this is the case? I say if Rats are smart enough to get off a lost cause and survive, surely they deserve respect, not derision. Surely? But perhaps you say this is wrong because we are talking about dirty RATS!

Perhaps you want to argue some point here, saying that they are unfaithful, suffer no loyalty and are generally selfish without consideration as to what is for the good of the whole. Maybe so, but on the other hand what sort of fool thinks a sinking ship is worthy of respect? If it is going down, why stay on it?

It's a good example of everything that is upside down in our present world. I had a saying on my desk for many years. It read: *In a bureaucracy we*:
1. *Praise the non-participants,*
2. *Pay the thieves,*
3. *Blame the Innocent*
4. *Imprison the volunteers, and then*
5. *Fill it all out in Triplicate.*

Bureaucracy is an animal that wants everyone to stay in line, follow orders, and be treated as a nameless number. The 'Powers that Be' prefer people just toe the line and be 'good'.

It took me years to discover that being 'good' according to the social mores is really just obeying someone's rules. It is a subtle belief that if you obey you will be approved of - The Santa Clause, as I call it -This is a thinly disguised need for attention. So, drop the need for approval! Life is not about you being 'good' but about surviving. It took me years to get past the guilt and conditioning of my upbringing and get to a point where I asked "Does this work for me?" before I considered, "Will I be approved of?" It has taken me years to understand that being a Rat is not at all harmful to others, but that when I ignore the messages it sends, I am being harmful to myself.

What is often forgotten by the rank and file who are mired in convention (But never the bosses) is the Ratology Motto: *"When the ship is sinking, jump!"*

Society holds up many fine ideals: Notions like Loyalty, Respect and Faithfulness, and these are all wonderful concepts that sound great when you are applying for admission at the Pearly Gates, and in the right time and place these virtues are good. However, it can be taken too far. Ideals can become a hindrance to the successful living of your life.

Consider: If you are in a marriage that is dead and buried, you are a fool to remain faithful, loyal or even respectful if the partner is abusive or unkind.

To succeed in the Moment we need to understand 'Like meets Like'. We must get past notions of good or bad being the directors of our life, and get down to what is here, now. What is being presented to us, how can we grasp it, how can we get in charge of the process, or otherwise, how do we leave it? And from here we come to a very important step in our ability to survive. We come to an understanding of what is USEFUL to us. We need to always ask ourselves: *What serves a useful purpose for me here?*

USEFUL is the watchword. If something is Useful it has a BENEFIT to you. So when faced with a question of loyalty, the real behavioural question is: *When is Loyalty no longer useful in this situation?* If we find inside our self in a place or situation where a particular trait no longer serves a purpose, how do we dispose of it? There is a boundary line between what is USEFUL and what is merely a trapping of respectability (and respectability can indeed be a trap) and we need to define this zone for ourselves.

Here is our first significant hurdle. Society and its values will invariably tend to prefer respectability to purpose. It at this point of your growth that you will re-discover one of the first conflicts you ever experienced as a child, between doing what you WANT to do, as opposed to what you are EXPECTED to do. It's a dilemma that can only be answered when we discover what is USEFUL. What is Necessary? What is Essential? What is it that will work for you in this moment? These things are all part of what is Useful.

Society's ideals are generally employed to send you in the direction of what supports it. This is often spiritually and emotionally useless for yourself. Why? Society simply wants to control you, and to train you to do what is expected. Society wants you to fit into the machine. This is all good for society, but at some point when we get sick of just fitting in and we want to start expressing our self as we are - What then? It's the paralysing question: *What to do?*

Well, let's just wheel out the tried and true warhorses. The noble notions of service and sacrifice: Ask not what your country can do for you, etc. And this is not a bad thing. These ideals can convince ordinary, well-meaning souls to become something greater than they presently believe themselves to be. As an example: The sportsman who goes for Gold at the Olympics because of a noble sense of competition and improving self. It works but only because in this process the individual transforms their spirit.

I am not saying ideals are wrong, far from it, only that we need to know when something is useful or otherwise in our life. Blind obedience is a Ratology Sin.

Ideals can be a good thing and such is the power of ideals that they can elevate the spirit. Yet in the hands of the 'Powers that Be' these same ideals can just as easily be used to turn you into willing cannon fodder. It's NOBLE to go fight in Iraq and free the poor people from Tyranny! Surely you still believe this, don't you? The upshot (If you can bear the pun) is that nobility is good for self-esteem, but it is not necessarily a good survival tool. The Noble Truths of Ratology are very simple:

1. *Loyalty does not feed hungry children.*
2. *Courage does not pay rent.*
3. *Truth is not Superannuation.*

If you remember these practical RAT truths as you go through your life, you will do significantly better for yourself in everything you seek to achieve.

Let's recap the start of this book, 'The Proverbial Truth'. An old proverb speaks of an angel that visits three old monks who have dedicated their lives to understanding life and living. The angel says to the aged leader, "You have earned a right to one gift from the heavens. You will be given the choice to attain Wisdom, Beauty, or Money. What will you choose?"

The monk is ecstatic and instantly chooses Wisdom, and thus is immediately enveloped in a deep, contemplative thought. He is then immediately thrown into a deep, gut-wrenching sob that lasts for hours. The angel is now long gone, and the night is upon the group - Finally, his friends can take the weeping and the pain no longer and ask him "What's it like? What is this pain? What is it that this wisdom has revealed to you?"

The man looks up, weeping. With great misery and tears of sorrow in his eyes, he says with his newfound wisdom, "Don't you understand? I should have asked for the Money!"

Being a little mercenary in our dealings with life is not a bad thing. Being noble is all well and good, but it does not pay the bills and often it does not even engender respect from others. I knew a woman who loved sex, but one day she realised she needed money and some guy wanted her, so she decided to charge him. Suddenly she had a whole lot of guys more interested in her because she was charging them - what really surprised her was how she was now treated with respect from the same men who last week treated her with scorn. Go figure!

The rule is simple: *Offer it for nothing, and it has the same value - Nothing.* 'Free' usually means worthless, even though Freedom can cost everything.

OK, let's just presume you are intelligent enough to figure out that wasting your life for someone else's cause is not such a great idea. What? Are you really telling me that you don't want to be cannon fodder? Do you actually want to think for yourself?

Excellent. Ok, I kind of doubt you really mean it, but let me be a little less cynical, and give you a small clue to help you on the path: *Avoiding other people's battles significantly reduces the risk of you suffering for your ideals.*

We all know ideals are wonderful in their right place, but they certainly do not make life easier, or even better. Ideals can be a good motivation, a kick start, but they do not give you to happiness or success. In fact, your ideals can often become a burden - a burden that can send you to an early grave.

Imagine if you were a soldier in Hitler's army who openly stated that you disagreed with the extermination of the Gypsy, the Slavic's and the Jews? Well, you would soon be joining them in the gas chambers, wouldn't you?

A friend of mine (the very wonderful Henri Melianaus) told me his extraordinary story before he passed away. He had been in the Lithuanian Army, which in World War Two got taken over by the Russians. The Russians put them in their uniform and sent them the Lithuanians up as cannon fodder for the Germans. But the Germans recognised the situation and invited the Lithuanians over to the German Army, which they promptly agreed to.

Henry was a competent administrator, a Staff Sergeant with Bavarian heritage, who was blond haired and blue eyed. Obviously, he qualified for the SS and he was given a role at his former rank in the Lithuanian army. So in the space of one week, from facing certain death from the Russians, and then the Germans, he was now a Sergeant in the Nazi SS. Of course, he didn't mention he was Jewish. He quickly saw exactly what was going on with the movement of Slavs, Jews and what happened to any critics of Hitler.

Henri was not completely stupid. No matter how you might abhor this business of extermination (and he informed me it was absolute BS that anyone in the SS didn't know what was going on) he said nothing. Instead, he used his new position to secretly organised passes for people to get into Switzerland. He survived the war because he CONTAINED his ideals and turned them to practical, useful purposes. He QUIETLY he put them to use. He even got caught, a few times, but he was an amazingly good RAT and somehow survived to tell me his tale.

There is something very basic that Ideals-orientated people rarely grasp: *Ideals without a useful application are a death sentence.* We need to understand that ideals have their place but being useful has a higher priority. Why? Because when we are dead, so are our ideals. If we have been useful, we survive better in the minds of friends, and some would say in the after-life as well. We need to grasp this very simple basic concept: *Ideals, for and of themselves, do not pay a dividend to anything but our vanity.*

It is not about money, recognition or friends we talk about here. It is simply catching the vibe of waking up each day feeling useful. There is really not a lot that is better than this. (Well, maybe a few things I won't mention here) The Ancient Greeks held that the argument of life and truth was between the Idealist and the Hedonist, but I say the real question to ask is "What is useful".

Being useful gives us a sense of independence, confidence and a better grasp on reality. A man who can fix his own car, build a house, and read a book has a far better chance of being happy in his old age than a public servant who sits on his butt pushing papers around. Why? Because one person is clearing the decks of any personal compromise every day and is living life on agreeable terms with themselves. The other sits in a self-imposed prison, obeying other people's rules. It is this simple: Being useful gives you greater freedom. Being useless enslaves you.

The Mystic Rat Says: *To be truly Free means we experience the Un-Damming of Self in every moment of experience.*

Have you ever noticed how a baby never doubts that Life loves it? A baby holds nothing back. It has complete and total faith in its mother and inherently trusts. However, when a baby is not given love and instead is given hatred and anger, it will die. Die is the wrong word: The baby will simply leave this ugly vibration and return to a happier place. Being useful is the same thing to our Soul as a mother loving her child. Being useless is to live in frustration and anger, and this kills us.

When you are useless, no one will give you respect or genuine affection and you die emotionally. You become just another human blobby-toy wandering around sucking up the jello. Useful people, however, engender respect and develop an aura of strength. A baby is not particularly useful per se, but it does help its family to become useful. IE: Mother must care for it, Dad must earn money to feed the child, etc. The baby helps the family become useful.

But if you were still wiping the bum of a twelve-year-old you would get a little concerned, yes?

What we DO has a bearing on our life and how others react to us. Obviously, the first thing we have to DO is to survive. Ideally, we survive in a way that is in accord with Life rather than our usual abrasion with it. This sense of harmony tells the universe that you are working with it, and working with the universe really means doing something useful. Get it? But maybe you are a blob with no idea and no place to start to grasp this 'being useful' business. Well, start by doing something useful. What could be simpler?

QUES: *Why DO you exist?* Any ideas? (Please, no deep philosophy. Being a good RAT means to keep things simple) No ideas yet? I will keep it simple.

ANS: *We exist to become USEFUL to life.* "Wait a minute," you say, "Useful to life? Are you suggesting that Life needs ME? I thought it was the other way around?? How can Life need ME?"

That was quick! You are doing better than I expected. These are sensible thoughts. These are the types of thought that will help you solve the puzzle box.

Life is about consciousness. Life IS consciousness and Life (consciousness) is in us, around us, running through us, part of us, and part of our environment. Every native culture knew this and yet we clever people called them primitive, superstitious fools for this simple faith: the belief that Life spoke to you through nature, the land and through all things living. J Allen Boone in "Kinship with all life" speaks of how life runs through all life and communicates in ITS way with all things. I have found in this notion a profound understanding and a far greater truth than what is generally presented in the manufactured world of religions and philosophy.

For thousands of years, the spiritual people have asked "How do I awaken? How do I become Enlightened? How do I find God?" Well, one day we wake up and realise most of the answers to all of the above revolve around the notion of becoming USEFUL. There is a Secret Equation written in every person's heart. It goes: *Consciousness flows in exact proportion to the size of the usefulness provided for it.*

So if you want Consciousness, if you want to Awaken, then simply become USEFUL in some way to someone or some thing. *Useful = Purpose = Freedom*

Useful! This is the keynote word that strikes the Chord of Purpose. USEFUL is what attracts Consciousness. Becoming USEFUL fills the heart with being, which makes your world complete, which makes you more useful. Usefulness is the bait you lay in your heart to attract the NOW, the single Drop of Life.

Here is where your RAT comes in, and it is where your RAT will save you from yourself. You see, simply put, your Inner Rat knows when something is a dead loss, when it is useless when it is full of lies, and when it is false. So, if you happen to notice that the ship is sinking, LEAVE!

Your Rat wants nothing to do with this, not for any high ideal, but because it prefers to PLAY. It prefers to play in the sandpit rather than sit in school learning social sciences about what it 'should' do. Your RAT knows that Play = Freedom, and that the Social Shoulds are chains. Your RAT is that brat inside you, you own personal Bart Simpson. It may seem rude and disrespectful, but underneath the apparent and callous disregard for tradition, there is a mine of USEFUL stuff. Your Rat is all common sense, practicality, and no-nonsense see-it-like-it-is reality. But do NOT expect a heart of gold or a nest of sweet ideals, do NOT look for 'nice' when playing with your Rat. Your Rat has but one goal, survive.

Rats are not so smart as they are sensible. They are not so Loving as they are aware of the natural equality of Souls. (In time you will discover that this is a very powerful thing) Rats desert a sinking ship in the same way as you avoid a restaurant that serves lousy food. It just makes sense to not go there. You would be a fool to go back to a place where they can't cook a decent steak, yes?

So please, can you tell me why on earth do you keep going back to old attitudes and habits which sabotage your life?

As an Example: I had this fellow, we will call him "Sam", stay with me for a period of some weeks. It became clear in short shrift that he thought his way of life was right, and that my way of living was wrong. He even declared the writing of this book to be an utter and complete waste of time. It puzzled me because the man was a depressive who depended on pills to get by. He had lost his house, his job, his wife, his entire life to the many stupid decisions he had made. I was essentially looking after him, and being insulted for my kindness.

It was terribly obvious to any who saw from outside this mans limited viewpoint that the fellow was in complete drift mode on life's ocean. It was equally clear that he would never see the lack of a rudder in his own life because his own rudderless self-conviction (that was the cause for the problems) was what he thought was his saviour. It was so obvious to me, yet do you really want to pull a person living on a thread aside, and snip it? This would destroy the last vestige of pride they had left.

Seeing the Obvious; it's is a powerful phrase. When we are finished with you dear reader you will see how powerful a thing the OBVIOUS truly is. Learning to see the Obvious is the greatest gift you can give yourself. (Apart from losing the obvious and falling madly in love) Let's put aside that delightful madness for the moment and look at what your RAT will help you achieve: The Obvious.

Once more: Rats DO desert a Sinking Ship. And that is the SMART thing to do. It's a lot harder to survive in life and feed a family when you are DEAD, yes? So what is this negative concept of the RAT getting off the Sinking Ship? Au Contraire mes amies! It is very obviously the best course of action for survival.

Dear Reader, what I will show you in these coming pages will possibly shock you. It may certainly surprise you, and for some on the edges of respectability it may come as a relief to understand how they have already chosen to live is OK. The message is simple: *It's OK to be a RAT*! That's the core message I am here to give you. It may not seem profound, let alone worth the cost of admission, but that's how it is.

So, what is a Rat? How do you find it? And how am I going to give you this message in a way you will understand? Well, I cannot. I simply cannot give you this message, for the same simple reason that my former house guest could not see his own problems and thought everyone else had the issue.

Your own conditioning will prevent you from seeing things clearly. The best I can do is to give you some thoughts, try to make it fun, and hope that you catch the message in the same way you catch a cold: You wake up one morning and you realise you have got it!

First, we have to start by recognising where the conditioning hides inside us. Our social and emotional conditionings form the core of the logjams that block us from being free. A clue: *It is not about finding anything. It is all about getting rid of those blocks and logjams inside us.* Quite apart from the pun I could not resist, this is why I called this book: *RATOLOGY: Way of the Un-Dammed.*

The greatest single source of internal logjams come from our upbringing and the process of socialization. So let's look at the social sham.

Think about it: It is the holes that give Swiss Cheese its character, importance, and place in the world

Social Values = Sham + Necessity

"If you want to be thought a liar, always tell the truth." Logan Pearsall Smith

In the next few chapters, we are beating up on the socialization process and the way we have to deal with the hand-me-down notions we have been given as children, and which subsequently become accepted as our reality. It's a bit to plough through but if you can cope, the message will become clear.

In life we all have an invisible question hanging over us: Do we join the tribe or follow the beat of our own drum? The obvious tells us that socialization has institutionalised us to some degree, but what can we do about it?

We need to look at where things start if we are to understand how to end them. So, where and how did we first lose the natural flow of our being and get dammed up with shoulds? The primary area of concern is socialization, but let's not forget sexualization as a core factor. Let's look at society and its values and how we slot in with these things individually, and then we will look at Sexualization.

I used to love calling up random telephone numbers from the phone book when I was a kid, and asking the person if Mr. Wall was home. They would say "No" so I asked if Mrs. Wall was home. They again say "No" and I reply "What! There are no Walls at all where you live?" They, of course, say "No" - So I say "GET OUT - Get out before the roof hits you!"

It was a favourite game, that and calling up people with Jewish names, asking in a very German Accent if they wanted to contribute to the Nazi Youth Movement. Very Politically Incorrect of me, yes?

The plain truth is that almost everything you have ever been taught as being 'correct' is a sham, a mock-up that gets you to behave according to the Rule Book of your society. However, it is also necessary. We invent 'walls', which are the internal Rules of Conduct. Every should is a brick in an internal wall. The walls define what to do in a given situation, how to speak, how to behave, etc. These rules (we imagine) keep the roof from falling in. Yet imagine a building without walls, and you get the picture.

When I was young, a show came to town that had a curious exhibit. A blank polystyrene form, roughly in the shape of a head, had a film projected over the 'face'. It appeared to make the head come alive and start talking. You could see the fake head, and yet it still looked real.

Even so, it was a sham. The majority of what we believe is like this film, a projection of a hand-me-down patchwork of notions derived from the systems of belief that fell into our lap from other cultures and ancient times. These are played over your child-self and now they now appear as your present beliefs. Think about it: Our beliefs are simply what we believe to be true, but our baby self - the blank slate - believed nothing of the sort.

At heart, the framework of our life is largely a lie, a fraud. It's no one person's fault. It is just a snowball of notions that got larger as it rolled down the hill. You started out great as a baby, but as we all roll down a slope largely full of crap, like a dirty snowball we all end up at the bottom well and truly covered in shit.

A Liberal Education at Harvard has the following as the noted goals: *"Individuals should learn to think for themselves. They should be skeptical of pre-existing arrangements. They should break free from the way they were raised, examine life from the outside and discover their own values."*

It sounds great, but this is an institution speaking of breaking free from institutionalisation! Please note that it starts with "Individuals SHOULD learn ..." What more can I say? The reality is that we are ALL institutionalised to some degree. We are all raised in cultures where only set behaviours are accepted. Because of your low 'round peg in square hole' fit-ability quotient, in order fit in you had to think and feel in ways that often oppose what was natural to you.

I had a friend who was an extraordinarily talented artist. Teresa painted things with pristine clarity and could even do miniatures. But she felt she needed a qualification, so she went to art school, where she was ridiculed. She was told "realism is dead" by people who are were unable to do what she did. My friend felt very insecure and tried to paint their way, but no matter what she did, it always came out as something recognisable.

Finally she got really angry with it all and for her final exam just threw paint at a canvas, then presented it, saying, "Is THIS the sort of garbage you are looking for?" Her teacher was impressed and passed her with honours.

Institutional thinking is presented as the secure base on which ventures are built. Tell that to Galileo. It sounds great as the dictum comes down from on high as to what is IN and what is OUT, but the facts remain there is just so much wrong thinking in society that it begs the imagination as to how it could possibly continue. I guess our not so beloved Terrorists think along the same lines because this is the same reasoning they use to justify blowing people up. Like my short-term guest of the last chapter; self-conviction in our personal truth despite the obvious and contrary evidence is pretty damn common. What isn't too common is common sense.

The Mystic Rat Says: *We always believe in our belief.*

This brings us to ask the obvious question about seeing through the illusions: *How do we see the Obvious?* You would imagine the obvious is, well, obvious. But this is rarely the case. It is like those 3D picture books - It's all just a jumble of dots until it comes into focus, and then it seems clear and obvious. That's when we 'get it'. You either get it, or you don't.

There are three things that are certain in life:
1. *We live many fictions in our life and we call them truth.*
2. *We believe in so many truths that are really fiction.*
3. *Unless this is obvious, it is worth nothing to you*

Think for a moment about the first two statements, they seem the same but they are really quite different. The first is our experience, the second is our perception. It is the combination of these two that cause the Fixed Belief. A Fixed Belief is that which dwells within us as an unshakable certainty, one that defies all argument.

A simple example: A bricklayers experience tells him he makes money through hard work and that's that. That is his EXPERIENCE. But he has also been taught by the attitude of friends and family that working class is his culture. Combine the acceptance of his status as Working Class (Perception) with his work (Experience) and his reality becomes a statement that reads: "Don't expect to be more than a bricklayer"

His neighbour might become a Doctor, and the woman down the road may become a Surgeon, but his fixed belief will hold him in place as a Bricklayer despite all the very obvious evidence that it does not have to be this way.

The Mystic Rat Says: *Experience + Perception = Reality*.

However, when we alter the experience or the perception we enact change upon our reality. Doing things a little differently - This is the simplest way to change our reality. But this is far easier to say than do.

Change the experience, give the bricklayer a job as a banker for instance, and things will change for a time, but he will most likely fail. Like a rubber band, a person will generally rebound back to what they 'know' to be true. Even if by some stroke of fate he remains in the Banker position, he will still tend to see everything he does as a different way of laying bricks.

Change the PERCEPTION, however, and everything shifts. If a Bricklayer gets a job as a Car Salesman and makes three times the money in his first week, his PERCEPTION might alter and he might say "Hey - I can sell cars!" This shift of attitude can get him out of 'bricklayer' thinking and accordingly he will change his reality. When we see the obvious, we change our perspective.

True perception is all about becoming something more rather than less. A good deal of this book is about you and your ability to first SEE what is in front of you (The Obvious) and from this point allowing our inner Rat to guide us through the change of perception about yourself and the world around you.

The Mystic Rat Says: *Change perception and you change reality.*

Changing our perception is the hard part. Why? Because we need some common sense, and not many people want to be common! The hard part about altering our own view of ourselves is not so much as doing it, is as easy as changing a shirt: The hard part is WANTING to. It is the easiest thing in the world to change is our way of looking at things but we do not want to. Can you possibly suggest to me why?

My former house guest had a life that was a complete disaster. Everything worked out badly for him, he drove a crappy car, had no girlfriend, he even was in debt to his few remaining friends.

Yet he still believed 'I' was the one who had the problem. And who can say, maybe he is right! Maybe I am the short-sighted one here.

Of course, I was the one living in the luxury house on acreage in the middle of town with two Porsches in the garage, raising the family and enjoying life - But maybe this was all a dream and he was right.

Generally speaking, we are all just a little bit Myopic, Miserable and Misinformed. It is not entirely our fault. We have been programmed at every turn by authorities; starting with parents, but running through every aspect of society with the warmongers, priests, and politicians. Like willing sheep, we have obeyed the bark of the dog that runs us because if we don't we might get a nip on the heels. Woof, go left. Woof, go right. Woof, stop here. We obey because it is easy to obey and for the fear of the consequences of disobeying.

Fear of Consequence: This is part of what Dams us.

Socialization occurs because of the institutional energies around us. We are the good cucumber who gets pickled by our environment. The 'pickle sauce' of conventional thinking creates structures of fixed belief and patterns of behaviour. However, we can break down the institutions inside us by learning to see things more clearly. But in order to do this, we need to move past the obscuring lens of fear, guilt, and shame.

We need to let go of our fixed perception of how things are in order to see how things are!

However, the problem is we are INSIDE the puzzle box. It is very hard to sort a jigsaw when you believe you are one of the pieces. We need to think OUTSIDE the box, to be BIGGER than our circumstances - then we can start the journey to personal freedom.

Trust your Inner Rat to sniff out the Cheese of Destiny

SEX and SEPARATION

> *I can remember when the air was clean and sex was dirty.*
> *George Burns*

Socialization is a process of instilling a set of Shoulds. The first stage is to train you to speak, go to the loo, wash yourself, etc. The second and more injurious to the psyche part of socialization is designed to contain the enormous powers that are unleashed during puberty. Ah, puberty and the SEX thing. We think we are OK as kids then a whole new ball gets tossed into play. We go from children versus the adults to boys versus girls, and vice versa.

I had over 80 teenagers rock up to my place on my youngest sons sixteenth birthday party and I witnessed first hand the curious process of control that somehow keeps everything in its place. Girls off their face on some pill were going up to boys saying, "I have a boyfriend, and I shouldn't do this, but I really want to kiss a boy!"

Their friends are pulling them away, reminding them that they HAVE a boyfriend, or it goes the other way and their friends are joining in. One girl, with breasts bulging out from her very small bra, came up to me saying, "These boys are so coarse. They just call us girls sluts. It's really disgusting!"

Odd, I thought, this girl is wearing next to nothing at this party and I was fairly certain she was advertising something, but maybe I got the message wrong? Perhaps she had almost bare breasts because she wanted the boys to see her pure heart?

Now, as I just happened to be writing this book at the time, I felt it was appropriate to say something - But really, what can you say? It is pretty obvious why she dresses that way, and why she gets the comments, just as it was obvious why she was coming up to the older man. She wants attention, which in puberty translates to sexual attraction, which translates to power.

But the 'shoulds' hold her back and leaves her with just a flirtatious expression rather than being a full-blown orgy girl. This is, obviously, not such a bad thing for her future husband. In the end, the only sardonic comment (which I knew would fly high above her head) I made was "They shouldn't act that way, should they?" The irony was entirely missed, of course.

The socialization process helps contain the wild energy of puberty. It is also where the real blockages start to embed themselves and cause life-long suffering for individuals. The 'Shoulds' that hold us back from complete abandon are, at this point, necessary. A young mind does not grasp the effect their actions have on others, so a degree of containment is needed. But when you start to grow past the need to have external discipline applied to your thinking the same blockages that got embedded at puberty are still there, blocking you.

Sex and Separation: Sexual activity defines and proves the gender separation between the species as much as it forms the process of connection that teaches us our boundaries, our manners, and defines our behaviours. In other words: Communication skills are a necessary-to-learn bridge-building activity if we want to get some sex. We learn this through non-verbal and verbal signals, which in turn will hopefully form the path to positively releasing the pent up frustrations of growth that are unleashed in puberty.

However, the nature of our upbringing is such is that this almost never happens easily, if it happens at all. Most people NEVER learn to bridge the gender gap and so sex and sexual activity remain for them proof of separation, rather than the natural state of connection. Obviously, sex, beyond survival of the race, is an ideal process of union but the reality is our internal blockages tend to prevent this.

Now I am not going down the road of listing all the blockages and how to deal with them. We don't have the time nor enough pages in this book for this. The point we need to grasp is that IF you feel generally separated from the opposite sex, it is because you have childhood blockages that in puberty became a fixed wall.

Shakespeare's "Midsummer Nights Dream" is one of the best explorations of this subject and is recommended reading. In an argument about whether someone is a Lover or a Tyrant, Bottom Exclaims:

> **The raging rocks**
> **And shivering shocks**
> **Should break the locks**
> **Of prison gates**

This is a way of saying that true, passionate love will break us free from the prison where we sit as tyrants over ourselves. That's why I say the only better thing then an ability to see the obvious is to fall madly and deeply in love. *T'is truly better to have loved and lost than never to have loved at all.*

So WHY are these girls not throwing off all their clothes and having an orgy? It is not just the upbringing, because the passion of Puberty will break this up if left to its own devices. The peer pressure to conform is the cause. EG: If your friend will sex any boy at the party, then she will also sex YOUR boyfriend, so it is self-interest to keep your friends in line. It is for our personal security that we retain these invisible rules and regulations, thus keeping ourselves in line with the social norm. But I ask: *Where did the Wild Things go?*

Where has the true worship of Dionysius gone? Why has the drinking and the drugs taken over, but not the sexual abandon? The simple answer is; because our passions make it so. Jealousy, attachment, fear of loss, insecurity, poor communication, ownership issues, etc. etc. All these negatives roll up into a ball of crap that tells us to keep our friends in line to stop them going for OUR partner next.

When Captain Cook got to Tahiti, his sailors were amazed at how free the women were. There was NO repression and the girls slept with whoever they wanted. Unfortunately, this freedom stirred up the jealousy inside Cook's men and they started to become aggressive and ugly. Imagine that: even in paradise, our passions come forward to disturb the joy.

Why do I mention this? Unresolved blockages, specifically sexual ones, will not just ruin our communication with others, they will destroy our natural connection to life, and create hell from the stuff of heaven. Blockages create separation, isolation, unwanted aggression and emotional poverty. All those boys down the bar wanting a fight? It's all repression, fear and blockages they are trying to knock out of the way.

The baggage of 'shoulds' hangs over us individually like a depressive cloud of concern. Take more than 90% of people on anti-depressants and teach them to renegotiate their 'should' agreements with life, and they will perk up within thirty days. Most will no longer need their prescription medicine for depression. (There are hormonal and physical forms of depression that are not so easily treated, of course)

Instead of dealing with our blockages and repressions, however, we get on a millwheel of confusion and generally seek external remedies. Specifically, we seek things we do not have, believing this to be a cure for what we DO possess. (blockages, fears, and concerns) Because we don't like what we have got, we look for something else. This might seem obvious, but people rarely see things in clear terms such as this.

In truth we 'could' seek deeper states of being. This is something we already have but have not yet realised - Yet we don't. We pursue dreams and in the process become enslaved to the pursuit. Sex is a driving force that pretty much enslaves the senses. By chasing tail, we end up chasing our own tail.

We have all seen a dog doing this, and occasionally they DO get their own tail. He thinks he got something, and he DID - a sore tail.

The Mystic Rat Says: *In Western society we worship sex but find separation. It's a sorry tale of chasing tail.*

Practicing acceptance of an unlovable soul is not an approval of their profanity or base desires, it is the recognition these exists and must be dealt with. Greed, lust, vanity, anger, and attachment are the big 'wants', the primal forces ruling the heart and mind of the majority of folk.

These show up clearly in relationships. We can hide these things from our social connections, but it is much harder to disguise our driving forces from our partner. Here's the thing: If we feel acceptance, rather than judgement, we are more able to let them things go and move to a deeper place.

Why Authority?

> *"What's brave, what's noble?*
> *Let's do it after the high **Roman** fashion,*
> *And make death proud to take us."*
> Shakespeare

Why do we blindly obey the rules of society? It's not just the threat of punishment from the courts that stops us, it is ourselves. There is some part deep within us that believes authority needs to be obeyed. Yet we also hate being told what to do! We are often torn between the two desires: Run or Fight - Obey or Rebel.

There is a very real and basic urge we all possess to OBEY. Just as we have another urge to REBEL. They both come from the same source, our parental influence. All our physical senses are trained from the get-go with an authority figure that feeds us, supports us, and clothes us. We are used to feeling helpless in the embrace of authority and even when we 'grow up' we still tend to become a helpless kitten whenever a strong authority figure appears.

But when puberty arrives, everything is turned on its head.

At age fourteen, after ten years of obeying what others did in church, (sitting, kneeling, praying, standing, etc.) I decided to just sit there. To my surprise, no one paid any attention! They kept going through the ritual, and the fact that I ignored it made no difference to anyone. That was when I realised that the *first choice* we make for personal freedom is simply not to follow the crowd.

The power inherent in all forms of authority exists because people will do as they are instructed. Authority rules! We all see the 'talking heads' on the TV and for some reason, we tend to believe them. Every day, as Media Authorities, these people are handing out ideals and beliefs which they themselves do not practice. We know this, but we still watch and listen.

"You need ethics and rules to feel safe and secure?" our TV and Political rulers will say - "Sure, we have batches of them, fresh and unused. How many do you want?" They the good shepherds who exist to shear the flock, yet the flock knows it needs to be shorn. Blessed by the Lord of Ratings, media specialists hand out indoctrination! Like the cane in boarding school, everyone gets a dose. The world of Media, Politics, and Religion give out unwritten rules of behaviour like free show bags at an exhibition. Well, they seem free, but once you wake up to them, you soon discover how expensive they.

HINT: The Mystic Rat Recommends: *Anytime you want to believe what any media person, politician or priest say, chant 'Weapons of Mass Delusion' to yourself to awaken from the hypnotic slumber that took you to that belief.*

Many so-called Social Authorities are now Tools of Mass Deception.

The Warlords of Mass Delusion have always been with us. They come in many disguises, yet like Dictators such as Hitler and Mussolini, they only become transparently obvious when we stop obeying the dogs they employ (the ones that are herding the sheep to the abattoir) and start to see the obvious. Seeing the obvious - That's the first step in awakening your Inner Rat.

Do you remember when many people in the US thought invading Iraq was a GOOD idea? Now, almost no-one is saying this apart from the loony fringe of Neo-Con intellectualism. How on earth did anyone get the notion that Saddam Hussein posed a threat to world peace? It seems insane now, but so many were hypnotised by the beating of war drums that they just didn't see it. Rah Rah Rah, beat the patriotic drum and let's go get that slimy Iraqi toad.

Now that the green glasses are off and the Wizard of OZ looks ordinary. In fact it now seems incredibly stupid to have gotten involved at all. In the meantime, the 'War on Terror' has turned the US administration into a new terrorist organisation with rendition, drone attacks, Guantanamo Bay. Administration has moved into the right-wing of the White House!

Iraq was made into a flashpoint. But tell me this: Can you remember when your perception of things in Iraq changed? At some point, most people seemed to think it was OK to go into Iraq and sort it all out. Many presumed it was about oil, but overall, the media had everyone cheering more Go than No.

We had an evil Dictator who wanted to take over the world, so maybe it was a good idea, yes? Apparently, he was going to destroy the world, just like the Twin Towers. (Rah Rah Rah, off to war we go) For some reason, people at the time were completely unable to see the obvious.

Now it seems overt to most that it was a beat up by the Neo-Con right-wingers, whose agenda before coming to power was the invasion of Iraq. The Twin Towers simply provided a gift-wrapped opportunity to feed the US people the lie the Neo-Cons wanted them to swallow - the lie that said a war in Iraq was necessary.

The propaganda machine that created that war has now faltered. Even Republican Senators now think the whole thing was a dud and a waste of money! Like Vietnam before it, the people have slowly opened their eyes and started to see the **obvious**. In the end, Governments just follow the public decision. And what does seeing the Obvious really mean? It usually means we are getting the crap and BS out of the way in order to see reality. Seeing the Obvious really means you have become UN-DAMMED in that area!

This is a good thing. Even if it has to be beaten out of us, it's a good thing.

The Mystic Rat Says: *It is more difficult for a serious man to put his tongue in his cheek than it is to enter into the Kingdom of Fun!*

Ratology: Getting Un-Dammed by seeing the Obvious.

"Sometimes the first duty of intelligent men is the restatement of the obvious." George Orwell

The Obvious is Obvious. As an example: It is pretty damn obvious that if there were no OIL to protect in the Middle East that the US would not have bothered to go there. After all, there were a lot of terrible governments abusing millions of people in the world, but where was George W Bush? We KNOW the Iraq War is about having a foot in the door of the Middle East. All the blather to the contrary barely dents the sides of common sense and even the most red-necked freckle-faced yellow-bellied dog lover knows it.

We are starting to see the OBVIOUS in this arena called Iraq. This is yet another proof that finally, the world is ready for Ratology.

So, what does seeing what is obvious do to help us? Seeing the obvious is seeing reality. Here is the entire book in a sentence - Inside you, there is a faculty that sees the obvious in all things. It is what RATOLOGY calls your RAT. Your RAT is your REALITY ATTENTION TRIGGER. That is all it is. It's that hair-trigger of awareness inside you that smells where the crap is.

In most people, their Rat is soundly asleep under layers of convention and compromise. However, wake it up and things will change. When your Rat is awake you will experience the **Hallmarks of Consciousness**:

1. You will discover your path, your truth, and your light.
2. In doing this, you will realise that you are Good Enough
3. You will then understand how all your past moments are like bricks, and that you can re-stack them into a more useful form, and
4. In doing so you will create a new house for your consciousness to live in.
5. You will then more fully appreciate this incredible gift called Life.

Seeing the Obvious is to see reality as it IS. This is important because only this is what gives us a new perception, and from this, we discover a new reality, a place where we grow up just a little bit more. Growing up and seeing the obvious means we tend to make fewer mistakes. This means:

1. We buy a home at the right time
2. We take a job that has better prospects
3. We choose a partner who helps rather than hinders us.
4. We raise Children with greater awareness and perception
5. They raise children who are free
6. We all get a better, clearer, and vastly more honest society

All we have to do is to grasp and understand our Inner Rat. This is just the first step, of course. Seeing the obvious of itself does not cure us of our real problem. Oh, that's right - I haven't mentioned our real problem yet, have I?

The Mystic Rat Says: *Our REAL problem is our sick addiction to rules, whereby we want to be told what to do by an authority.*

Like a child, we like to believe. We WANT to believe, we NEED to Believe. Despite our cynicism and doubt, we WANT to believe that our elders have our best interests at heart. We need to feel the person we vote for has some sort of clue as to how to run the country. We have to believe that things will get better, or we would all commit suicide right now.

And here's the weird thing - most people who are in authority believe they are doing the right thing. Even when they are killing Monks in Burma, the rulers of that country are convinced they are doing the right thing. Society, for the better part, is a case of the blind leading the blind.

In the past, we have willingly accepted the guidance of those whom we *believed* would look after us. And for the most part, this is what parents do. But in life, we quickly discover that most people are really just looking after themselves. People will say they have your interests at heart, but really, who wants to look after you? Even our parents and loved ones, who generally DO have purely our interests at heart, usually have hooks and conditions tied to their love. It's not a conspiracy, everyone has personal limitations guiding their actions. Your Mother means well, but really she wants you to be the person SHE wants you to be. Your Father will be proud of you according to HIS standards of right and wrong. Family is important, but so is freedom and independence. Are we prepared to let it all go and grow up? Growing up means we lessen our reliance on external authority - But most do not really want the terrible burden of freedom. They need to believe someone is looking after them. You might call it God, or you might call your local dominatrix, but people LIKE being contained within a safe set of predictable rules.

The simple truth is that Governments and Religions and Universities and used car salesmen are not interested in helping YOU - Governments and Religions would become dysfunctional if they actually sought to help each member of the society they are (supposedly) responsible for. A University would not function if it catered for the slow. A used car salesperson would starve if they actually wanted to give you the best deal.

Governments (and all institutions) exist to feed themselves. Otherwise they would starve and die and you would have no-one to govern you! Religions are not here to HELP you, they are here to fleece the flock. (And surely the flock is happiest if it is shorn at least once a year, yes?)

Self-Interest is the Law. It is the One True God of the practical man.

Your boss employs you to make HIMSELF money. If slavery were still permitted, he would fire you and buy slaves. Know and understand this and start to work out your personal relations along the lines of self-interest. If you do, the paradox is that you will have a better marriage, get a better job, and make enough money to be more generous.

Do you want Humpty Dumpty to become functional again? Well, the first thing to do is distrust all the Kings Horses and all the Kings Men. Why? Because they couldn't put you back together again! Remember? (No opposable thumbs on the horses, to begin with) Humpty Dumpty in real life was a murderous cannon who killed hundreds of men, he was a canon that served the Royalists. Humpty had no free will, no choice to act independently, so maybe he jumped! Perhaps he committed suicide to get away from his slavery?

On this subject of Slavery, it's back with a vengeance and indeed has become the new dynamic in the world of commerce. What? You are surprised? Tell me, do you have a Mortgage? Then you are a slave to the bank. Sorry to be blunt, but that's how it is. You have chosen to have restricted choice and limited independence because you have chosen to have a debt. And if that's OK with you, be happy about it.

At least you have an end point for your chosen position. The real question. The whole point of seeing the obvious and freeing ourselves from external control, is a very basic self-evident one: **Are you doing what you want, or what you must?**

Summary: Authority and the trapping of respectability are veneers - An image used to control things. On the surface, this is good because it keeps the various cracked eggs in society together and functional - But it is important not to internalise external authority. This is when we start to imagine that others know better than ourselves what we must do in life. To crack the illusion we must practice seeing the Obvious in all things in our life. When we see the obvious, we ALSO discover what we need to do in any situation.

The New Slavery - It's a Question of Money

> *Our forefathers made one mistake. What they should have fought for was representation without taxation.* Fletcher Knebel

Iron bars do not a prison make. Most people are slaves to authority and to their habits - Slavery still exists, it has just changed its face and become more insidious. Right at this moment, we are facing possibly the worst financial crisis the world has seen since the Fall of Rome, yet it remains completely invisible. This is NOT the financial crisis of 2008. It is connected to this, yet that is but a small part of the problem.

We are in the midst of a greater disturbance to the fabric of society, one that will cripple the energy that created the Renaissance, yet so one seems to be taking any notice. What are our newspapers telling us about it? Nothing! Where is the clarion call to arms, in order to stop this evil from destroying what is left of Western Democracy? An invisible plague has swept into our culture and we are destined to be in its grip for generations.

We are experiencing the fall of Western Civilization right now. The re-run of the collapse of the Roman Republic is playing out once more before our eyes.

But it is not Barbarian Invaders that are doing this, it is our banks. It has taken hundreds of years, but finally, the BANKS have taken over and enslaved the Middle Classes. There is a subtle yet powerful 180-degree turn in the World of Freedom we experience in the West. Once, if you had money, you were free to choose what you wanted. Now it is the paradoxical OPPOSITE!

With the apparent gift of wealth, Banks (Uniting with Government Tax Policy) have lent out enough money to enslave the one class of people who set us free from the Tyranny of the Church: The Middle Classes! via the Merchant Princes, the Merchant class gained their independence from the Catholic Church essentially because they had money. Money paid for the energy of artists and musicians and sculptors. Money is what allowed Da Vinci and Michelangelo to create - to be acknowledged and, in this process, open up possibilities for young minds to imagine something new.

It was this creative force, funded by free and independent middle classes, that broke up the complete control the church had through the Dark Ages. We freed ourselves from autocracy during the Renaissance but we have now willingly trapped and cornered ourselves within a virtual financial slavery to the Banks and corporate brokering.

And HOW did this happen? It is surprisingly simple: *Taxation without representation.*

This needs to be explained. Our society is full of hidden charges that feed Government and quasi-government offices. No matter what government you vote in, the taxes you pay will never lessen. Go on, vote in a different government and watch how nothing changes. Your money is being leached, abused and used - spent in areas without you having any say about it.

This started with World War One, which drove personal taxation through the roof. Prior to World War One, there was a personal tax rate of 1% but now it can be anything up to 70%. But tax is not used for revenue in the way people think - Tax is used as a lever to direct money to specific areas of the economy and one of these main areas is getting you to take out a second mortgage.

Only a few people know how to live in Western Society and not pay personal tax to the government. You can do it, legally and ethically, and it is fairly simple to arrange but there is a risk - Tax law is such that if you are accused of wrongdoing by the Tax Department, you are effectively deemed guilty until you prove your innocence. Plus ANY Western Government can change the Tax Laws, backdate them, and then jail you for what used to be a legal tax deduction under the former laws. There is no comeback.

Don't laugh. It has already been done, many times. Habeas Corpus means little when you are already guilty before you enter a plea. Tax-wise you have fewer rights than an inmate at Guantanamo Bay.

For "Joe Six Pack" there is only ONE SIMPLE AND LEGAL WAY to avoid this heavy taxation. (I presume you don't want to become a drug baron) This is to take out a second mortgage. Your investment becomes your tax deduction and suddenly it appears that all this tax money you used to pay is now deductible. Your tax is now going into YOUR portfolio. It looks great. Your former 'lost' tax money is now buying you an investment house! However, this 'gift' enslaves you to the chains of the Bank. Which is fine if all goes well, but will it?

You are handing your fate over to the whim of the economy. And we all know the economy goes up, and then down. Thus you are giving your financial future over to those who CONTROL the economy. IE: Government and Banks. Tax is being used as a weapon to effectively force you to take out a second mortgage, but who controls the cost of your Second Mortgage? Oh dear, it seems that the Reserve Bank is now holding your purse strings. What's more, you have no vote what-so-ever on what the Reserve Bank will do to Interest Rates, or who runs it, or what it does with its revenue - All these people taking out a second mortgage have effectively elected the Reserve Bank as their Government.

The Mystic Rat Says: *Tax is now a weapon of the State and it is being used against us like a cattle prod, pushing us in the direction of the slaughterhouse.*

This book is being written in the Year of the Rat: Oct 2007 – Dec 2008. Tight now Global Markets are taking a tumble supposedly because of Sub-Prime lenders who took in VAST sums of cash in return for granting highly suspect mortgages. What is more, this same greed is reversing the former "generosity" of banks and the lending capital is evaporating, propelling us inexorably towards recession and hardship. This is the story we have been sold. It's not correct.

Sub-Prime was just a catalyst of a far deeper concern - the deregulation of the derivatives market, which was a direct consequence of GREED. Further, the money the Federal Reserve is using to 'Bail Out' the banks is really just going back to itself in repayments that would have otherwise not been made.

Confused? We need to stop here and get a brief overview of how Money really works. Money is a Liquid Asset. It is a river of cash that flows through the banks, yet it is a river without a source because the money you borrow doesn't actually exist. When you put in a mortgage a valuation is done. This goes to your bank, who shows it to the Reserve, and they say, "Look, the country is now worth $(The value of YOUR mortgage) dollars more, so Iwe can release this into the economy." So they give the seller the money, or more correctly, they give you the debt. The money doesn't actually exist.

It is Money from Nothing created on the basis of a piece of paper and the belief that you will enslave yourself to repay the debt. Why do we need to understand this? Money and debt are the currency of existence in the West at the moment and we need to have a grasp on what this is about if we are to learn the rules and thus learn to free ourselves from its slavery.

In 1879 the total cash reserve of the US, which included Gold and Silver coin as well as cash and cash certificates, was over $144 Million. Of this $99 Million was lent out. (New York Times, Jan 21, 1880) This means that if all loans defaulted in the US (Which could happen if there were an invasion, etc.) the country would still survive. This is pretty much the ONLY reason the US survived the civil war. Having cash and assets in reserve meant that the country could still trade and thus recover from the shock and expense of the war.

Of the $144 Million in Reserve, only $99 Million dollars was in circulation. Most of the Federal Reserve was classed as "Species" which was Gold and Silver Coin. These were REAL Coins of Gold and Silver as well as Gold in reserve. This was what was meant when people referred to the Gold Standard.

But the US moved off the Gold Standard. It moved to a fictitious standard of "net worth" rather than real value. This is what the book "The Wizard of Oz" is all about. (OZ is a direct pun on Ounce, which was abbreviated to "oz" in the old terminology - Green glasses = The Greenback)

Let's put the result of this change as statistics rather than general concepts.
1. In 1998 the net cash money (monetary base) available in the US was $525 Billion.
2. By 2002 the figure had risen to $640 Billion.
3. That is an increase of $115 Billion Dollars in circulation, yet during the same period, the agreed net reserve **dropped** from $178 to $162 Billion.
4. THEREFORE: The US lost $16 Billion of reserves, but floated $115 Billion in available cash.

In other words, there is a net effective cash increase of over $130 Billion in just four years. What does this mean in real terms?

This constitutes an INVENTION of over $32 BILLION DOLLARS A YEAR despite a LOSS of Reserves. This is NET CASH, not total reserve, and of course, this amount is paltry compared the spiraling debt - but it tells you the direction things were going in. *(Author Note: This was first written in March 2008, just before the Financial Collapse)*

In anyone's language this doesn't make a whole lot of sense, does it?

To date, the bailout by the US Treasury is getting up to over One Trillion Dollars. And how do they bailout loans that have defaulted? It is done by inventing the money. To balance the books and work in with world accounting practices, Governments invent the money they need. Of course, too much invention and this generates a loss of faith in a currency, which creates inflation. Yet the US consistently spends more than twice what it earns, and has done so for DECADES. Add this to the debt created by the War in Iraq (on top of the Ten Trillion in national debt) and it all starts to look like nonsense.

Now we look on the Reserve Bank side of the equation. Despite the rumours, the Reserve Bank is NOT privately owned, it is owned and run by the US Treasury. Yet, the US Senate has no real control over the Fed. It is an animal that has a mind of its own. If it says there's too much liquidity, it dries up the money source. (Liquidity effectively means the CASH FLOW being spent in those areas that directly feed the commercial wheels of the country.)

Let me translate this for you: What the term "Too much Liquidity" really means is that people are spending money in areas that sends cash to China, or otherwise out of the country. This results in a constriction of monetary policy (in order to stop the bleeding) by causing LESS liquid cash to flow into the system. This is NOT an increase in Interest rates, though this is another basic mechanism used to control cash flow, it is simply a process where money is not created at the same rate as it used to be. In other words: How DARE you want a cheaper air conditioner!

The "Fed" and Government combined seek to control where you spend your money. It does this in two ways:

1. Via Government Taxation Incentive. This drives your money towards cars and houses. This causes liquidity to stay in the country. This is all done with interest rate policy in conjunction with Governmental Tax Breaks.
2. Via increasing/decreasing Interest Rates and Cash Reserve allocations. This controls spending by taking away the money you MIGHT have sent to China, and putting it where it belongs: In the Reserve Bank coffers.

Administrators long ago figured out that in order to keep your country prosperous you have to control the Cash Flow. Business is one thing. Business gives jobs and activity which in turn garner taxation and generates economic activity, but it is the mortgages and loans (in tandem with the HUGE money market that follows these) that are the real driving forces behind money circulation.

It may sound like madness let loose, but the system works. It's all fine. Everything moves through a process that involves countless small checks and balances and it works out in the end.

There is only one rule: *As long as people keep spending, it all keeps working.* But what happens when there is a bump in the road? (And we know history proves that there WILL be a bump) The facts are simple: If consumers this year in the US spend just 3% less than last year the whole country will slip into recession. And what does this mean?

Two normal options: Mortgage prices go up, house prices go down, and the dream home becomes a nightmare. Or, mortgage prices go down, house prices go up, and the dream home lives up to its name. But this time, the cards are stacked so mortgages go down, housing prices go down, and the dream house has to be sold for peanuts, leaving you bankrupt.

The Bump in the Road

Folks, we have come to the bump. Soon enough it all starts. With the US down it's dominos away! China produces less because there is less demand, so China buys fewer raw materials. That means jobs get lost in mining economies all over the world. THIS means that the second 'tax deducting' mortgage that our $150K a year miner has taken out is now a problem. He is laid off and a second mortgage is suddenly a very large liability he cannot afford - So the house gets sold at any price to get out of it. And I do mean at any price because on the open market a LOT of houses are getting sold off, so the prices are well down. And when your neighbour's house sells under the hammer for 30% less than yours, your equity dies as well.

So the subsequent bankruptcy spreads a loss of value to ALL the neighbours, and thus all house prices plummet. This means that every one of those valuation certificates that every mortgage is based on is now worth a lot less. To keep it simple, the net result is that to maintain the value of currency the Reserve Bank has to remove as much cash as it can out of the economy. This is when the real collapse comes.

THIS is why the US Treasury bailed out the failing banks on Wall Street. It knew that to withdraw cash meant that the wheels would fall off the circus wagons and the show would grind to a stop. So they created MORE money to buy back worthless investments, because they figure it will cost more not to.

So boig business is saved, but let's face it, if your house is now worth less than the cost of your mortgage, you are going to be less interested in paying it off. We start to think of Bankruptcy as a solution - This is where it starts - The noose tightens, the fear takes hold, then the DEPRESSION hits and people stop spending. This kills the economy and puts it into a tailspin. Finally, the stock market collapses, jobs dry up, and inflation goes on a spree.

And what becomes of those Second Mortgages taken out by once prosperous miners and tradesmen who sought to lessen their tax? Well, you got no job so you don't need a tax deduction, so it gets fire sold.

Why do you think they call it a MORT Gauge - A Death Gauge? Face it, people, we THINK we are free in the West. We believe we have rights and freedom, but we do NOT. We are trapped like a fly in the web of commerce and should we try to leave, the spider will come along and EAT us.

Let's suggest an example: If you default on your bills because someone died in your family, your credit cards will be killed, and you die financially. In worse case scenarios the house is taken, or your credit rating is so badly affected that you cannot to even RENT a house anymore.

Suddenly you realize how the third world lives. Without CREDIT and CREDIT WORTHINESS it is very hard to survive in Western culture.

You want to survive, so you learn to JUGGLE your Credit - Using Peter to pay Paul, as they say. This is a reality for many in today's world. We have entered an absurd way of life where Credit Cards, that imaginary money provided at 15%, has become the New Reality. Credits cards are fast becoming the new slave lords of the modern world. We all know what happens when one card is hard to repay. You get a new card to do a balance transfer in order to get the interest down and get some more play money. Then you run them BOTH to the hilt - Which means ANOTHER card, and so on.

And you wonder WHY you are not happy? Do you wonder WHY you reach for the anti-depressant pills? Your whole life has been contained, restrained and inflamed by sets of invisible controls. Your whole cultural existence has become a Pinocchio puppet show where you think you are free to become a 'real boy'. But the NOSE keeps growing and the NOOSE keeps tightening with every new credit application you fill out.

That damn NOOSE that keeps growing is like the Social Lie that runs your outer life. You have to LIE in order to keep getting more credit. You have to manufacture stories that make the Credit Card companies happy. You NEED to tell lies to get more credit because without it, your life as you know it ENDS. If you want to pick up the girl, take her out, you need a Credit Card for the restaurant. You want a new car to impress your friends, etc. etc. It all requires Credit, and you end up "running in your own debt" as Emerson put it.

We are all tarred with the same brush to some degree. Some have better cash flow and sail the financial seas OK, but when everything starts going pear-shaped no-one is safe. We are all tied to a thousand social, political, governmental and financial rules and regulations that have us stuck like glue to the millwheel, and if the millwheel fails, we all go down. That is unless we wake up and work the system to OUR advantage. And how do we do this?

It's so simple - Get out of debt.

We have to break the credit slavery cycle. Let's face it, in most people's life their job is now a process to keep the little treadmill of finance turning. Our jobs are often BORING, UNINTERESTING, and just plain SAD but we cannot stop the millwheel because if we do the house of credit cards will fall.

Shop Shop Shop

Usually, we look to escape in other ways. We look for EXCLUSIONS, interests, activities outside our normal routine, and SHOPPING. Shop, shop, shop, and get more debt. Folks, I hate to tell you this - But getting excited as you wait out the last 10 seconds to buy things on Ebay is not really living. Yet for so many people it IS. Online bidding, shopping, these are the new adrenalin highs. If you get nothing else from this book, remember the simple Jewish adage. *Credit for Necessities, Cash for Luxuries.*

There is a curious Law in the Business Bible called, *The Commercial Law of Disposal.* It reads: *People Love to Buy, so help them.*

We love to buy things. There is a tape inside us that says: *You have heartache? BUYING is the Aspirin you need.* All business counts on the fact that the consumer will feel happier when they BUY. All advertising targets this response, yet my personal research has shown conclusively that almost every self-made rich person has a polar OPPOSITE response.

Rich people HATE to buy. They HATE spending money and will bargain for the lowest possible price. They will walk a mile to save a dollar. They are made happy only when they get something well under market value because they know they can RESELL this item for more than they paid for it. They are PRAISED for frugality! People worship Money, thus those with money are worshipped.

For the rich with a golden-touch reputation, wealth can become a self-fulfilling prophecy. Donald Trump went into partnership with an Australian Millionaire (Rodney Adler) to buy a hotel. Word spread out that Trump had bought in the Caribbean, therefore people started looking at the purchase and the general area. Whatever Trump buys is always worth more than he pays, so the Caribbean must be about to boom. Within weeks of them signing to purchase for $55 Million, the Hotel was resold to new buyers (with NOTHING done to it to improve net value) for $89 Million.

That's 34 Million Dollars profit before the contract settled. It cost Adler and Trump absolutely nothing - ZERO - to pocket $34,000,000 in cold hard cash.

Insane? Crazy? Wake up people, this is the NORM for highly successful people. Their success creates an aura where people rush to follow, hoping to get a little of the magic aura for themselves. But there is no magic. It is simply a story of the shepherd fleecing the flock.

The Commercial Law of Profit reads: *Buy Cheap, Sell Dear.* If you just practice this simple rule, your life will improve.

However, the punters have NO idea. Why? Because they are addicted to buying. The rush and adrenalin of the PURCHASE is the new high. Ignore the

Laws of Economy, forget the reality of repayment, just BUY. Spend and feed the wheels of commerce with your lust for trinkets and don't forget to sell Manhattan Island for some beads while you are at it.

People laugh and think how stupid the Indians were for selling off Manhattan for a few trinkets - yet, here we are, selling our Soul for a buzz on Ebay.

Don't worry because the value of your house is going UP. It is all getting paid for by the rising economy. YES! The Rising Economy is the new omnipresent, all giving God of choice. Of course, the house price that goes up can only buy you another house that has also gone up. (Read "A Connecticut Yankee in King Arthur's Court" by Mark Twain) Prices 'going up' are meaningless unless you own more than one property. The reality is that when you take commissions and taxes into account, you are actually worse off when house prices increase UNLESS you move to a cheaper area. But what if the property market goes DOWN? Oops! Double Whammy and Catch 22 all rolled into one.

(May the ever present God of Commerce forbid)

But is there is a way to beat the Laws of Economy as we know it? Is there a way to mysteriously grow rich and free from the constraints of social rules? Rather than make life easy on myself and just say "NO", or worse, just give a simplistic "Yes" - I say, "Depends on how well you get on with your Inner Rat!"

Not everyone is trapped by the consequences of the Social Lie and the Laws of shoul. There are a few adventurous ones who are outside the square, do what they want, and live life on their own terms. Almost without exception, these explorers (in business, travel, etc.) are those who have learned to adjust reality in some way to suit themselves. Rather than be confined by what they experience, most travellers of this type have learned the Art of Bending the Rules to suit themselves.

And here's the REAL message: *Without fail, these few who are FREE are people who are in contact with, and are listening to, their Inner Rat.* They may not recognize the terms I use, they may not imagine this is what they are doing, but in my study of people who are successful and free and living outside the square, I have noted one constant - They trust their Inner perception and instincts - and they LISTEN to their Alarm Bells.

This alarm bell, dear reader, is your RAT: Your **Reality Attention Trigger**. This is the part of you that does not accept face value. It is your Fire Alarm, it is your signal light, and it is your one true friend in a dark world of lies and deception.

Your RAT is that part of you that, literally, smells a rat. It is that part that has antennas that go "Hmmm..." and knows something is either not right, too good to be true, or really worth looking into. Your RAT is your saving grace, your doubting Thomas and your Devil Self all rolled into one.

Unfortunately, most of us ignore our RAT and prefer social nicety and political correctness. As a result, we pay far more than we need to for just about everything we get. We pay financially, emotionally, spiritually and mentally for a failure to listen clearly to the alarms bells within us.

As a result of our failure to listen to our RAT, Some go overboard and fall into an ocean paranoia while others fail to look up and drown in convention.

But we have OTHER friends in here. We have one specific helper who works alongside your RAT - an inner person who will show us the light at the end of the tunnel. It may surprise you to hear me say this, but your Humour Button is your Saving grace. The JESTER within guides you to your RAT. It is your John the Baptist to every Holy Cheezus in Waiting.

Summary: *If you want to get broker, trust your broker.*

FACT: We all Lie. It is a given that, in our present society, the lies we are taught have osmosed into our being. The problem comes when we are unaware of our lies. This is when they can take over the driving seat and start directing our lives.

The Paradox of the Lie reads: No Truth is greater than the Lie that is believed by two or more people. (It can take a while to grasp what this one means)

The Jesters

"Truth is often the jester"   Anon

My siblings used to say: Funny 'ha ha' or funny 'strange'? How we define humor is based on how it connects and, when it DOES connect, it changes the world. Surely you Jest? I jest not, dear reader - JESTERS are the social and political early warning system that speak of troubles about to arrive. Go on You Tube and see how many of today's woes were predicted by the Funny Men and Women of the world. (George Carlin in particular) If you are unhappy, it is often because you have a shortage of irony in your veins. Listen to the voice of humor within and you shall be saved, my child.

Your Jester can be the mouthpiece and cohort for your RAT. The Rat senses the trouble, then the Jester can pour oil on the troubled water and allow you to escape the situation - even if it means putting a match to the oil! It knows: Irony is mightier than the Lie that defines you.

Let's look at the context in which I speak - In times of old, the jester was the mouthpiece for the disgruntled parties in the Kingdom. He was the Satirist who was paid to give out the message when any member of the court had gone too far because, in a dictatorship, if you spoke up personally your life was on the line. Many Jesters experienced a short existence as a result of their subversive humour. An old Jester was one with quick feet, not just a quick mind.

People would pay the Jester to put a twist onto something. An example: When someone was about to get themselves a bacon selling franchise at the local fair which would disadvantage a butcher in town, that butcher would pay for the Jester to mock the fellow and make him look foolish in the eyes of the King. This gave the butcher a shot at snapping up the deal for himself.

That's the real role of the Jester. He is the intercessionary agent between the *Powers that Be* and the *Powerless that Want.* When Catholics want something from God, they pray to Mary or Jesus, so THEY will go ask him. This is a good way to discover the Rat Within, pay attention to your Jester, and IT will find a way to knock on your Inner Rat's door. Find your jester within!

I liked David Letterman! He was a full on court jester. He was up there prodding the rich and powerful mercilessly and loved getting ordinary people to do whatever he asked them to. He played, twisted, tweaked and hammered away at the American funny button for years. He is also the person most responsible for giving writers fair pay and helping to break the writers' strike of 2007-2008. He was an institution that became powerful because it was FUNNY.

Ain't that a laugh? Laughter is the greatest prayer we can offer the Gods. It is one thing that the forces of the Universe actually pay serious attention to. (pun intended) And it is a NOW thing!

Look at the Greek Myths, they are full of irony and bittersweet truths, but who reads them? Yet Seinfeld - He's worth millions.

Today, Jesters are more in need than ever before. Western Culture is dying from a serious illness: It is simply getting FAR too serious, with laws against scratching your butt, picking your nose and eating your earwax. (Cats love licking earwax!) People are dying emotionally and financially as a result of ever-increasing seriousness that emanates from a central authority as CONTROL.

I was watching a TV news piece where a reporter was grilling the organizer of a fashion show for using a thirteen-year-old model in a catwalk display. "Don't you realize that there are men out there who think this is a perfect opportunity to express their sick desires?" the reporter accused, rather than asked.

The person in the firing line was clearly on the back foot. Of course, if she had a fully functioning RAT she would have been fine, and would possibly have quipped, "Yes, it is possible a paedophile might turn up. Of course, given the huge size of your audience in comparison to mine, I consider that it is far more likely that a sick person will be getting their rocks off watching how YOU are reporting on thirteen-year-old models. So tell me: How DO you feel about this?"

Sadly, the Jester's natural ability to flip the question to a reversal was not awake in that person. They were completely bamboozled and caught dead in the water, thus they looked GUILTY. In truth, it was an opportunity in disguise and they missed their chance to SHINE.

And that's what the Jester is for. *The JESTER is one who has learned to radiate the light of perception in a light-hearted way.* The JESTER is your ticket to freedom. It is the mouthpiece of your RAT and the eyes of your Soul and, what's more, this archetype has been in EVERY civilization and in EVERY culture.

He appears as the Trickster, the Fool, the Magician, the Gate Keeper: a thousand disguises, but always as the observant one that sees through the crap.

A woman we shall call Miss "C" had a very powerful Jester. It made her almost immune to the normal social mores, but she had married a high ranked Jewish man. This meant she was EXPECTED to convert to Judaism so that her children could be considered properly Jewish. Well, she happened to be German, blond-haired, blue-eyed and completely disinterested in being Jewish.

Respect for personal boundaries is never a strong point of any religion. In this case, the woman was pursued with phone calls, letters, and demands from wailing women in the street. Finally, her presence was demanded at a meeting of the "high up" Jewry, all women, many of them prison camp survivors.

They railed against her for her stubbornness, saying she was damaging their future. How could she do this to her children, but more importantly, how could she do this to THEM? They showed her the tattoos and said how much they had suffered, and WHY was she causing them more suffering. You would be amazed how many people crack under the guilt trip and say "OK - let the kids be Jewish"

However, Miss 'C' was unimpressed. Why would she join a religion she didn't believe in, for sake of what THEY believed?

So they continued *"For 6000 years we have been persecuted and suffered, and you sit here, looking smug, ignoring everything we have been through! How can you do this?"*

Finally, she spoke, *"6000 years of suffering, and you want me to put my own children through this? This is not a good sales pitch. But I have to add, I really thought that you might have recognized a pattern by now."* And with this, she walked out. She said it with humour because she saw the irony of what the women were saying and, maybe one day, one of them would as well. I doubt it.

They are too caught up in the Serious Illness that has them firmly in its grasp. Her husband left her, of course. He had a large inheritance at stake and would not swim too much against the tide. She figured she was better off without him.

The point is these people were trying to coerce her into making an agreement, using their personal stories of suffering as a rationale. She saw through this and pointed out the obvious. And, of course, now that I say this someone will accuse me of being anti-Semitic, which is just another form of controlling guilt trip.

Let's not play Semitics, folks - let play Semantics!

It is pretty obvious that I am simply talking about how we create our own reality and seek to impose this reality onto others in order to reinforce our own beliefs, but I can already see the TV journalist asking "Why do you hate Jews?" Remember, if you want evening current affairs rating success, your job is to twist up the truth and present fiction as fact, and fact as fiction.

Now, if I told this story without humour I would be lining myself up for attack by opposing forces. I am fully aware that many people suffering from the 'serious' illness will genuinely fail to grasp the irony of the above, but Res Ipsa Loquitur, your Honour. Obviously, someone asking you to join their religion because they suffered for 6000 years does not really make sense!

Remember: Humour is your shield, Irony is your defence, and barbed observation your weapon against the controllers and zombies of this world.

And that's just about everyone. People try all sorts of things to get you to do what THEY want. There are a hundred subtle traps to catch the sleeping soul in the webs of commerce, social conditioning, and familial expectations. You need to have a functioning sense of humour and a firm grasp of Irony to survive it.

Humour allows you to duck the arrows and slings of outrageous seriousness. My father always said 'Humour is the grease that oils grating opinions".

It's Shakespeare: *To be funny, or not to be funny, THAT is the question?*

Summary: *Finding the Humour in any given thing is a powerful way to free up your life. It also helps others around you feel free, which has a very positive knock-on effect with relationships and finding a sense of harmony in life.*

Irony releases Truth from the Absurd

"Irony is the hygiene of the mind."   Elizabeth Bibesco

How might I be thankful for the Catholic Brother who decided to cane me when I was eight years old? To explain: I had not done my religious homework and, as a result, I was taken out of the class to be given the cane. By age nine they left you in the class, as an example to others of what will happen should they think to stray - but at Eight you were expected to cry and that would be embarrassingly unmanly - you know, like caning a child might be?

I remember it well: The weapon of discipline is poised and about to fall when a strange word, one I did not recognize, popped into my mind. I have no idea where it came from, or what it meant so, out of pure curiosity, I asked, "Excuse me, Brother- What does the word IRONY mean?"

The question quite tweaked the fellow. The good Brother brought the cane down viciously, screaming, "Irony! I will show you bloody IRONY!"

He did - very effectively. I looked it up right after and I never forgot it. To this very day I can spot an ironic situation from three miles. As a note, that Brother never dared cane me again and I am told he eventually left the Brotherhood. Obviously, now I would thank him for putting into my memory such a powerful experience. In Book Two I go into when I was Aged Three and defeated the Kindergarten Gestapo, but suffice to say, my Ratty Friend has been at my side all my life - helping me with unseen awareness at critical points in my life.

Your RAT loves irony. It also appreciates the sardonic, sharp wit that comes from the wry perspective where we doubt everything, trust nothing, and never, ever forgive or forget. This might seem harsh, but understanding the greater hand of the Rat behind our adventures and misadventures tends to leave one in a place of acceptance - but not forgiveness.

Let me diverge for a moment, and point out something few will mention to you. *Forgiveness of others is unnecessary.* Acceptance is important as people do what they do and with acceptance we learn and gain experience. If a person hurts you and they apologize, or they don't, forgiving is really a vanity. It presumes you are above them. Forgiving yourself is the secret.

This will offend some people. Let me paint it a different way - think of ourselves as a radio station, we tune into specific frequencies which then become reality in our lives. Who is the person who dials up the station? That's you. YOU are responsible - YOU need to forgive YOURSELF.

When we forgive ourselves for the negative choices, it allows us to move on to better ones. Further, if we create your own reality, forgiving someone else is meaningless. More than this, to say "I forgive you" is often a silent judgement, a should in disguise, - Just accept the lesson and move on.

But let's stick with irony for the moment.

Irony is the time-honoured tool of the Jester. It provides both courage and ammunition under fire. All true wit uses the razor's edge of discrimination, one that only a sharpening stone of Irony will provide. What's more, an appreciation of the ironic frees us from our own vanities and obsessions and give us the breathing room to appreciate the moment for what it is.

The greatest weapon the Jester holds in his arsenal of humour is irony. Years ago, Bryant Gumbel, an American TV journalist, asked a leading Senator, "Don't you think the US Presidential Race has become somewhat a MEDIA CIRCUS?"

The Senator stopped, paused a moment, then smiled at the ironic question. He asked, "Gosh Bryant, and who do you think is to blame for THAT?"

Spotting IRONY in the moment means you are AWAKE. The alternative is to sit in the pat notions of the great unwashed. Sitting in pat notions is literally sitting in Cow Pats of the male variety. (That's otherwise called bullshit, people)

Of course, there are real issues that are serious and which damage innocent people. There is very little irony with paedophiles who get their rocks off with thirteen-year-old girls, but let's face it, the REAL paedophiles ask the little girls if they have a younger sister. Or, if they are Catholic priests, they may be looking for the younger brother. *Do not laugh!* Laughter removes the weight of your social expectations and obligations - and DESTROYS your sense of injustice.

Irony - If you tell me you are waiting for Jesus Christ to return, I might smile broadly, look at you, and say, "Well, here I am!".

Seriously - we need to see the funny side of things.

Facts are that, at any given point in the history of the world, there are a whole lot of things that are wrong. Does this mean we can't find the absurdity inside the wrongness? Just as every cloud has a silver lining, every situation has a funny bone. If you have misplaced this, look for it beside your suffering bone. But be warned, the funny bone is made from rare irony, which is a banned import in any serious nation.

The New War and our Buying Addiction

At this very moment we are in the middle of a new war - Not WW3 - this time it is called WWW. The World Wide Web is information overload. We are getting attacked on all sides with a plethora of opinions from a hundred different sources, bits and bytes of dislocated opinions. It's not people talking face to face, but talking heads with moving pixels performing a mimicry of life.

This war has come about because of computers and the new information superhighway. There is INFORMATION everywhere and, hot on the heels to try and contain it, we now find there are NEW RULES. Further, as a follow on from this, there are now unpaid TAX COLLECTORS.

"What?" You ask.

Everything you buy is provided by an unpaid Tax Collector, the shop owner. Anything you buy sends a percentage of that little item back to your government as a VAT, GST or Sales Tax. What this ALSO means is that every detail is recorded and going into some computer somewhere. Your entire financial history can now be tracked.

What this does is to make everyone a little bit more serious because now, if you make a mistake in a tax return, you will suffer. You will be fined as it can be proven that you spent the money on a hooker, not "entertainment", and claimed it as a business expense. That's no fun and it's all on computer.

You can even be physically tracked and followed by technology now. Once your name is flagged, everything you do, every time you use a credit card, every time you fill up the car, everywhere you go - it is all being ticked off by a computer. Satellites way up in space can get tagged to your home, watching every person when they leave, and tracking them as to where they go. Big brother IS watching - It's not Hollywood any more, it's real.

The net result of this is a curious one - The increasing lack of personal space creates pressure. It is a stress factor and the solution many find is a BUYING ADDICTION. We are turning into Ebay Junkies. People have always loved to buy, but the net makes it so easy, and cheap. With all the external pressure from Facebook opinions, government taxes, and the huge levels of social injustice the EASY solution is to do the Ostrich and just buy more stuff.

Spending is an aphrodisiac, panacea and confidence booster. Forget dealing with the impossible to solve external world, just spend more.

How does this work, you ask?

Buying stuff gives a temporary high, a way to coax the brain with a buzz. The whole of society has been engineered on the basis that people will buy. Buying keeps the wheels turning. Buying and selling creates the market and a healthy market is a healthy society, or so we are told. The Free Market is supposedly the great liberator of human endeavour.

Control Factors

I discovered an interesting statistic some years ago that completely defies this notion of the free market. During the 12th Century in Europe, the average working week was 15 hours. The average family was well fed. There was a great deal of travelling entertainment and a good deal of disposable income. The people were happy and content, by all accounts, yet there was no merchant class to speak of. Nor was their ownership of property, mortgages, or banks. The Feudal system meant your local Lord owned everything and you paid a stipend, usually a percentage of what you produced, as rent. But your holding was yours as long as you paid this and it could be handed down to your children .

Spin forward 300 years and by the end of the 15th century, people were in poverty, forced to work long hours, cast out from family farms, and constantly feeding the taxes of some government funded war. How come?

Well, by this time we had a Banking System and a Middle Class to support.

And how do you support a middle class? You sell minions crap they don't really need. Add the threat of war, one that will possibly burn down your farm, and your Government can now pressure on people to cough up even more tax.

ERGO: Convince a populace that terrorists lurk around the corner and you can confine them in a room full of regulations (for their safety) and force them to march to the beat of someone else's drum. Doesn't this sound all too familiar? Linger WAR over the heads of the populace and they become docile.

Add to the fact that people are unwilling to argue and fight with establishment because the battle is too overwhelming. For one, they can just print any money they need while you have to earn it. For two, arguing with the State is a little like being locked in a room with a hungry lion and feeding it pieces of ourselves in order to stop the beast from eating us.

Opposing this way of doing things is to actually run a country for the people by the people. Capitalism is fine but it is understood and accepted that happy, content people do not need anything like the degree of STUFF that unhappy people need. So, obviously, the real job of government is to keep 'em on edge. Keep 'em under threat, tax them higher, and get them to spend more

Remember the Cold War? What about the Korean War, the Vietnam War, and Iraq One and Two? Now we have the War on Terror, and I reckon that will be good for at least thirty years. And who pays for these wars? YOU do.

Goddamnit, I need some SPACE to get away from all this doom and gloom! We need a little relief from all this suffering, so let's go buy something! That will give us that glimmer of joy, that small sense of fleeting freedom we want. If I can get that new car, and a better house, I am sure Utopia will be mine.

Summary: *The struggle to survive is often a simple struggle to find clear space to BE. If we understand that clear space is wealth, then we can work to achieve this as a goal. When uncluttered space is not a luxury or a convenience, but a determined goal, we are setting right priorities. Clear space means you have room for new events in your life.*

Negotiation

A sailor on the ocean knows it is ALL negotiation. You have to pick the wind and the currents and set your sails and your rudder in order to make the difference between what IS and what you want. What you WANT gives you a direction, while your understanding of what IS shows the best way there.

Goodbye Utopia – Hello Freedom

"Our life dreams the Utopia. Our death achieves the Ideal." Victor Hugo

We all need to give ourselves some elbow room to breath, to be ourselves, and to just tune OUT of the humdrum. Yet the vibes of modern society are all pervasive. TV creeps tendrils of energy creep through the walls of your home and into your brain. Media rhubarb is everywhere. Your JESTER is the only one who will save you! Only when we learn to see the obvious and employ Irony and Humour in the various situations of our life will we be free. Only then shall the lies of society lose their grip over our subconscious.

But there is a cost! We must sacrifice an ideal or three in order to allow this change to happen. Number One: *We must let go of the dream of Utopia, the concept that there is a perfect world or even a world that is acceptably equal.* Just accept the facts: the world just isn't fair. It never will be anything but a bunfight. Yet, inside this we can develop our own space, our own free zone. When we grasp that this treasure is, of itself, a goal worthy of Kings, then we will come closer to true independence than any 'perfect' world could offer.

Ok - How do we get rid of Utopia? Come on folks, get real. It doesn't exist, there is nothing to remove. Have you ever seen a passport with a stamp on it that says 'Eternal Happiness'? We remove Utopia when we stop telling ourselves lies that it exists. Maybe when you die you will find a better place, but in the here and now, forget the notion. Rather, aim for room to breathe and enjoy your life with what is here right now. Give yourself some SPACE and the freedom you find here is a type of utopia.

Clear, free, personal Space is a worthy goal. With this in mind, and in heart, your Jester will be more inspired. This is the place it loves to live, dance, and breath. Give some space to your Jester and it will excite you. To do this effectively, we need SPACE, an area where your personal self is free of the crap. A sardonic doubt of everything you hear and see in media (which is basically gossip) helps to make this zone a reality. Sitting in this place you find it easier to compare the goals you seek with the reality you experience.

When you have SPACE as a goal, you find breathing room. Now you can ask if a situation enhances your freedom, or detracts from it. This is where the Humpty Dumpty wall is MEANT to be employed: Creating a protection around your personal space, so that the garden within that feeds you is protected. This makes your life simple, clear and uncluttered. This makes it easier to deal with the inevitable ups and downs we all get. If you take my advice and ignore the 'big' goal of perfection, you will paradoxically discover a far more perfect way of living. Or perhaps I should say, a less imperfect way to live.

In a world full of sleepwalkers, the fuzzy, warm, huggy, dream-like Utopia seems a perfect goal. Utopia is the desire for the perfect everything, and it is completely stupid: The perfect marriage, the perfect wife, the perfect family, the perfect house, the perfect job. It's a nonsense.

These ideals are painted as a goal we should seek, but even if you did somehow managed to pull the rabbit out of the hat and magically get it all, you would quickly become dissatisfied. Why? It's Human Nature. We always want more. There is no rationale for this, it is just what humans do. It is why we go to the Moon, why we get divorced, and why we cannot see the wood for the trees.

We just want MORE.

Harmony and happiness are a temporary form of balance which can only grow in a bed of contentment you have watered with smiles. Dreams of a perfect forever, however, sprout from the opposite - discontent and a fear of loss. Utopia and Harmony are, paradoxically, polar opposites.

I do not wish to disparage the person who is hoping for a better life, but you will not find this in a dream of Utopia. It is an illusion, and a dangerous one.

We tend to fall somewhere in the middle: Wishing for better, working for more. When we have worked for something, we can appreciate it for what it is and will be more willing to preserve and hold it. But a 'perfect' marriage? If you DO have a good relationship, you already understand that it is earned every day and that after every short period of happiness we are back at the coal face.

The underlying rule is one of "nothing too much." We learn that being greedy and always wanting more only seems to only provide less, whereas contentment provides harmony - But none of this is stagnant. Life lives at the very edge of uncertainty. Life is a moveable feast, a very vibrant place.

Life is a living ocean of circumstance where anything can happen. Waves of change from shifting tides are a given, and so all of the above leads us to our only true choice: *Do we surf our circumstances, or drown in them.*

Let us presume you choose not to drown. What is the best way to surf? You cannot demand life provide anything, but you can relax and wait for the waves. Let's give ourselves a mantra: *Go With The Flow*. More to the point, do not struggle. Stress and tension creates a rigidity that drowns us. Instead: Less urgency, less stress, more focus, and higher expectation.

The Gratitude Attitude

The Mystic Rat Says: *Perfection equals Stagnation. Less than Perfect is Perfect*

Let me add to this, the gifts and good things come to all, it's just that the greedy, the grasping and the lazy never appreciate them. When we develop **gratitude** for all the small things in our life, then a remarkable and surprising event starts to germinate deep within us. We start to discover we are the creators of our fate, not creatures of circumstance. This may seem innocuous, but it is one of the loudest things this book can announce: *Gratitude opens the door to manifesting true wealth and freedom.* It is so very simple: a deep and sincere appreciation of living invites more life into our lives.

The Mystic Rat Says: *Gratitude is the Great Rat Attitude.*

Gratitude is the right attitude. It is the way the Rat inside you sees every opportunity and piece of luck that comes its way. Do you think your RAT is an opportunist? Of course he is! But he/she is a grateful opportunist, and that's why the opportunities keep coming. Hint: Even if you are grateful only because you know it keeps the door open, that's enough.

Gratitude teaches us HOW to possess things, yet remain free of them. Gratitude allows us to have, to hold, yet not to be OWNED by the object of our desire. All we can really possess is this moment, and a sense of Gratitude for this moment enlarges the experience, makes it deeper, and helps it to last longer. This is true wealth.

There are days when I just look outside, feel the wind, see the sunshine and find myself completely HERE. I know there is stuff to get back to, but the moment is strong and I just want to stay in it. Linger longer, as they say.

I asked Jack Thompson, an Australian movie star who is regularly seen in major support roles in Hollywood, "Jack, you have done a lot, acted, directed, developed scripts, but is there more? Is there anything you most want to do?" We were sitting on the balcony of his country home, and he said: "Sit here, and look at the view." I got the message. Sit HERE, and appreciate the moment.

To have everything, but not possess the internal freedom to truly enjoy it makes the getting of any particular thing a Pyrrhic Victory. Working for something creates the space where it can live (this is what 'earning it' really means) but APPRECIATING it means you cherish your Moment of Victory. This appreciation becomes a habit that trains your mind to look for Victory Moments. Appreciation and Gratitude of this moment polarises you to NOW. As a result of this message you send, live gives you more NOW.

If you don't believe me, look at all those people who win millions in the lotteries. Precious few have anything left after two years, and their lives are ruined. Why? Apart from the fact that the majority of poor people are poor because they don't understand money, many times they are not truly grateful for any luck that does come their way.

Like the person who can't really play poker, they win a lucky pile of chips, but within a few hands, they are all gone, given to people who can play. It appears that their luck deserted them. Like the proverbial rats from the sinking ship, their luck HAS left them. Yes, your Rat can and will abandon you to your fate if it sees the ship being driven towards the rocks of failure. Keep this in mind: A sense of futility is your greatest evil. A lack of gratitude is really a lack of respect for the moment, and it presents itself in many ways. Some of these are:

1. Unmindful purchasing,
2. Lack of consideration for another's space, and worst of all -
3. Deafness to the Rat within.

All of this invites into our moments the greedy little white ants of discontent. These will eat away at the frame of our life, causing it to collapse into loss and despair.

The Tibetans from the Amdo Tribe have a saying, *"As soon as there is joy in the toy, the pleasure turns to pain, and the wheel of life starts all over again"*

Consumers are largely mindless sleep walkers. They are pedaled goods that promise a perfect life, whereas the usual result of getting any particular 'perfection' such as a new car, etc. is the slow painful death by finance. It just keeps getting worse as people borrow ever larger sums to pay for their addiction to impossible standards of perfection.

Buying 'stuff' is often a disguised need for personal space. Dreams of Utopia are generally a fear of failing painted over with ideals of perfection. Appreciating the moment, being grateful for what life brings, these are the things that free the heart and give us room to breath.

Yet in all this, we have not mentioned the great, overriding force that controls the lives of most people: *The Cross of Time*.

Summary: *Perfection is simply not realistic. Allow your failings, allow other people their flaws, and focus on where you are going. Being grateful for the things that go right, and for what we have in our life, this is the most productive tool in the RAT arsenal. Acceptance of what IS, and a Gratitude for same, sets us free to explore our truest desires.*

The Cross of TIME

Time flies like an arrow, fruit flies like a banana.   Groucho Marx

Time waits for no man, they say. You have limited time to correct your attitude towards life before life removes itself from your body. (IE: You Die) Time has become an enemy in our modern world. We are always trying to beat it, yet we know it can't be defeated. And the paradox: Every little luxury we obtain to give us more time costs us money, which forces us to invest more of our time in earning it.

We all know how standards of housing have improved in the last forty years, which is great - But the COST has gone up so much that, for many, the concept of owning their own home is now a dream from the Good Old Days. Legal padding and regulations have increased the cost of subdivision exponentially. What was once a matter of putting a line on a piece of paper has become enmeshed in thousands of expensive rules that all add up to more COST.

Look at Singapore. It increased its population four-fold but kept the same boundaries, therefore everything had to go UP. So what happened? In Singapore, you have to buy space in the AIR. What! Space now costs money! It is true - Nothing now costs a fortune. It's twisty stuff.

However, most western cities are expanding outward. What does this mean? In our ever-growing cities, unlike Singapore, it means a Loss of TIME.

It is so obvious, yet so few see it. Land that is a two-hour commute to the city now costs what land twenty minutes away from the CBD used to cost twenty years ago. (Price adjusted for inflation and wages). Yet it is costing you more than money to buy this block of land, it is costing you TIME. That land now costs you one hour and forty minutes in to work, and one hour and forty minutes out, EVERY WORKING DAY. Overall, your two hour commute now costs two hundred minutes MORE than it did twenty years ago, and we haven't counted the added cost of travel.

What this means is that simple commuting is taking two hundred minutes of every day out of many peoples lives. Just getting to work and back is COSTING you an extra 200 Minutes a day. In any given city over One Million People are losing 200 minutes a day. That's 200,000,000 minutes every single day. That is 3,333,333.33 (recurring) HOURS that go nowhere in every city, in every country, on every day. Can you imagine how much productivity is lost? Can you begin to see some of the real cost of what we call 'progress'?

It is not just money that this new world is costing us, it is TIME. As a result, the space to enjoy even our time is becoming diminished. We are all paying more, and getting less.

It gets more complicated: Population expansion necessitates a degree of added regulation, to make sure everything works. But an addiction by public authorities to rules and regulations has taken hold of the collective government. We have become excessively over-regulated and traffic fines, traffic queues, and petrol bills have all gone far beyond what is necessary.

This is what unfettered bureaucracy does. Your world is made smaller by every decision and requirement made by some anonymous public official. Rarely do these decisions serve a useful purpose and, in reality, many laws are simply a process of people in useless jobs giving themselves something to do that they believe to be useful. Life in the public service is more about finding a personal promotion than finding anyone who serves the public, or even a purpose of any real value. You will truly need your Jester to see you through and help you to survive these eroding values of life.

The net result of all this LOSS is simple: People get tired of it all and fall asleep at the wheel. They get tired of driving their world down the endless highway of regulation, the endless traffic queues as they travel two hours into work - SO, what then happens? The eyes start to close in order to stop seeing the problems that only seem to multiply. The brain goes into neutral, and your mental wheels find themselves convenient ruts to follow.

In order to keep the car running you fuel up on what amounts to nothing - You drink more wine, tell more dinner stories, and spend more time with friends. But your PERSONAL life, the one that is YOURS, is slowly eroding away. It gets worse: As the space to enjoy your life diminishes, the stark, cold, hard reality hits you - You are ALONE.

Your commute time is a bubble. On the train, you are into Facebook, or your I-pod. In the car, you are into your radio. As the rules and regulations close in, we slip into a bubble of self. The I-Phone generation had retreated into their phone. Despite the fact they are in constant communication with everyone, they remain extraordinarily alone.

What happens is that in place of real social interaction, actually seeing and talking with people, is lessened so we have Facebook friends. We begin to avoid reality and discover that relationships, communication, and natural sharing begin to diminish. Day by day, we invest more in the ethereal friends, talk less to real people, and as a result disappear into a prison of ourselves.

It would be OK if we had something to show for it! When we have lots of great experiences hung like paintings on the walls of our being, it is truly marvellous to feel alone in a large room of our self. That is a fabulous feeling of rightness, a sense of presence earned by really living.

But when you are cramped into a room under the stairs with debts larger than the space you have to stretch out in, it just gets ugly. You close your eyes, but all you can dream of is some distant perfection in order to avoid your life. When this doesn't happen the next solution is generally found in a pill or a bottle. Pretty soon, the rut you are in becomes the only thing that is stopping your world from falling off the rails - Do you know the definition of a Rut? *It's a grave without the ends filled in*. At least, not yet!

You fall into the empty space inside. You stop listening to what people are saying, and instead all you hear is your own voice, talking incessantly about what could have been. A thick wall of unconsciousness grows around you, like ivy over an old house, and slowly but surely the childlike vitality drains - You take on that zombie-like half-dead vicissitude of existence. Can you hear the snoring? I can. It's everywhere!

My God (if it/she/he happens to be listening) - It is EVERYWHERE.

Please, read this book and WAKE UP. I am starting to feel very alone here as I type out these pixels. Please remember that your life to date has been a dream and please consider it important to wake up. But even if you manage this, what is to stop those eyelids from closing on you once more? What will you do when the pressure builds up and the hard times come? Are you panicking yet?

The question is: *How do we stay awake?* Simple - Keep your eyes open. That's not so hard is it? So, you ask: *How do we keep our eyes open?* It's simple:

1. *Keep your Jester to the fore*
2. *Look for the ironic, the whimsical, the humorous in life's situations.*
3. *Stop believing that you know anything - and just feel the moment.*

This keeps us awake, this keeps us alive. This way of living keeps us real. This 'awake' state then becomes the fertile ground for your Rat to grow. Grow your Rat with the right food, friend, and it will set you free. And believe me; it feeds on Irony, whimsy and light-hearted humour.

Your **Reality Attention Trigger** (RAT) is that part of you that is AWAKE. It is that which WAKES up the sleeping minions of your Soul. Your RAT rallies the splintered pieces of yourself to ACTION. Your RAT is your HERO, your SAVIOUR, and your FREEDOM FIGHTER.

Yet, even as I say this - you cannot really trust your Rat. Are you shocked? You may well be, but in my view neither can you really trust yourself. Why? We are all fragile creatures, prone to lying to ourselves as we hide in the next corner we have just painted ourselves into. You can't blame God for it, you can't even blame yourself. We simply have been given a curious nature and we follow it.

There is a Garden, nice place, with a tree whose fruit I must not eat. Why? That doesn't make a whole lot of sense. Why put fruit from the tree of knowledge in reach and then say, "You have to remain ignorant!" I wonder what it tastes like?

So, if you must blame anyone, blame Eve - This is the easiest, most convenient rational that absolves you from personal fault. Blaming another absolves you from guilt and stops God watching you. That's how it works, yes?

What? You do not believe me?

I blame you for that, because it's not MY fault.

Time to Pause

All of the aforementioned leads us to a single, solitary conclusion. We need TIME to do NOTHING. We need to make time to reflect, consider and contemplate without the gnawing pressure of achievement or competition nibbling away at the edges.

We need to make time start to work for us, to reverse the dog chasing its tail syndrome, and find a place of secure contentment in the NOW. How do we achieve this? Well, by shifting our focus.

The reason WHY people are chasing their tails is because they believe they have to - When you start to break down your beliefs and find they are mostly air, then your life will change course. We need to take time to recalibrate, to reset the compass, and rediscover what is truly important to us.

In this regard, the measure of how long we can survive WITHOUT something gives us a measure. We can survive without food for 3 months, without water for up to five days, but without air, we don't survive five minutes. If we lose out house tomorrow, how long will we live? We would just go rent one, or move in with friends. If we lost our job, we would just look for another one.

The things we are so focussed on as important really are just details that make life convenient. Shift your focus to things that matter, and what we find is that friendship is a primary importance. Without a friend, mammals such as we are suffer and fade. Family is important. A sense of love and connection is important. A new house or a fast car really aren't.

Try investing your time in recognizing and developing friendships, seek to value the moments we experience, and you discover that contentment will be as natural as the sun shining.

Summary: We waste a lot of time, competing, getting ahead, beating the clock, etc. It is our fault that we cannot see through the illusions placed in front of us, and believe that joining the rat race is the thing to do. But, as my father once said, if you MUST paint yourself into a corner, try and make it a nice one.

God is Dust

> *They say that God is everywhere, and yet we think of Him as somewhat of a recluse.* **Emily Dickinson**

The word 'God' of itself represents an absurd fiction to some and a precious notion to others. However, if we are to have a Way of the Un-Dammed it implies some sort of God-Like destiny is afoot! So, we need to address the issue and better to get it out of the way ASAP.

There is an old French saying that goes: *God is Watching*. It's about the attitude of fear and repression that people get when they suffer guilt and believe they are been observed by some distant authority. Of course, the truth is that no-one particularly cares what you are doing unless it impinges upon their own freedom in some way, but even so, some truly fear that a higher power is watching their every move, recording their faults and getting it all ready for judgement day. This can be a fear of disapproval from the father/mother image in the mind as easily as a distant God.

So 'The Dammed' come to their favourite excuse for not doing what they want to do, *"God (parent/society/friend) is watching"*.

What can we say about God? We must suppose that SOMETHING gave us our nature, our inherent beingness, but what? We need to take at least a cursory inspection of this notion of a God or, if our ancestors are right, of Gods.

Let me suggest something that you may never have expected: **God is Dust**. What was that? Ridiculous, you say? But wait, I have evidence! It's in the Bible! *"From Dust you came and unto Dust you shall return"*. There it is, simple. You are made in the Image of God - And you came from Dust. Logically, God is Dust.

But we can take it further if you wish. Jesus said that the Kingdom of Heaven is within. Everyone says that God is within, so what is left when all is said and done? What remains of your body after 100 years in the ground? Dust! That's what is within. This proves absolutely that God is Dust.

You still think this is absurd? Piffle I say to you! How can you say it is ridiculous? How could you possibly still doubt me? Consider the immutable facts. No matter how tightly you close up a house, tape up the windows, and seal the cracks - No matter what you do - Dust gets in. Dust gets over everything, given enough time. Even those tombs in Egypt that have been perfectly sealed for thousands of years, you open them up and dust is over everything. Obviously, as most of the Egyptians forgot the feather duster with all their artefacts, this would have made life uncomfortable for the Mummies.

Well, now we can clearly proven one aspect of God. Dust is Omni-Present - We can tick that one off. Dust is everywhere. It is in the Heavens, (from dust we came) probably even worse in Hell, (from dust we shall return) and we certainly have no shortage of it here on Earth.

Is it Omni-Potent? Yes! Given enough time, everything returns to dust. You just can't get more powerful than this, can you? Dust conquers all.

Could it also be Omni-scient? Perhaps. We can't prove it is, yet we can't prove it isn't. But given that we already have two positive results, and that the third cannot be disproved, then we may as well count it as a proxy vote. Yes, it is pretty clear - DUST covers all the necessary aspects you require of a God. It appears to me that Dust is at the creative heart of everything. Dust is the Alpha and the Omega: the IS, the NOW, and the HERE in all things.

And yet, you still do not believe me when I say Dust is God? I am shocked, deeply shocked that you could doubt me. Even when I point out it is in the Bible, you still argue I am wrong? Obviously, I have presented an uncomfortable truth, one you cannot reconcile, therefore reject out of hand.

I hear you say, "Dust has no consciousness. It cannot create of its own accord" Well, who is to say this is correct? Maybe God is in the Nano-Particles and merely uses Dust as a vehicle, a space suit of sorts, for living in an environment that is too un-Godlike for its true nature. Dust may be ITS protection. Perhaps Dust is merely the representative of God, or perhaps it is the SON of God? Maybe even the daughter?

You think I am an ignorant fool? Please, listen to the facts before you ridicule. For over a thousand years people have recited a creed (Nicene Creed) that states God has a mother. This is even more absurd than God being Dust. At least Dust is an original, not a DNA replicant. And when we think about this, Dust is born without a mother, therefore it possesses ANOTHER God-Like quality. Surely Dust at least qualifies for a role as Messiah? Yes? No?

I see you remain unconvinced. Good. If you believed Dust was God with a few simple tricks of reasoning, we may as well give up now and sell your bones to the knackery. However, while I would not really seek to explain God in a few paragraphs, I wonder if you caught the curveball that is the REAL point of this discussion? Have you ever wondered why people would reject the notion that God is Dust out of hand, yet accept a hundred other significantly more absurd concepts? People continually take sheer insanity, wrap it up in belief and then call it absolute truth. Do you have any thoughts as to why?

Absurdity is everywhere, yet rarely spotted. Why? For one - You possibly believe that POLITICIANS run the country? What nonsense - Next you will be trying to say the Churches exist to help their followers, or that Big Business really wants to pay you more money because this will help the economy.

The question remains as to why so many people blindly accept so many things as true when they are patently false - and it is also vice versa! - Some things that are clearly the obvious truth, few will accept. I know from experience that Vitamin C lessens the effects of colds and flu - but it rejected out of hand.

We have guiding lights - authorities - that determine what is true or otherwise. It used to be the Church, now it is science, but mostly it is the desire to control the money and attain the power that is the driving force behind it all. We have an authority addiction, a part inside us that bows to the parent OR which does a Bart Simpson and rebels. It all comes down to a few areas in our psyche, less complicated than any psychiatrist would want to believe, yet so intensely simple that it takes a lifetime to come to grips with the reasoning. But in ALL of it, we want to love and be loved. So God may as well be Dust! It changes nothing if it is true or false.

Reason says: Dust cannot be destroyed. Even if you place it into the heart of a Sun and convert it to pure energy, it still exists, though transformed. Dust is Immanent. Energy is Immanent. If we had an authority that said God is Dust, we would have people worshipping the stuff and saying feather dusters come from the devil. The real truth? We may as well believe that God is Dust, or call God an Energy Field, or see IT as a wise Duck which carries the Rock of Knowing. ALL this is equal to the myth of an Old Man sitting on a cloud.

Let's not argue unprovable concepts. The REAL questions about God are:
1. Is it CONSCIOUS?
2. Is it INTELLIGENT?
3. Is it AWARE?

And really, *might we not ask these questions about ourselves?*

Let's look at the obvious - If, for example, you are 'not' A: Conscious, B: Intelligent and C: Aware, then you have very little chance of discovering if anything else is. Yes? Because we can't really recognize anything unless we know what it is, can we? In other words: *Work on YOU before you go seeking God or any other assorted nefariously nebulous, niggling, niceties.*

Let's cut to the chase. Our REAL message here is to stop the notional patterns of belief we have picked up and start with the practical understanding of NOW. And here another curious fact emerges from the Dust of Experience: If we can stop practicing BELIEF, and start experiencing NOW, we will learn how so little of our lives, our feelings, and our thoughts are actually our own.

This will really surprise you when you discover it, but one day, with enough attention on your Rat, you will understand we are REPLICAS. When you do, you will find everything you 'thought' is really a 'tag' - an attachment usually tied to you by a parent or your society. It is all just something we picked up, like second-hand clothes from an Opportunity Shop. We are all wearing second-hand notions, feelings, thoughts, beliefs and opinions.

This gestalt of beliefs, whatever they may be, are exactly what are damming us up. Our beliefs are what prevent us from experiencing the fullness of NOW.

This is one reason why I like Animism, or the worship of just about everything as God. Animists pray to the sun for warmth (fair enough I say) and they pray to the ocean if they are fishermen (Again, quite fitting). If they walk through a forest they pray to the God of Trees, and if they are hunting they pray to the God of Hunting. Really, what could be more sensible?

But our good Christian Society ridiculed these notions and said, "There is but one true God". This was shortly before they started killing themselves as to who owned the correct franchise for that particular God.

I pray to the Poker Gods when playing Poker. I don't know if it works, but at the same time, I sure as hell win a lot of hands that I play. I don't really believe in a God of Poker watching over my cards, looking after me personally and wilfully going against the other players who do NOT pray to him or her or it. But I do 'believe' that when I clear out the clutter of 'believing' (paradox intended) that I see things more clearly. I have learned never to Love my Cards, and I am continually re-learning this, and my praying to the Poker Gods is a way to remind myself to let things go.

But what do I know! Maybe everything I am writing is just another belief of my own playing itself out and everything is an endless loop? The question here becomes *"Where is the Yardstick?"* Is there something we can all measure our lives against? Well, there is a measuring stick, but we need to let go of some of our beliefs in order to see it. May I please ask you to suspend both your doubt and belief for a little while longer? We first need to understand emotions and how they tie us into beliefs - then we can look further.

Summary: *Using notions such as rational and Irrational do not form a good basis to judge things in your life. Everything can be made to sound reasonable, or vice versa. When you meet a persuasive person or walk into a situation where you 'love your cards', you can be swayed into believing nonsense is truth.*

A better alternative to belief is to look at past performance. How did things work out in a similar situation in the past? How did that person deal with things in their past? This gives us a better perspective of how our NOW will unfold.

A Dream of Intimacy

> *What if everything is an illusion and nothing exists?*
> *In that case, I definitely overpaid for my carpet.* Woody Allen

Intimacy is a tricky area to discuss. Most of us would accept that there is a deep level of emotional truth in a mother loving a child, but how deeply felt are the emotions of an adolescent falling in love for the first time? Can we judge one better than the other? The depth of commitment and care the mother gives over many years surely outweighs the fleeting passions of the teen, yes? You and I may think this, but try and tell that to the teen!

First love is an all consuming passion, one where logic, common sense or any view to the contrary will simply not be heard by the person experiencing it.

It seems utterly real, and yet it is a complete dream. I had a real issue with emotion when I was young. I would fall in love with a shadow, but even as I fell deeply and truly and hopelessly for some girl, part of me always wondered if it was real. Was I fooling myself? The real question was: *I might love them, but was it possible for another to love ME?* I was pretty confused by the whole boy-girl thing. In fact, the entire 'feeling business' seemed pretty damn unstable and, rather than me feeling good about things, all I felt were feelings.

I found it easy to be loving, but very hard to be lovable. This is because I was not connected to my true emotional state. I was caught up in a web of untruths: Shame, guilt, and unworthiness were controlling my feelings, not my heart.

At age fourteen I saw a hippie girl on a bus, wearing a transparent cheesecloth shirt and no bra. I vaguely recall she had a pretty smile, but all I could see were those wonderful boobs. I was in love - with them! This was an utter certainty and I have to say, the way she smiled at me indicated she didn't seem to mind my gawking. They jiggled so perfectly as the bus moved along.

This was not my problem: The total and complete uncertainty I felt about everything else was the issue. With the girl on the bus, I could be fairly certain my passionate love for her breasts was a safe, one-way street. I didn't expect a return of this abiding affection. But when I had to meet and deal with another, form a relationship, cope with peoples emotions, it was very different. The looming question lingered that dammed everything us: I could feel all this love and lust, but did she feel anything in return? Could she love ME?

My conditioning told me I was unlovable, but I wanted to be loved. I had no way to cross this gaping hole in my psyche. No one whispered into my ear the simple secret that we know as intimacy. No one told me open and honest fears are normal, that having concern that another will love you is normal, or that felling unworthy was OK. I had no way to bridge the chasm, no way of knowing whether this love I felt was returned, and I felt terribly isolated in my own head.

The real problem was that this tsunami of feeling I was experiencing was drowning out my ability to LISTEN to the signals coming back to me from the object of my affection. Where was the path to connect my dream of love to the reality of relationship? I couldn't find it because I was blind, deaf and dumb to the NOW, and completely wrapped up in feelings. They OWNED me.

Yet my feelings emerged out of genuine needs, real emotions, and natural desires. Why was just talking to a girl and saying how I felt so difficult? NOW I get it - My lack of understanding of the difference between true and natural emotions versus false feelings was the culprit.

How do we recognise a true emotion from the thousands of feelings that pass through us? Shakespeare in Sonnet 116 gives a pretty good definition:

> Let me not to the marriage of true minds admit impediments
> Love is not love which alters when it alteration finds
> Or bends with the remover to remove.
> Oh no! It is the ever fixed mark
> That looks on tempest and is never shaken;
> It is the star to every wandering bark,
> Whose worth's unknown even though his height be taken.
> Love's not times fool, though rosy lips and cheeks
> Within its bending sickles compass come;
> Love alters not with his brief hours and weeks,
> But bears it out, even to the edge of doom.
> If this be in error, and upon me proved
> I never writ, nor no man ever loved.

True emotion stands alone, yet it is not a solo affair. It forms the 'marriage of true minds' that creates harmony. True love is a song that seeks to turn melody into harmony, sincerity into intimacy and each moment into an eternity. True emotions are a resonance within you that naturally and wonderfully turns your solitary note into a harmony when a like resonance is met.

True emotion has INTIMACY as it's cornerstone. It is pivotal to the nature of true communications that people share in an intimate trust. This natural closeness is what breaks down fear, shame, doubt, and uncertainty.

I had a good friend, she had many lovers during her life, and in her middle years, she explained to me, "I discovered that being 'in love' was a lie, but that being loving was my natural truth." Then she paused, and said, "What most people think of as their emotions are just unclear feelings, shadows without substance, things that pass like the wind. But I discovered within myself a sense of permanence: I knew I was a loving heart and that loving was my nature. I no longer fall in love, but I do grow in lovingness."

I see this in tribal groups, a sense of connective ambiance where each shares an intimacy with another, though no words are spoken. Some Aboriginal tribes have such a depth of intimacy that they hear each other's thoughts. An elder explained to me how his grandfather did not understand how the white people had the will to live, because their existence must be so isolated and lonely.

Feelings that are without Intimacy are selfish creatures that want to possess the object of desire. They are self-serving dreams that cut us off from the flow of life, whereas true emotions fill us with the experience of sharing. Sadly, the majority of people in Western society do not understand the difference. This brings us to the first question: *How DO we determine what is a mere feeling or a true emotion?*

But talking 'about' emotions is that it not exactly thrilling. Dissecting things with the mind holds as much excitement as a science experiment, but it is important we understand this element.

So, let's do our best and get it over with as quickly as we can. Like ripping the wax off the bikini line, grit your teeth and just get it done!

Riding My High Horse

I have a High Horse
Everyday, walking from my Ivory Tower
I go down and saddle up.
Then I ride out - past the shadows of humanity
Safe and secure in my certainty.

Then one day I saw a fair maiden
I rode towards her, and got down to speak.
Only now I was a peasant - like everyone else.
Weeping for my loss I climbed back on my horse.
And sighed - Once more, safe and secure.

But so lonely

EMOTIONS: Real and Unreal

"Where we have strong emotions, we're liable to fool ourselves." Carl Sagan

I find it curious that one of the world's leading scientists advised people to distrust their emotions. It is not unreasonable, because many of the emotions that we experience are really just passing feelings - an echo of our natural state, a little piece of truth bouncing off our beliefs and prejudices. Add to this the fact that most of our beliefs are essentially incorrect and those echoes we listen to become more distorted. It's a very tricky situation. How do we determine a real emotion from a manufactured feeling?

One thing is certain, people living in false beliefs and false emotions rarely think they are wrong. I can go up to the person who firmly holds the truth that the Earth is flat, show them photos from space proving it is round, and they will be good, yes? We all know the answer is: "Yes, it is round - like a plate!" Logically, if they realized how wrong they were, they would no longer believe.

Seek to tell a 'true believer' they are wrong and most will argue to exhaustion their case of personal rightness - based on what they believe to be truth. That's fair initially, but then, when proven wrong most true believers will ignore this and fall back onto the view of their tribe, saying, "But We Believe". Group agreement is the basis for their continuing belief. It's a Catch 22.

It's not just the fundamental types who do this, but these are an easier example to put up in order to isolate a condition. We all know fundamentalists adhere to fixed positions: ascending bodily into heaven, rapture, all manner of absurdities. When you ask them "Where do you actually go when you ascend bodily into heaven?" they respond "Well - God knows". I mean, let's face it, we have telescopes that look to the ends of the universe, but we haven't seen a Heaven Planet reported as yet. Yet this means the quantum of Zero, Zilch, Nothing and Nada to the believer. Heaven is in some other dimension - it's hidden from the eyes of the profane - God will show us in his own good time, etc. Who knows, there may even be some truth in it!

But WHY do we need to believe in our little absurdities? It's just so simple, we are all Humpty Dumpty Post Wall, and our beliefs are what hold the cracked egg together. *Our beliefs give us the sense that we will survive.*

Here is the difficulty: Most persons belief in any particular 'truth' is usually an emotional entanglement of both fact and fiction. It's a half-truth / half-lie that creates a self-perpetuating story. This story whispers it sweet nothings into our ears until, like falling in love, it becomes our REALITY. Look at the Gollum creature in the "Lord of the Rings" movies. This is a perfect example of self-suggestion taking control of external beliefs and creating a perceived reality.

Let us not underestimate this power. Your beliefs are not just mental constructs, as some would suggest, but real and tangible energies that direct your every move. Beliefs are an EMOTIONAL and ENERGETIC condition, which would would be fine if they were not invariably wrong to some degree.

Erroneous beliefs create the main stumbling blocks on the Road to Freedom.

OK, so now we have two problems. HOW do we pick a false emotion or belief? It is easy: *False things are devoid of intimacy*. Yes, I can pay lip service and believe that Jesus loves me intimately, but it is a one-way street. Jesus is not there to love me back. I might imagine he is, believe he is, but he isn't. There is the image of Jesus in your mind, but it cannot hug you, kiss you, or hold anything but a promise. True intimacy needs more than an imaginary friend.

I can feel the stones flying in my direction already. Let me clarify: *True Emotions require True Intimacy to Exist*. Intimacy is not some imaginary flight of fancy, it is a very secure, harmonic state of being. Of course, it is fine to act 'as if' something is real, but until it IS, you are imagining it.

Let me repeat this: *True Emotions require Intimacy*. The intimacy that is natural to the baby and its mother is a truth. We 'unlearn' it in the socialisation process. We can regain it only through the practice of Trust, Honesty, and Respect. The way we find these qualities in another is to develop a solid basis of sincerity and trust in ourselves, and a high level of ethics. Yes, I know I haven't really spoken much about those things, but this is because most people's ethical basis revolves around what they believe, not what they really feel.

To explain, ideals such a nobility, loyalty, and honour are quite useless to the mind and often form impediments to natural communication. They are usually the 'high horse', or aloof attitude, we ride that keeps us distant from each other. Yet these same ideals are ESSENTIAL to the heart. Honesty, nobility and loyalty are the wires that holds the Bridge of Trust between two hearts in place.

Let me put it another way: When we hold a true and open intimacy with another, you have no desire to harm them in any way. You would as soon cut these connections to another as you would cut off your own foot.

More importantly, when you are in a truly intimate relationship with yourself, *your mind and heart no longer argue*. You find that space within that can do a straight business on a crooked road. It as at this point your true emotions emerge, not as some excited pup yapping over every changing moment, but as a deep, resonant hum that comes from within.

Read Mandela's 'Long Walk to Freedom' for a guidebook. He says: *And as we let our light shine, we unconsciously give other people permission to do the same. As we are liberated from our own fear, our presence automatically liberates others.* These words come from a place of deep Emotional Truth.

There is a basic belief (incorrectly based on the Pythagorean notion of rational and Irrational forces) that there is a fight between heart and mind. We have the view that the mind is rational, while the emotions are Irrational. We tend to have the equation: "Logic = Rational" while "Passions = Irrational". A person governed and directed by logic is seen as rational, while the person impelled by inspiration and creative impulse is seen as irrational.

But what little hidden secret do we find in BOTH the rational and irrational? Lo and behold, the RAT. This lies in both the 'rat'ional and ir'rat'ional. It is more than a play on words - when you discover the truth of THIS in your waking thoughts and emotions, all will seem parts of the whole, not opposites at all.

When you grasp the whole you might begin to see how irrational the 'rational' man can be, and how oddly rational the mad artist is. Working nine to five in an office doing a job you hate really is entirely irrational, ye easily justified as necessary for bread on the table, etc. No one can argue the logic, even though the job is killing you. Working on a painting for three weeks which proves to be commercially worthless is apparently irrational, but the person doing it had more fun than the office worker - So where is the greater payout?

It comes down to where we place our focus. If the focus is on fun, the artist wins the rationality of the day award. If it is on money, the office worker wins.

However, the true 'Raison D'Etre' for our existence only comes when we understand what the true emotions are that are driving us. True Emotion is an EXPRESSION of our BEING. Your RAT is one of the few 'people' inside you that can help you uncover your inner motivations and reveal to you your real causation, your real motivations, your real self. We discover this by understanding (not suppressing) our emotions.

Master the Wild Horses

Emotions: They are like wild horses we are struggling to master. We like to think of our emotions as sources of delight, horror, fear, joy, the whole range of human - well - emotions. This is partly true, yet partly false. When we 'feel' sad, we have a FEELING - But is it 'real'? A feeling is NOT a true emotion, but the *echo of one*. Feeling something certainly has an emotional element but most of what we feel is NOT pure emotion. Feelings ECHO Emotion. Feelings for the most part are an emotion bouncing off our shoulds and beliefs. Generally, they are a lie that we feed ourselves on, and are largely illusionary.

Yet here comes the paradox: The Tsunami of feeling that happens when you are in love, in hate, etc. is completely real - in that moment of experience. But as soon as we stop riding the wave of passion, it then turns into just another wave onto the beach. Here's the difference: Pure Emotion is not subject to conditional change, whether by the course of time, or the altering of opinion.

Pure emotion is, as Shakespeare says, 'The star to every wandering bark'

Feelings are not to be discounted entirely, because they are a pointer towards true emotion. Feelings are like the refection of the Moon on the Lake - They always point towards the moon, but they are not IT. On this physical plane, no one is divorced from the effect of feeling, but we can learn to master this element within ourselves by learning to choose the waves we surf. Even if you choose unwisely and wipe out, you are still better off than being continually led by blind feelings.

Let me ask: *Would you marry a complete stranger just because you feel good around them? Would you give someone a mortgage over your life because you felt it might be ok?* Feelings are a bad judge of character.

All surfers will tell you the secret of fun is picking the right wave. They always come in sets and there is a clear message each sets sends about the type of wave you can expect. So look at your potential agreements BEFORE you step into them. We all know how a Wedding Ring turns into the Suffer Ring.

Plus, like any wave you catch, every feeling will have its time before it fades. You KNOW the love you feel for someone will change with the passing of time. True mastery over our emotions only comes when we accept that change is the only permanence. Our security comes by allowing change to occur.

This is called trusting life.

All is just another passing moment of experience. This is how it is, and seeking to keep things confined and safe simply denies the passing nature of the universe. Accept that all things will pass, especially your feelings, and you will discover the true certainty that lies underneath all experience. This is YOU.

When the builders of Temple of Apollo at Delphi inscribed "Man Know Thyself" on the right-hand side of the entrance, they were talking about YOU. They are talking about finding that still certain point within. We might otherwise call this Soul.

In the meantime, we all suffer from the effect of uncontrolled feeling. We all make choices that drop us into the dumpers at some point. And thank God we do. How dull it would be if the world were beige and full of accountants who always play it safe. The world is in flux, yet in the process of accepting change we can find inner certainty - Here we find that the true e-motions are just that Energy MOTIONS that come in waves. We can learn to SURF our Emotional Waves and as a result, get to have ourselves some FUN

Summary: *All things in life are an energy exchange. Tying things down, making them 'safe' constricts the free flow of energy, thus the life we live becomes truncated. Learning to surf the waves of change allows you to take charge of the energy that comes with it. When you are adept at catching waves, you learn from a seat of the pants feel to just know when there is no real substance in what you are being presented. This can save you a lot of time and trouble.*

The Mystic Rat Says: Follow the cheese to your destiny. Follow your nose and remember, the best purpose for your tongue is tasting, not talking.

Playing the Heart Strings

> *"Emotion has the power to attract, where Feelings wants to possess. The desire to OWN drives natural attraction away."* The Lord High Rat

PURE Emotion is a very different animal to the swirling cloud of feelings that sweep us up on the roller coaster. Real Emotion is more of a basic instinct, a sense of portent more than a sense stimulated by happenstance. Pure Emotion has the scent of destiny about it.

Take courage, for instance. Saint Exupery wrote that courage was not found in big events, but in the small, day-to-day details of our life. People think of it as going into a fire and saving someone's life, and this IS courageous. However, real courage is a way of life. It is every day facing what needs to be done, pushing ourselves on despite the fleas of discontent biting at our feet. This is REAL emotion. This is a state where your feelings do not rule you, but where the heart (courage comes from the Latin word "Cour", for heart) carries you on.

There is no actual feeling attached to this state. It is more correctly called an URGE, or rather an Urgency. Despite the associated feelings that are part of a moment, the tide of truth that flows from the heart commands you, involves you, yet leaves you separate at the same time.

It may be as simple as a sigh, for instance. This may surprise you, but a genuine sigh comes from a very deep place within us. Also, a mother's love can be this way. It is a reflex, an undirected, pure emotion that has no conditions attached. It is a state where you just completely wish the Soul that is your child well. It feels wonderful yet it is far more than a feeling, it is a complete reality. Pure Emotion is a State of BEING that flows from the heart. Feeling are fragile creatures, true emotions are robust and strong.

Now, the point to ALL of this is simple: *It is what we DO with this energy that shapes our lives for good or ill.*

Take the mother's love. After the initial urge subsides, the well-wishing sense of absolute love converts to feelings. But which way will it go? Usually, the emotions of love combine with a mental image, such as, "This is my child" more than, "This is my blessing". This can then turn a true emotion into a sense of ownership. Or the mother maintains clarity and simply enjoy the nature of the child, only doing what she must in order to socialize it.

When energies like the *'This is Mine'* concept start to run we get subtlety trapped. As much as we might believe we can own another person or thing, we cannot - And if we try, it will own US in the exact degree that we believe we own it. The main reason for rebellious teenagers is the need to shake off this ownership issue so many parents carry about. "Ye must hate thy Father and thy Mother, thy brother, and thy sister if ye are to find the kingdom of Heaven!" as

Jesus said in the Bible. He is talking about breaking the binds of social conditioning and familial ownership.

All kids rebel to some degree and if they don't, be very worried: They are hiding things. When my youngest son started on this path, which is so completely normal during puberty, I took him aside and said "I am really happy for you to object, to demand things, to say what you think. It means you are thinking for yourself. What's more, I would prefer this behaviour to you sitting and sulking in your room believing you have been done wrong. So object and disagree all you like! I enjoy it."

A few days later he objected to me holding the TV controller. "Why is it that YOU always have the say on what we will watch, huh?" he demanded. I smiled and just handed him the controller. Soon after this he left it on the table and went to watch the TV in his own room.

Ownership is a habit and it is not a good one. It is fine to own your issues or to own up to stepping out of line, or to own the consequences of our actions, but we cannot ever own anyone else. It does not stop people from trying, however. The main reason for ownership is to give a sense you are in charge, that YOU are the one running the show. This is when we place shoulds and restrictions all over those in our charge. The equation runs "Ownership = Control". Which, when you think about it, sounds an awful lot like slavery, yes?

I met a pretty girl at some New Years Eve gathering in Byron Bay, Australia. The place is renown for its free and easy lifestyle and its very 'out there' approach to life. We were getting on well and she mentioned it was her birthday - I started doing a quick number analysis, telling her what to expect in the year ahead. It was interesting and all sorts of things were opening up. Then her boyfriend came into the picture and, putting his arm around the girl, he looked at me as if to say, "What do YOU want?"

It was interesting - the really clear flow on information that was running through my mind stopped. I mean, it just stopped. I may as well have run into a brick wall it was so total. I looked at the guy and said, "Nice ownership issues. Good luck!" and moved on. I started to put attention on how 'owning' someone or something locks up the free flow of energy.

Now I am NOT saying you cannot own a house or a car, but when your sense of ownership goes past the *purpose* for that house or car, the 'thing' can own you as much as you own the 'thing'.

The point is this: *When we stay in the State of Being of Pure Emotion (Love) with the Rationale of Responsibility governing our actions, we do not generate a sense of OWNERSHIP.* Instead, we develop a sense of "land rights" - A sense of PLACE. A desire to protect and cherish what is in our care without the need to nail it down. In this State of Being, a whole raft of negatives simply cannot grow. You cannot have jealousy, small-mindedness or petty desires that need to control others in this 'zone'.

Mother Issues

Of course, I paint an almost impossible world of perfection. In reality, Daddy pays the mortgage, then is off with his mates, leaving Mum to raise the kids as best she can. But for a moment I want to look at the extraordinary dynamic of motherhood, and what it means to you. It is the source of the greatest love, yet also the creator of the greatest, most stubborn logjams in people's lives.

Most of the time, women are exercising their emotional energy to raise the child. Mothers throw tendrils of energy out, they use these like strings on a puppet to direct their child where they wish them to go. These are control wires and when you learn to see them, you see them everywhere. These are the invisible conditions of 'should' and 'should not' that quietly rule us.

Some women, in particular, have mastered the emotional energy and use it to control external events with relative ease. Projected Emotions can be used to shape your beliefs to a far greater degree than you would imagine. And once you are brought to the place where you BELIEVE, you will follow the rut of your conditioning without question. This is the basis of every cult.

Emotion is used by mothers as a conditioning tool. EG: If a child behaves, you love it. When the kitten pees in the litter tray, you praise it. When the child hits another you scold it. It's basically Pavlov's Dog for the most part, with affection or anger used in place of food. But it gets far more subtle than this.

I have seen women who have learned to 'fan' their sexual energy to control men. They play out feelings of desire, lust or even childlike, coy innocence without a word being said. The male picks up on the emotional scent and follows like a hungry puppy. Some women will play this in such a calculated way that they can actually generate the pheromones used in nature to attract a male - and it works. The "Vamp" (as this type is called) uses the natural forces to subvert the sense of the male. Yet here is the really curious part - This is not done to attract the male, but to dominate potential female competitors.

It is very common, and you will see this sort of thing being played out in every bar in the world. It is everywhere, in every culture, in every town. Media uses this aspect all the time, with sexy reporters, etc. competing to get your attention. Extreme examples are some of the highly sexual Pop Stars (Male and Female) who use sexual attraction to control and dominate their audience. It is a powerful thing, this power of attraction.

Perhaps surprisingly, a Porn Star does NOT use this energy to the same degree. Blatant sexual display is far more honest than the type of thing we are talking about here, which are subtle signals - A flick of an eye, the holding of a hand near the breast, etc. It is the small things that catch the eye and tease the hunger of emotionally starved people.

Women do this better than men because they live in an emotional world. As a general rule, women like to control events from an emotional pivot while men like to control them from a mental one. This is the Venus and Mars story in a nutshell. Women use their emotional energy to draw a male's attention, but again I stress, it is usually to get the attention and focus of the male AWAY from another woman. It's a competitive thing used to improve ones self-image at another's expense. Sadly, real love is rarely seen in Western Society.

Observe any night club or gathering place where sexually hungry people like to frequent. If a single man walks into the room there is far less urgency from the women to attract him. Women KNOW how easy it is to attract the male, so there's no fun in that. But causing a man's partner to wince and thus prove you are the superior attraction, now THAT is worth the effort! But if the male walks in with TWO beautiful girls, the rest of the Vamps in the room buzz over like flies to dog crap and you have to swat them off.

All women have a Vamp inside, just as they have an Angel, a Mother, a Child - or any one of the archetypal states. But the Vamp is the controller. Sometimes the Vamp will use her charms to make their OWN partner suffer. She wants to condition him through pain. It's all about CONTROL, and causing suffering can be quite an emotional charge for this type. Smart men work this to their advantage. They turn up at a nightclub with three beautiful women and watch the fur fly. Hugh Hefner was the classic example of this.

Why do I mention this? There is an emotional war going on around us right now. Someone you know is at war with their emotions against someone else you know. It is a simple fact, one that we call the 'Human Condition'.

Tell me, would you normally stroll into a war zone without armour or a weapon? Most men do, it is called getting married! This is not a quip: Marriage is a play of hug and tease at first, and it's great. Yet it generally degenerates into a game of tug and hate and a curious co-dependency within seven years. Why?

Women pretend they are vulnerable, tender and caring in order to attract the male, and for a time they are this. Most women usually believe they are in love when they marry or enter into a relationship, but precious few really believe all will be rosy. Women don't really believe in the 'happy ever after' myth, thus few will put down their emotional weapons and disarm. Why do we keep these things? Because, for a woman, they work just so damn well in helping her get what she wants.

The reality is that in a relationship, few people discover true intimacy. But when they DO, tension is easy to resolve. The Beatles would have heated arguments, but then John would look over his glasses and say "It's only me!" This would settle everyone down. It was an open-hearted recognition of the natural intimacy, love, and equality between them all.

"it's only me!" If a person understands this, and expresses it earnestly, they will impress their partner far more deeply than someone with good looks or money ever can. As a result, if you can grasp what I speak about here you will have a far better chance of surviving relationships with the heart intact.

Now, here the 'Men are from Mars' bit rears its ugly head. Men do understand there is a war going on somewhere, and their metabolism is designed to deal with it. The male body produces steroids specifically designed for battle - This is the tricky part. When the woman objects to something, anything, it triggers off his war steroids. This is when the fur flies.

Even in single-sex relationships, this is the same. One partner takes the male energy, the other the female. We have both inside us you know, it is not just a matter of having XY versus XX chromosomes.

While arguments between people are not my cup of tea, it happens. In all relationships there are waves of harmony and disharmony. When we learn to surf these natural waves, rather than play out our own game of emotional war, we grow the relationship into a real marriage. If we do not, the fur will fly.

A favourite story of mine was about a well-known Sydney artist who was somewhat of a womanizer. A gossip columnist called up his partner to ask, "Is it true that your husband was seen at lunch today with a Blonde?" It's a nasty way to say, "He's cheating on you, dear" and watch for the reaction. But this was a true marriage - the woman was totally cool, and responded, "It is absolutely false, a purely speculative rumour. I detest such ludicrous gossip - The woman was a Brunette."

And here you see the perfect riposte to the Emotion Wars. The rationale is clear: *Why buy into gossip?* Yet it is more than just not buying into the wave created, it is learning to surf WITHIN the situation. This is where a powerful law comes into play, one where you practise excluding non-intimate others from your personal concerns. Here we need to grasp the Law of Three, which states: "Whenever there are Two, a Third must appear."

Summary: *True Emotion is a powerful thing and it has a natural, sustaining quality - one that gives you energy and focus to achieve your goals. Simple feelings do not possess this power. When you grasp true emotion you will be able to easily spot false emotions in people, and accordingly, you will rarely be caught out unawares in personal dealings and relationships.*

Principle of Ratology: *Blame and shifting our focus into guilt or shame is simply not productive. Rather, we seek to remain clear about the purpose of our present moment and remind ourselves of our goals. We must do this every day. This is a necessary part of staying Awake.*

The Law of Three

> *"Where there is Two, a Third must appear."* Paracelsus

The Law of Three creates stability within us. When we understand and apply it correctly, we find a place of permanency inside. The Greeks called this, 'The Still Certain Point', and it is represented by the Omphalos at Delphi - The belly button of the world. This is the point of creation and the place of harmony within. Just like you disconnected from your mother and started the journey in life, this point is where you disconnect from society and find your own person, rather than continue as the programmed robot of your culture.

Your belly button represents the Law of Three: You are the result of your father and mother joining forces. Mother + Father = You! The principle is simple, you cannot find stability on a two-legged stool. In all relationships, you need an active third principle to give everything a sense of being able to stand on it's 'own three feet' so to speak.

It is all about building certainty within us. The Law of Three is about connectivity, creativity, and communication. We would see this in all human relationships - IF they obeyed this principle.

Most understand, when we have a problem and are going head-to-head with someone, the best thing to do is call in a third party. A counsellor who has no axe to grind can see both sides clearly and help each person see the other's point of view. It makes sense. The Law of Three makes sense.

It's a bit of a given that if we are to be happy as humans we need to be able to fit comfortably within a relationship of some sort. Now we all know that many relationships often end in relation-sinking-ships and, of course, in this instance your RAT jumps up and runs away, leaving you high and dry (or wet behind the ears if you went down with it) during these periods.

The breakdown of relationships, the inability to form good relationships and/or the sense of unworthiness that leads us to choose bad relationships can be confusing and deeply depressing, for some to the point of suicide. There are many reasons for this downturn but in every single case, it comes about because people are not obeying the Law of Three. Unsolvable problems come from people TRIANGULATING outside of the one-on-one energy of the relationship. This is the negative charge to the Law of Three, and this destroys relationships. So let's spend some time and look at this area.

We are not talking dogs and cats here. A dog will love you no matter what, and a cat doesn't care either way. We are looking at relationships that are based on the notion of equal partnerships. These may be personal, business or social experiences, but in all one thing is certain: *If we do not understand the basics of connecting with others, we are destined for trouble.*

Your RAT knows something very simple: If you appeal to people's natural instincts, making a connection is easy. Your Rat also knows how important it is to have the field of communication free from debris. However, most people's thoughts and emotions are a jumble sale. This creates a 'noise' that deafens people to their present moment. Communication here is impossible, because of the clanging stuff they are carting about, any conversation means talking louder than their problems and issues. It is why people shout at each other.

Here I am being a hypocrite. I am the least qualified person in the world to talk about successful, harmonious relationships - but as far as having numbers under the belt - I am your man! For some reason, I seem to burn people out after a couple of years, but because of this, I have hit most of the pitfalls and potholes you can find on Relationship Road. So in this sense, I am well qualified.

First, why do relationships fail? Primarily it is specifically because people do not set out their agreements in clear communication before they enter into an attempted union with another. Most will happily believe they are entering a love nest, when in truth it is a Cage of Karma. We come in with one set of expectations only to find reality bites, usually within 18 months, and we discover our Sugar Daddy / Mummy has become the Lemon Man / Woman.

Pre-nuptial agreements are NOT what I am talking about. They are lopsided affairs. However, the old days of arranged marriages DID work. Third Parties would meet, discuss, and go through in the finest degree what was expected in the upcoming marriage. Things like sleeping in on Sunday Morning, having Wednesday afternoon at tea with friends, really clear specifics such as how much sex was expected and how many children were planned. All these things were agreed to and written down.

And guess what? These arrangements have proven to be the most successful as far as marriages go. The whole point is that a THIRD PARTY was brought in to discuss things in a cool, calm fashion. This is one aspect of the Law of Three. Always respect the power of the Third Party, but ALSO be aware that this is a force to be reckoned with in all relationships.

As an example, I was working for a company and got on fine with the bosses. They loved me and were offering more money, a company car, and lots of benefits. It was looking good but then it all collapsed and I was fired for no apparent reason. Third Party Law: When relationships change for no apparent reason, a third party is involved. How did it happen? I made a passing comment to a woman at the office Christmas party who did get an obvious joke. I offended her, or at least my RAT did, by opening my mouth and making a flippant, sardonic quip. Everyone was laughing at a joke she didn't get and I said, "It's OK - the joke was only for smart people."

That got another huge laugh, but not from Rhonda. It had been said as a joke, but of course - Truth can hurt. She took it seriously and was deeply insulted. As a result, she whispered in company managers ear until I was removed.

The Third Party is a powerful thing. It can assist or it can destroy. The thing to remember: *We create a third party force with the subtle agreements we make.* As an example - If we have honesty and integrity as our base 'call ups' in any relationship, we will attract the energy of honesty and integrity into them. Likewise, if we whisper and gossip behind our partners back, talk about them to our friends, and discuss intimate details outside of the relationship bonds, then guess what? Your partner will feel it and find intimacy outside of your relationship. It is an absolute given that this is so.

The choices we make determine directly the sort of energy we invoke. This 'energy' is the third party we manifest and THIS will steer the direction of a relationship. These choices are reflected by the other party in the relationship. *Our choices determine outcomes!* This will surprise many people, but the facts are very simple: YOUR choices determine YOUR outcomes. There are no victims, only those slow to see the reality and those who fail to get out of the way.

Gossip is poison to relationships. If you gossip to another about your partner, this is a breach of intimacy and it breeds disharmony. Gossip brings other people's energy invisibly into the home circle with their whispers. People are intuitive, they FEEL things. As a result, the madness of the primate can be triggered. There is little rage greater than the Killer Ape (which is what we are) who feels the need to defend turf. Obviously, this tends to put a large dent in any further invitation to intimacy and so the downward spiral continues.

Rather than gossip, we can choose freedom and trust, and offer this with an open heart. Can we accept that this is more likely to create a natural harmony? Of course, giving freedom and trust to a gossip monger is not such a great idea, but ideally you will quickly recognize the mismatch and leave ASAP.

Triangulation

Good relationships are based on a one-to-one connection, or so we are told. Yet, so often we drag in all our past issues and fears to our present connection. This is another form of Third Party interference. By dragging our past into the present, we effectively triangulate the relationship between ourselves, the other person, and our fears and issues.

Triangulation is an important thing to grasp. One of the reason kids are so easy to get on with is because they do not triangulate. They are just themselves, and they accept you are as you are. An adult with problems is accepted as an adult with problems, but when we 'grow up' we see the adult, and we also see their problems. So THIS relationship becomes the adult, their problems, and ourselves. This is an unsolvable triangle.

Now consider that in most 'grown up' relationships we have TWO adults with problems - Can you how it gets even more complex? Each person sees the other person's issues, and it is a triangle between them, the person, and the issues.

But now we have TWO triangles, so it is even more unsolvable. Are we starting to see why relationships where people hold onto the past can be so difficult?

If you are going to have a successful relationship, you will need to call on a third force to harmonise things through the ups and downs. The greatest power in human relationships is, in reality, no force at all: It is simply ACCEPTANCE. By accepting the person as they are, we no longer triangulate them into the person and their issues. It's only me! ACCEPTANCE forms the third stabilising force.

Entering a relationship while carting all the baggage of our past problems and concerns is a guarantee of suffering. When TWO people do this it is like entering a four-way marriage with two unknown members who like nothing better than to interrupt and interfere. No one in their right mind would do it.

But we do, so the divorce, arguments, and hatred happens to us, like it happens to everyone. The whole show collapses in acrimony and negative sentiment. We react to all this in pretty much pre-set ways: *Once bitten, twice shy, three times lonely.* People get scared and reactive and start to become insular. Intimacy is ruined and, far worse, our connection with others becomes based on our needs rather than what we have to offer.

It is so easy to make things work! Try accepting someone as they are.

This is why Doctor Phil is so successful. Look at how he deals with people, and you will see he diagnoses and focuses on exactly this third party principle, but at all times he is ACCEPTING of the situation. This does not mean he is going to leave it as it is, but he STARTS with acceptance. As a Third Party, he can now effectively negotiate the stumbling blocks and reset people's compasses. SO many issues would be removed if we invoked acceptance of the other, and then brought in a third party to discuss our needs.

But there is another layer, the layer of need. People often enter into marriages because of hidden needs. SO many marriages would survive if we started out by looking at what we have to offer each other rather than what we can get. Acceptance and generosity, two old fashioned notions that still work.

It is rarely this way. A friend said it very simply. I asked him why he had chosen to remain single for the last six years. He answered, "I do not need another workshop. I just need a wife." Fair call, I thought.

Acceptance

How do we avoid a relationship ending up as a relation-shop? The Chinese read faces and go to counsellors who advise on how well two parties will get on in marriage. The solutions are generally very basic and simple. If a person has a dominant nose, for instance, it is recommended they find a person with a weak nose. Why? The dominant nose always likes to lead; the weak nose likes to follow. It's not that hard, is it? *It is simply matching up people who are most likely to accept the other party for what they are.*

That's it! We simply need to practice accepting people as they are, rather than move into their life and then try to change them. If someone in a relationship with you presents things you don't like, you have three choices: *Accept it, move on, or change it.* Trust me, the hard road is the 'change it' one.

"Most people lead lives of quiet desperation," said Thoreau. One of the very real reasons they do this is because they never chose compatible relationships. More to the point, most people never really chose anything but their impulse.

REMEMBER: *The main reason (by far) why most people do NOT experience harmonious relationships is simply because they call up their baggage to deal with a situation rather than their acceptance.*

The calling-up of baggage, this is the pictures from our past that we keep on the mental-shelf of the heart. It is what TRIANGULATES us away from dealing with the present. As a result, we are constantly being thrown backward into the ruts of past patterns. Like a train on its rails, these emotional and mental ruts take us in the direction of where we USED to go, never where we WANT to go.

This is another aspect to the consequences of the social and moral lies we have been imbued with, the 'should' and, in particular, the 'shoulds' around sexual infidelity. This is another reason why we need our RAT to get into the driving seat and take charge. Sure there are problems that occur in any relationship, but here I am going to say things that will have half the population of the world wanting to hunt me down - I say this anyway because it's true.

What Breaks Intimacy

May I suggest to you that the LEAST of your relationship problems are things like infidelity, flirting and sexual displays. Most imagine sexual fidelity as the top of the list of things that are important in a relationship, but the reality is that this is almost guaranteed to be breached at some point in a marriage. Masters and Johnson did the research way back in the 1960s and even then infidelity was pretty much a given. So let me ask you, what's the problem here?

The Romans had a practical view of such matters. They viewed marriage as more of a financial arrangement and, as such, it served a very useful purpose in matters of deciding inheritance, etc. They had four different levels of marriage and only one was the 'Till Death do us Part' type.

This fourth form of marriage was originally intended as a 'true love' match, but the reality was that it became a way to guarantee the dowry. When a patrician woman got married, she came with a money and valuables. If the couple got divorced, under this fourth type of marriage the dowry had to come back with her. It was more a form of insurance than a marriage vow.

We are animals and at some point, we will act like an animal. Now obviously I would prefer a faithful wife and I have no issue remaining faithful in every sense of the word. If there is true intimacy, I don't WANT to look elsewhere. But if she becomes disinterested in sex, why would I choose to remain faithful?

Why should I suffer because someone else has issues? I say this because a true marriage is not designed as a mutual suffering zone. I used to put up with things like this until I realized it was a waste of time. HOWEVER, it doesn't have to end the marriage! Acceptance cures everything bar the real issues.

The REAL Issues are things like gambling, which destroys the financial health of the family. Too many drugs or too much drink, THESE are real issues. Poverty is a real issue. Loss of a job or the death of a family member - these are real issues. But you know, unless someone catches aids, infidelity is a relatively small event UNLESS you have issues with trust.

And if you have issues of trust, why are you getting married? You are an empty glass and should stay on the shelf because there will be little to drink from in your presence. But here's the thing, when we can ACCEPT that there may be infidelity and allow whatever to happen, happen - it often doesn't. If you love someone enough there is a fairly huge possibility they will find this intimacy you offer far better value than casual relationships.

Personally, I could not imagine staying with a woman who slept around, I may as well go out with a hooker. I would add that I have known a lot of Hookers - I wrote articles on them for Playgirl magazine in the 1980s. They are great girls, as a rule, but useless for intimacy. I found many good friends, but no girlfriends.

What I want is INTIMACY - one on one. I want connection, breathing the Soul of that person sleeping beside me, gathering their sweet scent to my heart. I don't really want anyone interfering with this, but, if this does happen, I trust myself enough to survive the odd hiccup and get past issues such as this.

Yes, it does take time to rebuild the intimacy, but if the woman is not getting the same connection that I am, and needs more - Well I have to either say 'OK' or look somewhere else. But here is an important point: *Someone does not have to be sexually unfaithful to another person to break up the intimacy.* I went out with a damaged Soul who said she loved me. In her way she did but her past fears controlled her. As a result, when we were together she was worshipping the negative beliefs in her head rather than being part of this moment we shared. Now to me, THIS is a real breach of trust. This is unfaithfulness, because the dear girl had NO FAITH in me, or herself. Get it? Faith, trust, and charity all start at home, in your heart

Real Intimacy, real connection requires only one thing: That the two people be present and have nothing between them but the love they hold. Real intimacy shows as a kindness that comes when your loved one enters the room.

The Baggage We Carry

That is all it is, a sense of warmth in the heart. Unless you find this you will never enter a real relationship. So it boils down to Shakespeare's Sonnet: *"Let me not to the marriage of true minds admit impediments."* These impediments are anything within your being that is not based in intimacy and true emotions.

We need to understand the difference between our true emotions and the baggage we carry about. Our baggage will mock up feelings generated from fear, guilt, doubt, and ignorance - Fear-based realities based on hand-me-down beliefs with clichéd experiences, all stuck together with wishes and dreams. They are illusions, yet they surely seem real when we are living inside them.

I mean, technically everything is illusion. What we call 'matter' is an assemblage of atoms which are largely 'nothingness' strung together with infinitesimally small pieces of atomic structure. But if you are being chased in a field by a bull, it's real enough to make you run. Equally: You are stupid to say someone's distress is all illusion, or all in their head - Why? Because that illusion causes them great pain and, for them, it is real. Ever met a distrustful woman with a knife demanding to know where you were? Her jealousy may well be an illusion, but that illusion might just kill you. Run, little legs, run far, far away.

This is the core problem, the illusions we carry about. This is what we call our karma, which is essentially the set of pictures in our head. Karma is like the family photos we have on the shelf. Karma is the coach using images and beliefs to direct, telling us what to feel, how to think, what we are, and who to see. How do we get around our karma? We need to be able to stop, understand our true emotions, and thus learn to rearrange our beliefs to be more one-to-one with life and with others. In the simplest of terms: We have to pull out the recorded tapes of our past that are whispering their truths in our ears, and insert our ASPIRATIONS. (We look at this in Ratology Two)

We all have two storage boxes on the mind-shelf inside us. They are both full of Memes. We must stop pulling instructions from the box of failure and misery and start taking suggestions from the box of possibility and opportunity.

Further: If we are to be free, we MUST learn to stop attaching our beliefs and feelings onto fearful expectations of outcomes, and we must absolutely stop trying to control how other people might behave. In any marriage of true minds we need to be, as Gibran wrote, the Two Full Cups - Not two cups constantly pouring into the other, but ones that stand free and proud, each cup full to the brim with their own understanding. When we ARE this, the Law of Three calls in a third energy that is likewise complete, and self-sufficient. With THIS sense of self it is easy to trust, both yourself and another. The Path is very clear:

1. With trust comes intimacy,
2. With intimacy comes confidence,
3. With confidence comes clear communication.

This is all tied together with ACCEPTANCE. Acceptance of self and of others allows us to suspend fear, doubt, belief, and all restrictive emotions. This lets the other person to demonstrate who and what they are without us pre-conditioning them. Acceptance gives us enough patience to observe what evolves in any given moment. Do this and confidence will grow in your heart.

This is a whole lot easier to say than do, because most people are usually projecting fears, anxiety, and confusion all over the place. In a relationship, this means they are usually projecting all over you - like a babies vomit.

Real harmony only comes with two full cups accepting each other . But it can be hard to find two full cups. Most are cracked and leaking.

Love: What is it, really? So often we give our love without any sense of hesitation when we believe the ideal 'Mr. Right' or 'Miss Perfect' turn up in our lives. We go 'ALL IN' on the belief that what we are feeling is IT. This is wishful thinking for the most part. Our notions of 'true love' that we hold are really just mockups. These notions are just another Humpty Dumpty we have tried to put together again. What 'love' is for most people is a badly assembled batch of heart felt concepts wrapped around a framework of basic needs and desires.

And yet here I will appear to break all the rules of Ratology. Please forget everything I have written and fall madly, deeply in love!

It is one of the best things that can ever happen to you. Even if it all stuffs up and you end up a miserable, lone cormorant on a lonely rock, you have at least broken the mold of fear and hesitation. In the heat of the fire of amore', the images of fear and confining beliefs will start to melt and, even if it fails, you are left with a new possibility for your life.

Sure, in a few years, when the lens is removed from our eyes, we may well see the beer-swilling thick-headed red-neck or the peroxided blond giggle-fest for what he or she really is. But prior to this, when his hairy masculine alcohol smelling charm really seemed wonderful, or her sweet, intoxicating overdose of perfumed notions were just marvellous - it was great. The fire of your passion burned away old notions and left you with a new reality. It has given you a step up! You are reaching one inch further than you ever have done before.

And THIS is the most useful purpose within both madness and love. It is all about reaching past our Glass Ceilings.

The Glass Ceiling

"The glass ceiling gets more pliable when you turn up the heat." Pauline R Kezer

Do you remember the chapter, *"You want the Truth"*? (p: 100) We talked about how fleas are trained in a flea circus. A flea trainer puts fleas into various boxes, each with glass lids set at different heights. After a few weeks of hitting their heads, the fleas in each box learn to jump just below the glass ceiling. This is where the term "glass ceiling" came from.

Once 'trained' he can take them out of the box and put them in an aquarium with no lid at all. All the fleas will continue to jump to exactly the height their society has trained them to jump to. It doesn't matter that other fleas jump at different heights, the fleas in the 'Four Inch High' club will continue to jump to four inches. They have been pre-conditioned to this set pattern.

Why is this important to talk about? The bulk of our so-called emotions and preconceptions that form our biased perceptions come to us specifically because of our pre-installed Glass Ceilings. These are the limitations of self that are often put in place prior to age six by our parents or our peers. So much of what we imagine to be our beliefs are really just our trained habits. (Often they are denials of self) These form our pre-set ceilings or limitations. Examples are:

1. *I love him, but he needs to be stable.*
2. *She's gorgeous, but I am not worthy of her.*
3. *I want to be free, but I am afraid to let go.*
4. *I adore him, but I can't say so. (Etc. etc. etc.)*

These fears are our glass ceilings. They are our controllers. They create false conditions for what constitutes acceptance in our relationships and there are many of these 'logjams' inside us. These self-imposed limitations (from inside yourself or from external sources such as friends who share your low-self esteem issues, etc.) determine our choices, which determines our outcomes.

You can only jump so high within any given emotion before something goes "Whoa Buddy!" This is your *emotional restriction point*. (ERP) This is your HURT or FEAR zone - The net result of this glass ceiling is that, like the fleas in a flea circus, you learn to jump not-so-high emotionally the next time and thus save yourself some pain. According to this default setting, usually created in childhood, most of our emotions are really restrictions.

Further: What we presently believe to be 'our' emotions are generally an inheritance from family and society, so in this sense, they are not even ours - They are like books we have borrowed from the library which we stumbled and fell into - Just like Alice fell through the Looking Glass, in reading your story you forget about the real world and the dream takes over your imagination. This is when it becomes your reality, your glass ceiling. You have to be quite brave to get your head out of the book of imagined-self and face the real world.

It is like in the movie "The Matrix" where you have to choose - The red pill or the blue one? It is a choice to be free of illusion, or to dwell in it.

Choose wisely - Your life will count on it, or should I say your happiness will be at stake. You are the ONE, your choice is the TWO, and the combination of these will create the THIRD. This is the Law of Three at work in your life. What we become is based on the choices we make. What you will become is based on the choices you are making right now. It is all RIGHT NOW, today, this moment, right here. This is IT, folks. NOW is the sum total of all that is YOURS and the choices you make within this moment will determine your future.

How can we learn to choose wisely? Well, it is so stupidly simple that almost everyone overlooks it: We just need to ACCEPT ourselves as we are. We need to be our own hero and, perhaps surprisingly, our own villain as well. We need to be brave, we need to be true and we yet we ALSO need to be fearful and a liar. We need EVERYTHING we are in order to be ourselves. ACCEPTANCE is the keystone in the Arch of Being. ACCEPTANCE is the first point of our personal CHOOSING. True acceptance is you are saying that you, yourself, are good enough as you are. This is genuine self-belief.

After this initial choice, it gets easier. Logically, if we choose what we do because of what we believe, doesn't it stand to reason that when you start to believe in yourself, then you will change your choices to something more positive - yes? Changing your choices means you will change your reality.

Now countering this notion is a set belief that reality is what it is. For example, a set scientific belief goes "Whatever you choose to believe will not affect the reality of what IS." Science loves the notion of a fixed, empirical reality that is unchanging and which follows fixed laws. Belief is, therefore, of no value in this hard, factual world of proof and experiment. Contrary to believing in belief, the good scientist believes in doubt: *Doubt is one true God in the Religion of Science.*

And you know what's so funny about this? Those good scientists never really get to see the irony of believing in doubt! I was once asked by a professor what my opinion of the New Age was: I said: "My opinion is that there are too many opinions". I expected him to laugh, but instead, he thought seriously for a few moments, and replied, "Yes, a very interesting opinion."

Despite this scientific attitude that is, of itself, is a self-limiting belief factor and despite the clear facts and numerous 'proofs' that show how belief does indeed create a reality, science, as a rule, will scoff at the notion. Those wonderful priests of the modern age, our scientists, those rational men of worldly wisdom, how come they almost always fail to grasp their perfect Irony, the belief in their disbelief. Let me put it another way:

It is an empirical fact is that if no one believed that science was real, it would not exist. Why is this true? There would be no science course at a university for something no one believed existed, therefore there would be no scientists! So it is the NECESSARY belief in science that created science.

It was during the Age of Reason and philosophers like Kant instructed the scientific mind to reject belief, but this 'rebellion against believing' was because of religious superstition controlling so much of the thought of that day.

And then there came Existentialism. The tree may well be in the forest, but if no one saw the forest, let alone the tree, would Descartes have even asked us, "Is it really there?" Existentialism claims: *If the tree falls, and no one cares or notices, then from the individuals Point of View, it does not exist.* But it does.

Of course it's there. Just because YOU don't see it - this means nothing. The laws of gravity still exist as the apples falls from the tree where you are not sitting. The laws of thermo-dynamics still cook your days catch over the campfire. These things are Basic Laws of Nature.

It is DELUSIONAL belief that is the issue. You may believe (when you are on your LSD trip) that you can fly - But one of my friends managed to get himself permanent brain damage while discovering that his belief was not sufficient enough to counter gravity. Yet contrary to this, in the Himalayas, there are regular reports of Monks that DO fly from place to place.

So what DOES determine reality? Is it belief, is it laws of nature, or is it our choices? Does it really matter? Our beliefs, and the choices we make as a result of these beliefs, are both man-made inventions: *Yet they control our lives.* Even so, our Emotions DO have specific Laws that govern them. (Law of Karma, etc.) They obviously have a reality, because they exist, but how MUCH do they exist? The real question is: *How much is dream and how much is reality?*

I can't answer all the above for you. The best gurus in the world can't answer this but I can say that when we accept ourselves as we are, a whole lot of these questions fade away. Yet it remains that our BELIEFS direct our CHOICES, and that our choices direct the energy of our life towards a conclusion.

There is only one absolute certainty: if you believe you can only jump four inches, then you can only jump four inches.

Breaking the Glass Ceiling

Nicola Tesla imagined a world radically different from what had come before. He created the generators that drive our towns, he invented radio, and so much more. He refused to be limited by existing beliefs.

The Laws of Emotion

"I Think Therefore I Am," said the penguin as it sat pondering on the ice. Then the ice broke apart from under him and he suddenly cried out -
"I Sink, Therefore I Swim"

Honestly? There are Laws of Emotion? Well, in a sense - They are not like gravity, but they are real and have a curious twist. The most important of the Emotional Laws States: *There is No Truth greater than the Lie agreed upon by two or more people.* If we see any particular thing as being right or true, it isn't until we find another person in the room, house or culture to agree with us. When another agrees and says it is so, then it is so. This is how our cultural law and social rules came about in the first place.

It is the Law of Majority-Minority working in our emotions.

The Laws of Behaviour (The collective shoulds of any culture) are sustained because we, as a culture, collectively 'believe' in them. Yet they change with the tide of social acceptance. Playing Rock and Roll no longer sends you to hell, however, apparently saying politically incorrect things on Facebook will.

These Laws are not as simple as saying 'I believe' in something and it becomes instantly real. It takes time and an acceptance by a significant weight of the people. It is a slow growth, like a tree in the forest. Over the course of generations, some manufactured 'laws of behaviour' (or beliefs) attain the presence and recognition as a 'truth'.

But consider this: Almost ALL behavioural laws came about as a result of some sort of threat to the society that believes in them.

Why do I mention all of this? If we want to un-dam ourselves from the generational conditioning we are presently living inside, we have to counter the weight of ages within. Let's put it into perspective: *When you break a 'should' you are really breaking years of conditioned behaviour that have been placed on you.* This is no small thing. Also, you need to be careful when breaking a 'should' because there will be a queue of people waiting to fix that broken egg and plaster that 'should' right back over you.

This is what the generational change in the 1960s was all about - breaking up the SHOULDS. So, is there any one single rule or condition that explains the process? Is there a simple way to approach all this complicated 'stuff'?

Let's look at where our 'stuff' came from: *The threat of disorder and chaos created the need for organisation. This created the Should, which became the Law, which built society, which in due course created the funds to pay the policemen and the courts to enforce this Law.* As simple as it sounds, the invention and maintenance of our shoulds are the nub of our social order.

It's all about what is believed. You 'believe' in money, yes? Money has value and can buy us things, but if any given society stops believing in its value, their money quickly becomes worthless. It is the same for everything - and most especially with the lies we believe to be real. But find a connection with your true and deepest natural emotions and they will dissipate your shoulds. Come to a place of true emotion within and you will see the lies that drive you.

The Mystic Rat Says: *Remove belief from any single institution in our culture, and that institution will fall rapidly into dust. Cease to believe in yourself and you will be controlled by every strong force you encounter. Believe too much in any one thing, and that thing will become the demon that possesses you.*

Belief is EVERYTHING in society yet nothing in reality. The Gods of Egypt were believed in for thousands of years. They formed the basis for an entire culture but now they are a mere curiosity for historians. Phillip Adams (an Australian journalist) had a parade of "failed Gods' as statues in his office, a reminder of how sacred cows invariably end up as steak sandwich.

Yet at one time, the overarching belief in these 'Dead Gods' set the course for millions of lives. What does this mean? Our beliefs affect our life in profound and comprehensive ways. Further, all beliefs have a kernel of truth within them. Like a seed, each piece of reality inside your beliefs is waiting for enlightenment, the dawn of understanding.

So now I will appear to say the exact opposite of everything I have said prior in this book. Rather than castigate yourself over your false beliefs, try to WATER them, treat them well, and see what comes forth as they sprout to fruition.

If you really want to believe Jesus will come and raise people from the dead, try living inside that belief with a complete totality. The more you live in it, the more awareness you will achieve, and the more awareness you have of your belief. But do not just BELIEVE, try and EXPERIENCE this belief. Imagine you are there with Jesus as people are raised from the dead, but leave off the emotions. Just look, just watch, and see what your heart and mind shows you.

If it is false, as it grows you will discover this, and the less believable it becomes. Obviously, people being raised from the dead? They are not so pretty after a hundred years, and are really only bones after two hundred or more. So they have to be "refleshed". Here we take the gloss out and ask, "Why?"

God can just remake bodies, so why bother raising bones?

The Tibetans say: "It is good to be born into a religion, bad to die in one!" In other words: When you finally accept and understand that you believe in really a load of crap, you may learn to grow some roses in it. When the rose blooms you will see WHY you chose to do what you have done in this life. This is destiny, this prospective rose is your CORE KARMA, and everyone has a seed or two of something waiting to blossom inside their heart.

Summary: *For any single thing in your life, there will always be two other related matters connected to it. This is a fixed immutable Law. If you love a woman, there will be something needed to make the connection between the two of you. Spot the THIRD ELEMENT and you will be able to take charge of all relationships.*

The Seed of Emotion

"All the world's a stage and we are but actors upon it" Shakespeare

Imagine you have five English pound coins in your pocket. They are all exactly the same, only one has a Scottish accent, another a Welsh one, another a Cornish one, the other two have an Irish and an English one. They are all the same, yet different. They are all the same TYPE, yet their experiences taught them to voice what they are with a different accent. We all accept the Human Genome. We all accept that we humans are a 'type'. We have distinct variations, yet a black African human is as 'human' as the yellow Asian 'type'.

Why then is it so hard for most professionals to accept that we have a source point inside ourselves, a karma if you will, that is not determined by upbringing or genetics? We are a type. We have a seed inside that we germinated from and, like any seed, it can only grow into what it IS. An acorn will only grow into an Oak, never a Poplar or Larch. (Though acorns are popular with the squirrels)

How we are brought up determines the potential nature of what we become, but it does not determine what we are. We get beliefs grafted onto us, we get pickled by shoulds and all manner of influences shape us, but nothing determines what we are other than what we are. I say: the way to find this core-self is through an understanding of the emotions that drive us, along with the imagination that inspires us.

Every belief, viewpoint, and notion you hold is portrayed in your psyche is very similar to an actor on a stage. Your view might be the hero or villain, star or humble chorus, it's all just elements of the play to the director, which is your imagination. The script is largely written by your upbringing and social influences but HOW you perform is not. You are given a role to play and it is your desire to make something of it that works to create the applause, or boos, from the crowd. Your imagination gives your character a voice and the subsequent action you create {hopefully} convinces the audience (which is yourself) that it is real. If it all works, you believe it!

We tend to imagine ourselves as heroes, or something important. (I have met SO many reincarnations of Cleopatra!) The reality is we play many roles: hero, villain, priest, scared fool - it's all there in the Tarot Deck. These are the archetypes, the roles we play. Did you know these were outlined by the Pharaoh Akhenaton in Ancient Egypt? He added these archetypes to the standard card deck of the day as part of his new religion, one intent on breaking the power of the priesthood. There's nothing new in any of it - we are all replaying the past.

Here is a secret: *Regardless whether we choose to be a hero OR a villain in our life (and either are perfectly valid choices) we still have the Seed Cause to understand as to why we chose this role.* This seed is our true reality and usually, it is a fear mixed with a love of some sort.

The key: WE ALL HAVE AT LEAST ONE SEED DRIVING OUR ACTIONS, MOST OF US HAVE SEVERAL. These seeds are the core issues or patterns that drive us to act as we do. As they germinate and sprout, these seeds sprout as experiences, which affect the shape of the garden that grows. The most impacting experiences occur to us between the ages zero to six. This mutates the vine, yet while it does affect the fruit that grows, the roots remain the same.

Which brings us to the basic question: *How do we resolve seed causes?*

Seed Causation, or Base Reality, is generally reflected inside the emotional conditioning. It is a puzzle box and the combination to unlock it is found in the common sense of the heart linked to the perception in the mind. Question: *Why would we care about any of the above?* Answer: *It is all part of solving the puzzle of self.* Essentially, if we are to solve the 'puzzle of self' we need to:

1. Rise above our Emotions and
2. Learn to direct our imagination.

Step by step: In order to do this, we need to understand what our true emotions might be and where our imagination is pointing.

Firstly, your emotions are your powerhouse, not your mind. Emotions are the true driving force of our nature, but the way we interpret them is generally false. Our Imagination is the culprit for our false interpretation of emotion and, generally, it is doing this because of trained fears and conditioning. All this is a Catch 22 until we understand how the process works. The way we crack the nut of this conundrum is to discover our Core Karma, or in other words, the genuine source of the emotions inside us.

No book can tell you how to do this, but I can share with you an experience I had some years ago. I was listening to a friend who was talking, when a part of me dislocated from the conversation. A new perception arrived: I saw this man's entire life like a movie reel being played before me. I could see how there were only three 'seeds' he had to solve in this lifetime, but that he would circulate around them, never seeing the seed causes that were secretly directing his life.

Then I came back to myself and understood the real message. 'I' had been circulating around my true self, hiding in opinions, notions, and beliefs. Until I resolved the seed causes that drove me, I would forever run around in circles. But seeing the truth and living it are two different animals.

Our emotions give us the energy we need to keep our life running and this all starts with our SURVIVAL emotions. These are the feelings that cause a baby to cry when hungry: Baby COULD just sit there and starve, but it goes, "whoa, hungry!" and the message comes out via a cry, saying, "Hey - FEED ME!"

Here is something that surprised me in the research for this book. Did you know that a baby does not just 'call out'? It calls out in a specific pitch that it knows will attract the mother.

A baby doesn't think, "Oh, if I cry then I will get attention, and perhaps someone will get the notion to give me food." A baby has an instinctual emotive response to the stimulus of hunger, which is to call out for help in a way that is TARGETED to appeal to the emotions of the Mother. Science has not yet figured quite how it works, but tests have been done that prove that even when a mother cannot physically hear her baby crying, she still registers the same emotional response as if she can.

Emotions are REAL. They travel out as energy wavelengths that others can read if they are attuned to them. Emotions are like radio waves - The baby and the mother are in resonance and, just as when a radio is tuned into a frequency, when one sends the signal the other 'hears it', even without physical contact. The total vulnerability of the child and the complete love of the mother is what allows this. In other words - Intimacy.

OK - Here is the real point to grasp: *This is how true intimacy works.*

In simple terms, we are ALL radios. We can ALL tune in and receive whatever wavelength we are capable of listening to. All we need learn is the flexibility to change channels from our set position and, in doing so, we experience an entirely new set of circumstances. We are all free to change, we only need discover the WISH to do so within us. This 'wish' comes from our true emotions and our true emotions only emerge when we are capable of intimacy.

Research has proven that the membranes of all living cells are extremely sensitive to radiation. It suggests that thought and feeling alone can help control cell biology. Stress will cause cells to 'hide' and in effect hibernate. Joy causes them to come alive and be productive. All cells are sensitive to the environment and our bodies respond to this with their instinctive protection mechanisms.

But common sense kicks in - survival of the fittest and all that. We realise that being vulnerable means that someone may spot us as an easy picking and thus abuse our good nature. We learn to MODIFY our biology to suit environment. We develop a Poker Face. We contain our emotional responses in order to survive better, especially around those who are more powerful than us.

In nature, if you do not modify your emotions to suit your environment, you die. But prior to this, our NEEDS trigger our emotions and our emotions drive our brain to figure out how to get these. Which raises an important question.

What are Our NEEDS?

The question we are really asking is: *What are our CORE NEEDS?*

Unfortunately, as a result of our fears and emotional imprisonment, we civilized humans tend to have no understanding of what we really want. We often suffer **too much** emotional response, with a lack of intimacy. It cripples us.

Because of the shoulds and the beliefs we have picked up, normal needs such as food and love can become twisted into greed and lust. An Example: The CORE emotion, 'I need food' gets tagged with the secondary emotion, 'I am not loved'. The answer we might come up with is to gorge on sweets, etc. The natural signal for food from the stomach gets combined with a need to stimulate starving emotions from another area of our psyche.

We think we are in charge of our mind, but we are not. We are a slave to a thousand impulses, the most powerful being Food and Sex, and mostly we live our lives in the fear of not getting either. Regardless, a thousand impulses are driving us until we stop, recognise, then acknowledge them. These core issues are generally not complicated: *I want to be listened to. I want to be important. I want to receive respect.* Nothing fancy or tricky - just basic stuff.

To discover what our true needs might be means we need to find a deeper connection to life. And the best way to uncover this is to listen, watch and observe how others react to us. *Oh wat gift the givee gee us, to see ourselves as others see us.* If someone hates you, or loves you, or ignores you, try to go up and communicate with them honestly. You can literally ask a person what it is they don't like about yourself. You will be amazed at how forthcoming people can be, given such an opportunity! And in such types of open conversation we often hear something life is trying to tell us.

The energy and image that others see will tell us more about our true needs than any workshop or psychiatrist. The trick is to listen and allow life to speak. Ask what it is we truly want, then listen to what life brings to you. We are the creators of our lives, by our attitudes and choices, but only through the mirror of others are we able to reflect what we are to ourselves.

In the end, everything that causes good or bad things to occur in your life is buried inside you, somewhere. Deep down there are emotions that are driving your bus! Natural emotions only drive us to places that help us survive. Negative emotions only drive us to depression, misery, lack of contentment and a sense of abrasion with life. Whatever the negative emotion might be - I promise you - it will be hidden in whatever you fear and hate in this life.

Most of us do not even recognise the fear-based beliefs that are driving us. (fears wear many disguises) Even if we did, would we know how to deal with it? This is where your emotions are picking you up and driving you.

The movie "Shallow Hal" is a very good examination of this curious aspect of human nature. It is all about how our perspective shapes our reality. It is recommended viewing should you wish to grasp how emotions and needs are tied to perception and belief.

Why is this important to understand? Only when you grasp how secret, internal forces direct your life, can you can begin to choose alternatives.

Summary: *We do not do what we want, we want what we do. Understanding the seed cause of the emotions that instruct your mind/heart how to act will give you the ability to maintain a hold on the emotive elements of your being. Even if you constantly give in to your emotions, when you really grasp how it works, you will have the power to control your own life.*

Understanding Our Stick It Notes

"KNOWING YOURSELF means being able to separate the true from the false in yourself - love from emotion, joy from sentiment, will from desire." Barry Long

The biggest problem many people have is not the mortgage, the partner who strays, or the kids using drugs - it is that they are not in the driving seat of their own lives. Most people are sitting in the back, with no brakes, letting their emotions, fears and personal lies run the show. We want whatever it is we want - but most don't get it because we are afraid to take the wheel.

When we want something but are afraid to take charge, we get a distorted perception of reality. Our mind gets twisted around what we DON'T have rather than what we do. We fall into LACK, where false emotion creates false realities. This *Sense of Lack* has a powerful effect:

1. Lack creates yearning
2. The yearning demonstrates that which we do not have,
3. Which creates an internal hole we need to escape from.
4. Our reality turns away from the NOW as we pursue dreams.
5. Which creates a whirlpool of energy, where our wheels are spinning, while we go nowhere fast.

An example: Jealousy is a powerful experience that takes us nowhere healthy. It can completely absorb us and it seems totally real, yet within short shrift the whole show passes and we realize that this 'urgent need' gained us nothing but pain and distrust. This is the definition of a false emotion!

When we are inside it, it appears real, but jealousy is one of the most transparent of our fear-based realities. Our jealousy creates the very destiny we are tring to avoid. IE: The object of our obsession runs away and they find someone else. Yet this ALSO paradoxically PROVES to us that the jealousy was correct! Do you see the problem of fear-based Emotional Realities?

The Mystic Rat Says: *Beware the wheel creating the road upon which it runs.*

I had a girlfriend once who was INCREDIBLY jealous. She was absolutely certain that everything I did in public was to attract girls. The reality was that I was simply a happy person who smiled a lot. Happiness is infectious and so people were often smiling at me. Happy people will attract smiles from others.

And I was happy! I was blissfully happy because I had money in the bank, sex in the bed, and a nice place to live. My God! For the first time in my life I even had my own place where there were no cockroaches. How could I have NOT been happy? My then girlfriend was clearly attracted to my happiness, just as others would have been.

Her NEEDS pulled me towards her, then her FEARS pushed me away.

At the time I was like the dog that found a friend to play with. *I was HAPPY!!* That's it - The end of loneness. The sex was good and life was great.

She made sure this happiness business got stopped.

When travelling to get away from her madness, I met a guy who had a smile plastered all over his face. I was in the bush and he was standing under a lean-to (a sheet of tin braced on a tree) in the bush. It was pouring rain and I noticed he had a bicycle beside him and a swag spread out on some dry ground under the tin. You may think "What's there to smile about?" He didn't seem to have a lot going for him, but he was HAPPY. I thought he may have been a nutter, but I was curious and asked what had brought him to this point.

He explained that he had spent one month riding around New Zealand in the rain and was wet, cold, and miserable the entire time. But tonight he had made it to a dry space before the rain fell and he was DRY. Now if I were the cynical type I might have said something to make him less ridiculously happy.

But why would I question it? Happiness is rare enough and only a fool seeks to lessen another's experience of joy. The jealous girlfriend was always looking for a negative reason for my happiness, and I was in the process of escaping that tyranny - I did not want to put it onto the shoulders of another.

This is another proof of true emotion, you have no desire to lessen the joy or happiness of another soul. I STILL FEEL that happiness radiating from him, I still have this in my heart because I welcomed it as a worthy and true emotion.

Irrational Beliefs Create Powerful Emotions

BUT! Looking through the filter of the jealous woman, my happiness had to be rejected. Why? To her, my smiling self was a clear sign that I was after - or worse, getting - something more than she offered. Now you may think this is strange and makes no sense - and you would be right. Why would anyone choose to believe this? Why do people CHOOSE to doubt another and make their own life a misery? Well, there is no WHY to Jealousy. It creates its own reality and its own rules as to how things work. The jealousy equation runs, *"He's Happy + I am Not = He cannot be happy with me: THEREFORE there must be a Third Party = He is having Sex with someone else!"*

I had no idea what her problem was at the time, nor was I particularly interested. After all, I was HAPPY. But the jealousy had the desired effect and I got pretty twisted up and unhappy. Finally, I got rid of the problem by ending the relationship, and that's when I came to a different space. Then it all flipped!

I got back to town and suddenly I see HER talking and laughing with other men, and I found MYSELF getting incredibly jealous. Even as I knew this was nonsense, even though I KNEW it wasn't real - It still FELT real, completely real. Even when I knew it was a lie, it still felt utterly and completely REAL.

My best friends, if they laughed with her, became my enemy. Strangers were a threat if they walked beside her. It was insane, and even at the time I knew it was insane, yet it just kept right on coming! This total sense of Jealously just kept drilling me, which was weird because I had never been Jealous before! At last a light dawned - I finally remembered how in the relationship I had ASKED, "What is this madness called jealousy?" Why? Because I had wanted to understand it. Life had heard my request and answered with the experience.

That's the law: *Just ask something earnestly of Life, and it will provide an answer.* If you earnestly ask Life what a banana tastes like, Life will provide a banana for you. *(This, by the way, is the REAL trick with manifestation - Ask for the EXPERIENCE, not the object of desire).* I had asked about Jealousy, now I was experiencing it.

It drove me mad. I simply could not control it and it was running my life to the point where I could not do anything. It was extremely distressing and I got to where I did not want to even eat - And lo and behold, the lights go on! I suddenly recalled how just before we broke up with the girl SHE had wanted to stop eating. Indeed, she was calling food Evil.

Was all this part of the Jealousy experience? When FINALLY I recognized I had ASKED for this, I relaxed. I went with it. I even stopped eating. In fact, I REALLY stopped eating and did a three month fast. Call me excessive, call me a fool, but this just came about. The triggers were there, the situation opened up for this to happen, and I fell into the experience as I pretty much seem to stumble into everything in my life.

The Three Month Fast

Now, to stop and explain - Without realizing it, what I was really doing was stopping the uncontrolled forces in my life. The need for food is a basic survival emotion and I denied it. I stopped the most basic core energies in my being from speaking. What this does is stop all the ancillary 'tags' to these core emotions from expressing themselves. Without consciously knowing it, I was saying to life, "I need to understand what is driving me."

Fasting, of itself, isn't a terrible thing at all. Sure, after five days on just water you get this horrible sense you are going to die, but after this, the whole thing passes and you lose the desire to eat. You start to feel great and you have lots of energy. I know it opposes what the scientists say, but have they ever done a forty five day water fast? I have a policy of doubting anything anyone says unless they have had actual experience on the subject.

A friend (a scientist, would you believe) turned up out of the blue saying he was travelling up the coast and did I want to come along? Sure - I found the timing perfect. We stayed in hostels and anywhere that was cheap, and generally had a great time for the next twelve weeks. I even wrote a Sci-Fi book in longhand, (This, by the way, became my stepping stone to learning how to type because it was such a pain to pay someone to transcribe - Therefore the Lie of Jealousy is a direct contributor to this book!)

Indeed, as events turned out, that hand-written book became my only proof that this period of my life existed. (Severe and prolonged fasting will dislocate you from your present sense of reality - part of the reason to do it!)

After six weeks I realised my body was starting to eat itself. I observed the fact, clinically, by noting my muscles were diminishing and understood that I should eat something. Quite reluctantly, I ate bread and fruit for another six weeks, and I do mean reluctantly because I was well adjusted to no food by this time. All up I was away travelling for almost three months: writing, hanging out, doodling along. Why? I have no real idea, but I had a general sense that something was up - and then FINALLY I had the Cosmic Realization I guess I had been secretly looking for. It was not the magic mushroom fuelled psychoactive type of explosive "Oh Yeah Baby", but a clear, straightforward, no-nonsense bell ringing of truth. My RAT had finally broken through with one, simple reality.

The Mystic Rat Said: **It's only me.**

Even at the time this was a pretty disappointing cosmic consciousness revelation. It was a very ordinary sort of epiphany, to the point of an anti-epiphany. In fact, it was downright dull. Yet it changed everything.

I did not grasp the importance at the time, but a CORE energy in my being had held a concern about what others thought. This stupidly simply realization set me free from this deeply buried fear - one that had been driving my bus!

Here's the rub, I almost tossed this notion aside. Though it seemed this 'should' be important - let's face it, this "revelation" just looked, and was, very ordinary. Given the extent of fasting and deprivation I had been through, I thought my "awakening" was a singularly unimpressive result. It took some time before it dawned on me what this pure, uncluttered viewpoint really meant. But when I did EVERYTHING took on a new understanding.

It's only ME. This meant that, if I knew enough to know what 'ME' is/was, then I could start to see the bits that were NOT me. And this is exactly the process that started to happen. I started finding pieces inside that I was not.

Slowly it came to light just how much crap I was carrying about, stuff I truly believed I was "supposed" to cart about. I woke up to how much I was SHOULDING on myself, and thus sabotaging every step of my life's journey.

BINGO! *I was doing what I SHOULD, not what I WOULD.*

And from this point, it flowed. All this "stuff"- Emotional Baggage, Mental Waffle, Stupid Beliefs, etc. came up to be reviewed in the new light of what 'ME' really was. And that's when it FINALLY clicked: It was ALL just me, even the lies, but now it was different. I had, up to recently, believed the crap and garbage WAS me, but in truth, it was all just 'Stuff' that I had stacked up and used to build a wall - A wall of Should that was now surrounding ME.

The Mystic Rat says: *From the One to the many to refold back to the One!*

We all have many aspects and shades to our being. But how do we bring these together as a collective working unit? This was when I realised that "It's Only Me" was the start of an apparent opposite understanding, the one which became *Rule One* in the *Rules of Rattyness*. Rule One: *"It's not about you."*

Now, this appears to conflict with "It's only me", but only on the surface - We have to understand that "It's not about you" relates to how you interact with OTHER people. What THEY do is all about themselves, and nothing to do with you. What YOU do is all about yourself, not them.

Get it? It's just US!

It's Just US

You may rightly think "It's only me" was not a cosmic realization of supreme truth, but for the 'ME' that existed right at that moment in time, it changed everything. Being able to see and recognize ME was the key that unlocked my internal door. I could now become free of my own beliefs because I had a way out. I recognised ALL my beliefs were part of the 'external' self, that I also was. It was still me, but the 'ME' that had been fed on a diet of lies until 'I' became a lie. Everything about myself was a lie, a paradox, and yet also a truth.

Completely nuts, hey?

Why did this satisfy me? This may surprise you, but I now saw everything differently. I had a massive shift of focus: T*his new understanding settled the question of competition within me*. I no longer needed to place myself higher or lower in relation to others. Now I fully grasped that I wasn't the smartest, but equally, I knew I was not the dumbest. I was not the brightest, nor the dullest. I wasn't the lightest or the fattest. I wasn't the tallest or the shortest. And all of this was perfectly FINE. It was exactly what it was, and that was FINE.

No one is the Cleverest or the Dumberest, the Greatest or the Least. And by really grasping this notion, you not only discover a tremendous release, you find a wonderful sense of the present moment. We are all simply what we are - With or without the tags of belief, doubt, and confusion that surround us, it is all just US. It never changes the fact that we are what we are.

"BINGO!" goes the light - SO THAT'S where Werner Erhardt got the notion of EST. So simple. When we look at the simple-est, the pure-est, the kind-est we discover it is the same 'est" that goes with the mean-est, the nasty-est and the savage-est. It all evens out when we wake up to the fact that it is only 'ME'.

But guess what? *There is no such thing as a Me-est or a You-est or a We-est.*
In other words, when you are truly yourself, you see what you are not.

Let me state this in a different way: The person inside us can be hungry, for truth, for food, for whatever. It is our PERSONALITY that determines hungrier, hungriest or Hungarian. Wait a minute, that's not right! The point is that the true emotion is only hungry. The personality you are wrapped in is what extends out and qualifies, compares and differentiates as to what it is hungry FOR.

Letting go off comparison, of the belief of what we are or what we are not, brings us to the point where we can see the person inside the personality.

'It's only Me' became an understanding that what I AM is sufficient unto the day. 'Sufficient Unto the Day' is a Latin proverb that effectively means to be self-contained, accepting of Life's gifts, and free to act according to your own will.

You figure it out - What counts is that alongside this simple reality came the other follow-on realities of: **It's only me. It is only you. It's only US.**

And what THIS means is extremely important - Letting go of comparison means we are all free to be exactly what we choose to be. It also means we finally understand the Stick-It notes on our back.

Stick it Notes

The truth shall set you free. This particular truth DID set me free. Free from beliefs in my own, as well as other peoples, superiority or inferiority. Free from the pain of fear that I was not good enough. Free from the need to impress myself with how good I was. I became free to be ME.

The long and the short of it: I finally grasped that not only is Jealousy just low self-esteem mixed with anger, I could NOW see that ALL emotions and States of Being were a mix of genuine self and 'additives' - These create Stick-It Notes on our backs, things others can easily read but which we ourselves rarely (if ever) comprehend. My personal insecurity stick-it note read "Kick Me! Treat me like crap - I deserve it!" to any passer-by who read it.

This became a HUGE revelation, one almost worthy of starving myself for all that time. What happens to us in life is largely the result of the Stick-It Note we have on our back. These labels are tags that others read and they deal with us in accordance with what they read.

And ALL of what I am now, have been, and will be, comes as a result of that apparently silly and inconsequential 'revelation' that is was only me. Because of this, I started looking at all my negative and positive emotions in a different light, and I discovered that I could accept myself.

This is a remarkable and liberating thing!

The Mystic rat Says: Forget supporting someone else's flag, become a patriot for the state of being you!

Summary: *By settling down and accepting ourselves, we learn a place exists within that is free of the need to impress. Losing the need to compete or to be greater or lesser than anything or anyone else means we start to understand what negative patterns have been driving us. Then we come to the point where we can break up the various aspects of ourselves as needed and piece them back together in a way that works better. Through the complete acceptance of Self we can learn to use our thoughts and emotions like a child uses a Lego set.*

Are We Still Pretending?

"The men the American people admire most extravagantly are the most daring liars; the men they detest most violently are those who try to tell them the truth."
                                                                Henry Lewis Menchen

This guy bets big into a pot because he peeked at his cards and saw two Aces. Other people like their card, and call, but he confidently bets in and raises every street. Finally, everyone folds and, triumphant, he decides to show his cards - Which happened to be two FOURS! He just saw the pointy bits and thought he had Aces. The real point: Pretending is not bad, believing in something false is not the problem. The dislocation starts when we turn over the fours, but insist they are still Aces. Belief does not change the facts, only how you arrive at them. And continuing a belief that opposes reality is pretence.

Even so: *Anything that helps us to survive is good*. Everything is OK as long as we are aware of what is around us. This means we pay attention to the hints and whispers life is constantly giving us. Pretending and believing we are something we are not makes us deaf to this dialogue. Does this mean we have to live in truth at all times? I am not sure we can.

It's a balancing act - Telling stories is what every novelist does, but they know it's a fiction. When we are the AUTHOR of our life, we may have our heads in the clouds - but to actually type it we must have our feet here on Earth. A novelist will write an interesting story, but they don't believe they are the character in it. The best writers are completely involved yet entirely separate.

The Mad Parade of Bacchus

I was sitting with an old school friend when he looked up at me one day, and said, "Time for the mad parade of Bacchus!" He was an alcoholic who was sober for extended periods, but when sobriety failed him, he went back to the bar and stayed there for months. I often wondered, who was the real person, the sober one, or the drunk?

After some time, I came to grasp that it was both and neither. My friend circulated around unanswerable questions inside himself. He wasn't gay, he believed, but he wanted relationships with men who dressed up as girls. He wasn't angry, but he hated everyone. He wasn't kind, yet he spent his life in service to helping the indigenous folk who could not help themselves. The one thing my dear friend never did was to pretend he wasn't fucked up, insecure, neurotic or emotional.

This person, dear reader, is one who taught me to be real. He may have never had any notion as to what or who he was, but neither would he pretend to be something he wasn't, in order to fit in.

So tell me - *Are we all still pretending to ourselves?* Are we pretending we are good citizens, obeying all the rules, and bobbing along just fine? Or are we happy to embrace the fact that we have a RAT inside us that needs to be expressed? The only valuable choices come from deeper within us, that same bit that just wants to live life, enjoy the moment, and have a laugh.

Remember the RAT Motto: *Half the Fun is Having Fun.*

I am not sure if there is anything else I can say other than to simply state that Ratology is a story that offers you a path to greater freedom. I can but trust that some part of you will recognize this. You don't need me to convince you - and I would not want to. The truth is it is more a case of you being able to trust yourself than trust me. Your next step will be either to accept the points outlined in this book, or to argue them. And if you want to argue it, feel free! I would suggest your engagement is inversely proving everything I have said about internal fractures, memes, and being dammed is 100% right. You can then rant on Facebook and watch people pretend they care. (Thumbs UP to that!)

Let us be clear - I do not care if you like me. I do not care if you think you are better or worse than me. I do not care for anything other than enjoying this moment. If you are an obstacle to this, I will not argue, I will just walk around you and find people I prefer to be with.

A final note of advice: You may have noted by now the rather total lack of advice in this book? There are many statements and things I present as facts, some you will argue with, some you will agree with. But I have assiduously sought to not 'should' on you, or tell you what you should do.

I am now going to almost break this rule and offer you some simple wisdom, which you can accept or reject.

For many years, if I wanted or needed anything I would buy whatever was serviceable and on special. I would shop in opportunity shops, unconcerned as to whether something was second-hand or not. Only one thing was certain, I never paid full asking price for anything. Then, one day in a store there were some thick purple towels for sale. They were over half an inch thick and really soft. I thought to myself, "Damn it, I need to have these!" I broke all my rules and bought two at full price because, obviously, one would need washing and if I am going to have a decent towel, I don't want to suddenly go from luxury to scratchy. Plus, what can I say, they were PURPLE!

I also had in the back of my mind the advice from Douglas Adams, in 'Hitch Hikers Guide to the Galaxy': *"A Towel is about the most massively useful thing an interstellar hitchhiker can have."*

I still delight in those towels, every day. So to my sage advice to you is this: *Buy a decent set of towels.*

Well, that's it! Book Two is available on Amazon, so come back for more punishment anytime you are ready.

The Yardstick

"When nobody around you seems to measure up, it's time to check your yardstick." Bill Lemley

Remember way back in the Chapter "God is Dust" (P 221) where we asked if there was a Yardstick we can use to measure if we are just living a dream or another belief, or if we have perchance stumbled into reality??

Well, now that we have come to the end of the book, I can reveal it to you. You have just read 136,000 words, but in the process of writing this, I have written over 1,000,000 of the little buggers. (My personal yardstick is more of an axe wielding maniac) Seriously: If you think I hold the secret that will reveal to you the difference between a dream and a reality, do you really think I would still be here? No chance - I would be off enjoying myself with all the incredible riches I received from selling that pearl.

Reality: It's like a song you really want to sing, but don't have the range for. The problem is this - It is so obvious to others when someone is singing out of key, but rarely is this the case for the person singing. We see this in the auditions for every talent quest show. The real trick in discovering what is real is NOT to sing out loud, it is to listen. It is to get out of the confined space of self-belief and listen to what life is telling us.

When we do this, we discover what's real. But here is the 'real' problem: In my experience, this state doesn't last for very long here on Planet Earth. We are surrounded by lies and illusions, while each and every experience we pass through tars the brush of our being ever so slightly. Whether this makes art, graffiti or just a mess is a personal interpretation, but the fact remains, it takes an effort to stay in clear space.

We are all affected, in some way, by the soil that grew us - but rather than argue our upbringing the best way to look at the manure that has been dumped upon our heads is as fertilizer. I will say one thing, however, a simple truth my father noted when he had a farm.

He showed me how a large clod of earth was being moved over the period of a days by a single shoot from a potato plant. The clod was FAR heavier than the plant stalk, yet that tiny thing had enormous power within it, enough to overcome an incredible obstacle. As he explained: *This is the Power of Growth.*

Life provides us with an opportunity for growth. It holds a vast resource, an unlimited font that you can tap into at any time you choose. All we have to do is open the heart, breath in, focus, and just go for it. Even a small shift in perception can give us a huge shift in reality, so my recommendation: *Learn to Love HOW you see, rather than WHAT you see.*

You may look up and see an open sky, or a glass ceiling, but HOW you see this determines what you will do. Do you wake, and breathe in the delight of a new day, or are you waking up fearful of calls from debt collectors? Are you stepping out and creating something new in your life, or are you stagnant and waiting for things to happen?

HOW we see these things determines our course more than WHAT we see. If we accept everything as what it is, HOW we see remains clear. With clarity, the path forward is easier to find.

Your Yardstick is best used as a WALKING Stick - and the road of reality we walk on is not any one thing, nor is it straight and simple. Reality is many things combined in a way that works well. It is your Attitude, and where you put your Attention. It is your level of Expectation, combined with your sense of Self-worth - In any given moment everything combines to create the reality we experience. However there is an eternal truth - A happy heart gives us happy moments, regardless of circumstance. Conversely: A sad song on a bright day darkens the mood. It is, as always, a choice. But HOW we see, not WHAT we see, will determine the nature of that choice.

The thing is, when you get on with yourself - truly and deeply - it really doesn't matter if you are living in total reality or a complete dream. If you have a good combination of the above somehow, like the potato shoot, you will find a way past the obstacles and find your day in the sun

Our only true 'Yardstick' is the sense of 'OK' that we get when we are in the flow of things. It is like a water dowser with his dowsing rods: he feels the pull when he is near the water. If we are aware of what life is whispering and if we follows its directions, the water of life will be found.

In the end, your Yardstick is your AWARENESS. Really, your Awareness is the sum total, the gestalt, that comes from Attention, Attitude, Expectation, and Self-Image ... This all forms the Yardstick that is your Reality Awareness Trigger, your RAT.

These are the things make up the Aces in your Poker Hand. Play with them as you will.

Remember: *We are looking for that which is looking.*

Happy Ratting Folks

QUESTION
A rabbit thinks the fox is evil, callous, indifferent and cruel. The fox sees the rabbit as food for the family table. Which one is right?

Ratology: Way of the Un-Dammed

SUMMARY

"And old rat is a brave rat." French Proverb

`Seven years and six months!' Humpty Dumpty repeated thoughtfully. `An uncomfortable sort of age. Now if you'd asked my advice, I'd have said "Leave off at seven" -- but it's too late now.'

`I never ask advice about growing,' Alice said indignantly.

`Too proud?' the other enquired.

Alice felt even more indignant at this suggestion. `I mean,' she said, `that one can't help growing older.'

`One can't, perhaps,' said Humpty Dumpty; `but two can. With proper assistance, you might have left off at seven.'

Through the Looking Glass: Chapter Six   Lewis Carroll

Do you remember the story of the Emperor's New Clothes? The Emperor is convinced by a shyster that he is wearing incredibly fine cloths of the most amazing material. Everyone is effectively hypnotized by this projection, until a child calls out that the Emperor is naked. This breaks the spell of illusion and the truth, that was always obvious, is made clear.

The whole point of this book is that truth is always obvious - But that you have to be close to the honest and basic child-like nature within yourself to realize this. The truth is that, for yourself, there is NO ONE closer to your divine source of truth than you are. However, you have to be awake to see it.

This is the job of your RAT. It is within you, but be warned, when you encourage it to come out it will shatter beliefs, disgorge wrong thinking, and start making you see the falsehood in your beliefs. In the Bible, this is what is meant when Jesus says *"Ye must hate your father and your mother (etc.) before ye can enter into the Kingdom of Heaven"*. Now add to this the fact he ALSO said, "the Kingdom of Heaven is within," and it gets curious.

For myself, Jesus is clearly stating that to break the barriers within, you have to break up all your social conditioning. He is talking about shattering your illusions of the world by using the negative power of doubt. He is talking about waking up your RAT and learning to see things as they really are.

In antiquity there was a thing known as the Orphic Mysteries - This was an Egyptian religion that spread over Greece and, in particular, was recognized and promoted by Pythagoras. The teaching instigated the notion of universities and a religion based on personal experience, all of which was a core element in creating the Golden Age of Greece, democracy, and so much we value today.

The spiritual teacher of the Orphic Mysteries was a mysterious being called Orpheus. (He was reinvented in "The Matrix" as Morpheus) Orpheus taught three basic principles, governed by the overriding concept that we are all children of the Universe. This credo went:

1. You are a child of the Universe. As such you contain all the elements of the universe including the power of creation. You have the power to mold the stuff of life via the way you think, how you feel, and by what you expect.
2. What we think feel and expect comes to pass in our lives, thus we learn by experience. Experience can teach us to modify our thoughts, feelings, and expectations.
3. By learning to modify our inner being and how it expresses itself, we come to realize we are free to act as we choose. We come into the Liberty of Spirit, which is the very nature of creation.

In Book Two of Ratology (*Ratology Two: Who Gives a Rats!*) we take a look at the inner process of creation: Spiritual Arithmetic, Bubble Consciousness, and the ways we structure our inner thoughts and feeling. (Available on Amazon)

Book Three, still to be named, will be out 2021. This is a comprehensive book on health and healing that reveals many of the new trends in medicine as well as common place and simple remedies for many diseases.

Ratology: Way of the Un-Dammed

Ode to Bernie - The Financial Crisis in an Eggshell
or: How to cook the books, have your cake, and eat them all

Once upon a time, not so very long ago, the EggMan stood up in a moment of epiphany and said, "I am going to become a chicken!" It was an instant hit with everyone in the forest where he lived. All around there was rousing applause from the animals, the rocks and trees.

"What a fine notion." said the tree.

"Excellent idea." said the stream.

So the EggMan imagined his chicken-self emerging. He dreamed of everything that was needed to become a Chicken. He created all sorts of plans, and talked about it to everyone. Soon the whole forest was buzzing about the forthcoming chicken creation.

Meetings were held, concepts were drawn up, 3D models were made, experimental mechanical chickens were built and then, on anticipation of the new chicken becoming a boon to the fast food industry, the Chicken Concept was registered on the forest stock exchange.

Everyone bought into the chicken stock. It became the new 'thing'! Mums and dads enthusiastically brought their sons and daughters to see how much their stocks were heating up. It was the buzz of the forest. The excitement was infectious! It spread to the fields beyond and even to the mountains in the distance. Soon everyone was buying into Chicken Stocks.

There was only one problem, something the EggMan was feeling increasingly embarrassed about. The sad truth was, he really had no idea how to become a chicken. In fact, he was becoming increasingly worried that he may have been destined to become something else: a turkey maybe, or worse, a Dodo. The ancient question arose: What to do, what to do?

So, off went EggMan to see the Old Forest Tree, who was ancient beyond belief and wise beyond imagination. He knocked on the trunk, waking the sleeping Soul up. Then he asked, "How do I become a chicken?"

Old Forest Tree looked down, mystified as to why anyone would want to become a chicken, but then realised it was an Egg before him. "Well," said the tree, "It all depends on what is inside you. Life will grow what it will and you have to trust it. You are what you are, dear Egg."

Well, that didn't answer things at all. EggMan had all these stocks invested in the fact he was going to become a Chicken and what he needed was a little certainty. He pondered, and wondered, and worried about it for many days, but then he realised the solution was right there before him! The EggMan gathered up all the chicken stocks he had sold, made them into books, then put them all into a pot and cooked them.

The next day he gathered all the denizens of the forest around the pot and, with a great flourish, started serving out the broth he made from the Chicken Stocks. What is more, he charged them for the soup, declaring: "See! Here is my special Chicken Stock soup, as promised! Which, of course, as you must realize, we would not be able to eat if there were no chicken to start it off!"

Now, with the adding of a little salt and pepper, and a few other spices, this new Chicken Stock soup didn't taste too bad. Not too bad at all! Soon everyone started buying it. Even the rocks in the forest, who didn't need to eat at all, were buying chicken stock soup.

Of course, as a result the chicken stocks were getting eaten through at a shocking rate. Soon there would be none left, so the EggMan solved this by creating more of them. And as the raging demand for Chicken Stock soup increased, this made even the increased stock options even MORE valuable, and these too were sold like there was no tomorrow.

"It can go on like this forever" said the EggMan triumphantly to the Old Forest Tree as he paid the fellow a visit with the amazingly good news.

The Old Tree was puzzled. "But, where is the chicken you were going to become?"

"It's in the soup" answered the EggMan, blithely.

"Then how is it you are still here?" the Old Tree asked, not understanding this new way of doing things in the modern economy.

"There it is," said the EggMan. "The clear, shocking proof that you are too old and too out of touch to grasp the reality of post-war economics."

Of course, under his breath, the EggMan was muttering, "And here before me is the next logical source for something to print my new chicken stocks on."

'*It's very* provoking,' *Humpty Dumpty* said after a long silence, looking away from Alice as he spoke, 'to be *called an egg— very*!'

RATOLOGY
Way of the Un-Dammed
Stop Shoulding on Yourself
Set Your Heart Free

RATOLOGY: Way of the Un-Dammed
COPYRIGHT 2009-2020 Ecallaw Leachim
ISBN: 978-0-9756994-2-3

This book is published under the Berne Convention. All rights are reserved. Apart from any fair dealing for the purpose of private study, research, criticism or review, as permitted under the Copyright Act, 1966, no part of this publication may be reproduced, stored in a retrieval system, or transmitted, in any form or by any means, electronic, electrical, chemical, mechanical, optical, photocopying, recording or otherwise, without the prior permission of the copyright holder. Inquiries should be sent to the publishers at the under mentioned address.

Copyright 2009-2020 Ecallaw Leachim

Publisher: Ladder to the Moon Productions
Email: mrmichaelmouse@hotmail.com

Did you enjoy Ratology?
Go for ROUND TWO!

Book Two is now available on Amazon. Explore the deep patterns that control every person and learn to renegotiate your agreement with life.

Available on Amazon

Advice on buying a decent Towel

"A towel, The Hitchhiker's Guide to the Galaxy says, is about the most massively useful thing an interstellar hitchhiker can have. Partly it has great practical value. You can wrap it around you for warmth as you bound across the cold moons of Jaglan Beta; you can lie on it on the brilliant marble-sanded beaches of Santraginus V, inhaling the heady sea vapors; you can sleep under it beneath the stars which shine so redly on the desert world of Kakrafoon; use it to sail a miniraft down the slow heavy River Moth; wet it for use in hand-to-hand-combat; wrap it round your head to ward off noxious fumes or avoid the gaze of the Ravenous Bugblatter Beast of Traal (such a mind-boggingly stupid animal, it assumes that if you can't see it, it can't see you); you can wave your towel in emergencies as a distress signal, and of course dry yourself off with it if it still seems to be clean enough."

"More importantly, a towel has immense psychological value. For some reason, if a strag (strag: non-hitch hiker) discovers that a hitch hiker has his towel with him, he will automatically assume that he is also in possession of a toothbrush, face flannel, soap, tin of biscuits, flask, compass, map, ball of string, gnat spray, wet weather gear, space suit etc. etc. Furthermore, the strag will then happily lend the hitch hiker any of these or a dozen other items that the hitch hiker might accidentally have 'lost'. What the strag will think is that any man who can hitch the length and breadth of the galaxy, rough it, slum it, struggle against terrible odds, win through, and still knows where his towel is, is clearly a man to be reckoned with."

Douglas Adams

About the Author

"History is a set of lies agreed upon."
Napoleon Bonaparte

Little can be said of the author other than he is a complete rat who likes poker. Otherwise, he has raised the children, done the divorce, fed the cats, played with the dog, buried the dead fish, and generally had a life like most people.

Ecallaw Leachim is an Australian, raised in New Guinea for a time and brought up by such a strict Catholic mother that he actually ASKED to be sent to Boarding School. Prison, he quipped, was the other option not open to him at the time.

Ecallaw apologises in advance if this book has insulted or offended you in any way, but stresses that if this is the case, then he probably WAS talking about you and it wasn't your imagination. Clearly, a psychic connection has been formed that allowed you to relate to the book in a deeply offended way and it is strongly suggested that you take THAT to your lawyer and smoke it.

At Age Four, the author saw that people he spoke to after church appeared to have two faces: one that said the socially polite thing, the other that said what they really thought. He was shocked when he realized that everyone was, in his view, lying. In his early twenties, Ecallaw discovered another profound truth - after three months of fasting in the wilderness: He had a cosmic realization that went, "It's only me."

He was distinctly depressed when he got the picture that, after three months of starvation, he got such an ordinary cosmic insight. Yet, to his enormous curiosity, he later discovered that these were the exact words that John Lennon said to the other members of the Beatle's when they had arguments.

John would tilt his glasses down and say, "It's only me."

Gathering this self-evident viewpoint into a larger understanding, he came to understand: *It's only me, it's only you, it's only US.* Adding to this the notion that *we are all in this together,* Ecallaw progressed on. He plucked further snippets of truth from the garden maze of his life and it is from these seeds of truth and pithy observations that he germinated the substance of the book you now hold.

If you loved it, tell him. If you hated it, it's your problem.

The BLACK ART of HOLDEM

Appeasing the Poker Gods by:

Reading the O.D.D.S
Building OPPORTUNITY
Creating YOUR LUCK

Don't just PLAY Holdem!
WIN the Damn Game!
Make MONEY from it!

Ecallaw "Ratty" Leachim

The Black Art of Holdem

Did you like Ratology: Way of the Un-Dammed?
Well, there's more! Go to www.laddertothemoon.com

"Possibly the best book on how to make money out of the game of Texas Holdem that exists"

Available from AMAZON or
WWW.LADDERTOTHEMOON.COM

laddertothemoon.com.au

The Power to Publish Is in Your Hands

TURNING DREAMS into REALITY

Do you have a story you wish to share? Ladder to the Moon specialise in uplifting books that open the heart, but we also help publish the "ordinary" stories of people who have something they simply wish to share with friends and relatives.

These are usually short run books, or 50 to 100 copies. We can either just print your story, or we can take your digital files and covert them into a more professional publication. Great for family memoirs!

The cost is not high, from $850 to just print an existing file in a run of 50 books, or up to $2500 for full publishing services - sourcing images, designing covers, etc.

We also will register you with an ISBN and get you listed on Amazon if you wish for a wider audience.

I was amazed how my little story came up so well. Friends in Europe are buying copies for their families. This is a truly wonderful service.

Manu Lai

Ladder to the Moon
qrcaustralia@gmail.com

Other Books by this Author

Ecallaw has written a number of books, from non-fiction study books on Numerology and the art of Dice Divination, to franchising workbooks, to children's stories and science fiction, all the way through to short stories and a genre known as Modern Myth.

"Give Caesar an army, and he will conquer Gaul ... But give Caesar a BICYCLE, and he will take over the WHOLE WORLD!" Pliny the Elder

Ecallaw Leachim

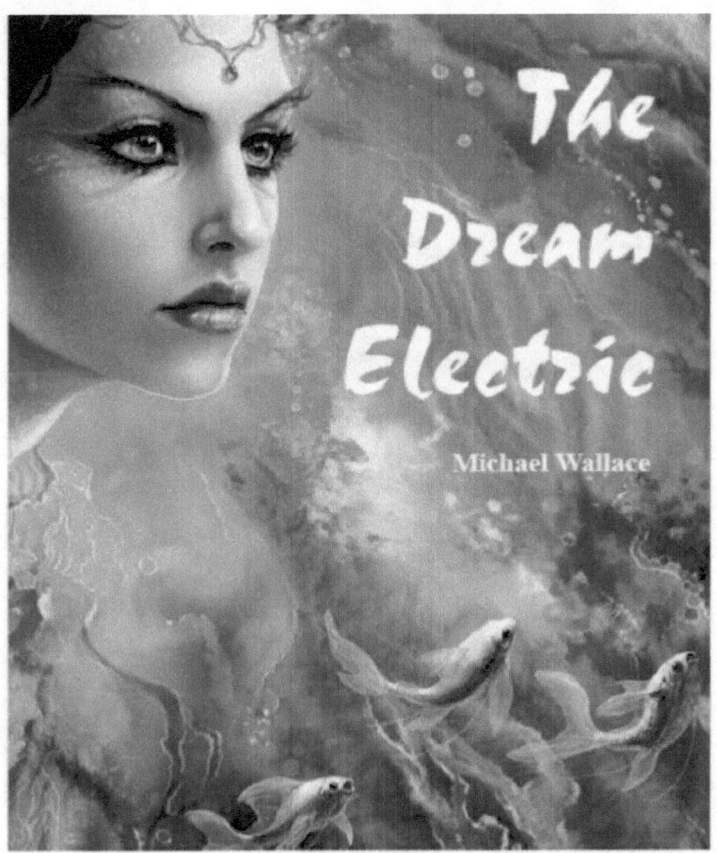

OLD EARTH, THE HOME OF MAN, HAS BEEN RENEWED WITH THE MIRACLE GENESIS BOTS .... BUT THERE IS A PROBLEM

Captain Childs, Master of the SS Orient, is given an impossible task. He must save mankind from the most destructive force ever imagined, an uncontrolled artificial intelligence that only knows how to create.

Yet his own superiors do not understand or even believe the threat is real. He must circumvent their influence, and to do so, he uses all his family and political connections. Yet, to his shock, he discovers the source of this horror comes from his OWN family.

The Dream Electric is a remarkable and inventive story that gives a nod to Bladerunner and Phillip K Dick's "Do Androids Dream of Electric Sheep".

AVAILABLE on AMAZON

AVAILABLE on AMAZON

End of Days Trilogy: Eat Your Fill, Eat Your Religion, Eat Your God

Be a VICTOR, not a VICTIM!

To a spider, the fly in the web is not a victim, it is food. When it is finished being food, it is dead and it is useless. Does this make spiders cruel? No, they are hungry, The real message is simple: If your mentality is that of a poor week helpless thing, then you will look like food to the carnivore.

Your inner Rat is what awakens you to the webs of deceit and lies woven all around you. These things are designed to catch your attention, to hypnotize you and make you supper. But when you listen to your Rat, you will see the trap, thus you won't be their next meal.

There are no victims, there are only those who did not listen to, or understand, their inner whispers.

www.laddertothemoon.com.au

Aiming for the Stars is much easier if we stop off at the Moon. We are then out of the atmosphere of our past, and can see things more clearly. We are lighter, can jump higher and further than ever before, and it takes far less energy to start each journey.

The hard part is climbing that Ladder to the Moon.

Other Books by this Author:

The Wolves of Planet Hope (Sci Fi)

ROME Too / ROME Tree (Parody)

Psychic Nazi Hunter
(The Extraordinary Biography of Alan Wood-Thomas)

End of Times Trilogy (Sci Fi)
Eat Your Fill - Eat Your Religion - Eat Your God

The Book of Number Trilogy (Non-Fiction Reference)
Workbook - Interpretations - Practitioner Guide

Jermimiah Versus the Grabblesnatch (out of print)

The Divinity Dice Series (Non-Fiction Reference)
Decimal Dice - Divinity Dice - Book of Aspects

Ratology: Way of the Un-Dammed (Self Help)

Ratology II: Who Gives a Rats? (Self Help)

Fragments of the Mirror (Short Stories)

The Witch Hunters (Short Stories)

Water: More Precious than Gold (out of print)

The Borringbar War (Auto-biography - Written in three days)

Hello Planet Earth (Modern Myth)

The Dream Electric (Sci Fi)

Parables of Geoff (Biography)

The WAND (Modern Myth)

**Available on Amazon or at
www.laddertothemoon.com.au**

The Nature of Truth

The nature of Truth, by it's very definition, is simple.

A TRUTH is an indivisible reality, a thing distilled to an essence - This is WHY it is a Truth. A Lie, on the other hand, is complicated. It contains an element of truth, but has things attached - usually fear, doubt and shame.

Learning to see the obvious in all things really means that you can more easily spot the bits that are attached to 'truth' - These are the things that turn out natural state of truth into a lie.

"At First - Through the Glass Darkly and then, Face to Face"

Saint Paul

"The Dark Art of Holdem"

Almost forgot, I was going to give you the secrets of how to win at Poker. The secret is there is no secret - It is about understanding people and understanding yourself. You win by surviving your internal demons and recognising when your opponents negatives are ruling them.

Never bluff! Merely ask questions with a bet to see how others respond. They may CALL it bluffing but it is simply creating a dialogue.

Capitalize on weakness. Never trust your cards,. Never fall in love with Aces. There are precious few hands that cannot be beaten by the next turn of a card.

In any hand, if you cannot be beaten try and encourage others to bet. If you can be beaten, encourage others to fold. You are there to get paid - Winning chips is the only thing that matters. You win the most chips by observing where your opponents are at, not by looking at how good your cards are.

Poker is checkers, not chess. If the opponents look weak, bet. If they look strong, don't. If you are hitting cards, play more hands. If you are not, fold more than you play. But if there IS a secret, here it is: You only really learn to play poker when your luck deserts you. Why? Because then you can only survive by how well you read the other players and by placing the right bet at the right time, regardless of whether you have anything.

This is when you need your Rat. It will sniff out opportunity, weakness and confusion in the others at your table, and it recognises the shifting of the tide. And here's the thing, all games have movements of luck, in and out. Know this, and never bet into a lucky player unless you know you can bluff them out of the hand. Good luck comes in waves and the trick is surviving until you get a break.

And when you do, how well you ride this wave determines the chips you get. *Your luck, your emotions, they are all waves onto the beach.* Highs and lows are the norm, catching the tide at its zenith is the art.

Remember: You can get big chips from little cards, so don't be a 'card-Ist'. (You know, like a person who judges another by colour is a racist, a person who judges their cards by their paint is a cardist)

Wait for opportunity, pray to the Poker Gods and always remember - Its not about you. Most of all, keep in mind the fact that we win at poker by not losing. Thus the Golden Rule: *There is an endless supply of cards, but a limited number of chips.*

That's it! Get my book, "The Dark Art of Holdem" (Amazon) to learn more.

www.ingramcontent.com/pod-product-compliance
Lightning Source LLC
Chambersburg PA
CBHW030531230426
43665CB00010B/845